The Bible Speaks Today

Series Editors: J. A. Motyer (OT)
John R. W. Stott (NT)

The Message of Romans

God's good news for the world

Titles in this series

The Message of
Romans

God's good news for the world

John R. W. Stott

*Rector Emeritus of All Souls Church,
Langham Place, London
and President of Christian Impact*

Inter-Varsity Press

Inter-Varsity Press
38 De Montfort Street, Leicester LE1 7GP, England

First published 1994
Reprinted 1995

British Library Cataloguing in Publication Data
A catalogue record for this book is available from the British Library.

ISBN 0–85111–143–2

Set in 10/11pt Linotron Garamond
Typeset in Great Britain by Parker Typesetting Service, Leicester
Printed in Great Britain by Clays Ltd, Bungay, Suffolk

Inter-Varsity Press is the book-publishing division of the Universities and Colleges Christian Fellowship (formerly the Inter-Varsity Fellowship), a student movement linking Christian Unions in universities and colleges throughout the United Kingdom and the Republic of Ireland, and a member movement of the International Fellowship of Evangelical Students. For information about local and national activities write to UCCF, 38 De Montfort Street, Leicester LE1 7GP.

Contents

General preface

The Bible Speaks Today describes a series of both Old Testament and New Testament expositions, which are characterized by a threefold ideal: to expound the biblical text with accuracy, to relate it to contemporary life, and to be readable.

These books are, therefore, not 'commentaries', for the commentary seeks rather to elucidate the text than to apply it, and tends to be a work rather of reference than of literature. Nor, on the other hand, do they contain the kind of 'sermons' which attempt to be contemporary and readable without taking Scripture seriously enough.

The contributors to this series are all united in their convictions that God still speaks through what he has spoken, and that nothing is more necessary for the life, health and growth of Christians than that they should hear what the Spirit is saying to them through his ancient – yet ever modern – Word.

J. A. MOTYER
J. R. W. STOTT
Series Editors

Author's preface

'Not another commentary on Romans?' My friend groaned audibly. There was pain in his voice and in his eyes. And I sympathized with him. For the literature surrounding Romans is so massive as to be unmanageable. I have myself read about thirty commentaries, not to mention numerous other works which relate to Paul and Romans, and still there are many more which I have not had time to study. Is it not a folly then, even an impertinence, to add yet another book to this huge library? Yes, it would be, were it not for the three distinctives of *The Bible Speaks Today* (*BST*) series which perhaps, if taken together, may justify it.

First, *BST* authors (like all other commentators) are committed to a serious study of the text in its own integrity. Although a presuppositionless approach is impossible (and all the commentators tend to be recognizably Lutheran or Reformed, Protestant or Catholic, liberal or conservative), yet I have known that my first responsibility has been to seek a fresh encounter with the authentic Paul. Karl Barth, in his preface to the first edition of his famous *Römerbrief* (1918), called this an 'utter loyalty' to Paul, which would allow the apostle to say what he does say and would not force him to say what we might want him to say.

This principle has made it necessary for me to listen respectfully to those scholars who are offering us a 'new perspective on Paul', especially Professors Krister Stendahl, E. P. Sanders and J. D. G. Dunn. Their claims that both Paul and Palestinian Judaism have been gravely misunderstood have to be taken seriously, although I note that the most recent commentator, the American Jesuit scholar Joseph Fitzmyer, whose work appeared in 1993 and was hailed by the reviewers as 'monumental' and 'magisterial', almost entirely ignores this debate. All I have felt able to do is to sketch a brief explanation and evaluation of it in my Preliminary Essay.

But expositors should not be antiquarians, living only in the remote past. Reverting to Barth, it was his conviction that Paul, although 'a child of his age', who addressed his contemporaries, also 'speaks to all men of every age'. So he celebrated the 'creative energy' with which Luther and Calvin had wrestled with Paul's message 'till the walls which separated the sixteenth century from the first became transparent'. And the same dialectical process between ancient text and modern context must continue today, even though many commentators confine themselves to exegesis without application.

I confess that, ever since I became a Christian fifty-six years ago, I have enjoyed what could be termed a 'love–hate' relationship with Romans, because of its joyful–painful personal challenges. It began soon after my conversion, with chapter 6 and my longing to experience that 'death to sin' which it seemed to promise. I toyed for many years with the fantasy that Christians are supposed to be as insensitive to sin as a corpse is to external stimuli. My final deliverance from this chimera was sealed when I was invited to give the Keswick Convention 'Bible Readings' on Romans 5 – 8 in 1965, which were subsequently published under the title *Men Made New*.

Next, it was Paul's devastating exposure of universal human sin and guilt in Romans 1:18 – 3:20 which rescued me from that kind of superficial evangelism which is preoccupied only with people's 'felt needs'. The very first sermon I preached after my ordination in 1945, in St Peter's Church, Vere Street, was based on the repeated Romans statement that 'there is no distinction' between us (3:22 and 10:12), either in our sin or in Christ's salvation. Then there was Romans 12 and its demand for our whole-hearted commitment in response to God's mercies, and Romans 13, whose teaching about the use of force in the administration of justice made it impossible for me to remain a total pacifist in the Tolstoy-Gandhi tradition. As for Romans 8, although I have declaimed its final triumphant verses at innumerable funerals, I have never lost the thrill of them.

I have not been altogether surprised, therefore, in the course of writing this exposition, to observe how many contemporary issues are touched on by Paul in Romans: enthusiasm for evangelism in general and the propriety of Jewish evangelism in particular; whether homosexual relationships are 'natural' or 'unnatural'; whether we can still believe in such unfashionable concepts as God's 'wrath' and 'propitiation'; the historicity of Adam's fall and the origin of human death; what are the fundamental means to living a holy life; the place of law and of the Spirit in Christian discipleship; the distinction between assurance and presumption; the relation between divine sovereignty and human responsibility in salvation; the tension between ethnic identity and the solidarity of the body of Christ; relations between church and state; the respective duties of the individual citizen and the body politic; and how to handle differences of opinion within the Christian community. And this list is only a sample of the modern questions which, directly or indirectly, Romans raises and addresses.

The third characteristic of the *BST* series is that each book is intended to be both readable in style and manageable in size. A commentary, in distinction to an exposition, is a reference work and to that extent unreadable. Moreover, many of the most influential commentaries on Romans have been published in two volumes, such as those by C. H. Hodge, Robert Haldane and John Murray, and those in our own day by Professors Cranfield and Dunn. As for the late Dr Martyn Loyd-Jones, his penetrating exposition of Romans 1 – 9 runs to nine volumes, comprising more than 3,000 pages. By contrast with these multi-volume works, which I fear many busy Christian leaders do not have time to read, I have been determined from the beginning to limit this exposition to one volume (even though a bulky one!), while at the same time making available to readers some of the fruits of my study of the larger works.

I am grateful to Brian Rosner and David Coffey for reading the manuscript and making suggestions, a number of which I have adopted; to Colin Duriez and Jo Bramwell of IVP for their patient editorial skills; to David Stone for compiling the study guide; to Nelson González, my current study assistant, for giving himself the punishing task of reading the manuscript four times, and for deftly putting his finger on weak places where clarification or elaboration was needed; and, last but not least, to Frances Whitehead, whose undiminished enthusiasm, energy and efficiency have combined to produce yet another impeccable script.

At the beginning of his fourth-century exposition of Romans, Chrysostom spoke of how much he enjoyed hearing Paul's 'spiritual trumpet'.[1] My prayer is that we may hear it again in our day and may readily respond to its summons.

JOHN STOTT
Easter 1994

---

[1] Chrysostom, p. 335.

Chief abbreviations

AV	The Authorized (King James') Version of the Bible (1611).
BAGD	Walter Bauer, *A Greek–English Lexicon of the New Testament and Other Early Christian Literature*, translated and adapted by William F. Arndt and F. Wilbur Gingrich, second edition, revised and augmented by F. Wilbur Gingrich and Frederick W. Danker from Bauer's fifth edition, 1958 (University of Chicago Press, 1979).
ET	English translation.
GNB	The Good News Bible (NT, 1966, fourth edition 1976; OT, 1976).
GT	*A Greek–English Lexicon of the New Testament*, by C. L. W. Grimm and J. H. Thayer (T. and T. Clark, 1901).
JB	The Jerusalem Bible (1966).
JBP	*The New Testament in Modern English*, by J. B. Phillips (Collins, 1958).
LXX	The Old Testament in Greek according to the Septuagint, third century BC.
mg.	Margin.
Moffatt	James Moffatt, *A New Translation of the Bible* (Hodder and Stoughton, 1926, Old and New Testaments in one volume; revised 1935).
NEB	The New English Bible (NT, 1961, second edition 1970; OT, 1970).
NIV	The New International Version of the Bible (1973, 1978, 1984).
REB	The Revised English Bible (1989).
RSV	The Revised Standard Version of the Bible (NT, 1946; second edition, 1971; OT, 1952).
RV	The Revised Version of the Bible (1881–5); Apocrypha, 1895.
TDNT	*Theological Dictionary of the New Testament*, ed. G. Kittel and G. Friedrich, translated by G. W. Bromiley, 10 volumes (Eerdmans, 1964–76).

Bibliography

Works referred to in the footnotes are shown there by surname, or surname and date or volume number.

Commentaries

Barclay, William, *The Letter to the Romans*, in *The Daily Study Bible* (St Andrew Press, 1955; revised edition, 1990).

Barrett, C. K., *A Commentary on the Epistle to the Romans*, *Black's New Testament Commentaries* (Adam and Charles Black, 1957; second edition, 1962).

Barth, Karl, *The Epistle to the Romans* (1918; ET from the sixth edition, Oxford University Press, 1933).

Bengel, Johann Albrecht, *Gnomon of the New Testament* (1742; ET, T. and T. Clark, 1866).

Bruce, F. F., *The Letter of Paul to the Romans*, in *The Tyndale New Testament Commentaries* (Inter-Varsity Press and Eerdmans, 1963; second edition, 1985).

Brunner, Emil, *The Letter of Paul to the Romans – A Commentary* (Lutterworth Press, 1959).

Calvin, John, *The Epistle of Paul the Apostle to the Romans* (1540; Oliver and Boyd, 1961).

Chalmers, Thomas, *Lectures on the Epistle of Paul the Apostle to the Romans* (Collins, in four volumes, 1837–42).

Chrysostom, John, *Homilies on the Epistle to the Romans*, delivered in Antioch c. 387–397, in Philip Schaff, ed., *A Select Library of the Nicene and Post-Nicene Fathers*, vol. XI (1851; Eerdmans, 1975).

Cranfield, Charles E. B., *A Critical and Exegetical Commentary on the Epistle to the Romans*, in *The International Critical Commentaries* (T. and T. Clark; vol. I, 1975; vol. II, 1979; with corrections, 1983).

Denney, James, *St Paul's Epistle to the Romans*, in *The Expositor's Greek Testament*, vol. II (Hodder and Stoughton, 1901; Eerdmans, 1970).

Dodd, C. H., *The Epistle of Paul to the Romans*, in *The Moffatt*

New Testament Commentary (Hodder and Stoughton, 1932; eleventh edition, 1947).

Dunn, James D. G., *Romans*, in *The Word Biblical Commentary* (Word Books, in two volumes, 1988).

Fitzmyer, Joseph A., *Romans*, vol. 33 in *The Anchor Bible* (Doubleday, 1992; Geoffrey Chapman, 1993).

Godet, F. L., *Commentary on the Epistle to the Romans* (1879–80; ET, T. and T. Clark, 1880–82; one-volume edition, Zondervan, 1969).

Griffith Thomas, W. H., *St Paul's Epistle to the Romans, A Devotional Commentary* (Eerdmans, 1946).

Haldane, Robert, *Exposition of the Epistle to the Romans* (1835–39; Sovereign Grace Book Club, in two volumes, 1957).

Hodge, Charles H., *A Commentary on Romans*, in *The Geneva Series of Commentaries* (1835; Banner of Truth Trust, 1972).

Käsemann, Ernst, *Commentary on Romans* (1973; ET, SCM and Eerdmans, 1980).

Liddon, H. P., *Explanatory Analysis of St Paul's Epistle to the Romans* (privately distributed, 1876; Longmans, Green, and Co., 1893).

Lightfoot, J. B., *Notes on the Epistles of St Paul*, from unpublished commentaries (Macmillan, 1895; Baker, 1980).

Lloyd-Jones, D. Martyn, *Romans* (The Banner of Truth Trust and Zondervan).
1. *The Gospel of God* (Romans 1) (1985).
2. *The Righteous Judgment of God* (Romans 2:1 – 3:20) (1989).
3. *Atonement and Justification* (Romans 3:21 – 4:25) (1970).
4. *Assurance* (Romans 5) (1971).
5. *The New Man* (Romans 6) (1972).
6. *The Law: Its Function and Limits* (Romans 7:1 – 8:4) (1973).
7. *The Sons of God* (Romans 8:5–17) (1974).
8. *The Final Perseverance of the Saints* (Romans 8:17–39) (1975).
9. *God's Sovereign Purpose* (Romans 9) (1991).

Luther, Martin, *Lectures on Romans*, in *Luther's Works*, vol. 25 (1515; ET, Concordia, 1972).

Moo, Douglas, *Romans 1 – 8*, in *The Wycliffe Exegetical Commentary* (Moody, vol. 1, 1991).

Morris, Leon, *The Epistle to the Romans* (Eerdmans and Inter-Varsity Press, 1988).

Moule, H. C. G., *The Epistle of Paul the Apostle to the Romans*, in *The Cambridge Bible for Schools and Colleges* (Cambridge University Press, 1884).

——*The Epistle of St Paul to the Romans*, in *The Expositor's Bible* (Hodder and Stoughton, second edition, 1894).

Murray, John, *The Epistle to the Romans*, in *The New International Commentary on the New Testament* (Eerdmans, 1959–65; single-bound, two-volume edition, 1968).

Neill, Stephen C., *The Wrath and the Peace of God: Four Expositions of Romans 1–8* (CLS, 1943).

Nygren, Anders, *Commentary on Romans* (1944; ET, SCM and Fortress, 1949).

Sanday, William, and Headlam, Arthur C., *A Critical and Exegetical Commentary on the Epistle to the Romans*, in *The International Critical Commentary* (T. and T. Clark, 1895; fifth edition, 1902).

Vaughan, C. J., *St Paul's Epistle to the Romans* (Macmillan, 1859; sixth edition, 1885).

Ziesler, John, *Paul's Letter to the Romans*, in *The Trinity Press International New Testament Commentaries* (SCM and Trinity Press International, 1989).

Other works

Augustine, *Confessions* (*c.* 397; new translation by Henry Chadwick, Oxford University Press, 1992).

Campbell, William S., *Paul's Gospel in an Intercultural Context. Jew and Gentile in the Letter to the Romans* (Peter Lang, 1991).

Cranfield, Charles, 'Some Observations on Romans 8:19–21d', in Robert Banks, ed., *Reconciliation and Hope* (Eerdmans and Paternoster, 1974).

Cullmann, Oscar, *Christ and Time. The Primitive Christian Conceptions of Time and History* (1946; ET, 1951; third revised edition, SCM, 1962).

——*The State in the New Testament* (1956; ET, SCM, 1957).

Donfried, Karl P., ed., *The Romans Debate* (T. and T. Clark, 1991).

Hanson, A. T., *The Wrath of the Lamb* (SPCK, 1959).

Hengel, Martin, *The Pre-Christian Paul*, in collaboration with Roland Deines (SCM and Trinity Press International, 1991).

Hooker, Morna D., 'Adam in Romans 1', *New Testament Studies*, 1959–60.

Jeremias, Joachim, *The Central Message of the New Testament* (1955; ET, SCM, 1966).

Josephus, Flavius, *The Antiquities of the Jews*, from *Josephus: Complete Works* (*c.* 93–94; Pickering and Inglis, 1981).

Küng, Hans, *Justification: The Doctrine of Karl Barth and a Catholic Reflection* (1957; ET, Burnes and Oates, 1964).

Luther, Martin, *Preface to the Epistle of St Paul to the Romans*

(1546), in *Luther's Works*, ed. J. Pelikan and H. Lehmann, vol. 35 (Muhlenberg Press, 1960).

Metzger, Bruce, 'The Punctuation of Romans 9:5', in Barnabas Lindars and Stephen Smalley, eds., *Christ and Spirit in the New Testament* (Cambridge University Press, 1973).

——*A Textual Commentary on the Greek New Testament* (United Bible Societies, 1975).

Morris, Leon, *The Apostolic Preaching of the Cross* (Tyndale Press, 1955).

Räisänen, Heikki, *Paul and the Law* (J. C. B. Mohr, 1983).

Robinson, John A. T., *Wrestling with Romans* (SCM, 1979).

Sanders, E. P., *Paul and Palestinian Judaism* (SCM, 1977).

——*Paul, the Law, and the Jewish People* (Fortress, 1983; SCM, 1985).

——*Paul* (Oxford University Press, 1991).

Seifrid, Mark A., *Justification by Faith. The Origin and Development of a Central Pauline Theme* (E. and J. Brill, 1992).

Stendahl, Krister, *Paul Among Jews and Gentiles and Other Essays* (Fortress, 1976; SCM, 1977).

Thompson, Michael, *Clothed with Christ. The Example and Teaching of Jesus in Romans 12:1 – 15:13* (JSOT Press, Sheffield, 1991).

Wedderburn, A. J. M., *The Reasons for Romans* (1988; T. and T. Clark, 1991).

Westerholm, Stephen, *Israel's Law and the Church's Faith* (Eerdmans, 1988).

Wright, N. T., *The Climax of the Covenant. Christ and the Law in Pauline Theology* (T. and T. Clark, 1991).

Ziesler, John, *The Meaning of Righteousness in Paul, A Linguistic and Theological Inquiry* (Cambridge University Press, 1972).

Preliminary essay

Paul's letter to the Romans is a kind of Christian manifesto. To be sure, it is also a letter, whose contents were determined by the particular situations in which the apostle and the Romans found themselves at that time. Nevertheless, it remains a timeless manifesto, a manifesto of freedom through Jesus Christ. It is the fullest, plainest and grandest statement of the gospel in the New Testament. Its message is not that 'man was born free, and everywhere he is in chains', as Rousseau put it at the beginning of *The Social Contract* (1762); it is rather that human beings are born in sin and slavery, but that Jesus Christ came to set us free. For here is unfolded the good news of freedom, freedom from the holy wrath of God upon all ungodliness, freedom from alienation into reconciliation, freedom from the condemnation of God's law, freedom from what Malcolm Muggeridge used to call 'the dark little dungeon of our own ego', freedom from the fear of death, freedom one day from the decay of the groaning creation into the glorious liberty of God's children, and meanwhile freedom from ethnic conflict in the family of God, and freedom to give ourselves to the loving service of God and others.

It is not surprising that the church in every generation has acknowledged the importance of Romans, not least at the time of the Reformation. Luther called it 'really the chief part of the New Testament, and ... truly the purest gospel'. He continued: 'It is worthy not only that every Christian should know it word for word, by heart, but also that he should occupy himself with it every day, as the daily bread of the soul.'[1] Calvin wrote similarly, declaring that 'if we have gained a true understanding of this Epistle, we have an open door to all the most profound treasures of Scripture'.[2]

The same appreciation of Romans was expressed by British Reformers. William Tyndale, for example, the father of English Bible translators, in his prologue to Romans, described it as 'the principal and most excellent part of the New Testament, and most

[1] Luther (1546), p. 365.   [2] Calvin, p. 5.

pure Euangelion, that is to say, glad tidings . . . and also a light and a way in unto the whole Scripture'. He went on to urge his readers to learn it by heart. For, he assured them, 'the more it is studied, the easier it is; the more it is chewed, the pleasanter it is'.[3]

1. The influence of the letter

Several notable church leaders have testified, in different centuries, to the impact which Romans has made on their lives, in some cases being the means of their conversion. I mention five of them, in order to encourage us to take our study seriously.

Aurelius Augustinus, known to the world as Augustine of Hippo, destined to become the greatest Latin Father of the early church, was born on a small farm in what is now Algeria. During his turbulent youth he was both the slave of his sexual passions and the object of his mother Monica's prayers. As a teacher of literature and rhetoric he moved successively to Carthage, Rome, and then Milan, where he came under the spell of Bishop Ambrose's preaching. It was there during the summer of the year 386, when he was thirty-two years old, that he went out into the garden of his lodging, seeking solitude. 'The tumult of my heart took me out into the garden', he wrote later in his *Confessions*, 'where no-one could interfere with the burning struggle with myself in which I was engaged . . . I was twisting and turning in my chains . . . I threw myself down somehow under a certain fig tree, and let my tears flow freely.'

> Suddenly I heard a voice from the nearby house chanting as if it might be a boy or a girl . . . saying and repeating over and over again 'Pick up and read, pick up and read.' . . . I interpreted it solely as a divine command to me to open the book and read the first chapter I might find . . . So I hurried back to the place where . . . I had put down the book of the apostle when I got up. I seized it, opened it and in silence read the first passage on which my eye lit: 'Not in riots and drunken parties, not in eroticism and indecencies, not in strife and rivalry, but put on the Lord Jesus Christ and make no provision for the flesh in its lusts' (Rom. 13:13–14). I neither wished nor needed to read further. At once, with the last words of this sentence, it was as if a light of relief from all anxiety flooded into my heart. All the shadows of doubt were dispelled.[4]

In 1515 another professor was overtaken by a similar spiritual crisis. Like everybody else in medieval Christendom, Martin Luther had been brought up in the fear of God, death, judgment and hell.

---

[3] From William Tyndale's translation of the New Testament (1534).
[4] Augustine, Book VIII, 19–29, pp. 146–153.

Because the surest way to gain heaven (it was thought) was to become a monk, in 1505 at the age of twenty-one he entered the Augustinian cloister at Erfuhrt, where he prayed and fasted, sometimes for days on end, and adopted other extreme austerities. 'I was a good monk,' he wrote later. 'If ever a monk got to heaven by his monkery, it was I.'[5] 'Luther probed every resource of contemporary Catholicism for assuaging the anguish of a spirit alienated from God.'[6] But nothing pacified his tormented conscience until, having been appointed Professor of Bible at Wittenberg University, he studied and expounded first the Psalms (1513–15) and then Romans (1515–16). At first he was angry with God, he later confessed, because he seemed to him more a terrifying judge than a merciful saviour. Where might he find a gracious God? What could Paul mean in Romans 1:17 when he stated that 'the righteousness of God was revealed in the gospel'? Luther tells us how his dilemma was resolved:

> I had greatly longed to understand Paul's letter to the Romans, and nothing stood in the way but that one expression 'the righteousness of God', because I took it to mean that righteousness whereby God is righteous and acts righteously in punishing the unrighteous ... Night and day I pondered until ... I grasped the truth that the righteousness of God is that righteousness whereby, through grace and sheer mercy, he justifies us by faith. Thereupon I felt myself to be reborn and to have gone through open doors into paradise. The whole of Scripture took on a new meaning, and whereas before 'the righteousness of God' had filled me with hate, now it became to me inexpressibly sweet in greater love. This passage of Paul became to me a gateway into heaven.[7]

Some 200 years later, it was Luther's own God-given insight into the truth of justification by grace through faith which led to the similar illumination of John Wesley. His younger brother Charles had with some Oxford friends founded what came to be nicknamed 'the Holy Club', and in November 1729 John joined it and became its acknowledged leader. Its members engaged in sacred studies, self-examination, public and private religious

---

[5] Roland H. Bainton, *Here I Stand* (Hodder and Stoughton, 1951), p. 45.

[6] *Ibid.*, p. 54.

[7] This appears to be F. F. Bruce's free translation (p. 57) of Luther's own account of his 'tower experience', so called because it took place in the tower of Wittenberg's Black Cloister. His account appeared first in 1545 in his preface to the Wittenberg edition of his Latin works. It is reproduced in the American edition of *Luther's Works*, vol. 34 (Mühlenberg Press, 1960), pp. 336f., and by Fitzmyer, pp. 260f. See also Gordon E. Rupp's translation in his book *The Righteousness of God: Luther Studies* (Hodder and Stoughton, 1953), pp. 121f.

exercises, and philanthropic activities, apparently hoping to win salvation by such good works. Then in 1735 the brothers Wesley sailed for Georgia as chaplains to the settlers and missionaries to the Indians. Two years later they returned in a profound disillusionment, which was mitigated only by their admiration for the piety and faith of some Moravians. Then on 24 May 1738, during a Moravian meeting in Aldersgate Street, London, to which John Wesley had gone 'very unwillingly', he turned from self-confidence to faith in Christ. Somebody was reading Luther's *Preface to . . . Romans*. Wesley wrote in his journal:

> About a quarter before nine, while he was describing the change which God works in the heart through faith in Christ, I felt my heart strangely warmed. I felt I did trust in Christ, Christ alone, for salvation; and an assurance was given me that he had taken away *my* sins, even *mine*, and saved *me* from the law of sin and death.[8]

Coming now into our own era, two other Christian leaders may be mentioned. Both were Europeans, one Romanian, the other Swiss. Both were clergy, one Orthodox, the other Protestant. Both were born in the 1880s, although they never met and may never even have heard of each other. Yet, despite their different countries, cultures and churches, both were transformed by their study of Romans. I am referring to Dumitru Cornilescu and Karl Barth.

While studying at the Orthodox Theological Seminary in Bucharest, Dumitru Cornilescu[9] longed to experience a greater spiritual reality and depth. During his search he was introduced to some books by evangelical authors, who themselves directed him to the Bible. So he determined to translate the Bible into modern Romanian, began the work in 1916 and almost six years later completed it. Through his study of Romans he came to believe truths which previously had been unfamiliar and even unacceptable to him: that 'there is no-one righteous, not even one' (3:10), that 'all have sinned' (3:23), that 'the wages of sin is death' (6:23), and that sinners may be 'justified freely' through Christ (3:24), because 'God presented him as a sacrifice of atonement through faith in his blood' (3:25). Through these and other texts of Romans he came to see that God through Christ had done everything necessary for our salvation. 'I took this forgiveness for myself,' he said; 'I accepted Christ as my living Saviour.' 'From that point on,' writes Paul Negrut, 'Cornilescu was assured that he belonged to God, and that he was a

[8] *John Wesley's Journal* from the entry for 24 May 1738.
[9] I am grateful to Dr Paul Negrut of Oradea, Romania, for allowing me to read and quote from his unpublished paper entitled 'The Bible and the Question of Authority within the Orthodox Church of Romania'.

new person.' His translation, published in 1921, became the standard Bible Society text. But he himself was exiled by the Orthodox Patriarch in 1923, and died some years later in Switzerland.

Switzerland was also the home of Karl Barth. During his pre-war theological studies he came under the influence of some of the leading liberal scholars of the day and shared their utopic dream of human progress and social change. But the horrific carnage and bestiality of the First World War, and his reflection on the message of Romans, were enough in combination to shatter the illusions of liberal optimism. Even while writing his exposition, he said that 'it required only a little imagination . . . to hear the sound of the guns booming away in the north.'[10] The publication of the first edition of his commentary in 1918 marked his decisive break with theological liberalism. He had come to see that the kingdom of God was not a religious brand of socialism, achieved by human prowess, but a radically new beginning initiated by God.[11] In fact, the bedrock he had come up against was 'the Godness of God', that is, 'God's absolutely unique existence, power and initiation'.[12] Simultaneously he came to perceive the depths of human sin and guilt. He entitled his exposition of Romans 1:18ff. (Paul's exposé of Gentile depravity) 'The Night', and wrote about verse 18: 'Our relation to God is *ungodly* . . . We assume that . . . we are able to arrange our relation to him as we arrange our other relationships . . . We dare to deck ourselves out as his companions, patrons, advisers and commissioners . . . This is the *ungodliness* of our relation to God.'[13]

Barth confessed that he wrote 'with a joyful sense of discovery'. For, he added, 'the mighty voice of Paul was new to me: and if to me, no doubt to many others also'.[14] But his uncompromising emphasis on the sinner's absolute dependence on the sovereign, saving grace of God in Jesus Christ created what Sir Edwyn Hoskins (his English translator) described as a 'hubbub and commotion'.[15] Or, as the Roman Catholic theologian Karl Adam put it, using appropriate wartime imagery, Barth's commentary dropped 'like a bombshell on the theologians' playground'.[16]

F. F. Bruce, who drew attention – rather more briefly than I have done – to the influence of Romans on four of these five men, wisely added that its impact has not been confined to such giants, since 'very ordinary men and women' have been affected by it too. Indeed, 'there is no saying what may happen when people begin to study the letter to the Romans. So, let those who have read thus far

[10] Barth, p. v.   [11] See John Bowden, *Karl Barth, Theologian* (SCM, 1983).
[12] Eberhard Busch, *Karl Barth* (1975; ET, SCM, 1976), p. 119.
[13] *Ibid.*, p. 44.   [14] *Ibid.*, p. 2.   [15] *Ibid.*, p. xi.
[16] Quoted by Bruce, p. 58, and by Robinson, p. viii.

be prepared for the consequences of reading farther: you have been warned!'[17]

2. New challenges to old traditions

It has long been taken for granted, at least since the Reformation, that the apostle's chief emphasis in Romans is on God's justification of sinners by grace, in Christ, through faith. For example, Calvin wrote in his introductory essay on 'The Theme of the Epistle of Paul to the Romans' that 'the main subject of the whole Epistle . . . is that we are justified by faith'.[18] This is not to deny that Paul goes on to handle the further themes of assurance (chapter 5), sanctification (chapter 6), the place of the law (chapter 7), the ministry of the Spirit (chapter 8), God's plan for both Jews and Gentiles (chapters 9 – 11) and the varied responsibilities of the Christian life (chapters 12 – 15). Nevertheless, the assumption has been that Paul's main preoccupation was with justification, and that he developed those other topics only in relation to justification.

During this century, however, and in particular during the last thirty years, this thesis has been challenged. In 1963 an article by Professor Krister Stendahl, who later served as Lutheran Bishop of Stockholm, appeared in the *Harvard Theological Review*, entitled 'The Apostle Paul and the Introspective Conscience of the West', which was subsequently incorporated in his book *Paul Among Jews and Gentiles*.[19] He maintained that the traditional understanding of Paul in general and of Romans in particular, namely that their focus is on justification by faith, is wrong. This mistake, he continued, is due to the western church's morbid conscience,[20] and specially to the moral struggles of Augustine and Luther, which the church has tended to read back into Paul. Justification, according to Bishop Stendahl, is not '*the* pervasive, organizing doctrinal principle or insight of Paul',[21] but 'was hammered out by Paul for the very specific and limited purpose of defending the rights of Gentile converts to be full and genuine heirs to the promises of God to Israel'.[22] Paul's concern was not his own salvation, for he himself had a 'robust conscience',[23] claimed to be 'blameless',[24] and experienced 'no troubles, no problems, no qualms of conscience, no feelings of shortcomings',[25] but rather the salvation of the Gentiles, that they could come to Christ directly and not through the law. Consequently, 'the climax of Romans is actually chapters 9 – 11, *i.e.* his reflections on the relation between church and synagogue, the

---

[17] Bruce, p. 58.   [18] Calvin, p. 5.   [19] First published in 1976.
[20] *Ibid.*, pp. 11ff., 78ff.
[21] *Ibid.*, p. 27.   [22] *Ibid.*, p. 2.   [23] *Ibid.*, pp. 14, 40, 80.   [24] Phil. 3:6.
[25] Stendahl, p. 13.

church and the Jewish people',[26] and chapters 1 – 8 are 'a preface'.[27] Romans is 'about God's plan for the world and about how Paul's mission to the Gentiles fits into that plan'.[28]

To some degree this is a necessary corrective. For justification is certainly not Paul's exclusive preoccupation, as we have seen. Nevertheless, Romans 1 – 8 cannot be downgraded to the status of a mere 'preface'. Bishop Stendahl seems to have set up an unnecessarily sharp antithesis. Paul was indeed deeply exercised, as the apostle to the Gentiles, about the place of the law in salvation and about the unity of Jews and Gentiles in the one body of Christ. But he was also evidently concerned to expound and defend the gospel of justification by grace alone through faith alone. In fact, the two concerns, far from being incompatible, are inextricably interwoven. Only loyalty to the gospel can secure unity in the church.

Whether Paul's pre-conversion conscience was as cloudless as Dr Stendahl makes out, and whether we in the West have unduly introspective consciences which we have projected on to Paul, only careful exegesis of the crucial texts can settle. But in 1:18 – 3:20 it is Paul (not Augustine or Luther) who establishes universal and inexcusable human guilt. And Paul's own claim to have been 'blameless' in law-righteousness[29] must have referred to an *external* conformity to the law's demands. For in those revealing autobiographical verses in the middle of Romans 7 (if that is what they are) he tells how it was the commandment against covetousness, being an *internal* sin of heart, not action, which provoked in him 'every kind of evil desire' and so brought him to spiritual death. Professor Stendahl does not refer to this passage. Besides, it is not necessary to polarize between a 'morbid' and a 'robust' conscience. A truly healthy conscience disturbs our security and shames our pride, especially when the Holy Spirit comes to 'convict the world of guilt in regard to sin and righteousness and judgment'.[30] We should not therefore expect any unregenerate person to have a completely clear conscience.

In 1977 the major work of the American scholar Professor E. P. Sanders was published, *Paul and Palestinian Judaism*. Describing the prevailing picture of Palestinian Judaism as 'a religion of legalistic works-righteousness',[31] and of Paul's gospel as self-consciously antithetical to Judaism, he declared that his purpose was to 'destroy that view' as being 'completely wrong' and to show that it 'is based on a massive perversion and misunderstanding of the material'.[32] He conceded that his thesis was not altogether new, since, as Dr N. T. Wright has written, G. F. Moore 'set out substantially the same

[26] *Ibid.*, p. 4; *cf.* p. 28.   [27] *Ibid.*, p. 29.   [28] *Ibid.*, p. 27.   [29] Phil. 3:6.
[30] Jn. 16:8ff.   [31] Sanders (1977), p. 56.   [32] *Ibid.*, p. 59.

position' in the three volumes of his *Judaism in the First Centuries of the Christian Era* (1927–30).[33] Nevertheless, Professor Sanders went further. He surveyed with immense erudition the rabbinic, Qumranic and apocryphal literature of Judaism from 200 BC to AD 200. And the religion which emerged from this study he characterized as 'covenantal nomism'. That is, God had brought Israel into a covenant relationship with himself by his grace, and had then asked for obedience to his law (nomism) as their response. This led Professor Sanders to portray Judaism's 'pattern of religion' in terms of 'getting in' (by God's gracious election) and 'staying in' (by obedience). 'Obedience maintains one's position in the covenant, but it does not earn God's grace as such.'[34] Disobedience was atoned for by repentance.

Part II of Professor Sanders' book is simply headed 'Paul'. Even though it is only about a quarter the length of Part I, it is of course impossible to do it justice in a single paragraph. Highlights of Professor Sanders' thesis are as follows: (1) that Paul's starting-point was not the belief that all human beings are guilty sinners before God, but rather that Jesus Christ is Lord and Saviour of both Jews and Gentiles, so that 'for Paul the conviction of a universal solution preceded the conviction of a universal plight';[35] (2) that salvation is essentially a 'transfer' from the bondage of sin to the lordship of Christ; (3) that the means of transfer is 'participation' with Christ in his death and resurrection;[36] (4) that the reason salvation must be 'by faith' is not to obviate human pride, but that if it were 'by law' the Gentiles would be excluded and Christ's death would have been unnecessary ('the argument for faith is really an argument against the law');[37] and (5) that the resulting saved community is 'one person in Christ'.[38] Professor Sanders calls this way of thinking 'participationist eschatology'.[39] It will readily be seen, however, that in this attempted reconstruction of Paul's gospel the familiar categories of human sin and guilt, the wrath of God, justification by grace without works, and peace with God in consequence, are conspicuous by their absence.

In his second book, *Paul, the Law and the Jewish People*,[40] Professor Sanders replies to some of his critics and seeks to clarify and develop his thesis. He is surely right, in general, that Paul's 'argument concerns the equal standing of Jews and Gentiles – both are under the power of sin – and the identical ground on which they

[33] Stephen Neill and Tom Wright, *The Interpretation of the New Testament 1861–1986* (Oxford University Press, 2nd edn., 1988), p. 374.
[34] Sanders (1977), p. 420.   [35] *Ibid.*, p. 474.
[36] *Ibid.*, *e.g.* pp. 453ff., pp. 506ff.
[37] *Ibid.*, p. 491.   [38] *Ibid.*, pp. 547f.   [39] *Ibid.*, p. 549.
[40] Sanders (1983). See also Sanders (1991).

change that status – faith in Jesus Christ.'[41] But he then insists that 'the supposed objection to Jewish self-righteousness is as absent from Paul's letters as self-righteousness itself is from Jewish litera-ture.'[42] That is a much more questionable statement. At least five issues need to be raised.

First, the evidence is plain that the language of 'weighing', that is, of 'balancing merits against demerits',[43] does not occur in the litera-ture of Palestinian Judaism. But does the absence of this imagery of the scales prove the absence of the concept of merit? Cannot works-righteousness exist even when it is not 'weighed'? Paul was not mistaken to describe some Jews as 'pursuing' righteousness and not attaining it' (9:30ff.), and others as 'trying to be justified by law'.[44]

Secondly, in Judaism entry into the covenant was understood as depending on God's grace. This is hardly surprising, since in the Old Testament itself God is seen to take the initiative in his grace to establish his covenant with Israel. There could be no question of 'deserving' or 'earning' one's membership. Yet Professor Sanders goes on to show that 'the theme of reward and punishment is ubiquitous in the Tannaitic literature',[45] specially with regard to gaining life in the world to come. Does this not mean that human merit, while not the basis (in Judaism) of entering the covenant, was yet the basis of remaining in it? But Paul would have been vehement in his rejection of this. To him 'getting in' and 'staying in' are both by grace alone. Not only have we been justified by grace through faith (5:1), but we continue to stand in this grace into which we have been granted access by faith (5:2).

Thirdly, Professor Sanders concedes that 4 Ezra was the one exception to his thesis. For in this apocryphal book, he writes, 'one sees how Judaism works when it actually does become a religion of individual self-righteousness'. Here 'covenantal nomism has col-lapsed. All that is left is legalistic perfectionism.'[46] If one literary example has survived, may there not have been others which did not survive? May not the lapse into legalism have been more widespread than Professor Sanders admits? Besides, he has been criticized for reducing the complexity of first-century Judaism into 'a single, unitary, harmonious, and linear development'.[47] Professor Martin Hengel makes the same point. He writes that 'in contrast to the progressive "unification" of Palestinian Judaism under the leadership of the rabbinic scribes after AD 70, the spiritual face of Jerusalem before its destruction was a markedly "pluralistic" one'. After listing nine different groups he concludes: 'Jerusalem and its

[41] *Ibid.*, p. 30. [42] *Ibid.*, p. 156. [43] Sanders (1977), p. 146. [44] Gal. 5:4.
[45] Sanders (1977), p. 117. [46] *Ibid.*, p. 409.
[47] Jacob Neusner and Bruce Chilton, 'Uncleanness', *Bulletin for Biblical Research* 1 (1991), pp. 63ff.

environs must have presented the contemporary visitor with a confusingly varied picture.'[48] Again, 'perhaps there was no such thing as this *one* Palestinian Judaism with the *one* binding view of the law'.[49]

Fourthly, the case developed by E. P. Sanders and others rests on the meticulous examination of the relevant literature. But is it not well known that popular religion may diverge widely from the official literature of its leaders? It is this very distinction which leads Professor Sanders to write: 'The possibility cannot be completely excluded that there were Jews accurately hit by the polemic of Matthew 23 . . . Human nature being what it is, one supposes that there were some such. One must say, however, that the surviving Jewish literature does not reveal them.'[50] A parallel could be drawn with Anglicanism. The *Book of Common Prayer* and the Thirty-nine Articles, that is, the official literature of the church, insist that 'we are accounted righteous before God only for the merit of our Lord and Saviour Jesus Christ by faith, and not for our own works or deservings',[51] and that we may not 'presume' to approach God 'trusting in our own righteousness'.[52] Nothing could be clearer in the literature. Yet is it unfair to conjecture that the actual faith of many Anglicans remains one of works-righteousness?

Fifthly, it is clear that Paul had a horror of boasting. This has traditionally been taken as a rejection of self-righteousness. We are to boast in Christ and his cross,[53] not in ourselves or each other.[54] Professor Sanders, however, interprets Paul's antipathy to Jewish boasting (*e.g.* 3:27ff.; 4:1ff.) as being directed against pride in their favoured status (2:17, 23), which would be incompatible with the equal standing of Jews and Gentiles in Christ, not against pride in their merit,[55] which would be incompatible with a due humility before God. But one wonders if this distinction can be maintained as neatly as Professor Sanders does. Paul seems to bracket them in Philippians 3:3–9, where he contrasts 'glorying in Christ Jesus' with 'putting confidence in the flesh'. And the context shows that in 'the flesh' (what we are in our unredeemed self-centredness) Paul included both his status as 'a Hebrew of Hebrews' and his obedience to the law: 'in regard to the law a Pharisee . . . as for legalistic righteousness [that is, external conformity to the requirements of the law] faultless'. In other words, the boasting which Paul had himself renounced, and now condemned, was a self-righteousness compounded of both status-righteousness and works-righteousness. In

[48] Hengel, p. 44.   [49] *Ibid.*, p. xi.   [50] Sanders (1977), p. 426.
[51] Article XI.
[52] The Prayer of Humble Access in the Holy Communion Service.
[53] *E.g.* 1 Cor. 1:31; 2 Cor. 10:17; Gal. 6:14.
[54] *E.g.* 1 Cor. 1:29; 3:21; 4:6f.   [55] *Cf.* Eph. 2:9.

addition, the apostle twice writes of a righteousness which can be described as our 'own' either because we think we 'have' it or because we are seeking to 'establish' it.[56] Both passages indicate that this righteousness of our own (*i.e.* self-righteousness) is based on law-obedience, and that those who 'pursue' it thereby indicate that they are unwilling to 'submit' to God's righteousness. In Romans 4:4–5 Paul also makes a sharp contrast between 'working' and 'trusting', and so between a 'wage' and a 'gift'.

Finally, I am grateful for Professor Sanders' reference, quoted in paragraph 4 above, to 'human nature being what it is'. For our fallen human nature is incurably self-centred, and pride is the elemental human sin, whether the form it takes is self-importance, self-confidence, self-assertion or self-righteousness. If we human beings were left to our own self-absorption, even our religion would be pressed into the service of ourselves. Instead of being the vehicle for the selfless adoration of God, our piety would become the base on which we would presume to approach God and to attempt to establish a claim on him. The ethnic religions all seem to degenerate thus, *and so does Christianity.* In spite of the learned literary researches of E. P. Sanders, therefore, I cannot myself believe that Judaism is the one exception to this degenerative principle, being free from all taint of self-righteousness. As I have read and pondered his books, I have kept asking myself whether perhaps he knows more about Palestinian Judaism than he does about the human heart.

Certainly Jesus included 'arrogance' among the evils which issue from our hearts and defile us.[57] In consequence, he found it necessary in his teaching to combat self-righteousness. For example, in the parable of the Pharisee and the tax-collector he emphasized divine mercy, not human merit, as the proper object of justifying faith; in the parable of the labourers in the vineyard he undermined the mentality of those who demand payment and resent grace; and he saw little children as models of the humility which receives the kingdom as a free, unmerited gift.[58]

As for the apostle Paul, since he was well acquainted with the subtle pride of his own heart, could he not sniff it out in others, even when it hid under the cloak of religion?

In the end, however, it comes back to the question of exegesis. It is universally agreed that Paul's gospel in Romans was antithetical. He was expounding it over against some alternative. But what was this? We must allow Paul to speak for himself, and not make him say what either old traditions or new perspectives want him to say.

---

[56] Phil. 3:9; Rom. 10:3.   [57] Mk. 7:22ff.
[58] Lk. 18:9ff.; Mt. 20:1ff.; Mk. 10:13ff.

It is hard to see how any interpretation of Paul can explain away either his negative conclusion that 'no-one will be declared righteous in his sight by observing the law' (3:20), or his positive affirmation that sinners are 'justified freely by his grace' (3:24).

The debate about Paul in general and Romans in particular is now focused on the purpose and place of the law. A note of pessimism characterizes the writing of some contemporary scholars, since they are not persuaded that Paul knew his own mind on this topic. Professor Sanders is prepared to concede that Paul was 'a coherent thinker', while adding immediately that he was 'not a systematic theologian'.[59] Dr Heikki Räisänen, the Finnish theologian, is a good deal less complimentary. 'Contradictions and tensions have to be *accepted*', he writes, 'as *constant* features of Paul's theology of the law.'[60] In particular, Paul is said to have been inconsistent about the present status of the law. On the one hand, he states 'in unambiguous terms that the law has been abolished',[61] while on the other he claims that it is fulfilled in the lives of Christians. Thus Paul contradicts himself, asserting 'both the abolition of the law and also its permanently normative character'.[62] Also, 'we find Paul struggling with the problem that a *divine* institution has been *abolished* through what God has done in Christ . . .'. Most of Paul's difficulties are attributable to this. He even 'tries to hush up the abolition' by insisting that his teaching 'upholds' and 'fulfils' the law. But how can it be fulfilled by being set aside?[63]

The difficulties which Dr Räisänen finds, however, seem to be more in his own mind than in Paul's. It is true of course that, when Paul is responding to different situations, he makes different emphases. But it is not impossible to resolve the apparent discrepancies, as I hope will become clear in the exposition of the text. Our deliverance from the law is a rescue from its curse and its bondage, and so relates to the two particular functions of justification and sanctification. In both areas we are under grace, not law. For justification we look to the cross, not the law, and for sanctification to the Spirit, not the law. It is only by the Spirit that the law can be fulfilled in us.[64]

Professor James Dunn seems to have accepted the main theses of K. Stendahl, E. P. Sanders and H. Räisänen, and has sought to develop them further, especially in relation to the law. In a famous paper entitled 'The New Perspective on Paul' (1983), summarized in the introduction to his commentary, he portrays Paul in Romans as being in dialogue with himself, the Jewish rabbi with the

[59]Sanders (1977), p. 433. *Cf.* Sanders (1983), p. 148.   [60]Räisänen, p. 11.
[61]*Ibid.*, p. 199.
[62]*Ibid.*, p. 69.   [63]*Ibid.*, pp. 264f.
[64]Je. 31:33; Ezk. 36:27; Rom. 7:6; 8:4; Gal. 5:14ff.

Christian apostle. When he declared that nobody could be justified 'by the works of the law', he was not referring to 'good works' in a general and meritorous sense. He was thinking rather of circumcision, the sabbath and the food laws, which 'functioned as an "identity marker" and "boundary", reinforcing Israel's sense of distinctiveness and distinguishing Israel from the surrounding nations'. Further, this 'sense of distinctiveness' was accompanied by a 'sense of privilege'. The reason Paul was negative to 'the works of the law' was not that they were thought to earn salvation, but that (a) they led to a boastful pride in Israel's favoured status, and (b) they fostered an ethnic exclusiveness incompatible with the inclusion of the Gentiles, to which he was committed.[65]

There can be no doubt that Paul saw these two dangers clearly. But Dr Stephen Westerholm is right, in his fine survey *Israel's Law and the Church's Faith* (1988), to question aspects of this reconstruction. For Paul, he argues, used 'law' and 'works of law' interchangeably, so that his reference was wider than to particular Jewish rituals; it was boasting in good works, not just in favoured status, which Paul opposed, as is clear from the case of Abraham (3:27; 4:1–5); and 'the fundamental principle affirmed by Paul's thesis of justification by faith, not works of the law, is that of humanity's dependence on divine grace . . .'.[66]

Clearly the last word has not yet been spoken or written about these controversial issues in Romans. We may not feel able to agree that Paul's pre-conversion conscience was as cloudless as is now being claimed, or that he was as muddled over the law, and as preoccupied with its ritual regulations, as some are arguing; or that first-century Judaism was completely free from notions of merit and of works-righteousness. But we can be profoundly thankful for the scholarly insistence that the Gentile question is central to Romans. The redefinition and reconstitution of the people of God, as comprising Jewish and Gentile believers on equal terms, is a critical theme which pervades the letter.

3. Paul's purposes in writing

The older commentators tended to assume that Paul was providing in Romans what Philip Melanchthon termed 'a compendium of Christian doctrine', somewhat detached from any particular sociohistorical context. Contemporary scholars, on the other hand, have tended to over-react to this, and to focus entirely on the transient situation of writer and readers. Not all have made this mistake, however. Professor Bruce called Romans 'a sustained and coherent

---

[65]Dunn, vol. 38A, pp. lxiiiff.   [66]Westerholm, pp. 118ff., 167.

statement of the gospel'.[67] Professor Cranfield has described it as 'a theological whole from which nothing at all substantial can be taken away without some measure of disfigurement or distortion'.[68] And Günther Bornkamm could refer to Romans as 'the last will and testament of the apostle Paul'.[69]

Nevertheless, all the New Testament documents (the gospels, the Acts and the Revelation as well as the letters) were written from within a particular situation. And this situation concerned partly the circumstances in which the author found himself, partly those of his intended readers, and usually a combination of both. It is these which help us to grasp what prompted each author to write and why he wrote what he did write. Romans is no exception to this general rule, although Paul nowhere spells out his reasons in detail. So different reconstructions have been attempted.

In his helpful monograph *The Reasons for Romans* Dr Alexander Wedderburn has urged that three pairs of factors need to be borne in mind – both the epistolary framework of Romans (its beginning and end) and its theological substance in the middle, both Paul's situation and the Roman church's, both the Jewish and the Gentile sections of the church, and their particular problems.[70]

What, then, were Paul's own circumstances? He is probably writing from Corinth during those three months which he spent 'in Greece'[71] just before sailing east. He mentions three places which he is intending to visit. The first is Jerusalem, taking with him the money which the Greek churches have contributed for the poverty-stricken Christians in Judea (15:25ff). The second is Rome itself. Having been frustrated in his previous attempts to visit the Christians in Rome, he is confident that this time he will be successful (1:11ff.; 15:23ff.). Thirdly, he plans to go on to Spain, in order to continue his pioneer missionary work 'where Christ was not known' (15:20, 24, 28). His most obvious purposes in writing were related to these three destinations.

Indeed, Paul thought of Rome, being situated between Jerusalem and Spain, as a place of refreshment after he had been to Jerusalem and a place of preparation *en route* for Spain. In other words, his visits to Jerusalem and Spain were of special significance to him because they expressed his two continuing commitments: to the welfare of Israel (Jerusalem) and to the Gentile mission (Spain).

Paul was evidently apprehensive about his forthcoming visit to Jerusalem. He had invested much thought, time and energy in promoting his collection, and had staked his personal prestige on it.

---

[67] In Donfried, p. 182. [68] Cranfield, vol. II, p. 819.
[69] In Donfried, pp. 16ff. [70] Wedderburn (1988), p. 5.
[71] Acts 20:2f.

It was to him more than an expression of Christian generosity.[72] It was a symbol of Jewish–Gentile solidarity in the body of Christ, and of an appropriate reciprocity (Gentiles sharing with Jews their material blessings, having first shared in their spiritual blessings, 15:27). So he urged the Roman Christians to join him in his prayer-struggle (15:30), not only for his personal safety, that he might be 'rescued from the unbelievers in Judea', but especially for the success of his mission, that his service might be 'acceptable to the saints there' (15:31). Humanly speaking, its acceptability was in doubt. Many Jewish Christians regarded him with deep suspicion. Some condemned him for disloyalty to his Jewish heritage, since in his evangelization of Gentiles he championed their freedom from the necessity of circumcision and law-observance. For such Jewish Christians, to accept the offering which Paul was taking to Jerusalem would be tantamount to endorsing his liberal policy. The apostle felt the need of support from Rome's mixed Jewish–Gentile Christian community; he wrote to them to solicit their prayers.

If Paul's immediate destination was Jerusalem, his ultimate destination was Spain. The fact was that his evangelization of the four provinces of Galatia, Asia, Macedonia and Achaia was now complete, since 'from Jerusalem all the way around to Illyricum' (approximately modern Albania), he had fully preached the gospel (15:19b). So what next? His ambition, which indeed had become his fixed policy, was to evangelize only 'where Christ was not known', so that he would 'not be building on someone else's foundation' (15:20). Now, therefore, he put these two things together (the fact and the policy) and concluded that there was 'no more place' for him 'to work in these regions' (15:23). In consequence, his sights were set on Spain, which was regarded as part of the western frontier of the Roman Empire, and to which, so far as he knew, the gospel had not yet penetrated.

But he could have decided to go to Spain without either visiting Rome on the way or even telling the Romans his plans. So why did he write to them? Surely because he felt the need of their fellowship. Rome was about two-thirds of the way from Jerusalem to Spain. He asked therefore if they would 'assist' him on his journey there (15:24), presumably with their encouragement, financial support and prayers. Indeed, he wanted 'to use Rome as a base of operations in the Western Mediterranean, much as he had used Antioch (originally) as a base in the East'.[73]

So Paul's intermediate destination, between Jerusalem and Spain, was to be Rome. A church had already come into being there, perhaps through Jewish Christians who had returned home from

---

[72] 2 Cor. 8 – 9.   [73] Wright, p. 234.

Jerusalem after Pentecost.[74] But who the pioneer, church-planting missionary may have been is not known. If Paul's planned visit seems inconsistent with his policy not to build on another's foundation, we can only guess that Rome was not regarded as any one person's territory and/or that he was influenced by the countervailing truth that as the specially appointed apostle to the Gentiles (1:5f.; 11:13; 15:15f.) it would be appropriate for him to minister in the metropolis of the Gentile world (1:11ff.), although he tactfully added that he would visit them only 'while passing through' (15:24, 28).

We still have to ask why he should write to them, however. It was partly no doubt to prepare them for his visit. More than that, because he had not visited Rome before, and because most of the church members there were not known to him, he saw the need to establish his apostolic credentials by giving a full account of his gospel. How he did this was determined in the main by 'the inner logic of the gospel',[75] but at the same time he was addressing his readers' concerns and responding to criticism, as will emerge in the next paragraphs. Meanwhile, with regard to his own situation, he sent them a threefold request – to pray that his service in Jerusalem would be acceptable, to help him on his way to Spain, and to receive him during his stopover in Rome as the apostle to the Gentiles.

Paul's purposes in writing to the Romans are not traceable only to his own situation, however, and in particular to his plans to travel to Jerusalem, Rome and Spain. His letter also arose from the situation in which the Roman Christians found themselves. What was that?

Even the most casual reading of Romans betrays the fact that the church in Rome was a mixed community consisting of both Jews and Gentiles, with Gentiles in the majority (1:5f., 13; 11:13), and that there was considerable conflict between these groups. It is further recognized that this conflict was primarily not ethnic (different races and cultures), but theological (different convictions about the status of God's covenant and law, and so about salvation). Some scholars suggest that the house churches in the city (see 16:5, and also verses 14 and 15 which refer to the Christians 'with them') may have represented these different doctrinal positions. It may also be that the 'disturbances' made by the Jews in Rome 'at the instigation of Chrestus' (probably meaning Christ), which were mentioned by Suetonius,[76] and which led to their expulsion from Rome in AD 49 by the Emperor Claudius,[77] were due to this same conflict between Jewish and Gentile *Christians*.

---

[74] Acts 2:10.   [75] Cranfield, vol. II, p. 818.
[76] Suetonius, *Life of Claudius* (c. AD 120), 25.4.   [77] See Acts 18:2.

What then was the theological issue which lay beneath the ethnic and cultural tensions between Jews and Gentiles in Rome? Dr Wedderburn refers to the Jewish Christians in Rome as representatives of 'Judaizing Christianity', since they regarded Christianity 'as simply part of Judaism' and required their followers to 'observe the Jewish law',[78] while the Gentile Christians he calls 'supporters of a law-free gospel'.[79] Moreover, he and many other scholars have also seen in the former group 'the weak' and in the latter 'the strong' whom Paul addresses in chapters 14 – 15, although this may well be an over-simplification. The 'weak in faith', who scrupulously observed the ceremonial regulations like the food laws, condemned Paul for not doing so. They may also have regarded themselves as the sole beneficiaries of God's promises, and were not at all in favour of Gentile evangelization unless the converts were prepared to be circumcised and observe the law in full.[80] To them Paul was both a traitor to the covenant and an enemy of the law (that is, an 'antinomian'). The 'strong in faith', on the other hand, who like Paul himself were champions of a 'law-free gospel', made the mistake of despising the weak for being still in unnecessary bondage to the law. Thus the Jewish Christians were proud of their favoured status, and the Gentile Christians of their freedom, so that Paul saw the need to humble them both.

Echoes of this controversy, in both its theological and its practical implications, may be heard rumbling throughout Romans. And Paul is seen from beginning to end as an authentic peacemaker, pouring oil on troubled waters, anxious to preserve both truth and peace without sacrificing either to the other. He himself had, of course, a foot in both camps. On the one hand, he was a patriotic Jew ('I could wish that I myself were cursed and cut off from Christ for the sake of my brothers . . . the people of Israel', 9:3). On the other hand, he had been specially commissioned as the apostle to the Gentiles ('I am talking to you Gentiles . . . as I am the apostle to the Gentiles . . .', 11:13; *cf.* 1:5; 15:15f.). So he was in a unique position to be an agent of reconciliation. He was determined to make a full and fresh statement of the apostolic gospel, which would not compromise any of its revealed truths, but which would at the same time resolve the conflict between Jews and Gentiles over the covenant and the law, and so promote the unity of the church.

In his ministry of reconciliation, therefore, Paul develops two paramount themes, and interweaves them beautifully. The first is the justification of guilty sinners by God's grace alone in Christ alone through faith alone, irrespective of either status or works. This is the most humbling and levelling of all Christian truths and

---

[78] Wedderburn, p. 50.   [79] *Ibid.*, p. 62.   [80] *Cf.* Acts 15:1.

35

experiences, and so is the fundamental basis of Christian unity. In fact, as Martin Hengel has written, 'although people nowadays are fond of asserting otherwise, no-one understood the real essence of Pauline theology, the salvation given *sola gratia*, by grace alone, better than Augustine and Martin Luther.'[81]

Paul's second theme is the consequent redefinition of the people of God, no longer according to descent, circumcision or culture, but according to faith in Jesus, so that all believers are the true children of Abraham, regardless of their ethnic origin or religious practice. So 'there is no difference' now between Jews and Gentiles, either in the fact of their sin and guilt or in Christ's offer and gift of salvation (*e.g.* 3:21ff., 27f.; 4:9ff.; 10:11ff.). Indeed, 'the single most important theme of Romans is the equality of Jews and Gentiles'.[82]

And linked with this is the continuing validity both of God's covenant (which now embraces Gentiles and demonstrates his faithfulness) and of his law (so that, although 'released' from it as the way of salvation, we yet through the Spirit 'fulfil' it as the revelation of God's holy will).

A brief overview of the letter and its argument will throw further light on the intertwining of these related themes.

4. A brief overview of Romans

Paul's two main themes – the integrity of the gospel committed to him and the solidarity of Jews and Gentiles in the messianic community – are already apparent in the first half of the letter's first chapter.

Paul calls the good news 'the gospel of God' (1) because he is its author, and 'the gospel of his Son' (9) because he is its substance. In verses 1–5 he focuses on the person of Jesus Christ, David's son by descent and powerfully declared God's Son by the resurrection. In verse 16 he focuses on his work, since the gospel is God's power for the salvation of everyone who believes, 'first for the Jew, then for the Gentile'.

In between these succinct statements of the gospel, Paul seeks to establish a personal relationship with his readers. He is writing to 'all in Rome' who are believers (7), irrespective of their ethnic origin, although he knows that the majority of them are Gentiles (13). He thanks God for all of them, he prays for them constantly, he longs to see them, and he has tried many times (so far unsuccessfully) to visit them (8–13). He feels under obligation to preach the gospel in the capital city of the world. Indeed, he is

---

[81] Hengel, p. 86.   [82] Sanders (1991), p. 66.

eager to do so, because in the gospel God's righteous way of 'righteoussing' the unrighteous has been revealed (14–17).

The wrath of God (1:18 – 3:20)

The revelation of God's righteousness in the gospel is necessary because of the revelation of his wrath against unrighteousness (18). The wrath of God, his pure and perfect antagonism to evil, is directed against all those who deliberately suppress what they know to be true and right, in order to go their own way. For everybody has some knowledge of God and of goodness, whether through the created world (19f.), or through conscience (32), or through the moral law written on human hearts (2:12ff.), or through the law of Moses committed to the Jews (2:17ff.).

The apostle thus divides the human race into three sections – depraved pagan society (1:18–32), critical moralizers whether Jews or Gentiles (2:1–16), and well-instructed, self-confident Jews (2:17 – 3:8). He then concludes by accusing the whole human race (3:9–20). In each case his argument is the same, that nobody lives up to the knowledge which he or she has. Even the special privileges of the Jews do not exempt them from divine judgment. No, 'Jews and Gentiles alike are all under sin' (3:9), 'for God does not show favouritism' (2:11). All human beings are sinful, guilty and without excuse before God. The picture is one of unrelieved darkness.

The grace of God (3:21 – 8:39)

The 'But now' of 3:21 is one of the great adversatives of the Bible. For into the universal darkness of human sin and guilt the light of the gospel has shone. Paul again calls it 'the righteousness of [or from] God' (as in 1:17), that is, his just justification of the unjust. This is possible only through the cross, in which God has demonstrated his justice (3:25f.) as well as his love (5:8), and it is available to 'all who believe' (3:22), whether Jews or Gentiles. In explaining the cross, Paul resorts to the key words 'propitiation', 'redemption' and 'justification'. And then, in responding to Jewish objections (3:27–31), he argues that because justification is by faith alone, there can be no boasting before God, no discrimination between Jews and Gentiles and no disregard for the law.

Romans 4 is a brilliant essay in which Paul proves that Abraham, the founding father of Israel, was himself justified neither by his works (4–8), nor by his circumcision (9–12), nor by the law (13–15), but by faith. In consequence, Abraham is now 'the father of all who believe', irrespective of whether they are Jews or Gentiles (11, 16–25). The divine impartiality is evident.

Having established that God justifies even the wicked by faith (4:5), Paul affirms the great blessings enjoyed by his justified people (5:1–11). *Therefore*, he begins, we have peace with God, we are standing in his grace, and we rejoice in the prospect of seeing and sharing his glory. Even suffering does not shake our confidence, because of God's love which he has both poured into our hearts through his Spirit (5) and proved on the cross through his Son (8). Because of what God has already done for us, we dare to say that 'we shall be saved' on the last day (9–10).

Two human communities have now been portrayed, the one characterized by sin and guilt, the other by grace and faith. The head of the old humanity is Adam, the head of the new is Christ. So then, with almost mathematical precision, Paul compares and contrasts them (5:12–21). The comparison is simple. In both cases the one deed of one man has affected enormous numbers of people. The contrast, however, is much more significant. Whereas Adam's disobedience brought condemnation and death, Christ's obedience has brought justification and life. Indeed, Christ's saving work will prove far more successful than Adam's destructiveness.

In the middle of this antithesis between Adam and Christ, Paul introduces Moses: 'the law was added so that the trespass might increase. But where sin increased, grace increased all the more' (20). Both statements will have sounded shocking in Jewish ears, because they will have seemed incorrigibly antinomian. The first appeared to blame sin on the law, and the second to minimize sin by magnifying grace. Did Paul's gospel both disparage the law and encourage sin? Paul answers the second charge in Romans 6, and the first in Romans 7.

Twice in Romans 6 (verses I and 15) we hear Paul's critic asking whether Paul meant that we may go on sinning so that God's grace may go on forgiving. Both times Paul responds with an outraged 'God forbid!' For Christians to ask such a question shows that they have never understood the meaning of either their baptism (1–14) or their conversion (15–23). Did they not know that their baptism signified union with Christ in his death, that his death was a death 'unto sin' (meeting its demand, paying its penalty), and that they had shared in his resurrection too? By union with Christ they were themselves 'dead unto sin and alive unto God'. How then could they go on living in what they had died to? It was similar with their conversion. Had they not decisively offered themselves to God as his slaves? Then how could they contemplate lapsing into their old slavery to sin? Our baptism and conversion have both closed the door on to the old life, and opened a door on to a new life. It is not impossible for us to go back, but it is inconceivable that we should. Far from encouraging sin, grace prohibits it.

Paul's critics were also disturbed by his teaching on the law. So he clarifies it in Romans 7. He makes three points. First (1–6), Christians have 'died to the law' in Christ, just as they have 'died to sin'. Consequently, they are 'released' from the law, that is, from its condemnation, and are now free not to sin but to serve in the new way of the Spirit. Secondly, writing (I believe) out of his own past (7–13), Paul argues that, although the law reveals, provokes and condemns sin, it is not responsible for sin or death. No, the law is holy. Paul exonerates the law.

Thirdly (14–25), Paul describes in vivid terms a painful, continuing, inner moral struggle. Whether the 'wretched man' who cries for deliverance is a regenerate Christian or unregenerate (I take a third position), and whether he is Paul himself or somebody Paul is impersonating, his purpose in this paragraph is to demonstrate the weakness of the law. His defeat is due neither to the law (which is holy), nor even to his true self, but to 'sin living in me' (17, 20), and this the law has no power to control. But now (8:1–4) God has done through his Son and Spirit what the law, weakened by our sinful nature, was unable to do. In particular the remedy for indwelling sin is the indwelling Spirit (8:9), who has not been mentioned in chapter 7, apart from verse 6. Thus for both justification and sanctification we are 'not under law but under grace'.

As Romans 7 is full of the law, so Romans 8 is full of the Spirit. During the first half of the chapter Paul describes some of the very varied ministries of the Holy Spirit – liberating us, indwelling us, giving us life, leading us into self-control, witnessing with our spirit that we are God's children, and interceding for us. The fact that we are God's children reminds Paul that we are therefore also his heirs, and that suffering is the only road to glory. He then draws a parallel between the sufferings and glory of God's creation and the sufferings and glory of God's children. The creation has been subjected to frustration, he writes. But one day it will be liberated from its bondage. Meanwhile the creation is groaning as in the pains of childbirth, and we groan with it. We also wait with eager yet patient expectation for the final redemption of the universe, including our bodies.

In the last twelve verses of Romans 8 the apostle rises to sublime heights of Christian confidence. He expresses five convictions about God at work for our good, that is, for our final salvation (28). He outlines five stages of God's purpose from a past to a future eternity (29–30). And he flings out five defiant questions to which there is no answer. He thus fortifies us with fifteen assurances of God's steadfast love, from which nothing can ever separate us.

The plan of God (9 – 11)

Throughout the first half of his letter Paul has forgotten neither the ethnic mix of the Roman church nor the tensions which kept surfacing between the Jewish Christian minority and the Gentile Christian majority. The time has come for him to address head-on the underlying theological problem. How is it that the Jewish people as a whole had rejected their Messiah? How could their unbelief be reconciled with God's covenant and promises? How also did the inclusion of the Gentiles fit in with God's plan? It is notable that each of these three chapters begins with a personal and emotional statement of Paul's love for Israel – his anguish over their alienation (9:1ff.), his longing for their salvation (10:1) and his own continuing Jewishness (11:1).

In chapter 9 Paul defends God's covenant loyalty on the ground that his promises were not addressed to all Jacob's descendants, but to Israel within Israel, a remnant, since he has always worked according to his 'purpose of election' (11). This can be seen not only in his choosing Isaac rather than Ishmael, and Jacob rather than Esau, but also in his having mercy on Moses, while hardening Pharaoh (14–18), even though this was a judicial surrender of Pharaoh to the wilful hardening of his own heart. If we still have problems over election, we must remember that it is always inappropriate for human beings to talk back to God (19–21), that we must let God be God in his resolve to make known his power and mercy (22–23), and that Scripture itself foretold the calling of Gentiles as well as Jews to be his people (24–29).

It is plain from the end of chapter 9 and from chapter 10, however, that Israel's unbelief cannot be explained *tout simple* by God's purpose of election. For Paul goes on to affirm that Israel 'stumbled over the stumbling-stone', namely Christ and his cross. This is to accuse Israel of a proud unwillingness to submit to God's way of salvation, and of a religious zeal which was not based on knowledge (9:30 – 10:4). Paul goes on to contrast 'the righteousness that is by the law' with 'the righteousness that is by faith', and to emphasize from a skilful use of Deuteronomy 30 the ready accessibility of Christ to faith. There is no need for anybody to go in search of Christ, since he has come and died and risen, and is close to any who will call on him (5–11). Moreover, there is no difference in this between Jew and Gentile, since the same Lord is Lord of all and richly blesses all who call on him (12–13). But, for this, evangelism is necessary (14–15). Why then did Israel not accept the good news? It is not that they had not heard it or understood it. Why then? It is that all day long God had stretched out his hands to welcome them, but they were 'disobedient and obstinate' (16–21).

So then, the unbelief of Israel, which in Romans 9 is attributed to God's purpose of election, in Romans 10 is attributed to her pride, ignorance and stubbornness. The tension between divine sovereignty and human responsibility constitutes an antinomy which the finite mind cannot fathom.

With chapter 11 Paul looks into the future. He declares that Israel's fall is neither total, since there is a believing remnant (1–10), nor final, since God has not rejected his people and they will recover (11). If through Israel's fall salvation has come to the Gentiles, now through the Gentiles' salvation Israel will be made envious (12). Indeed, Paul sees his evangelistic ministry in terms of arousing his own people to envy, in order to save some of them (13–14). And then Israel's 'fulness' will bring 'much greater riches' to the world. Paul goes on to develop his allegory of the olive tree, and teaches two lessons from it. The first is a warning to the Gentiles (the wild olive shoot which has been grafted in) not to presume or boast (17–22). And the second is a promise to Israel (the natural branches) that if they do not persist in unbelief, they will be grafted back in again (23–24). Paul's vision for the future, which he calls a 'mystery' or revelation, is that when the fulness of the Gentiles has come in, 'all Israel will be saved' as well (25–27). And the ground of his assurance is that 'God's gift and call are irrevocable' (29). So we may confidently expect the 'fulness' of both Jews and Gentiles to be gathered in (12, 25). Indeed, God will 'have mercy on them all' (32), meaning not everybody without exception but rather both Jews and Gentiles without distinction. It is not surprising that this prospect leads Paul to break out into a doxology, in which he praises God for the depth of both his riches and his wisdom (33–36).

The will of God (12:1 – 15:13)

Calling the Roman Christians his 'brothers' (the old ethnic distinctions having been abolished), Paul now addresses to them an eloquent appeal. He bases it on 'the mercies of God' which he has been expounding, and he calls for both the consecration of their bodies and the renewal of their minds. He sets before them the stark alternative which has always and everywhere confronted the people of God, either to conform to the pattern of this world or to be transformed by renewed minds which discern God's 'good, pleasing and perfect will'. The choice is between the world's fashion and the Lord's will.

In the chapters which follow it becomes clear that God's good will is concerned with all our relationships, which are radically changed by the gospel. Paul treats eight of them, namely, our

41

relationship to God, ourselves, each other, our enemies, the state, the law, the last day and the 'weak'. Our renewed minds, which begin by seeking God's will (1–2), are also to evaluate ourselves and our gifts soberly, and not to have either too high or too low an opinion of ourselves (3–8). Our relationship to one another follows naturally from the mutual ministries which our gifts make possible. The love which binds members of the Christian family together will include sincerity, affection, honour, patience, hospitality, sympathy, harmony and humility (9–16).

Our relationship to our enemies or to evildoers comes next (17–21). Echoing the teaching of Jesus, Paul writes that we are not to retaliate or take revenge, but rather to leave the punishment of evil to God, since it is his prerogative, and meanwhile to seek peace, serve our enemies and overcome evil with good. Our relationship with the governing authorities (13:1–7) may well have been suggested to Paul's mind by his reference to God's wrath (12:19). If the punishment of evil is God's prerogative, one of the ways in which he does it is through the state's administration of justice, since the magistrate is God's 'minister' to punish the wrongdoer. The state also has a positive role to promote and reward good in the community. Our submission to the authorities is certainly not unconditional, however. If the state misuses its God-given authority, to command what God forbids or forbid what God commands, our clear Christian duty is to disobey the state in order to obey God.

Verses 8–10 revert to love, and teach that loving our neighbour is both an unpaid debt and the fulfilment of the law. For though we are 'not under law', in the sense that we look to Christ for justification and to the Holy Spirit for sanctification, we are still called to 'fulfil the law' in daily obedience to God's commandments. In this sense we must not set the Spirit and the law over against each other, since the Holy Spirit writes the law in our hearts. And this primacy of love is the more urgent as the day of Christ's return approaches. We are to wake up, to get up, to dress, and to live as those who belong to the day (verses 11–14).

Our relationship with the 'weak' is the one Paul treats at greatest length (14:1 – 15:13). They are evidently weak in faith or conviction, rather than in will or character. They must have been mainly Jewish Christians, who believed they should still observe both the food laws and the feasts and fasts of the Jewish calendar. Paul himself is one of the 'strong' and identifies with their position. His educated conscience tells him that foods and days are matters of secondary importance. But he refuses to ride roughshod over the sensitive consciences of the weak. His overall exhortation to the church is to 'accept' the weak as God has done (14:1, 3) and to 'accept' one another as Christ has done (15:7). If they welcome the weak into their hearts and their fellowship, they will not despise them, or condemn them, or damage them by persuading them to go against their consciences.

The most notable feature of these practical instructions is that Paul grounds them on his Christology, and in particular on the death, resurrection and parousia of Jesus. The weak are brothers and sisters for whom Christ died. Christ rose to be their Lord, and we have no right to interfere with his servants. He is also coming to be our judge; so we should not play the role of judge ourselves. We should also follow the example of Christ who did not please himself but became a servant – indeed a servant of both Jews and Gentiles. So Paul leaves his readers with a beautiful vision of the weak and the strong, Jewish believers and Gentile believers, who are bound together by such a 'spirit of unity' that 'with one heart and mouth' they glorify God together (15:5–6).

In his conclusion Paul describes his ministry as apostle to the Gentiles, together with his policy to preach the gospel only where Christ is not known (15:14–22); he shares with them his travel plans to visit them on his way to Spain, but first to take the offering to Jerusalem as a symbol of Jewish–Gentile solidarity (15:23–29); and he asks for their prayers (15:30–33). He then commends Phoebe to them, who is assumed to be the bearer of the letter to Rome (16:1–2); he sends greetings to twenty-six named individuals (16:3–16), men and women, slaves and free, Jews and Gentiles, who help us to grasp the extraordinary unity-in-diversity enjoyed by the church in Rome; he warns them against false teachers (16:17–20); he sends messages from eight individuals who are with him in Corinth (16:21–24); and he expresses a final doxology. Although the doxology's syntax is a little complex, its content is marvellous. It enables the apostle to end where he began (1:1–5), since the letter's introduction and conclusion both refer to the gospel of Christ, the commission of God, the outreach to the nations and the summons to the obedience of faith.

Introduction: The gospel of God and Paul's eagerness to share it
Romans 1:1–17

Paul begins his letter in a very personal way. The personal pronoun and possessive (I, me, my) occur more than twenty times in these opening verses. He is evidently anxious from the start to establish a close relationship with his readers. His introduction is in three parts, which I will call 'Paul and the gospel' (1–6), 'Paul and the Romans' (7–13) and 'Paul and evangelism' (14–17).

1:1–6
1. Paul and the gospel

Letter-writing conventions vary from culture to culture. Our modern way is to address our correspondent first ('Dear Joan') and to identify ourselves only at the end ('Yours sincerely, John'). In the ancient world, however, the custom was to reverse the order, the writer announcing himself or herself first and the correspondent next ('John to Joan, greetings!'). Paul normally followed the convention of his day, but here he deviates from it by giving a much more elaborate description of himself than usual, in relation to the gospel. The reason is probably that he did not found the church in Rome. Nor has he yet visited it. He feels the need, therefore, to establish his credentials as an apostle and to summarize his gospel. *Paul, a servant of Christ Jesus, called to be an apostle and set apart for the gospel of God*, he begins.

'Servant' is *doulos* and should really be translated 'slave'. In the Old Testament there was an honourable succession of individual Israelites, beginning with Moses and Joshua, who called themselves Yahweh's 'servants' or 'slaves' (*e.g.* 'O LORD, truly I am your servant'),[1] while Yahweh also designated Israel collectively 'my servant'.[2] In the New Testament, however, it is remarkable how easily the title 'Lord' has been transferred from Yahweh to Jesus (*e.g.* verses 4, 7), while the Lord's 'servants' are no longer Israel, but all his people, irrespective of whether they are Jews or Gentiles.

'Apostle', on the other hand, was a distinctively Christian name from the beginning, in that Jesus himself chose it as his designation of the Twelve,[3] and Paul claimed to have been added to their number.[4] The distinctive qualifications of the apostles were that they were directly and personally called and commissioned by Jesus, that they were eye-witnesses of the historical Jesus, at least (and specially) of his resurrection,[5] and that they were sent out by

[1] Ps 116:16. [2] *E.g.* Is. 43:1, 10. [3] Lk. 6:12f. [4] *E.g.* Gal. 1:1.
[5] Acts 1:21–26; 1 Cor. 9:1; 15:8f.

him to preach with his authority. The New Testament apostle thus resembled both the Old Testament prophet, who was 'called' and 'sent' by Yahweh to speak in his name, and the *shaliach* of rabbinic Judaism, who was 'an authorized representative or delegate, legally empowered to act (within prescribed limits) on behalf of his principal'.[6] It is against this double background that the apostle's authoritative teaching role is to be understood.

Paul's twofold designation as 'slave' and 'apostle' is particularly striking when these words are contrasted with one another. First, 'slave' is a title of great humility; it expressed Paul's sense of personal insignificance, without rights of his own, having been purchased to belong to Christ. 'Apostle', on the other hand, was a title of great authority; it expressed his sense of official privilege and dignity by reason of his appointment by Jesus Christ. Secondly, 'slave' is a general Christian word (every disciple looks to Jesus Christ as Lord), whereas 'apostle' is a special title (reserved for the Twelve and Paul and perhaps one or two others such as James). As an apostle, he had been *set apart for the gospel of God*.

How did Paul intend his readers to understand his reference to having been set apart? The verb *aphōrismenos* has the same root meaning as 'Pharisee' (*pharisaios*). Was this deliberate, since Paul had been a Pharisee?[7] Anders Nygren, for example, reflecting his Lutheran tradition, writes that 'as a Pharisee Paul had set himself apart for the law, but now God had set him apart for . . . the gospel . . . Thus in the very first verse of this epistle we encounter the letter's basic juxtaposition of law and gospel which, from one point of view, is the theme of Romans.'[8] It is questionable, however, whether Paul's readers would have picked up this play on words. In his own mind Paul is more likely to have seen a parallel between his consecration to be an apostle and Jeremiah's to be a prophet. For in Galatians Paul wrote that God had set him apart (using the same word) from birth, and then called him to preach Christ to the Gentiles,[9] just as God had said to Jeremiah: 'Before you were born I set you apart; I appointed you as a prophet to the nations.'[10] We need, therefore, to think of Paul's Damascus road encounter with Christ not only as his conversion but as his commissioning to be an apostle (*egō apostellō se*, 'I send you', 'I make you an apostle'),[11] and especially to be the apostle to the Gentiles.

Paul's two verbal expressions, then, *called to be an apostle* and *set apart for the gospel of God*, belong inseparably together. One cannot think of 'apostle' without thinking of 'gospel', and *vice versa*. As an apostle, it was Paul's responsibility to receive,

---

[6] Barrett, p. 16. [7] Phil. 3:5. [8] Nygren, pp. 45f. [9] Gal. 1:15f.
[10] Je. 1:5. [11] Acts 26:17.

formulate, defend, maintain and proclaim the gospel, and so combine the roles of trustee, advocate and herald. As Professor Cranfield has put it, the apostle's function was 'to serve the gospel by an authoritative and normative proclamation of it'.[12]

Paul now proceeds to give a six-point analysis of the gospel, to which he has been set apart.

1. The origin of the gospel is God

'God is the most important word in this epistle,' Dr Leon Morris has written. 'Romans is a book about God. No topic is treated with anything like the frequency of God. Everything Paul touches in this letter he relates to God . . . There is nothing like it elsewhere.'[13] So the Christian good news is *the gospel of God*. The apostles did not invent it; it was revealed and entrusted to them by God.

This is still the first and most basic conviction which underlies all authentic evangelism. What we have to share with others is neither a miscellany of human speculations, nor one more religion to add to the rest, nor really a religion at all. It is rather *the gospel of God*, God's own good news for a lost world. Without this conviction, evangelism is evacuated of its content, purpose and drive.

2. The attestation of the gospel is Scripture

Verse 2: *the gospel he promised beforehand through his prophets in the Holy Scriptures.* That is to say, although God revealed the gospel to the apostles, it did not come to them as a complete novelty, because he had already promised it through his prophets in Old Testament Scripture. There is, in fact, an essential continuity between the Old Testament and the New. Jesus himself was quite clear that the Scriptures bore witness to him, that he was the son of man of Daniel 7 and the suffering servant of Isaiah 53, and that, as it had been written, he had to suffer in order to enter into his glory.[14] In the Acts we hear Peter quoting the Old Testament in reference to Jesus' resurrection, exaltation and gift of the Spirit.[15] We also watch Paul reasoning with people out of the Scriptures that the Christ must suffer and rise, and that he was Jesus.[16] He similarly insisted that it was 'according to the Scriptures' that Christ both died for our sins and was raised on the third day.[17] It was thus that both the law and the prophets bore witness to the gospel (3:21; *cf.* 1:17).

We have reason, then, to be thankful that the gospel of God has a double attestation, namely the prophets in the Old Testament and

---

[12] Cranfield, vol. I, p. 53.   [13] Morris (1988), p. 40.
[14] Jn. 5:39; Lk. 24:25ff., 44f.   [15] Acts 2:14ff.; *cf.* 1 Pet. 1:10ff.
[16] Acts 17:2f.; *cf.* 13:32ff.   [17] 1 Cor. 15:3f.

the apostles in the New. Both bear witness to Jesus Christ, and this is what Paul comes to next.

3. The substance of the gospel is Jesus Christ

If we bring verses 1 and 3 together, by omitting the parenthesis of verse 2, we are left with the statement that Paul was set apart for the gospel of God *regarding his Son*. For the gospel of God is 'the gospel of his Son' (9). God's good news is about Jesus. As Luther put it in his gloss on this verse: 'Here the door is thrown open wide for the understanding of Holy Scripture, that is, that everything must be understood in relation to Christ.'[18] Calvin writes similarly that 'the whole gospel is contained in Christ'. Therefore, 'to move even a step from Christ means to withdraw oneself from the gospel'.[19]

Paul now describes him by two contrasting clauses: *who as to his human nature was a descendant of David* (3), *and who through the Spirit of holiness was declared with power to be the Son of God, by his resurrection from the dead: Jesus Christ our Lord* (4). Here are references, direct or indirect, to the birth (descended from David), death (presupposed by his resurrection), resurrection from the dead, and reign (on David's throne) of Jesus Christ. So neatly and carefully constructed is the parallelism that many scholars have guessed that Paul is making use of a fragment from an early creed. If so, he now gives it his apostolic endorsement. It expresses an antithesis between two titles (seed of David and Son of God), between two verbs (he 'became' or 'was born' David's descendant, but *was declared* or 'appointed' God's Son), and between two qualifying clauses (*kata sarka*, 'according to flesh', and *kata pneuma hagiōsynēs*, literally, 'according to spirit of holiness').

First, the two titles. 'Son of David' was a universally recognized messianic title.[20] So was 'Son of God', based particularly on Psalm 2:7. The way Jesus himself understood it, however, as seen both in his personal approach to God as '*Abba*, Father' and in referring to himself absolutely as 'the Son',[21] already indicates that the designation is divine, not merely messianic. Paul evidently used it thus (not only in 1:3–4 and 9, but also *e.g.* in 5:10 and 8:3, 32). The two titles together speak, therefore, of his humanity and his deity.

---

[18] Luther (1515), p. 4.   [19] Calvin, p. 15.

[20] The title goes back ultimately to 2 Sa. 7:12ff., where God promised to establish David's throne for ever; it was picked up by the prophets (*e.g.* Ps. 89; Is. 9:6ff.; 11:1, 10; Je. 23:5f.; and Ezk. 34:23f.; 37:24f.) and further developed in the Qumran literature. For the New Testament fulfilment see *e.g.* Mt. 1; Mk. 12:35ff.; Lk. 1 – 2; Jn. 7:42; Acts 2:29ff.; 13:22f.; 2 Tim. 2:8; Rev. 5:5; 22:16.

[21] *E.g.* Mt. 11:27.

Of the two verbs, the first causes little difficulty. Although it means no more than 'became', it evidently refers to Jesus' descent from David by birth (and maybe by adoption too, since Joseph acknowledged him as his son). The second verb, however, raises a problem. The translation *declared with power to be the Son of God by his resurrection from the dead* is readily intelligible. But the trouble is that *horizō* does not really (or usually) mean 'declare'. It is properly rendered 'appoint', as when God 'appointed' Jesus the judge of the world.[22] Yet the New Testament does not teach that Jesus was appointed, established or installed Son of God at or by the resurrection, since he has been the Son of God eternally. This leads to the suggestion that the words 'in power' should be attached to the noun 'Son of God' rather than to the verb 'appoint'. In this case Paul is affirming that Jesus was 'appointed Son-of-God-in-power'[23] or even 'declared to be the powerful Son of God' (BAGD). Nygren captures the antithesis well by writing: 'So *the resurrection is the turning point in the existence of the Son of God*. Before that he was the Son of God in weakness and lowliness. Through the resurrection he becomes the Son of God in power.'[24]

The third contrast is in the two qualifying clauses 'according to flesh' and 'according to spirit of holiness'. Although 'flesh' has a variety of meanings for Paul, here it evidently refers to Jesus' human nature or physical descent, though perhaps with an undertone of its weakness or vulnerability over against the power implicit in his resurrection and deity. Some commentators then insist that, in order to preserve the parallelism, 'according to spirit of holiness' must be translated 'according to his divine nature' or at least 'according to his holy human spirit'. But 'Spirit of holiness' is not at all an obvious reference to Jesus' divine nature. Moreover, it was not only a part of him, whether his divine nature or his human spirit, which was raised from the dead or appointed Son-of-God-in-power by the resurrection. On the contrary, it was the whole Jesus Christ, body and spirit, human and divine.

Other commentators point out that 'Spirit of holiness' was a natural Hebraism for the Holy Spirit, and that there were obvious links between the Holy Spirit and the resurrection, both because he is 'the Spirit of him who raised Jesus from the dead'[25] and – more important – because it was the risen and exalted Christ who demonstrated his power and authority by pouring out the Spirit,[26] and who thus inaugurated the new era, which is the age of the Spirit.

It seems then that the two expressions 'according to the flesh' and 'according to the Spirit' refer not to the two natures of Jesus Christ

---

[22] Acts 10:42; 17:31.   [23] *E.g.* Cranfield, vol. I, p. 62.
[24] Nygren, p. 51; *cf.* 2 Cor. 13:4.
[25] Rom. 8:11.   [26] Acts 2:33.

(human and divine), but to the two stages of his ministry, pre-resurrection and post-resurrection, the first frail and the second powerful through the outpoured Spirit. So here is a balanced statement of both the humiliation and the exaltation, the weakness and the power of God's Son, his human descent traced to David, his divine sonship-in-power established by the resurrection and gift of the Spirit. Moreover, this unique person, seed of David and Son of God, weak and powerful, incarnate and exalted, is *Jesus* (a human, historical figure), *Christ* (the Messiah of Old Testament Scripture), *our Lord*, who owns and rules our lives. Perhaps we could add that Jesus' two titles, 'the Christ' and 'the Lord', will have specially appealed to Jewish and Gentile Christians respectively.

4. The scope of the gospel is all the nations

Paul now comes back from his description of the gospel to his own apostleship and writes: *Through him* (sc. the risen Christ) *and for his name's sake* (a phrase to which I will return), *we received grace and apostleship to call people from among all the Gentiles to the obedience that comes from faith* (5). It is unlikely that by using the plural 'we', Paul is wanting to associate the other apostles with him, since he nowhere mentions them in this letter. Probably it is an editorial 'we', or the 'we' of apostolic authority, by which in reality he was referring to himself. What then did he 'receive' from God through Christ? He calls it *grace and apostleship*, which in the context seems to mean 'the undeserved privilege of being an apostle'. For Paul always attributed his apostleship to God's gracious decision and appointment.[27]

As Paul goes on to state the purpose of his apostleship, he discloses further aspects of the gospel. He defines its scope as *all the Gentiles*. This seems to imply that the Christians in Rome were predominantly Gentile, since he specifically mentions them: *And you also are among those who are called to belong to Jesus Christ* (6). Yet Paul will shortly describe the gospel as 'the power of God for the salvation of everyone who believes, first for the Jew, then for the Gentile' (1:16). What he is affirming is that the gospel is for everybody; its scope is universal. He himself was a patriotic Jew, who retained his love for his people and longed passionately for their salvation (9:1ff.; 10:1). At the same time, he had been called to be the apostle to the Gentiles.[28] We too, if we are to be committed to world mission, will have to be liberated from all pride of race, nation, tribe, caste and class, and acknowledge that God's gospel is

---

[27] *E.g.* Rom. 12:3; 15:15; 1 Cor. 15:10; Gal. 1:15; 2:9; Eph. 3:1f., 7f.
[28] Acts 9:15; 22:21; 26:17f.; Rom. 11:13; 15:16ff.; Gal. 1:16; 2:2ff.; Eph. 3:8.

for everybody, without exception and without distinction. This is a major theme of Romans.

5. The purpose of the gospel is the obedience of faith

Literally, Paul writes that he has received his apostleship 'unto obedience of faith among all the nations'. So 'obedience of faith' is his definition of the response which the gospel demands. It is a particularly notable expression, coming as it does at the beginning and the end of Romans (see 16:26), since it is in Romans that Paul insists more strongly than anywhere else that justification is 'through faith alone'. Yet here he apparently writes that it is not by faith alone, but by 'obedience of faith'. Has he lost his bearings? Does the apostle now contradict himself? No, we must give him credit for consistency of thought.

Three main explanations of the phrase are offered. The first is that it means 'obedience to the faith', taking 'faith' here as a body of belief. And certainly this is a New Testament expression.[29] Further, the apostles do refer to conversion in terms of obedience to truth or doctrine.[30] But when 'faith' has this meaning, one would expect the definite article to be in place ('the faith'), whereas the whole context of Romans really demands a reference here to 'faith' (as in 8, 16–17).

The second possibility is that this is a genitive of 'equivalence', and that the expression should be translated 'the obedience which consists of faith'. As John Murray puts it, 'the faith which the apostleship was intended to promote was not an evanescent act of emotion but the commitment of wholehearted devotion to Christ and to the truth of his gospel'.[31] And yet, although faith and obedience do always belong together, they are not synonymous, and the New Testament usually maintains a distinction between them.

The third option is that the genitive is one of source or origin. So NIV renders it *the obedience that comes from faith*, which immediately reminds one of Abraham who 'by faith . . . obeyed'.[32] At the same time we note that this is the obedience of faith, not the obedience of law. Perhaps, in fact, the second and third options do not exclude each other. For the proper response to the gospel is faith, indeed faith alone. Yet a true and living faith in Jesus Christ both includes within itself an element of submission (*cf.* 10:3), especially because its object is 'Jesus Christ our Lord' (4) or 'the Lord Jesus Christ' (7), and leads inevitably into a lifetime of obedience. That is why the response Paul looked for was a total,

---

[29] Acts 6:7. *Cf.* 2 Thes. 1:8; 1 Pet. 4:17.   [30] *E.g.* Rom. 6:17; 10:16; 1 Pet. 1:22.
[31] Murray, vol. I, p. 14.   [32] Heb. 11:8.

unreserved commitment to Jesus Christ, which he called 'the obedience of faith'. This is our answer to those who argue that it is
possible to accept Jesus Christ as Saviour without surrendering to
him as Lord. It is not. Certainly the Roman Christians had believed
and obeyed, for Paul describes them as being *among those who are
called to belong to Jesus Christ* (6).

6. The goal of the gospel is the honour of Christ's name

The words *for his name's sake*, which NIV places at the beginning of
verse 5, actually come at the end of the Greek sentence and so form
something of a climax. Why did Paul desire to bring the nations to
the obedience of faith? It was for the sake of the glory and honour
of Christ's name. For God had 'exalted him to the highest place' and
had given him 'the name that is above every name', in order that 'at
the name of Jesus every knee should bow ... and every tongue
confess that Jesus Christ is Lord'.[33] If, therefore, God desires every
knee to bow to Jesus and every tongue to confess him, so should
we. We should be 'jealous' (as Scripture sometimes puts it) for the
honour of his name – troubled when it remains unknown, hurt
when it is ignored, indignant when it is blasphemed, and all the time
anxious and determined that it shall be given the honour and glory
which are due to it. The highest of all missionary motives is neither
obedience to the Great Commission (important as that is), nor love
for sinners who are alienated and perishing (strong as that incentive
is, especially when we contemplate the wrath of God, verse 18), but
rather zeal – burning and passionate zeal – for the glory of Jesus
Christ.

Some evangelism, to be sure, is no better than a thinly disguised
form of imperialism, whenever our real ambition is for the honour
of our nation, church, organization, or ourselves. Only one
imperialism is Christian, however, and that is concern for His
Imperial Majesty Jesus Christ, and for the glory of his empire or
kingdom. The earliest Christians, John tells us, went out 'for the
sake of the Name'.[34] He does not even specify to which name he is
referring. But we know. And Paul tells us. It is the incomparable
name of Jesus. Before this supreme goal of the Christian mission, all
unworthy motives wither and die.

To sum up, here are six fundamental truths about the gospel. Its
origin is God the Father and its substance Jesus Christ his Son. Its
attestation is Old Testament Scripture and its scope all the nations.
Our immediate purpose in proclaiming it is to bring people to the
obedience of faith, but our ultimate goal is the greater glory of the

[33] Phil. 2:9ff.   [34] 3 Jn. 7.

name of Jesus Christ. Or, to simplify these truths by the use of six prepositions, we can say that the good news is the gospel *of* God, *about* Christ, *according to* Scripture, *for* the nations, *unto* the obedience of faith, and *for the sake of* the Name.

1:7–13
2. Paul and the Romans

Having described himself (both his apostleship and his gospel), Paul now addresses himself to his readers: *To all in Rome who are loved by God and called to be saints: Grace and peace to you from God our Father and from the Lord Jesus Christ* (7). It is hard for us to imagine the sensations which the mere mention of the word 'Rome' would arouse in first-century people who lived far away in one of the provinces. For 'she was the eternal city which had given them peace,' wrote Bishop Stephen Neill, 'the fount of law, the centre of civilisation, the Mecca of poets and orators and artists', while being at the same time 'a home of every kind of idolatrous worship'.[1] Yet God had his people there, whom the apostle describes in three ways.

First, they are *loved by God*, his own dear children. Secondly, they are *called to be saints*, as also they are 'called to belong to Jesus Christ' (6). 'The saints' or 'the holy people' was a regular Old Testament designation of Israel. Now, however, the Gentile Christians in Rome were also 'saints'. For all Christians without exception are called by God to belong to Christ and to his holy people.

Thirdly, the Roman Christians are the recipients of God's *grace and peace*. The Aaronic blessing in the Old Testament was a prayer that Yahweh would both 'be gracious' to his people and give them 'peace'.[2] As used by Paul, one could almost claim that these words epitomize two of his major purposes in writing this letter, 'grace' emphasizing the freeness of God's justification of sinners, and 'peace' the reconciliation of Jews and Gentiles in the body of Christ. Although he does not use the word 'church' (perhaps because the Roman Christians met in several house groups), he nevertheless sends his greetings to them *all* (7) and gives thanks for them *all* (8), irrespective of their ethnic origin. Since 'beloved', 'called' and 'saints' were all Old Testament epithets for Israel, it seems probable

[1] Neill, p. 2.   [2] Nu. 6:25f.

that Paul deliberately uses them here to indicate that all believers in Christ, Gentiles as well as Jews, now belong to the covenant people of God.[3]

After this introduction the apostle tells his Roman readers frankly of his feelings towards them. He makes four points.

1.   He thanks God for them all

First, I thank my God through Jesus Christ for all of you, because your faith is being reported all over the world (8). Allowing for a degree of legitimate hyperbole, it was still true that wherever the church had spread, the news that there were Christians in the capital had spread also. And although Paul had not been responsible for bringing the gospel to them, this did not inhibit him from giving thanks that Rome had been evangelized.

2.   He prays for them

God, whom I serve with my whole heart in preaching the gospel of his Son, is my witness how constantly I remember you (9) *in my prayers at all times; and I pray that now at last by God's will the way may be opened for me to come to you* (10). In Paul's apostolic ministry, preaching and praying go together. He assures them that, even though most of them are unknown to him personally, he yet intercedes for them *constantly* (9) and *at all times* (10a). This is no pious platitude. He is telling the truth, and he calls on God to witness his statement. In particular, he prays that *now at last by God's will*, that is, if it is his will, *the way may be opened* for him to come to them (10b). It is a humble, tentative petition. He presumes neither to impose his will on God, nor to claim to know what God's will may be. Instead, he submits his will to God's. When we reach chapter 15, we will consider how his prayer was answered.

3.   He longs to see them and he tells them why

His first reason is this: *so that I may impart to you some spiritual gift* (*charisma*) *to make you strong* (11). At first sight it seems natural to interpret such a gift as one of those *charismata* which Paul has listed in 1 Corinthians 12 and will list later in Romans 12 and Ephesians 4. There seems to be a fatal objection to this, however; namely that in those other passages the gifts are bestowed by the sovereign decision of God,[4] Christ[5] or the Spirit.[6] So the apostle could hardly claim to be able to 'impart' a *charisma* himself. He appears therefore

---

[3] *Cf.* Rom. 9:24f.   [4] Rom. 12:6.   [5] Eph. 4:11.   [6] 1 Cor. 12:11.

to be using the word in a more general sense. Perhaps he is referring to his own teaching or exhortation, which he hopes to give them when he arrives, although there is 'an intentional indefiniteness'[7] about his statement, perhaps because at this stage he does not know what their main spiritual needs will be.

No sooner has he dictated these words than he seems to sense their inappropriate one-sidedness, as if he has everything to give and nothing to receive. So he immediately explains (even corrects) himself: *that is, that you and I may be mutually encouraged by each other's faith* (12). He knows about the reciprocal blessings of Christian fellowship and, although he is an apostle, he is not too proud to acknowledge his need of it. Happy is the modern missionary who goes to another country and culture in the same spirit of receptivity, anxious to receive as well as give, to learn as well as teach, to be encouraged as well as to encourage! And happy is the congregation who have a pastor of the same humble mind!

4. He has often planned to visit them

I do not want you to be unaware, brothers, that I planned many times to come to you (but have been prevented from doing so until now)... (13a). Exactly what has foiled him he does not say. Perhaps the most likely explanation is the one he will mention towards the end of his letter, namely that his evangelistic work in and around Greece had not yet been completed (15:22ff.). Why had he tried to visit them? He now gives a third reason: *in order that I might have* (RSV 'reap') *a harvest among you.* 'Harvest' is literally 'fruit', and John Murray rightly comments: 'The idea expressed is that of gathering fruit, not that of bearing it.'[8] In other words, he hopes to win some converts in Rome, *just as ... among the other Gentiles* (13). It would surely be appropriate that the apostle to the Gentiles should engage in evangelistic reaping in the capital city of the Gentile world.

---

[7] Cranfield, vol. I, p. 79.   [8] Murray, vol. I, p. 24.

1:14–17
3. Paul and evangelism

The apostle now makes three strong personal statements about his anxiety to preach the gospel in Rome:

> verse 14   'I am bound . . .' (RSV 'under obligation')
> verse 15   'I am . . . eager . . .'
> verse 16   'I am not ashamed . . .'

The reason these affirmations are so striking is that they are in direct antithesis to the attitude of many in the contemporary church. People nowadays tend to regard evangelism as an optional extra and consider (if they engage in it) that they are conferring a favour on God; Paul spoke of it as an obligation. The modern mood is one of reluctance; Paul's was one of eagerness or enthusiasm. Many of us today would have to confess, if we are honest, that we *are* ashamed of the gospel; Paul declared that he was not.

Mind you, Paul had just as many reasons to feel reluctant or embarrassed as we do. Rome was the symbol of imperial pride and power. People spoke of it with awe. Everybody hoped to visit Rome at least once in their lifetime, in order to look and stare and wonder. But who was this fellow Paul who wanted to visit the capital city not as a tourist but as an evangelist, and who believed he had something to say which Rome needed to listen to? What folly and presumption was this? According to tradition, Paul was an ugly little guy with beetle brows, bandy legs, a bald pate, a hooked nose, bad eyesight and no great rhetorical gifts.[1] So what could he hope to accomplish against the proud might of imperial Rome? Would he not be wiser to stay away? Or, if he must visit Rome, would it not be prudent for him to keep his big mouth shut, lest he be laughed out of court and hustled out of town?

Evidently Paul did not think so. On the contrary, 'I am under

[1] From *The Acts of Paul and Thecla*, included in *The Apocryphal New Testament*, ed. M. R. James (Clarendon, 1924; corrected edition, 1953), p. 273. *Cf.* 2 Cor. 10:10; Gal. 4:13ff.

obligation', he wrote; 'I am . . . eager . . . I am not ashamed.' What, then, were the origins of his evangelistic enthusiasm? They were two.

1. The gospel is a debt to the world (14–15)

The NIV *I am bound* and the RSV 'I am under obligation' should properly be translated 'I am [a] debtor' (AV). It is perhaps puzzlement over how and why the gospel could be a debt which has led translators to write more generally of 'obligation'. There are, in fact, two possible ways of getting into debt. The first is to borrow money *from* someone; the second is to be given money *for* someone by a third party. For example, if I were to borrow £1,000 from you, I would be in your debt until I paid it back. Equally, if a friend of yours were to hand me £1,000 to give to you, I would be in your debt until I handed it over. In the former case I would have got myself into debt by borrowing; in the latter it is your friend who has put me in your debt by entrusting me with £1,000 for you.

It is in this second sense that Paul is in debt. He has not borrowed anything from the Romans which he must repay. But Jesus Christ has entrusted him with the gospel for them. Several times in his letters he writes of having been 'put in trust with the gospel'.[2] It is true that this metaphor is one of stewardship (or trusteeship) rather than indebtedness, but the underlying thought is the same. It is Jesus Christ who has made Paul a debtor by committing the gospel to his trust. He was in debt to the Romans. As apostle to the Gentiles he was particularly in debt to the Gentile world, *both to Greeks and non-Greeks* (literally 'barbarians'), *both to the wise and the foolish* (14). It is not certain how we are meant to understand this classification. Both couplets may denote the same contrasting groups, or the first may allude to differences of nationality, culture and language, the second of intelligence and education. Either way, these expressions together cover the whole of Gentile humanity. It was because of his sense of debt to them that he could write: *That is why I am so eager to preach the gospel also to you who are at Rome* (15).

Similarly, we are debtors to the world, even though we are not apostles. If the gospel has come to us (which it has), we have no liberty to keep it to ourselves. Nobody may claim a monopoly of the gospel. Good news is for sharing. We are under obligation to make it known to others.

Such was Paul's first incentive. He was eager because he was in debt. It is universally regarded as a dishonourable thing to leave a

[2] *E.g.* 1 Cor. 4:1f.; Gal. 2:7; 1 Thes. 2:4; 1 Tim. 1:11; Tit. 1:3.

debt unpaid. We should be as eager to discharge our debt as Paul was to discharge his.

2. The gospel is God's power for salvation (16)

Paul now gives a second reason for being eager to preach the gospel, and not ashamed of it: *I am not ashamed of the gospel, because it is the power of God for the salvation of everyone who believes: first for the Jew, then for the Gentile* (16).

Some commentators are so offended by the thought that Paul could feel ashamed of the gospel that they pronounce his statement a case of litotes, that is, an understatement made for rhetorical effect, especially the use of a negative in place of a positive (as when someone says, 'I am not amused', meaning 'I am upset and angry'). So Moffatt renders the phrase, 'I am proud of the gospel.' But surely this attempt to tone down Paul's statement, though grammatically permissible, is psychologically misguided. Jesus himself warned his disciples against being ashamed of him, which shows that he anticipated they might be,[3] and Paul gave Timothy a similar admonition.[4] I once heard James Stewart of Edinburgh, in a sermon on this text, make the perceptive comment that 'there's no sense in declaring that you're not ashamed of something unless you've been tempted to feel ashamed of it'. And without doubt Paul knew this temptation. He told the Corinthians that he came to them 'in weakness and fear, and with much trembling'.[5] He knew that the message of the cross was 'foolishness' to some and 'a stumbling-block' to others,[6] because it undermines self-righteousness and challenges self-indulgence. So whenever the gospel is faithfully preached, it arouses opposition, often contempt, and sometimes ridicule.

How then did Paul (and how shall we) overcome the temptation to be ashamed of the gospel? He tells us. It is by remembering that the very same message, which some people despise for its weakness, is in fact *the power of God for the salvation of everyone who believes.* How do we know this? In the long run, only because we have experienced its saving power in our own lives. Has God reconciled us to himself through Christ, forgiven our sins, made us his children, put his Spirit within us, begun to transform us, and introduced us into his new community? Then how can we possibly be ashamed of the gospel?

Moreover, the gospel is God's saving power for *everyone who believes: first for the Jew, then for the Gentile.* Saving faith, which is the necessary response to the gospel, is the great leveller. For

---

[3] Mk. 8:38.   [4] 2 Tim. 1:8, 12.   [5] 1 Cor. 2:3.   [6] 1 Cor. 1:18, 23.

everyone who is saved is saved in exactly the same way, by faith.[7] That goes for Jews and Gentiles equally. There is no distinction between them in respect of salvation.[8] The priority of the Jews ('first for the Jew') is both theological, because God chose them and made his covenant with them, and therefore historical ('We had to speak the word of God to you first').[9]

Reflecting on the apostle's three personal affirmations in verses 14–16, we have seen that his eagerness to evangelize in Rome arose from his recognition that the gospel is an unpaid debt to the world and the saving power of God. The first gave him a sense of obligation (he had been put in trust with the good news), and the second a sense of conviction (if it had saved him, it could save others). Still today the gospel is both a debt to discharge and a power to experience. Only when we have grasped and felt these truths shall we be able to say with Paul, 'I am not ashamed . . . I am under obligation . . . So I am eager to share the gospel with the world.'

3. The gospel reveals God's righteousness (17)

For in the gospel a righteousness from God is revealed, a righteousness that is by faith from first to last, just as it is written: 'The righteous will live by faith' (17).

We note the logic of Paul's statement in verses 16–17: 'I am not ashamed of the gospel, *because* it is the power of God for . . . salvation . . . For (gar, because) in the gospel a righteousness from God is being revealed . . . .' That is, the reason the gospel is God's saving power is that in it God's righteousness is revealed. Moreover, this righteousness is 'from faith to faith' (AV), in fulfilment of Habakkuk 2:4: 'the righteous will live by his faith'. Many commentators have called verses 16–17 the 'text' of which the rest of Romans is the exposition. They are certainly crucial to our understanding. But three basic questions confront us. First, what is 'the righteousness of God'? Secondly, what is the meaning of 'from faith to faith' (AV) or 'through faith for faith' (RSV)? Thirdly, how should we interpret the Habakkuk quotation and Paul's use of it?

a. The righteousness of God

The meaning of the expression *dikaiosynē theou* ('righteousness of – or from – God') has been discussed throughout church history and has in consequence attracted an enormous, even unmanageable, literature. It is not easy to summarize, let alone to systematize, the debate.

[7] *Cf.* Rom. 3:22; 4:11; 10:4, 11. [8] Rom. 10:12; *cf.* Gal. 3:28. [9] Acts 13:46.

First, some emphasize that 'the righteousness of God' is *a divine attribute* or quality. 'Righteousness' describes his character, together with his actions which are in keeping with his character. Since he is 'the Judge of all the earth', it stands to reason that he will himself always 'do right'.[10] For he loves righteousness and hates wickedness, and righteousness is the sceptre of his kingdom.[11]

In Romans God's personal righteousness is supremely seen in the cross of Christ. When God 'presented him as a sacrifice of atonement', he did it 'to demonstrate his justice' (*dikaiosynē*, 3:25, repeated in 3:26), and in order that he might be both himself 'just' and 'the one who justifies those who have faith in Jesus' (3:26b). Throughout Romans Paul is at pains to defend the righteous character and behaviour of God. For he is convinced that whatever God does – in salvation (3:25) or in judgment (2:5) – is absolutely consistent with his righteousness. This is William Campbell's emphasis, namely that 'the righteousness of God' is 'first and foremost a righteousness that demonstrates God's faithfulness to his own righteous nature',[12] his integrity, his self-consistency. This attribute of God cannot be, however, either the only or even the main truth which Paul declares to be revealed in the gospel (1:17), since it was already fully revealed in the law.

Others stress, secondly, that 'the righteousness of God' is *a divine activity*, namely his saving intervention on behalf of his people. Indeed, his 'salvation' and his 'righteousness' are frequently coupled in the parallelism of Hebrew poetry, especially in the Psalms and in Isaiah 40 – 66. For example, 'the LORD has made his salvation known and revealed his righteousness to the nations.'[13] Similarly, God declares: 'I am bringing my righteousness near . . . and my salvation will not be delayed,'[14] and describes himself as 'a righteous God and a Saviour'.[15] It would perhaps be an exaggeration to claim in the light of these texts that God's righteousness and God's salvation are synonyms. It is rather that his righteousness denotes his loyalty to his covenant promises, in the light of which he may be implored – and expected – to come to the salvation of his people. For example, 'Vindicate me in your righteousness, O LORD my God.'[16] As John Ziesler has put it, 'salvation is the *form* that God's righteousness . . . takes'.[17] Ernst Käsemann writes of God's righteousness in terms of power, God's saving power, in loyalty to his covenant, overthrowing the forces of evil and vindicating his

---

[10] Gn. 18:25.   [11] Ps. 45:6f., quoted in Heb. 1:8f.; *cf.* Ps. 11:1ff.
[12] Campbell, p. 162.
[13] Ps. 98:2; *cf.* 51:14; 65:5; 71:2, 15; 143:11.
[14] Is. 46:13; *cf.* 45:8; 51:5f.; 56:1; 63:1.
[15] Is. 45:21.   [16] Ps. 35:24.
[17] Ziesler (1989), p. 70. See also Zeisler (1972), p. 42.

people.[18] N. T. Wright's understanding is similar. The righteousness of God, he writes, is 'essentially the covenant faithfulness, the
covenant justice, of the God who made promises to Abraham,
promises of a worldwide family characterized by faith, in and
through whom the evil of the world would be undone'.[19]

Thirdly, 'the righteousness of God' revealed in the gospel is *a
divine achievement*. The genitive is now no longer subjective (as in
reference to God's character and activity), but objective ('a
righteousness from God', as NIV renders the phrase in both 1:17 and
3:21). Indeed in Philippians 3:9 the simple genitive ('the righteousness of God') is replaced by a prepositional phrase ('the righteousness ... *from* God, *ek theou*). It is a righteous status which God
requires if we are ever to stand before him, which he achieves
through the atoning sacrifice of the cross, which he reveals in the
gospel, and which he bestows freely on all who trust in Jesus Christ.

There can be little doubt that Paul uses the expression 'the
righteousness of God' in this third way. He contrasts it with our
own righteousness,[20] which we are tempted to establish instead of
submitting to God's righteousness (10:3). God's righteousness is a
gift (5:17) which is offered to faith (3:22) and which we can have or
enjoy.[21] Charles Cranfield, who opts for this interpretation, paraphrases 1:17 in this way: 'For in it (*i.e.* in the gospel as it is being
preached) a righteous status which is God's gift is being revealed
(and so offered to men) – a righteous status which is altogether by
faith.'[22] Further, in 2 Corinthians 5:21 Paul has written that in
Christ we actually 'become the righteousness of God'; in Romans 4
he will write about righteousness being 'credited' ('reckoned' or
'imputed') to us, as it was to Abraham (verses 3, 24); and in 1
Corinthians 1:30 it is Christ himself 'who has become for us ... our
righteousness'.

Thus 'the righteousness of God' can be thought of as a divine
attribute (our God is a righteous God), or activity (he comes to our
rescue), or achievement (he bestows on us a righteous status). All
three are true and have been held by different scholars, sometimes in
relation to each other. For myself, I have never been able to see why
we have to choose, and why all three should not be combined. Even
Professor Fitzmyer, who uses the strange expression 'the uprightness of God', and affirms that it is 'descriptive of God's upright
being and of his upright activity',[23] goes on to concede that it also
expresses 'the status of uprightness communicated to human beings
by God's gracious gift'.[24] In other words, it is at one and the same
time a quality, an activity and a gift.

---

[18] Käsemann, pp. 23ff.   [19] Wright, p. 234.   [20] Phil. 3:9; *cf*. Rom. 10:3.
[21] Phil. 3:9.   [22] Cranfield, vol. I, p. 100.
[23] Fitzmyer, p. 257.   [24] *Ibid.*, p. 258.

It seems legitimate to affirm, therefore, that 'the righteousness of God' is God's righteous initiative in putting sinners right with himself, by bestowing on them a righteousness which is not their own but his. 'The righteousness of God' is God's just justification of the unjust, his righteous way of pronouncing the unrighteous righteous, in which he both demonstrates his righteousness and gives righteousness to us. He has done it through Christ, the righteous one, who died for the unrighteous, as Paul will explain later. And he does it by faith when we put our trust in him, and cry to him for mercy.

b.   'From faith to faith'

The righteousness of God, which is revealed in the gospel and offered to us, is (literally) 'out of faith into faith' or 'from faith to faith' (av). Many explanations of this phrase have been proposed, some more ingenious than others. I mention what seem to me to be the four most plausible. The first relates to faith's *origin*, as Bengel puts it: 'from the faith of God, who makes the offer, to the faith of men who receive it'.[25] More simply, it is 'from God's faith (better, faithfulness) to our faith'. God's faithfulness always comes first, and ours is never other than a response. This was Karl Barth's understanding.[26] Secondly, the *spread* of faith by evangelism may be in Paul's mind: 'from one believer to another'. Thirdly, he may be alluding to faith's *growth*, 'from one degree of faith to another' (*cf.* 2 Cor. 3:18, rsv). Fourthly, it may be faith's *primacy* which is being stressed. In this case the expression is purely rhetorical, and has been rendered, for example, *by faith from first to last* (niv) or 'by faith through and through'.[27]

c.   The Habakkuk quotation

The apostle now confirms his emphasis on faith from Scripture and quotes Habakkuk 2:4: *The righteous will live by faith*. The prophet had complained that God intended to raise up the ruthless Babylonians to punish Israel. How could he use the wicked to judge the wicked? Habakkuk was told that whereas the proud Babylonians would fall, the righteous Israelite would live by his faith, that is, in the context, by his humble, steadfast trust in God.

Many scholars, however, like rsv, translate Paul's quotation of Habakkuk differently: 'he who through faith is righteous shall live'. There are strong arguments in favour of this epigram. First, Paul has

---

[25] Bengel, p. 17.   [26] Barth, p. 41. See also Dunn, vol. I, pp. 44ff.
[27] Murray, vol. I, p. 70.

already used this text, in Galatians[28] written some years earlier, as biblical support for justification by faith, not law. So this seems to be how he understands it. Secondly, the context almost demands this rendering, being an endorsement from Scripture of 'from faith to faith'. Paul's concern here is not how righteous people live, but how sinful people become righteous. Thirdly, this translation fits the structure of the letter. Thus Anders Nygren points out that in Romans 1 – 4 'faith' occurs at least twenty-five times and 'life' only twice, whereas in Romans 5 – 8 'life' occurs twenty-five times and 'faith' only twice. These statistics establish, he concludes, 'that the theme for chapters 1 – 4 is "he who through faith is righteous" and for chapters 5 – 8 "he shall live" '.[29]

But is it legitimate to translate the Habakkuk text in this way, and so to make faith the way to righteousness instead of the way to life? I think so. We note that it characterizes God's people in terms of righteousness, faith and life. Whichever way the sentence is understood, both renderings affirm that 'the righteous shall live' and that faith is essential. The only question is whether the righteous by faith will live, or the righteous will live by faith. Are not both true? Righteousness and life are both by faith. Those who are righteous by faith also live by faith. Having begun in faith, they continue in the same path. This also fits in with the expression 'from faith to faith', which stresses that the Christian life is by faith from beginning to end. So I think F. F. Bruce was correct to write: 'The terms of Habakkuk's oracle are sufficiently general to make room for Paul's application of them – an application which, far from doing violence to the prophet's intention, expresses the abiding validity of his message.'[30]

---

[28] Gal. 3:11.   [29] Nygren, p. 87.   [30] Bruce, p. 76.

A.   The wrath of God against all humankind
Romans 1:18 – 3:20

Nothing keeps people away from Christ more than their inability to see their need of him or their unwillingness to admit it. As Jesus put it: 'It is not the healthy who need a doctor, but the sick. I have not come to call the righteous, but sinners.'[1] He was defending against the criticism of the Pharisees his policy of fraternizing with 'tax collectors and "sinners"'. He did not mean by his epigram about the doctor that some people *are* righteous, so that they do not need salvation, but that some people *think* they are. In that condition of self-righteousness they will never come to Christ. For just as we go to the doctor only when we admit that we are ill and cannot cure ourselves, so we will go to Christ only when we admit that we are guilty sinners and cannot save ourselves. The same principle applies to all our difficulties. Deny the problem, and nothing can be done about it; admit the problem, and at once there is the possibility of a solution. It is significant that the first of the 'twelve steps' of Alcoholics Anonymous is: 'We admitted we were powerless over alcohol – that our lives had become unmanageable.'

To be sure, some people insist with great bravado that they are neither sinful nor guilty, and that they do not need Christ. It would be quite wrong to seek to induce guilty feelings in them artificially. But if sin and guilt are universal (as they are), we cannot leave people alone in their false paradise of supposed innocence. The most irresponsible action of a doctor would be to acquiesce in a patient's inaccurate self-diagnosis. Our Christian duty is rather, through prayer and teaching, to bring people to accept the true diagnosis of their condition in the sight of God. Otherwise, they will never respond to the gospel.

It is this plain and unpopular principle which lies behind Romans 1:18 – 3:20. Before Paul can show that salvation is equally available to Jews and Gentiles (which he says it is in 1:16), he must prove that

---

[1] Mk. 2:17.

they are equally in need of it. So his purpose in this passage is to draw up 'the indictment that all, Jews and Greeks alike, are under the power of sin',[2] so that 'the whole world may be exposed to God's judgment'.[3] He does more than bring an accusation; he marshalls the evidence against us, in order to prove our guilt and secure our conviction. All men and women (Jesus being the solitary exception) are sinful, guilty and without excuse before God. Already they are under his wrath. Already they stand condemned. It is a theme of great solemnity. It is also the necessarily dark background against which the gospel shines brightly, and an indispensable foundation for world evangelization.

The way Paul demonstrates the universality of human sin and guilt is to divide the human race into several sections and to accuse them one by one. In each case his procedure is identical. He begins by reminding each group of their knowledge of God and of goodness. He then confronts them with the uncomfortable fact that they have not lived up to their knowledge. Instead, they have deliberately suppressed it, even contradicted it, by continuing to live in unrighteousness. And therefore they are guilty, inexcusably guilty, before God. Nobody can plead innocence, because nobody can plead ignorance.

First (1:18–32), he portrays *depraved Gentile society* in its idolatry, immorality and antisocial behaviour.

Secondly (2:1–16), he addresses *critical moralizers* (whether Gentiles or Jews), who profess high ethical standards and apply them to everybody except themselves.

Thirdly (2:17 – 3:8), he turns to *self-confident Jews*, who boast of their knowledge of God's law, but do not obey it.

Fourthly (3:9–20), he encompasses *the whole human race* and concludes that we are all guilty and without excuse before God.

Throughout this long passage, in which the apostle gradually but relentlessly builds his case, he never loses sight of the good news of Christ. Indeed, 'the righteousness of God' (that is, as we have seen, his righteous way of 'righteoussing' the unrighteous) is the only possible context in which he could dare to expose the squalor of human unrighteousness. In 1:17 he has stated that 'in the gospel a righteousness from God is revealed'. In 3:21 he will repeat this statement almost word for word: 'But now a righteousness from God ... has been made known.' It is in between these two great affirmations of the revelation of God's gracious righteousness that Paul sandwiches his terrible exposure of human unrighteousness (1:8 – 3:20).

---

[2] Rom. 3:9b, REB.   [3] Rom. 3:19b, REB.

1:18–32
4. Depraved Gentile society

It is important that we grasp the connection between this section ('The wrath of God') and the last ('The gospel of God'). In verses 16–20 the apostle develops an argument of sustained logic. He refers successively to the power of God (16), the righteousness of God (17), the wrath of God (18) and the glory of God in creation (19–20). Moreover, each statement he makes is linked to the preceding one by the Greek conjunction *gar* or *dioti*, meaning 'for' or 'because'. Let me try to clarify the stages of the argument by engaging Paul in dialogue.

Paul: *I am not ashamed of the gospel* (16a).
Q: Why not, Paul?
Paul: *Because it is the power of God for the salvation of everyone who believes* (16b).
Q: How so, Paul?
Paul: Because *in the gospel a righteousness from God is revealed,* that is, God's way of justifying sinners (17).
Q: But why is this necessary, Paul?
Paul: Because *the wrath of God is being revealed from heaven against all the godlessness and wickedness of men who suppress the truth by their wickedness* (18).
Q: But how have people suppressed the truth, Paul?
Paul: Because *what may be known about God is plain to them ... For since the creation of the world God's invisible qualities ... have been clearly seen ...* (19–20).

One might, then, speak of a fourfold self-revelation of God, although the vocabulary of revelation is not used consistently throughout. For the sake of theological clarity I will state these divine disclosures in the opposite order:

First, God reveals his glory (*his eternal power and divine nature*) in his creation (19–20).

Secondly, he reveals his wrath against the sin of those who suppress their knowledge of the Creator (18).

Thirdly, he reveals his righteousness (his righteous way of putting sinners right with himself) in the gospel (17).

Fourthly, he reveals his power in believers by saving them (16).

A careful study of the devastating exposure of Gentile decadence which follows has suggested to some scholars that Paul was influenced both by the story of Adam's fall in Genesis and by the Jewish critique of pagan idolatry in the book of Wisdom.

Professor Morna Hooker has written that Paul was portraying 'man's sin in relation to its true biblical setting – the Genesis narrative of the Creation and the Fall'.[1] Others have taken this up, and it is not difficult to find parallels which could be claimed as reminiscences. For example, like Genesis 1 – 3, Paul refers to *the creation of the world* (20) and to the classification of its creatures into *birds and animals and reptiles* (23); he uses the vocabulary of *glory* and 'image' or 'likeness' (23); he alludes to the human being's knowledge of God (19, 21), the resolve to become *wise* (22), the refusal to remain a dependent creature (18, 21), the exchange of God's *truth* for Satan's *lie* (25), and the understanding that rebellion *death* (32; *cf.* 5:12ff.). From this it seems clear that Paul was writing against the general biblical background of creation and fall, although the case has not been proved that he was intentionally re-telling Adam's story.

The case is stronger that Paul was alluding to the apocryphal book of Wisdom, especially to its chapters 13 – 14, which is a Hellenistic Jewish polemic against pagan idolatry. Sanday and Headlam provide a table, whose columns draw attention to possible parallels between Wisdom and Romans.[2] Certainly the Wisdom chapters contain references to the human failure to know God from his works ('from the good things that are seen they gained not power to know him that is');[3] to the sin and folly of idolatry ('they . . . called them gods which are works of men's hands');[4] to the fact that 'the worship of those nameless idols is a beginning and cause and end of every evil',[5] including 'the confusion of sex', 'disorder in and various social ills;[6] and to the conclusion that those who fail to find God in his works 'are not to be excused'.[7] But these similarities are picked out from a mass of inferior material, and are not close enough to suggest conscious borrowing. It seems likely that Paul was drawing more on the Old Testament prophets' criticism of idolatry than on the book of Wisdom. I agree with Godet

---

[1] M. D. Hooker, 'Adam in Romans 1' in *New Testament Studies* 6, 1959–60.
[2] Sanday and Headlam, pp. 51f.
[3] Wisdom 13:1.   [4] Wisdom 13:10.   [5] Wisdom 14:27.   [6] Wisdom 14:25.
[7] Wisdom 13:8f.

that there is a huge difference between Wisdom's 'tame and super-ficial explanation of idolatry' and Paul's 'profound psychological analysis'.[8]

In returning now to Paul's text, we are confronted by his state-ment that *the wrath of God is being revealed from heaven against all . . .* human *wickedness* (18).

The very mention of God's wrath is calculated nowadays to cause people embarrassment and even incredulity. How can anger, they ask, which Jesus in the Sermon on the Mount equated with mur-der,[9] and which Paul identified as a manifestation of our sinful human nature and as incompatible with our new life in Christ,[10] possibly be attributed to the all-holy God? Indeed, reflection on the wrath of God raises three questions, about its nature, objects and outworking.

1. What is the wrath of God?

If we are to preserve the balance of Scripture, our definition of God's anger must avoid opposite extremes. On the one hand, there are those who see it as no different from sinful human anger. On the other, there are those who declare that the very notion of anger as a personal attribute or attitude of God must be abandoned.

Human anger, although there is such a thing as righteous indigna-tion, is mostly very unrighteous. It is an irrational and uncontrol-lable emotion, containing much vanity, animosity, malice and the desire for revenge. It should go without saying that God's anger is absolutely free of all such poisonous ingredients.

The desire to eliminate any notion of God's personal anger, as being altogether unworthy of him, is usually associated with the name of C. H. Dodd, whose commentary on Romans was pub-lished in 1932. He argued that 'Paul never uses the verb "to be angry" with God as subject', although he is often said to love, and that the noun *orgē* (anger) is used only three times in the expression 'the anger of God', whereas it occurs constantly as 'wrath' or 'the wrath', without reference to God, 'in a curiously impersonal way'.[11] Dodd's conclusion is that Paul retains the concept 'not to describe the attitude of God to man, but to describe an inevitable process of cause and effect in a moral universe'.[12] A. T. Hanson elaborated this view in *The Wrath of the Lamb* (1959), maintaining that God's wrath is 'wholly impersonal'[13] and is 'the inevitable process of sin working itself out in history'.[14]

[8] Godet, p. 106.   [9] Mt. 5:22.   [10] Gal. 5:19f.; Eph. 4:31; Col. 3:8.
[11] Dodd, p. 21.   [12] *Ibid.*, p. 23.
[13] Hanson, *The Wrath of the Lamb* (SPCK, 1959), p. 69.
[14] *Ibid.*, pp. 21, 37.

But the argument based on the comparative absence of the expression 'the wrath of God' in favour of 'wrath' or 'the wrath' is weak. For Paul treats grace similarly. At the end of Romans 5 he writes both of 'the grace of God' (15), and about 'the grace' which he nevertheless personifies as both 'increasing' (20) and 'reigning' (21), and which is the most personal of all God's attributes. If then 'grace' is God acting graciously, 'wrath' must be God reacting in revulsion against sin. It is his 'deeply personal abhorrence' of evil.[15]

The wrath of God, then, is almost totally different from human anger. It does not mean that God loses his temper, flies into a rage, or is ever malicious, spiteful or vindictive. The alternative to 'wrath' is not 'love' but 'neutrality' in the moral conflict.[16] And God is not neutral. On the contrary, his wrath is his holy hostility to evil, his refusal to condone it or come to terms with it, his just judgment upon it.

2. Against what is God's wrath revealed?

In general, the wrath of God is directed against evil alone. We get angry when our pride has been wounded; but there is no personal pique in the anger of God. Nothing arouses it except evil, and evil always does.

More particularly, Paul writes that God's wrath is being revealed *against all the godlessness (asebeia) and wickedness (adikia) of men who suppress the truth by their wickedness* (18). According to J. B. Lightfoot, *asebeia* is 'against God' and *adikia* 'against men'. Further, 'the first precedes and entails the second: witness the teaching of this chapter'.[17] Scripture is quite clear that the essence of sin is godlessness. It is the attempt to get rid of God and, since that is impossible, the determination to live as though one had succeeded in doing so. 'There is no fear of God before their eyes' (3:18). The converse is also true. essence of goodness is godliness, to love him with all our being and to obey him with joy.

God's wrath is directed, however, not against 'godlessness and wickedness' *in vacuo*, but against the godlessness and wickedness of those people *who suppress the truth by their wickedness* (*adikia* again). It is not just that they do wrong, though they know better. It is that they have made an *a priori* decision to live for themselves, rather than for God and others, and therefore deliberately stifle any truth which challenges their self-centredness.

What 'truth' has Paul in mind? He tells us in verses 19–20. It is that knowledge of God which is available to us through the natural order. For *what may be known about God* (and what is knowable

---

[15] Robinson, p. 19.   [16] Neill, p. 10.   [17] Lightfoot, p. 251.

to finite, fallen creatures like us is inevitably limited) is nevertheless *plain* or open. And the reason it is plain is that God has taken the initiative and has *made it plain*. How? Verse 20 explains. It is that ever *since the creation of the world God's invisible qualities – his eternal power and divine nature* (which together constitute something of his 'glory', 23) – *have been clearly seen, being understood from what has been made*. In other words, the God who in himself is invisible and unknowable has made himself both visible and knowable through what he has made. The creation is a visible disclosure of the invisible God, an intelligible disclosure of the otherwise unknown God. Just as artists reveal themselves in what they draw, paint and sculpt, so the Divine Artist has revealed himself in his creation.

This truth of revelation through creation is a regular theme of Scripture. 'The heavens declare the glory of God', and 'the whole earth is full of his glory'.[18] The Job who confessed that hitherto he had only 'heard' of Yahweh, finally affirmed that through the ingenuity of the natural order his eyes had 'seen' him.[19] For the living God who made all things, as Paul proclaimed to his pagan audience in Lystra, 'has not left himself without testimony', but has shown his kindness to the human race by his gifts of rain and crops, abundant food and overflowing joy.[20]

Because Romans 1:19–20 is one of the principal New Testament passages on the topic of 'general revelation', it may be helpful to summarize how 'general' differs from 'special' revelation. God's self-revelation through 'what has been made' has four main characteristics. First, it is 'general' because made to everybody everywhere, as opposed to 'special' because made to particular people in particular places, through Christ and the biblical authors. Secondly, it is 'natural' because made through the natural order, as opposed to 'supernatural', involving the incarnation of the Son and the inspiration of the Scriptures. Thirdly, it is 'continuous' because since the creation of the world it has gone on 'day after day ... night after night',[21] as opposed to 'final' and finished in Christ and in Scripture. And fourthly it is 'creational', revealing God's glory through creation, as opposed to 'salvific', revealing God's grace in Christ.

The conviction that God reveals himself through the created universe is still meaningful to us in the twentieth century. Although the five so-called 'classical' arguments for the existence of God, formulated by Thomas Aquinas in his *Summa* in the thirteenth century, are no longer in vogue, Christians still believe that God's power, skill and goodness are displayed in the beauty and balance,

[18] Ps. 19:1; Is. 6:3.   [19] Jb. 37 – 41; 42:5.
[20] Acts 14:14ff.; *cf.* Mt. 5:45; Acts 17:22ff.
[21] Ps. 19:2.

intricacy and intelligibility of the universe, as scientists keep on probing it.

For example, after the satellite detection of the birthpangs of the universe was announced to the American Physical Society in April 1992, an anonymous *Guardian* contributor wrote: 'It is difficult to know what the appropriate reaction to such mind-expanding discoveries should be, except to get down on one's knees in total humility and give thanks to God or Big Bang or both, for cunningly contriving to allow this infinitesimal part of the universe called Earth to be bestowed with something called Air.' At the opposite end of the size scale, a consultant surgeon wrote to me a few years ago: 'I am filled with the same awe and humility when I contemplate something of what goes on in a single cell as when I contemplate the sky on a clear night. The coordination of the complex activities of the cell in a common purpose hits the scientific part of me as the best evidence for an Ultimate Purpose.' Anthropologists have also found a worldwide moral sense in human beings so that, although conscience is of course to some extent conditioned by culture, it still testifies to everybody everywhere both that there is a difference between right and wrong, and that evil deserves to be punished (32).

Paul ends his statement with the words: *so that men are without excuse* (20). This shows that what he has been asserting is 'natural revelation' and not 'natural theology (or religion)'. The latter expresses the belief that it is possible for human beings through nature to come to know God, and that therefore, as the way to God, creation is an alternative to Christ. Some people base this belief on Romans 1, especially on the expressions that *they knew God* (21) and that they possessed *the knowledge of God* (28). But there are degrees to the knowledge of God, and these phrases cannot possibly refer to the full knowledge of him enjoyed by those who have been reconciled to him through Christ. For what Paul says here is that through general revelation people can know God's power, deity and glory (not his saving grace through Christ), and that this knowledge is enough not to save them but rather to condemn them, because they do not live up to it. Instead, they *suppress the truth by their wickedness* (18), so that they *are without excuse* (20). It is against this wilful human rebellion that God's wrath is revealed.

3. How is God's wrath revealed?

The first answer to this question is that God's wrath will be revealed in the future, at the end, in the judgment of the last day. There is such a thing as 'the coming wrath',[22] and Paul calls Judgment Day 'the day

[22] 1 Thes. 1:10.

of God's wrath'.[23] Secondly, there is a present disclosure of God's wrath through the public administration of justice, to which Paul will come later in his letter (13:4). But this is not in his mind here.

Thirdly, there is another kind of present disclosure of the anger of God, to which the apostle will devote the rest of Romans 1. It *is being revealed from heaven* now, he says (18), and he goes on to explain it by his terrible threefold refrain *God gave them over* (24, 26, 28). When we hear of God's wrath, we usually think of 'thunderbolts from heaven, and earthly cataclysms and flaming majesty', instead of which his anger goes 'quietly and invisibly' to work in handing sinners over to themselves.[24] As John Ziesler writes, it 'operates not by God's intervention but precisely by his *not* intervening, by letting men and women go their own way'.[25] God abandons stubborn sinners to their wilful self-centredness,[26] and the resulting process of moral and spiritual degeneration is to be understood as a judicial act of God. This is the revelation of God's wrath from heaven (18).

Let me sum up our reflection thus far on the wrath of God. It is God's settled and perfectly righteous antagonism to evil. It is directed against people who have some knowledge of God's truth through the created order, but deliberately suppress it in order to pursue their own self-centred path. And it is already being revealed, in a preliminary way, in the moral and social corruption which Paul saw in much of the Greco-Roman world of his day, and which we can see in the permissive societies of ours.

In Paul's exposition of the outworking of the wrath of God, he develops the same logical process of deterioration, according to the principle he has established in verses 18–20. That is, the general pattern of his argument recurs in verses 21–24, 25–27 and 28–31, 'repeated with horrifying emphasis'.[27]

First, he asserts the people's knowledge of God: *they knew God* (21), *the truth of God* (25), and *the knowledge of God* (28).

Secondly, he draws attention to their rejection of their knowledge in favour of idolatry: *they neither glorified him as God nor gave thanks to him* (21); *they exchanged the truth of God for a lie, and worshipped and served created things rather than the Creator* (25); *they did not think it worth while to retain the knowledge of God* (28).

Thirdly, he describes the reaction of God's wrath: *he gave them over . . . to sexual impurity* (24); *to shameful lusts* (26); and *to a depraved mind* (28), leading to antisocial behaviour.

---

[23] Rom. 2:5, 8; *cf.* 3:5; 4:15; 5:9; 9:22.   [24] Neill, pp. 12f.
[25] Ziesler (1990), p. 75.   [26] *Cf.* Ps. 81:12; Ho. 4:17; Acts 7:42; 14:16.
[27] Barrett, p. 38.

These are the three stages of the downward spiral of pagan depravity.

a. Verses 21–24

The opening statement that *they knew God* cannot be taken absolutely, since elsewhere Paul writes that people outside Christ do not know God.[28] It refers rather to the limited knowledge of God's power and glory which is available to everybody through general revelation (19–20).

Instead of their knowledge of God leading to the worship of God, they *neither glorified him as God nor gave thanks to him.* Rather *their thinking became futile and their foolish hearts were darkened* (21), and (despite their claim to wisdom) *they became fools* (22). Their futility, darkness and folly were seen in their idolatry, and in the absurd 'exchange' which their idolatry involved: *they exchanged the glory of the immortal God for images made to look like mortal man and birds and animals and reptiles* (23).[29]

What Paul saw plainly, wrote C. H. Dodd, was that Greek philosophy 'easily came to terms with the grossest forms of superstition and immorality. And so it did, just as it is a grave count against the lofty philosophy of Hinduism that it utters no effective protest against the most degrading practices of popular religion in India today.'[30] But the cultural idolatry of the West is no better. To exchange the worship of the living God for the modern obsession with wealth, fame and power is equally foolish and equally blameworthy.

God's judgment on the people's idolatry was to give them over *in the sinful desires of their hearts to sexual impurity.* The history of the world confirms that idolatry tends to immorality. A false image of God leads to a false understanding of sex. Paul does not tell us what kind of immorality he has in mind, except that it involved *the degrading of their bodies with one another* (24). He is right. Illicit sex degrades people's humanness; sex in marriage, as God intended, ennobles it.

b. Verses 25–27

Here another 'exchange' is mentioned, not the exchanging of the glory of God for images (23), but the exchanging of *the truth of God for a lie,* indeed 'the' lie, the ultimate lie. For this is what the falsehood of idolatry is, since it involves transferring our worship to

---

[28] *E.g.* Gal. 4:8; 1 Thes. 4:5; 2 Thes. 1:8.   [29] *Cf.* Ps. 106:20; Je. 2:11.
[30] Dodd, p. 25.

created things from *the Creator*, whom Paul in a spontaneous doxology declares worthy of eternal adoration: *who is for ever praised* (25).

This time *God gave them over to shameful lusts*, which Paul specifies as lesbian practices (26) and male homosexual relationships (27). In both cases he describes the people concerned as guilty of a third 'exchange': the *women exchanged natural relations for unnatural ones* (26), while *the men also abandoned natural relations with women and were inflamed with lust for one another* (27a). Twice he uses the adjective *physikos* ('natural') and once the expression *para physin* ('against nature' or 'unnatural'). *Men committed indecent acts with other men, and received in themselves the due penalty for their perversion* (27b). Paul does not specify what this penalty is; only that it is received 'in themselves'.

Verses 26–27 are a crucial text in the contemporary debate about homosexuality. The traditional interpretation, that they describe and condemn all homosexual behaviour, is being challenged by the gay lobby. Three arguments are advanced. First, it is claimed that the passage is irrelevant, on the ground that its purpose is neither to teach sexual ethics, nor to expose vice, but rather to portray the outworking of God's wrath. This is true. But if a certain sexual conduct is to be seen as the consequence of God's wrath, it must be displeasing to him. Secondly, 'the likelihood is that Paul is thinking only about pederasty' since 'there was no other form of male homosexuality in the Greco-Roman world', and that he is opposing it because of the humiliation and exploitation experienced by the youths involved.[31] All one can say in response to this suggestion is that the text itself contains no hint of it.

Thirdly, there is the question what Paul meant by 'nature'. Some homosexual people are urging that their relationships cannot be described as 'unnatural', since they are perfectly natural to them. John Boswell has written, for example, that 'the persons Paul condemns are manifestly not homosexual: what he derogates are homosexual acts committed by apparently heterosexual people'. Hence Paul's statement that they 'abandoned' natural relations, and 'exchanged' them for unnatural (26–27).[32] Richard Hays has written a thorough exegetical rebuttal of this interpretation of Romans 1, however. He provides ample contemporary evidence that the opposition of 'natural' (*kata physin*) and 'unnatural' (*para physin*) was 'very frequently used . . . as a way of distinguishing between

[31] Robin Scroggs, *The New Testament and Homosexuality* (Fortress, 1983), pp. 115ff., 130f.

[32] John Boswell, *Christianity, Social Tolerance and Homosexuality* (University of Chicago Press, 1980), pp. 107ff.

heterosexual and homosexual behaviour'.[33] Besides, differentiating between sexual orientation and sexual practice is a modern concept; 'to suggest that Paul intends to condemn homosexual acts only when they are committed by persons who are constitutionally heterosexual is to introduce a distinction entirely foreign to Paul's thought-world',[34] in fact a complete anachronism.

So then, we have no liberty to interpret the noun 'nature' as meaning 'my' nature, or the adjective 'natural' as meaning 'what seems natural to me'. On the contrary, *physis* ('natural') means God's created order. To act 'against nature' means to violate the order which God has established, whereas to act 'according to nature' means to behave 'in accordance with the intention of the Creator'.[35] Moreover, the intention of the Creator means his original intention. What this was Genesis tells us and Jesus confirmed: 'At the beginning the Creator "made them male and female", and said, "For this reason a man will leave his father and mother and be united to his wife, and the two will become one flesh." So they are no longer two, but one.' Then Jesus added his personal endorsement and deduction: 'Therefore what God has joined together, let man not separate.'[36] In other words, God created humankind male and female; God instituted marriage as a heterosexual union; and what God has thus united, we have no liberty to separate. This threefold action of God established that the only context which he intends for the 'one flesh' experience is heterosexual monogamy, and that a homosexual partnership (however loving and committed it may claim to be) is 'against nature' and can never be regarded as a legitimate alternative to marriage.

c. Verses 28–32

Paul's opening statement in verse 28 this time includes a play on words between *ouk edokimasan* ('they did not think it worth while') and *adokimon noun* ('a depraved mind'). It is not easy to reproduce it in English. One might say that 'since they did not see fit to retain the knowledge of God, he gave them over to an unfit mind'.

And their *depraved mind* led this time not to immorality but to a whole variety of antisocial practices, which *ought not to be done* (28), and which together describe the breakdown of human community, as standards disappear and society disintegrates. Paul gives

---

[33] Richard B. Hays, 'Relations Natural and Unnatural: A Response to John Boswell's Exegesis of Romans 1', *Journal of Religious Ethics*, Spring 1986, p. 192.
[34] *Ibid.*, pp. 200f.   [35] Cranfield, vol. I, p. 125.
[36] Mt. 19:4ff., quoting Gn. 2:24.

a catalogue of twenty-one vices. Such lists were not uncommon in those days in Stoic, Jewish and early Christian literature. All commentators seem to agree that the list defies neat classification. It begins with four general sins with which these people *have become filled*, namely *every kind of wickedness, evil, greed and depravity*. Then come five more sins which they are *full of* and which all depict broken human relationships: *envy, murder, strife, deceit and malice* (29). Next come a couple on their own, which seem to refer to libel and slander, although JBP offers a characteristically imaginative translation: 'whisperers-behind-doors' and 'stabbers-in-the-back'. These two are followed by four which seem to portray different and extreme forms of pride: *God-haters, insolent, arrogant and boastful*. Now comes another independent couple of words, denoting people who are 'inventive' in relation to evil and rebellious in relation to parents (30). And the list ends with four negatives, *senseless, faithless, heartless, ruthless* (31), which JB rather neatly renders 'without brains, honour, love or pity'.

Verse 32 is a concluding summary of the human perversity Paul has been describing. First, *they know*. Yet again he begins with the knowledge possessed by the people he is depicting. It is not now God's truth that they know, however, but *God's righteous decree*, namely *that those who do such things deserve death*. As he will write later, 'the wages of sin is death' (6:23). And they know it. Their conscience condemns them.

Secondly, they nevertheless disregard their knowledge. *They not only continue to do these very things*, which they know deserve death, *but* (which is worse) they actively encourage others to do the same, and so flagrantly *approve* the evil behaviour of which God has expressed his disapproval.

We have come to the end of Paul's portrayal of depraved Gentile society. Its essence lies in the antithesis between what people know and what they do. God's wrath is specifically directed against those who deliberately suppress truth for the sake of evil. 'Dark as the picture here drawn is,' wrote Charles Hodge, 'it is not so dark as that presented by the most distinguished Greek and Latin authors, of their own countrymen.'[37] Paul was not exaggerating.

[37] Hodge, p. 43.

2:1–16
5. Critical moralizers

Having declared the depraved Gentile world to be guilty and in-excusable (1:20, 32), Paul now passes the same verdict on a person whom he addresses in direct speech: *You, therefore, have no excuse, you who pass judgment on someone else* ... (2:1). Who is this person? He or she is an imaginary character whom, in the long-standing tradition of the Greek 'diatribe', the apostle engages in dialogue. Indeed this individual, together with the category which he or she represents, is in the forefront of Paul's mind throughout the first sixteen verses of Romans 2.

Many commentators (perhaps most) believe that, having portrayed and condemned Gentile society in 1:18–32, Paul now turns his attention to Jewish people. This is an understandable viewpoint, since the classification of the human race into Jews and Gentiles is mentioned on numerous occasions throughout the letter,[1] and one of the apostle's main purposes in writing is to demonstrate that Jews and Gentiles are equal in sin and equal in salvation. There are two objections, however, to the straightforward identification of Paul's interlocutor at the beginning of Romans 2 as a Jew. First, it is not until verse 17 that he involves a Jew in direct conversation ('Now you, if you call yourself a Jew ...'). Instead, in the earlier verses, although this is obscured by NIV, he twice addresses his partner in the dialogue as 'O man' (1, 3), deliberately emphasizing that he or she is a human being, rather than specifically a Jew or a Gentile.

Secondly, if this section refers exclusively to the Jewish world, then 1:18–32 is the only picture Paul gives us of the ancient Gentile world, in which case it would seem to be an unbalanced one. For not all Gentiles preferred darkness to light, became idolaters, and were abandoned by God to sexually and socially promiscuous behaviour. There were others, as F. F. Bruce has pointed out:

[1] *E.g.* 1:16; 2:9f.; 3:9, 29; 9:24; 10:12; 15:8f.

We know that there was another side to the pagan world of the first century than that which Paul has portrayed in the preceding paragraphs. What about a man like Paul's illustrious contemporary Seneca, the Stoic moralist, the tutor of Nero? Seneca might have listened to Paul's indictment and said, 'Yes, that is perfectly true of great masses of mankind, and I concur in the judgment which you pass on them – but there are others, of course, like myself, who deplore these tendencies as much as you do.'

Bruce continues:

Not only did he [sc. Seneca] exalt the great moral virtues; he exposed hypocrisy, he preached the equality of all human beings, he acknowledged the pervasive character of evil ... he practised and inculcated daily self-examination, he ridiculed vulgar idolatry, he assumed the role of a moral guide ....[2]

It seems probable, therefore, that Paul has such Gentiles in mind as he dictates verses 1–16. He is evidently thinking of Jews too, however, since he twice uses the expression 'first for the Jew, then for the Gentile' (9, 10). It may even be that the Jews are his 'hidden target' throughout,[3] and that he begins in more general terms only to win their endorsement of his condemnation before turning the tables on them. But his main emphasis is clearly seen in his turning from the world of shameless immorality (1:18–32) to the world of self-conscious moralism. The person he now addresses is not just 'O man' but 'O man who judges' (1, 3), 'O critical, moralizing human being'. He seems to be confronting every human being (Jew or Gentile) who is a moralizer, who presumes to pass moral judgments on other people.

This becomes clearer when we compare the people envisaged in 1:32 and 2:1–3. The similarities are evident. Both groups have a certain knowledge of God as creator (1:20) or judge (1:32; 2:2), and both contradict their knowledge by their behaviour; they 'do such things' as Paul has been describing (1:32; 2:2). What, then, is the difference between them? It is that the first group do things they know to be wrong and *approve* of others who do them (1:32), which is at least consistent; whereas the second group do what they know to be wrong and *condemn* others who do them, which is hypocritical. The first group disassociate themselves entirely from God's righteous decree, in regard to both themselves and others; whereas the second group deliberately identify themselves with it by setting themselves up as judges, only to find that they are being judged for doing the same things.

[2] Bruce, p. 82.   [3] Moo, pp. 127, 135.

The underlying theme of this section, then, is the judgment of God upon self-appointed judges. His judgment is inescapable (1–4), righteous (5–11) and impartial (12–16).

1.   God's judgment is inescapable (1–4)

Paul uncovers in these verses a strange human foible, namely our tendency to be critical of everybody except ourselves. We are often as harsh in our judgment of others as we are lenient towards ourselves. We work ourselves up into a state of self-righteous indignation over the disgraceful behaviour of other people, while the very same behaviour seems not nearly so serious when it is ours rather than theirs. We even gain a vicarious satisfaction from condemning in others the very faults we excuse in ourselves. Freud called this moral gymnastic 'projection', but Paul described it centuries before Freud. Similarly, Thomas Hobbes, the seventeenth-century political philosopher, wrote of people who 'are forced to keep themselves in their own favour by observing the imperfections of other men'.[4] This device enables us simultaneously to retain our sins and our self-respect. It is a convenient arrangement, but also both slick and sick.

In addition, Paul argues, we expose ourselves to the judgment of God, and we leave ourselves without either excuse or escape. For if our critical faculties are so well developed that we become experts in our moral evaluation of others, we can hardly plead ignorance of moral issues ourselves. On the contrary, in judging other people, we thereby condemn ourselves, because we *who pass judgment do the same things* (1). For *we know* perfectly well *that God's judgment against those who do such things is based on truth* (2). How then can we suppose (we who, though mere human beings, play God and *pass judgment on* others for doing what we do) that we *will escape God's judgment* (3)? This is not a call either to suspend our critical faculties or to renounce all criticism and rebuke of others as illegitimate; it is rather a prohibition of standing in judgment on other people and condemning them (which as human beings we have no right to do), especially when we fail to condemn ourselves. For this is the hypocrisy of the double standard, a high standard for other people and a comfortably low one for ourselves.

Sometimes, in a futile attempt to escape the inescapable, namely *God's judgment*, we take refuge in a theological argument. For theology can be turned to bad uses as well as good. We appeal to God's character, especially to *the riches of his kindness, tolerance and patience* (4a). We maintain that he is much too kind and

---

[4] Thomas Hobbes, *Leviathan* (1651; Penguin, 1981), p. 125.

longsuffering to punish anybody, and that we can therefore sin with impunity. We even misapply Scripture to our advantage and quote such statements as, 'The LORD is compassionate and gracious, slow to anger, abounding in love.'[5] But this kind of manipulative theologizing is to *show contempt* for God, not honour. It is not faith; it is presumption. For *God's kindness leads* us *towards repentance* (4b). That is its goal. It is intended to give us space in which to repent, not to give us an excuse for sinning.[6]

2. God's judgment is righteous (5–11)

To presume on God's patient kindness, as if its purpose were to encourage licence, not penitence, is a sure sign of *stubbornness* and of an *unrepentant heart* (5a). Such obstinacy can have only one end. It means that we are *storing up* for ourselves not some precious treasure (which is what the verb *thēsaurizō* would normally mean) but the awful experience of divine *wrath* on *the day of God's wrath, when his righteous judgment will be revealed* (5). Far from escaping God's judgment (3), we will bring it all the more surely upon ourselves.

Paul now enlarges on his expression *God's . . . righteous judgment* (5b), and begins by stating the inflexible principle on which it is based. The NIV rightly puts this in inverted commas, since it is a quotation from Old Testament Scripture, namely that God '*will give to each person according to what he has done*' (6). The verse quoted is probably Psalm 62:12, although Proverbs 24:12 says the same thing in the form of a question. It also occurs in the prophecies of Hosea and Jeremiah,[7] and is sometimes elaborated in the vivid expression, 'I will bring down on their own heads what they have done.'[8] Jesus himself repeated it.[9] So did Paul,[10] and it is a recurring theme in the book of Revelation.[11] It is the principle of exact retribution, which is the foundation of justice.

Some Christians, however, are immediately up in arms. Has the apostle taken leave of his senses? Does he begin by declaring that salvation is by faith alone (*e.g.* 1:16f.), and then destroy his own gospel by saying that it is by good works after all? No, Paul is not contradicting himself. What he is affirming is that, although justification is indeed by faith, judgment will be according to works. The reason for this is not hard to find. It is that the day of judgment will be a public occasion. Its purpose will be less to determine God's judgment than to announce it and to vindicate it. The divine

---

[5] Ps. 103:8; Ex. 34:5ff.   [6] *Cf.* Ezk. 33:11; 2 Pet. 3:9.
[7] Ho. 12:2; Je. 17:10; 32:19.   [8] *E.g.* Ezk. 9:10; 11:21; *cf.* 2 Ch. 6:23.
[9] Mt. 16:27.   [10] *E.g.* 2 Cor. 5:10.
[11] *E.g.* Rev. 2:23; 20:12f.; 22:12.

judgment, which is a process of sifting and separating, is going on secretly all the time, as people range themselves for or against Christ, but on the last day its results will be made public. *The day of God's wrath* will also be the time *when his righteous judgment will be revealed* (5b).

Such a public occasion, on which a public verdict will be given and a public sentence passed, will require public and verifiable evidence to support them. And the only public evidence available will be our works, what we have done and have been seen to do. The presence or absence of saving faith in our hearts will be disclosed by the presence or absence of good works of love in our lives. The apostles Paul and James both teach this same truth, that authentic saving faith invariably issues in good works, and that if it does not, it is bogus, even dead. 'I by my works will show you my faith,' wrote James.[12] 'Faith [works] through love,' echoed Paul.[13]

Verses 7–10 elaborate verse 6, namely the principle that the basis of God's righteous judgment will be what we have done. The alternatives are now presented to us in two carefully constructed parallel sentences, which concern our goal (what we seek), our works (what we do), and our end (where we are going). The two final destinies of humankind are called *eternal life* (7), which Jesus defined in terms of knowing him and knowing the Father,[14] and *wrath and anger* (8), the awful outpouring of God's judgment. And the basis on which this separation is to be made will be a combination of what we seek (our ultimate goal in life) and what we do (our actions in the service either of ourselves or of others). It is very similar to the teaching of Jesus in the Sermon on the Mount, in which he delineated the alternative human ambitions (seeking our material welfare or seeking God's kingdom),[15] and the alternative human activities (practising or not practising his teaching).[16]

Returning to Paul, on the one hand there are those who *seek glory* (the manifestation of God himself), *honour* (God's approval) *and immortality* (the unfading joy of his presence), and moreover who seek these God-centred blessings *by persistence in doing good* (7). That is, they persevere in the way, for perseverance is the hallmark of genuine believers.[17] On the other hand there are those who are characterized by the single derogatory epithet *self-seeking* (8a). *Eritheia* was used by Aristotle of 'a self-seeking pursuit of political office by unfair means', and so here probably means 'selfishness, selfish ambition' (BAGD). Further, those who are infatuated with themselves, and engrossed in self-centred goals, inevitably *reject the truth and follow evil* (8b). Indeed, they 'suppress the truth by their

---

[12] Jas. 2:18, RSV.   [13] Gal. 5:6, RSV.   [14] Jn. 17:3.   [15] Mt. 6:31ff.
[16] Mt. 7:24ff.   [17] Cf. Heb. 3:14.

wickedness' (1:18). Both these expressions blame the repudiation of truth on *adikia*, 'evil' or 'wickedness'. To sum up, those who seek God and persevere in goodness will receive eternal life, while those who are self-seeking and follow evil will experience God's wrath.

In verses 9–10 Paul restates the same solemn alternatives, with three differences. First, he simplifies the two categories of people into *every human being who does evil* (9) and *everyone who does good* (10). Jesus made exactly the same division between 'those who have done evil' and 'those who have done good'.[18] Secondly, Paul elaborates the two destinies. He describes the one as *trouble and distress* (9), emphasizing its anguish, and the other as *glory, honour and peace* (10a), taking up the 'glory' and 'honour' of verse 7 which form part of the goal believers seek, and adding 'peace', that comprehensive word for reconciled relationships with God and with each other. Thirdly, Paul adds to both sentences, *first for the Jew, then for the Gentile* (9–10), affirming the priority of the Jew alike in judgment and in salvation, and thus declaring the absolute impartiality of God: *For God does not show favouritism* (11).

3. God's judgment is impartial (12–16)

That the judgment of God will be righteous (according to what we have done, 6–8) and impartial (as between Jews and Gentiles, without favouritism, 9–11) Paul now develops in relation to the Mosaic law, which is mentioned here for the first time and has a prominent place in the rest of the letter.

Jews and Gentiles appear to differ fundamentally from one another, in that the Jews *hear the law* (13), possessing it and listening to it being read in the synagogue every sabbath day, whereas the Gentiles *do not have the law* (14). It was neither revealed to them nor given to them. Nevertheless, Paul insists, this difference can be exaggerated. For there is no fundamental distinction between them in the moral knowledge they have (since *the requirements of the law are written on* all human *hearts*, 15), or in the sin they have committed (by disobeying the law they know), or in the guilt they have incurred, or in the judgment they will receive.

Verse 12 puts Jews and Gentiles into the same category of sin and death. Paul makes two parallel statements, beginning with the words *All who sin*. The verb is in the aorist tense, however, and should be translated 'All who sinned' (*hēmarton*). Paul is summing up their life of sin from the perspective of the last day. The point he is making is that all who have sinned *will also perish* or *will be judged*, irrespective of whether they are Jews or Gentiles, that is,

---

[18] Jn. 5:29.

whether they have the Mosaic law or not. All who have sinned *apart from the law* (Gentiles) *will also perish apart from the law* (12a). They will not be judged by a standard they have not known. They will perish because of their sin, not because of their ignorance of the law. Similarly, all who have sinned *under the law* (Jews) *will be judged by the law* (12b). They too will be judged by the standard they have known. God will be absolutely even-handed in judgment. The way people have sinned (in knowledge or ignorance of the law) will be the way they will be judged. 'The ground of judgment is their works; the rule of judgment is their knowledge,'[19] and whether they have lived up to their knowledge. *For it is not those who hear the law who are righteous in God's sight, but it is those who obey the law who will be declared righteous* (13). This is a theoretical or hypothetical statement, of course, since no human being has ever fully obeyed the law (*cf.* 3:20). So there is no possibility of salvation by that road. But Paul is writing about judgment, not about salvation. He is emphasizing that the law itself did not guarantee the Jews immunity to judgment, as they thought. For what mattered was not possession but obedience.

The same principle of judgment according to knowledge and performance is now applied more fully to Gentiles. Two complementary facts about them are self-evident. The first is that they *do not have the law* (*sc.* of Moses). This is stated twice in verse 14. Externally, they do not possess it. Secondly, however, they do have some knowledge of its standards internally. For Gentiles who do not have the law nevertheless *do by nature*, instinctively, *things required by the law*. This is not a universal claim, for Paul does not use the definite article and refer to 'the Gentiles'. He is simply saying that some Gentiles sometimes do some of what the law requires. This is an observable, verifiable fact, which anthropologists have everywhere discovered. Not all human beings are crooks, blackguards, thieves, adulterers and murderers. On the contrary, some honour their parents, recognize the sanctity of human life, are loyal to their spouses, practise honesty, speak the truth and cultivate contentment, just as the last six of the ten commandments require.

How then are we to explain this paradoxical phenomenon, that although they do not have the law, they yet appear to know it? Paul's answer is that *they are a law for themselves*, not in the popular – albeit mistaken – sense that they can frame their own laws, but in the sense that their own human being is their law. This is because God created them self-conscious moral persons, and *they show* by their behaviour *that the requirements of the law are written*

[19] Hodge, p. 53.

on their hearts (15a). So then, although they do not have the law in their hands, they do have its requirements in their hearts, because God has written them there. This surely cannot be a reference to God's new-covenant promise to put his law in his people's minds and write it on their hearts,[20] as Barth, Charles Cranfield and other commentators have suggested, since the whole context is one of judgment, not salvation. Paul is referring not to regeneration but to creation, to the fact that 'the work of the law' (literally), its 'requirements' (NIV), its 'effect' (NEB, JBP), its 'business',[21] has been written on the hearts of all human beings by their Maker. That God has written his law on our hearts by creation means that we have some knowledge of it; when he writes his law on our hearts in the new creation he also gives us a love for it and the power to obey it.

In addition, *their consciences* are *bearing witness*, especially by a negative, disapproving voice when they have done wrong, and so are *their thoughts* in a kind of interior dialogue, *now accusing, now even defending them* (15b), as if in a lawcourt in which the prosecution and the defence develop their respective cases. It seems that Paul is envisaging a debate in which three parties are involved: our *hearts* (on which the requirements of the law have been written), our *consciences* (prodding and reproving us), and our *thoughts* (usually accusing us, but sometimes even excusing us).

Verse 16 concludes this section. Verses 14–15 seem to form a parenthesis (as in NIV). Verse 16 then resumes the theme of judgment, and NIV indicates this by adding the introductory words *This will take place*. Paul has stressed that we cannot escape God's judgment (1–4); that it will be a righteous judgment (5–11), according to our works, including the fundamental ambition or direction of our lives (what we 'seek'); and that it will be impartial as between Jews and Gentiles (12–15). In both cases, the greater our moral knowledge, the greater our moral accountability will be. Now he adds three further truths about judgment day, 'the day of God's wrath' (5).

First, God's judgment will include the hidden areas of our lives: *God will judge men's secrets.* Scripture tells us repeatedly that God knows our hearts.[22] In consequence, there will be no possibility of a miscarriage of justice on the last day. For all the facts will be known, including those which at present are not, for example, our motives.

Secondly, God's judgment will take place *through Jesus Christ.* He claimed that the Father had entrusted all judgment to him,[23] and he regularly spoke of himself as the central figure on the day of judgment.[24] Paul declared in Athens that God had both fixed the

---

[20] Je. 31:33; *cf.* 2 Cor. 3:3. [21] Dunn, vol. 38A, p. 100.
[22] *E.g.* 1 Sa. 16:7; Ps. 139:1ff.; Je. 17:10; Lk. 16:15; Heb. 4:12f.
[23] Jn. 5:22, 27. [24] *E.g.* Mt. 7:21ff.; 25:31ff.

day and appointed the judge,[25] as Peter had earlier told Cornelius.[26] It is a great comfort to know that our judge will be none other than our saviour.

Thirdly, God's judgment is part of the gospel. For *God will judge men's secrets*, Paul wrote, *through Jesus Christ, as my gospel declares* (16). Probably this means that the good news of salvation shines forth brightly when it is seen against the dark background of divine judgment. We cheapen the gospel if we represent it as a deliverance only from unhappiness, fear, guilt and other felt needs, instead of as a rescue from the coming wrath.[27]

4.   Conclusion: God's judgment and God's law

The universal knowledge of God's law, which Paul has been demonstrating in verses 12–16, is an indispensable basis both of the divine judgment and of the Christian mission.

First, the law is *a basis of divine judgment*. Paul's thrust has been that God has no favourites; that Jews and Gentiles will be judged by him without discrimination; and that both groups have some knowledge of his law. Consequently, no human being can plead complete ignorance. We have all sinned against a moral law we have known. Whether we have come to know it by special or general revelation, by grace or nature, outwardly or inwardly, in the Scripture or in the heart, is largely irrelevant. The point is that all human beings have known something of God (1:20) and of goodness (1:32; 2:15), but have suppressed the truth in order to indulge in wickedness (1:18; 2:8). So we all come under the righteous judgment of God.

Verses 12–16 were not written to give us hope that human beings can gain salvation by morality. Natural law can no more save sinners than natural religion. For whatever we may have known of God from creation (1:19f.), or of goodness from conscience (1:32; 2:15), we have stifled it in order to go our own self-seeking way (2:8). Besides, the purpose of these chapters is to prove that all human beings are guilty and inexcusable before God (3:9, 19), and in particular that nobody can be justified by observing the law (3:20).

Secondly, the law is *a basis of Christian mission*, of both evangelism and social action. Take evangelism. Dietrich Bonhoeffer was quite correct to write from prison, 'I don't think it is Christian to want to get to the New Testament too soon or too directly.'[28] What he meant is that, until the law has done its work of exposing and condemning our sin, we are not ready to hear the gospel of

---

[25] Acts 17:31.   [26] Acts 10:42.   [27] 1 Thes. 1:10.
[28] Dietrich Bonhoeffer, *Letters and Papers from Prison* (Fontana, 1959), p. 50.

justification. True, it is often said that we should address ourselves to people's conscious needs, and not try to induce in them feelings of guilt which they do not have. This is a misconception, however. Human beings are moral beings by creation.[29] That is to say, not only do we experience an inner urge to do what we believe to be right, but we also have a sense of guilt and remorse when we have done what we know to be wrong. This is an essential feature of our humanness. There is of course such a thing as false guilt. But guilt feelings which are aroused by wrongdoing are healthy. They rebuke us for betraying our humanity, and they impel us to seek forgiveness in Christ. Thus conscience is our ally. In all evangelism, I find it a constant encouragement to say to myself, 'The other person's conscience is on my side.'

The possibility of securing justice in society is another legitimate deduction from Paul's teaching in verses 12–16, even though it is not part of his direct purpose in the context. What he is saying is that the same moral law, which God has revealed in Scripture, he has also stamped (even if not so legibly) on human nature. Since he has in fact written his law twice, internally as well as externally, it is not to be regarded as an alien system, which we impose on people arbitrarily, and which it is altogether unnatural to expect human beings to obey. On the contrary, there is a fundamental correspondence between the law in Scripture and the law in human nature. God's law fits us; it is the law of our own being. We are authentically human only when we obey it. When we disobey it, we not only rebel against God, we also contradict our true selves.

In every human community, therefore, there is a basic recognition of the difference between right and wrong, and an accepted set of values. True, conscience is not infallible, and standards are influenced by cultures. Nevertheless, a substratum of good and evil remains, and love is always acknowledged as superior to selfishness. This has important social and political implications. It means that legislators and educators can assume that God's law is good for society and that at least to some degree people know it. It is not a case of Christians trying to force their standards on an unwilling public, but of helping the public to see that God's law is 'for our own good at all times',[30] because it is the law of human being and of human community. If democracy is government by consent, consent depends on consensus, consensus on argument, and argument on ethical apologists who will develop a case for the goodness of God's law.

---

[29] Young children and the mentally handicapped are obviously not as morally responsible as adults and the mentally mature.
[30] Dt. 6:24, REB.

2:17 – 3:8
6.   Self-confident Jews

Paul now moves on, in his wide-ranging critique of the human race, from critical moralizers in general (2:1–16), whether Jews or Gentiles, to Jewish people in particular in their self-confidence (2:17–29). In the first half of the chapter his interlocutor has been a human being ('O man', 1, 3, RSV); now in the second half it is a Jew (*Now you, if you call yourself a Jew . . .* , 17).

Paul anticipates and responds to Jewish objections to what he has written. He imagines Jews protesting somewhat as follows: 'Surely, Paul, you can't possibly treat us as if we were no different from Gentile outsiders? Have you forgotten that we have been given both the law (the revelation of God) and circumcision (the sign of the covenant of God)? Have you overlooked the fact that these three privileges (covenant, circumcision and law) are themselves tokens of the greatest privilege of all, that God chose us to be his special people? Are you saying that we Jews (who have been uniquely favoured by God's election) are no better off than the Gentiles? How can you disregard these peculiar blessings of ours, which distinguish us from the Gentiles and protect us from God's judgment?'

In reply to such questions Paul writes about the law in verses 17–24 and about circumcision in verses 25–29, and insists that neither guarantees Jewish immunity to divine judgment. His words are 'a pricking of the balloon of Jewish pride and presumption'.[1]

1.   The law (17–24)

Paul uses eight verbs to describe aspects of Jewish self-consciousness and self-confidence. First, *you call yourself a Jew*, being proud of the chosen people's honourable name. Second, *you rely on the law* given you at Sinai, trusting in your possession of it as

[1] Dunn, vol. 38A, p. 108.

a shield against disaster. Third, *you . . . brag about your relationship to God* (17). The Greek phrase is identical with the climax of Paul's portrayal of Christians who have been justified by faith, namely 'we rejoice in God' (5:11). But NIV is surely right to elaborate the translation here in order to express the Jews' pride in their monotheism and in their supposed monopoly of God. Fourth, *you know his will*, literally 'the will' absolutely, to which all other wills are relative. Fifth, *you . . . approve of what is superior*. Both here and in Philippians 1:10 this expression could mean either 'you test things which differ' or, having done so, 'you approve those things which the test has shown to excel'. Sixth, the reason for your moral discernment is that *you are instructed by the law* (18). And a further consequence of your instruction and discernment is (seventh) that *you are convinced* that you are competent to teach others. So *you are a guide for the blind* and *a light for those who are in the dark* (19), *i.e.* the Gentiles, since this is the stated vocation of the servant of the Lord.[2] You are also *an instructor of the foolish* and *a teacher of infants*, probably meaning spiritual babies, *i.e.* proselytes or converts. And all this *because* (eighth) *you have in the law the embodiment of knowledge and truth* (20). In these eight statements Paul has given a straightforward account of Jewish people in their double relation to the law. Being instructed, they instruct. Being taught, they teach.

But now Paul turns the tables on them. They do not live up to their knowledge (*cf.* 13). They do not practise what they preach. Following his eight verbs which portray their identity, he asks five rhetorical questions, which draw attention to their inconsistency. The first is general: *You, then, who teach others, do you not teach yourself?* (21a). It is followed by three questions about particular sins: *You who preach against stealing, do you steal?* (21b). *You who say that people should not commit adultery, do you commit adultery? You who abhor idols, do you rob temples?* (22). The last-named might refer to the misappropriation of funds intended for the temple, since Josephus tells the story of just such a scandal,[3] but Paul is more likely to have pagan temples in mind. *You who abhor idols* is an accurate portrayal of Jews. They recoiled from idolatry in horror. They would not dream of going anywhere near an idol temple, therefore – except for the purpose of robbery. In such cases 'scruple broke down before thievish avarice'.[4] Some commentators think all three sins so unlikely in Jewish leaders that they suggest a non-literal interpretation. 'When theft, adultery and sacrilege are strictly and radically understood, there is no man who is not guilty of all three,' writes C. K.

[2] Is. 42:6f.; 49:6.   [3] Josephus, 18:81ff.   [4] Moule (1884), p. 75.

91

Barrett,[5] and reminds us of Jesus' teaching in the Sermon on the Mount about the thoughts of our hearts.[6] But Paul seems to have actions rather than thoughts in mind, and Dodd quotes Rabbi Jochanan ben Zakkai, a contemporary of Paul's, who bewailed in his day 'the increase of murder, adultery, sexual vice, commercial and judicial corruption, bitter sectarian strife, and other evils'.[7]

Paul's fifth rhetorical question is again more general: *You who brag about the law* (which the Jews did, see verse 17), *do you dishonour God by breaking the law?* (23). *As it is written, 'God's name is blasphemed among the Gentiles because of you'* (24). This quotation seems to combine Isaiah 52:5 and Ezekiel 36:22. In both texts God's name had been mocked because his people had been defeated and enslaved. Could Yahweh not protect his own people? Just so, moral defeat, like military defeat, brings discredit on the name of God.

The argument of verses 17–24 is the same in principle as that of verses 1–3, and is just as applicable to us as to first-century critical moralizers and self-confident Jews. If we judge others, we should be able to judge ourselves (1–3). If we teach others, we should be able to teach ourselves (21–24). If we set ourselves up as either teachers or judges of others, we can have no excuse if we do not teach or judge ourselves. We cannot possibly plead ignorance of moral rectitude. On the contrary, we invite God's condemnation of our hypocrisy.

2. Circumcision (25–29)

If the Jews' possession and knowledge of the law did not exempt them from the judgment of God, neither did their circumcision. To be sure, circumcision was a God-given sign and seal of his covenant with them.[8] But it was not a magical ceremony or a charm. It did not provide them with permanent insurance cover against the wrath of God. It was no substitute for obedience; it constituted rather a commitment to obedience. Yet the Jews had an almost superstitious confidence in the saving power of their circumcision. Rabbinic epigrams expressed it. For example, 'Circumcised men do not descend into Gehenna,' and 'Circumcision will deliver Israel from Gehenna.'[9]

How does Paul counter this false assurance? He begins with an epigram of his own: *Circumcision has value if you observe the law*

[5] Barrett, p. 56.   [6] Mt. 5:21ff.   [7] Dodd, p. 39.   [8] Gn. 17:9ff.

[9] Quoted by Cranfield, vol. I, p. 172, footnote 1. Compare the saying in *Mishnah Sanhedrin* that 'all Israelites have a share in the world to come', quoted by Sanders (1977), p. 147. But Jesus himself taught that covenant membership was no guarantee of immunity to God's judgment (*e.g.* Mt. 21:28ff.). So had John the Baptist before him (*e.g.* Mt. 3:7ff.).

(25a). He does not deny the divine origin of circumcision, but he relativizes its value on the ground that he who is circumcised 'is required to obey the whole law'.[10] For circumcision is the sign of covenant membership, and covenant membership demands obedience. On this basis, namely that circumcision and the law belong together in God's covenant, Paul now makes two bold complementary statements. On the one hand, *if you* who are circumcised *break the law, you have become as though you had not been circumcised* (25b). On the other hand, *if those who are not circumcised keep the law's requirements, will they not be regarded as though they were circumcised?* (26). We may perhaps express Paul's double assertion in terms of two simple equations. Circumcision minus obedience equals uncircumcision, while uncircumcision plus obedience equals circumcision.

The consequence Paul infers from this will have been profoundly shocking to Jewish people. In contrast to their traditional picture of themselves sitting in judgment on the uncircumcised pagans (*cf.* 2:1–3), the roles will be reversed, and *the one who is not circumcised physically*, who *yet obeys the law, will* actually *condemn you* (a Jew) *who, even though you have the written code* (*i.e.* the law) *and circumcision, are a law-breaker* (27). The ultimate sign, the *bona fide* evidence, of membership of the covenant of God is neither circumcision nor possession of the law, but the obedience which both circumcision and the law demand. Their circumcision did not make them what their disobedience proved they were not. This is not salvation by obedience, but obedience as the evidence of salvation. The corollary is that Jews are just as much exposed to the judgment of God as Gentiles.

The extraordinary reversal of roles which Paul has described in verse 27, by which the Gentile condemns the Jew instead of the Jew condemning the Gentile, is due to a necessary redefinition of Jewish identity, which Paul proceeds to give, in contrast to the Jewish self-definition of 2:17ff. First he states negatively what a Jew is not (28), and then defines positively what a true Jew is (29). *A man is not a Jew if he is only one outwardly* (en tō phanerō, 'in the open' or 'visibly'), *nor is circumcision merely outward* (en tō phanerō, repeated) *and physical* (en sarki, 'in flesh') (28). No, *a man is a Jew if he is one inwardly* (en tō kryptō, 'in secret'); *and circumcision is circumcision of the heart* (29a). This concept is not new with Paul, since it occurs regularly in the Old Testament. In the Pentateuch God complains of his people's 'uncircumcised hearts', appeals to them to circumcise their hearts, and promises that he will do it to them himself so that they may love him with all their being.[11] Then

---

[10] Gal. 5:3.   [11] Lv. 26:41; Dt. 10:16; 30:6.

the prophets use the same imagery. Foreigners are significantly described as 'uncircumcised in heart and flesh'; those who are 'circumcised only in the flesh' and 'uncircumcised in heart' will be punished; Yahweh calls on his people to circumcise their hearts, and promises to give them a 'new heart'.[12]

What Paul looks for is something more than this, however, namely 'a circumcision of the heart that completely *replaces* the physical rite and does not merely complement it'.[13] It will also be *by the Spirit, not by the written code* (29b). That is, it will be an inward work of the Holy Spirit, such as the law as an external written code could never effect. This contrast between *gramma* (letter or code) and *pneuma* (the Spirit) sums up for Paul the difference between the old covenant (an external law) and the new (the gift of the Spirit). He anticipates here what he will elaborate in 7:6 and 8:4, indeed throughout the whole first half of chapter 8.[14] Further, *such a man's praise is not from men, but from God* (29c). This probably alludes to a play on Hebrew words, since Jews were named from their ancestor Judah, and his name in Hebrew was associated with, and may have been derived from, the word for 'praise'.[15]

In his redefinition of what it means to be a Jew, an authentic member of God's covenant people, then, Paul draws a fourfold contrast. First, the essence of being a true Jew (who may indeed be ethnically a Gentile) is not something outward and visible, but inward and invisible. For the true circumcision is, secondly, in the heart, not the flesh. Thirdly, it is effected by the Spirit, not the law, and fourthly, it wins the approval of God rather than human beings. Human beings are comfortable with what is outward, visible, material and superficial. What matters to God is a deep, inward, secret work of the Holy Spirit in our hearts.

Moreover, what Paul writes here about circumcision and being a Jew could also be said about baptism and being a Christian. The real Christian, like the real Jew, is one inwardly; and the true baptism, like the true circumcision, is in the heart and by the Spirit. It is not in this case that the inward and spiritual *replace* the outward and physical, but rather that the visible sign (baptism) derives its importance from the invisible reality (washing from sin and the gift of the Spirit), to which it bears witness. It is a grave mistake to exalt the sign at the expense of what it signifies.

3. Some Jewish objections (3:1–8)

It is not difficult to imagine the reactions of at least some of Paul's

---

[12] Ezk. 44:9; Je. 9:25f.; 4:4; Ezk. 36:26f.   [13] Dunn, vol. 38A, p. 127.
[14] *Cf.* 2 Cor. 3:6.   [15] *Cf.* Gn. 29:35; 49:8.

Jewish readers. They will have responded to him with a mixture of incredulity and indignation. For his thesis will have seemed to them an outrageous undermining of the very foundations of Judaism, namely God's character and covenant.

Paul's method of handling Jewish objections to his teaching takes the form of a 'diatribe', as we have seen – a literary convention well known to philosophers in the ancient world. In it a teacher would set up a dialogue with his critics or students, first posing and then answering their questions. Paul has already begun to use this genre when addressing both the critical moralizer (2:1ff.) and the Jew (2:17ff.); but now he develops it further. It is not necessary to suppose that his debating opponent is imaginary or his debate fictitious. It seems more probable that he is reconstructing the actual arguments which Jews have flung at him during his synagogue evangelism.[16] 'It often becomes easier to follow Paul's arguments', writes C. K. Barrett, 'if the reader imagines the apostle face to face with a heckler, who makes interjections and receives replies which sometimes are withering and brusque.'[17] We may go further than this. 'Paul's interlocutor was no straw man,' Professor Dunn writes. 'In fact we would probably not be far from the mark if we were to conclude that Paul's interlocutor is Paul himself – Paul the unconverted Pharisee, expressing attitudes Paul remembered so well as having been his own!'[18] In this way Paul the Pharisee and Paul the Christian are in debate with each other, as in Philippians 3.

The details of the debate are a little hard to grasp, not because Paul's position is 'obscure and feeble',[19] but because he gives it to us in only the briefest outline. For the elaboration we shall have to wait for Romans 9 – 11. We do have before us in 2:25–29, however, the teaching of Paul which prompts the objections, namely that there was no fundamental difference between Jews and Gentiles, and that the law and circumcision guaranteed neither Jewish immunity to the judgment of God nor Jewish identity as the people of God. This seemed to call in question God's covenant, promises and character. It prompted four distinct but related questions.

Objection 1: Paul's teaching undermines God's covenant (1–2). Paul and his critics are agreed that God chose Israel out of all the nations, made a covenant with them, and gave them circumcision as its sign and seal. But if the words 'Jew' and 'circumcision' are now to be radically redefined, then *What advantage . . . is there in being a Jew* in the old sense of the term, and *what value is there in circumcision* in its traditional meaning (1)? For these things do not protect Jews from judgment, according to Paul.

[16] *E.g.* Acts 17:1ff., 17; 18:4ff.; 19:8.   [17] Barrett, p. 43.
[18] Dunn, vol. 38A, p. 91.   [19] Dodd, p. 46.

In his answer Paul does not go back on what he has written about the real Jew and the true circumcision. The fact that being an ethnic Jew has no value in protecting from God's judgment, however, does not mean that it is valueless. It has *much* value *in every way*, but a different kind of value, that is, responsibility rather than security. *First of all* (Paul is evidently intending to list several privileges, but he does not get round to it until 9:4f.), *they have been entrusted with the very words of God* (2). It seems clear that these 'oracles of God'[20] are not just God's commandments or promises, but the whole Old Testament Scripture which contains them and which was committed to Israel's care. Indeed, to be the custodians of God's special revelation was an immensely privileged responsibility; it had been given to 'no other nation'.[21]

Objection 2: Paul's teaching nullifies God's faithfulness (3). Perhaps God's 'oracles' or 'very words' (2) allude in particular to his promises, notably to his promise of the Messiah. If so, the objector argues, what has become of God's promise, and (more important) of his faithfulness to his promise? *What if some did not have faith*, and so failed to inherit the promise? *Will their lack of faith nullify God's faithfulness* (3)? Paul's teaching seemed to imply this. The play on words relating to *pistis* (faith or faithfulness) is more obvious in the Greek sentence than in the English. It might be rendered as follows: 'If some to whom God's promises were entrusted (*episteuthēsan*, 2) did not respond to them in trust (*ēpistēsan*, 3a), will their lack of trust (*apistia*) destroy God's trustworthiness (*pistis*, 3b)?' If God's people are unfaithful, does that necessarily mean that he is?

Paul's riposte (*mē genoito*) is more violent than is suggested by the expressions 'Not at all!' (NIV), 'By no means!' (RSV), 'Certainly not!' (REB) or even 'God forbid!' (AV). John Ziesler suggests that '"not on your life" or "not in a thousand years" gives something of the flavour.'[22] For God will never never break his covenant, as Paul will elaborate in chapters 9–11. His truth or faithfulness is an *a priori*. Indeed, *Let God be true, and every man a liar* (4a). The first of these two propositions, writes Calvin, 'is the primary axiom of all Christian philosophy';[23] the second is a quotation of Psalm 116:11. So far is it from the case that human unfaithfulness undermines God's faithfulness, that even if every single human being were a liar, God would still be true, because he remains invariably himself and true to himself. Moreover, Scripture confirms this. David even acknowledged that he had sinned and done evil in God's sight in order that God's word might be proved right and his verdict

---

[20] AV, RSV, REB. [21] Ps. 147:19f.; *cf.* Dt. 4:8. [22] Ziesler (1989), p. 97.
[23] Calvin, p. 60.

justified: *'So that you may be proved right when you speak and prevail when you judge'* (4b).[24]

Objection 3: Paul's teaching impugns God's justice (5–6). Perhaps the reference to God as judge (4) leads Paul to mention his justice, which is displayed in his judgments. In this case the objector is making the general point that *our unrighteousness brings out God's righteousness more clearly.* The more unrighteous the criminal is, the more righteous the judge appears. Or the objector may be alluding to *God's righteousness* revealed in the gospel (1:17), his way of salvation. In this case he is arguing that the more sinful we are, the more glorious the gospel seems. Either way, according to Paul's teaching, says the objector, our unrighteousness benefits God, because it displays his character all the more brightly. This being so, *what shall we say?* Shall we conclude (as, according to the Jewish objector, the logic of Paul's position demands) *that God is unjust in bringing his wrath on us* (5a)? God's wrath is certainly on the immoral Gentiles (1:18) and will fall on the critical moralizers (2:5); but will he really bring it on his own people, the Jews? Would it not be unfair of him to punish them for something which is to his advantage? Even as he expresses this tortuous reasoning, Paul feels embarrassed and adds apologetically in parenthesis: *(I am using a human argument)* (5b).

He goes beyond an apology, however. He continues with another categorical denial (*Certainly not!*) and then asks his heckler a counter-question. If he really were unjust, *how could God judge the world?* (6). Paul takes it as axiomatic both that God is the universal judge and that therefore, as Abraham said, the Judge of all the earth will do right.[25] To impugn God's justice is to undercut his competence to judge and so to show up the absurdity of the original question.

Objection 4: Paul's teaching falsely promotes God's glory (7–8). *Someone might argue,* Paul continues, and goes on to develop the previous argument. In doing so, he also impersonates the objector by using the first person singular. *If my falsehood enhances God's truthfulness,* just as our unrighteousness displays God's righteousness more brightly (5), *and so increases his glory,* then surely God ought to be pleased, even grateful? Am I not doing him a service? This being so, Paul's teaching prompts two subsidiary questions. First, *why am I still condemned as a sinner* (7), if my sin is to God's advantage? How can God condemn me for glorifying him? Secondly, *why not say* (as, Paul adds, he is *being slanderously reported as saying* and as *some claim that* he does say), *'Let us do evil that good may result'*? This is the cry of the antinomian, who

[24] Ps. 51:4.   [25] Gn. 18:25.

rationalizes his lawlessness: 'If evil behaviour causes good consequences, such as manifesting God's character and so promoting his glory, then let's increase evil in order thereby to increase good. The end obviously justifies the means.' C. H. Hodge puts it well: 'According to this reasoning, says Paul, the worse we are, the better: for the more wicked we are, the more conspicuous will be the mercy of God in our pardon.'[26]

This time Paul does not answer the questions which his teaching is supposed to raise. For they do not merit a serious refutation; they are self-evidently perverse. It is enough to say of these objectors that *their condemnation is deserved* (8). For no good results can justify the encouragement of evil. Evil never promotes the glory of God.

We note from this passage (3:1–8) that Paul was not content only to proclaim and expound the gospel. He also argued its truth and reasonableness, and defended it against misunderstanding and misrepresentation. Whether these Jewish objections were genuine (because he had actually heard them advanced) or imaginary (because he had made them up), he took them seriously and responded to them. He saw that the character of God was at stake. So he reaffirmed God's covenant as having abiding value, God's faithfulness to his promises, God's justice as judge, and God's true glory which is promoted only by good, never by evil.

We too in our day must include apologetics in our evangelism. We need to anticipate people's objections to the gospel, listen carefully to their problems, respond to them with due seriousness, and proclaim the gospel in such a way as to affirm God's goodness and further his glory. Such dialogical preaching has a powerful apostolic precedent in this passage.

---

[26] Hodge, p. 75.

3:9–20
7. The whole human race

The apostle is approaching the end of his lengthy argument, and asks himself how to wrap it all up, how to rest his case: *What shall we conclude then?* (9a).

He has exposed in succession the blatant unrighteousness of much of the ancient Gentile world (1:18–32), the hypocritical righteousness of moralizers (2:1–16), and the confident self-righteousness of Jewish people, whose anomaly is that they boast of God's law but break it (2:17 – 3:8). So now he arraigns and condemns the whole human race.

Although there is considerable uncertainty about both the form and the meaning of the second verb in verse 9, I am content to accept the NIV rendering: *Are we any better?* That is, is there any benefit in being a Jew? If this is correct, then Paul asks the same question twice within the space of a few verses, and proceeds to give himself apparently opposite answers. In verse 1 he has asked: 'What advantage, then, is there in being a Jew?' And he has answered: 'Much in every way!' Now in verse 9 he asks: *Are we* (Jews) *any better* or 'any better off' (REB)? And he replies: *Not at all!* He certainly sounds as if he is contradicting himself, asserting first that there is great advantage in being a Jew and then that there is none. How can we resolve this discrepancy? Only by clarifying what benefit or 'advantage' he has in mind. If he means privilege and responsibility, then the Jews have much because God has entrusted his revelation to them. But if he means favouritism, then the Jews have none, because God will not exempt them from judgment: *We have already made the charge* (i.e. in 1:18 – 2:29) *that Jews and Gentiles alike are all under sin* (9), or 'under the power of sin' (RSV, REB, *cf.* Gal. 3:22). Paul appears almost to personify sin as a cruel tyrant who holds the human race imprisoned in guilt and under judgment. Sin is on top of us, weighs us down, and is a crushing burden.

This fact of the universal bondage of sin and guilt Paul goes on to support from Scripture. He supplies a series of seven Old Testament quotations, the first probably from Ecclesiastes, then five from the Psalms and one from Isaiah, all of which bear witness in different ways to human unrighteousness. Paul 'follows here a common rabbinical practice of stringing passages together like pearls'.[1]

> [10]*As it is written:*
> *'There is no-one righteous, not even one;*
> [11] *there is no-one who understands,*
>   *no-one who seeks God (Ec. 7:20).*
> [12]*All have turned away,*
>   *they have together become worthless;*
> *there is no-one who does good,*
>   *not even one' (Ps. 14:1–3 = Ps. 53:1–3).*
> [13]*'Their throats are open graves;*
>   *their tongues practise deceit' (Ps. 5:9).*
> *'The poison of vipers is on their lips' (Ps. 140:3).*
> [14] *'Their mouths are full of cursing and bitterness' (Ps. 10:7).*
> [15]*'Their feet are swift to shed blood;*
> [16] *ruin and misery mark their ways,*
> [17]*and the way of peace they do not know' (Is. 59:7f.; cf. Pr. 1:16).*
> [18] *'There is no fear of God before their eyes' (Ps. 36:1).*

Three features of this grim biblical picture stand out.

First, it declares the *ungodliness* of sin. Near the beginning comes the statement that *there is . . . no-one who seeks God* (11), and at the end *there is no fear of God before their eyes* (18). This is more than an assertion that when people renounce God they tend to plunge recklessly into evil, whereas when they fear God, they shun evil.[2] It is rather that Scripture identifies the essence of sin as ungodliness (*cf.* 1:18). God's complaint is that we do not really 'seek' him at all, making his glory or supreme concern,[3] that we have not set him before us,[4] that there is no room for him in our thoughts,[5] and that we do not love him with all our powers. Sin is the revolt of the self against God, the dethronement of God with a view to the enthronement of oneself. Ultimately, sin is self-deification, the reckless determination to occupy the throne which belongs to God alone.

Secondly, this catena of Old Testament verses teaches the *pervasiveness* of sin. For sin affects every part of our human constitution, every faculty and function, including our mind, emotions, sexuality, conscience and will. In verses 13–17 there is a deliberate listing of different parts of the body. Thus, *their throats are open graves*, full of corruption and infection; *their tongues practise deceit,*

---

[1] Morris (1988), p. 166. He quotes in support A. Edersheim's *The Life and Times of Jesus the Messiah,* vol. I (1890), p. 449.
[2] *E.g.* Jb. 28:28.　　[3] Ps. 14:2.　　[4] Ps. 54:3, RV; *cf.* Ps. 16:8.　　[5] Ps. 10:4.

instead of being dedicated to the truth; *their lips* spread *poison* like snakes; *their mouths* are filled with bitter curses; *their feet are swift* in the pursuit of violence, and scatter ruin and misery in their path, instead of walking in *the way of peace*; and *their eyes are* looking in the wrong direction; they do not reverence God.

These bodily limbs and organs were created and given us so that through them we might serve people and glorify God. Instead, they are used to harm people and in rebellion against God. This is the biblical doctrine of 'total depravity', which I suspect is repudiated only by those who misunderstand it. It has never meant that human beings are as depraved as they could possibly be. Such a notion is manifestly absurd and untrue, and is contradicted by our everyday observation. Not all human beings are drunkards, felons, adulterers or murderers. Besides, Paul has shown how some people sometimes are able 'by nature' to obey the law (2:14, 27). No, the 'totality' of our corruption refers to its *extent* (twisting and tainting every part of our humanness), not to its *degree* (depraving every part of us absolutely). As Dr J. I. Packer has put it succinctly, on the one hand 'no one is as bad as he or she might be', while on the other 'no action of ours is as good as it should be'.[6]

Thirdly, the Old Testament quotations teach the *universality* of sin, both negatively and positively. Negatively, *there is no-one righteous, not even one* (10); *there is no-one who understands, no-one who seeks God* (11); *there is no-one who does good, not even one* (12b). Positively, 'all have swerved aside, all alike have become debased' (12a, REB). The repetition hammers home the point. Twice we are told that 'all' have gone their own way, four times that 'no-one' is righteous, and twice that 'not even one' is an exception. For to be 'righteous' is to live in conformity to God's law, and 'the best man, the noblest, the most learned, the most philanthropic; the greatest idealist, the greatest thinker, say what you like – there has never been a man who can stand up to the test of the law. Drop your plumb-line, and he is not true to it.'[7]

Verse 19 has proved a puzzle to commentators. Its purpose is clear, namely that *every mouth may be silenced* and that *the whole world* may be *held accountable to God* (19b). But how is this conclusion reached? The probable explanation is that Jewish people reading the series of Old Testament quotations would assume that they applied to those wicked and lawless Gentiles. And of course God's judgment would fall on them. But Paul reminds Jews of their common knowledge: *we know that whatever the law says* (here meaning the Old Testament in general), *it says to those who are*

---

[6] J. I. Packer, *Concise Theology* (Tyndale House and Inter-Varsity Press, 1993), pp. 83f.

[7] Lloyd-Jones, vol. 2, p. 198. *Cf.* 1 Ki. 8:46; Ec. 7:20.

under the law (19a, literally, 'within' the law), namely themselves as Jews, so that they will be included in the judgment as well. In this way every mouth is stopped, every excuse silenced, and the whole world, having been found guilty, is liable to God's judgment. These words, writes Professor Cranfield, 'evoke the picture of the defendant in court who, given the opportunity to speak in his own defence, is speechless because of the weight of the evidence which has been brought against him'.[8] There is nothing to wait for but the pronouncement and execution of the sentence.

So this is the point to which the apostle has been relentlessly moving. The idolatrous and immoral Gentiles are 'without excuse' (1:20). All critical moralists, whether Jews or Gentiles, equally 'have no excuse' (2:1). The special status of the Jews does not exonerate them. In fact, all the inhabitants of the whole world (3:19), without any exception, are inexcusable (*hypodikos*) before God, that is, 'under accusation with no possibility of defence'.[9] And by now the reason is plain. It is because all have known something of God and of morality (through Scripture in the case of the Jews, through nature in the case of the Gentiles), but all have disregarded and even stifled their knowledge in order to go their own way. So all are guilty and condemned before God.

Therefore, Paul concludes, *no-one will be declared righteous in his sight by observing the law* (20a), literally 'by works of the law' (RSV). What does he mean by this expression? 'This is the first appearance', writes Professor Dunn, 'of a key phrase whose importance for understanding Paul's thought in this letter can hardly be overemphasized, but which has in fact frequently been misunderstood by successive generations of commentators.'[10]

The traditional understanding of 'works of the law', promoted particularly by Lutheran scholars, is that Paul is referring to good works of righteousness and philanthropy, done in obedience to the law, and regarded by the Jews as the meritorious ground on which God accepted them.

This tradition is now being challenged, especially by Professor E. P. Sanders, on the ground that Palestinian Judaism was not a religion of works-righteousness and that therefore Paul cannot have been denying what the Jews were not affirming, namely salvation by meritorious works. Instead, as Professor Dunn elaborates, Paul's target was narrower and quite specific, namely the 'devout Jew' who took it for granted that he was securely within God's covenant, provided that he maintained his membership by 'works of the law', namely those 'boundary markers' like sabbath observance and the

---

[8] Cranfield, vol. I, pp. 196f.   [9] Käsemann, pp. 88f.
[10] Dunn, vol. 38A, p. 158. The phrase occurs also in 3:28; 9:32; Gal. 2:16; 3:2, 5, 10.

food laws which distinguished him from the Gentiles.[11] Further, the reason Paul denied salvation by these works is that he was opposing privilege, not merit. For if salvation was by circumcision and cultural practices, only Jews and proselytes were included and Gentiles were excluded. In reaction to this, Paul emphasized not so much the freeness of God's grace (against merit) as its impartiality (against élitism). Salvation 'by works of the law' bolstered pride and privilege; salvation by faith abolished them.

How shall we respond to this increasingly popular reconstruction? At least, I think, in two ways. First, Professor Dunn's thesis (what he calls 'the new perspective on Paul'), namely that by 'works of the law' Paul meant distinctively Jewish 'identity markers' like sabbath, circumcision and food regulations, is far from proved. The expression contains no hint within itself that the 'works' in mind are only cultural-ceremonial and not moral. Nor does Paul's use of it suggest this limitation. For example, Romans 3:20 concludes Paul's long argument that all human beings are morally sinful and guilty, including Jews whose transgressions include stealing and adultery (2:21f.), not ritual offences; the second part of Romans 3:20 defines the law's function as revealing sin; Romans 3:28 contrasts justification by faith with 'works of the law', which cannot mean Mosaic ceremonial rules, as is clear from the example of Abraham (4:2) who lived long before Moses. Dr Stephen Westerholm, who develops a powerful argument along these lines, writes: 'The "works of the law" which do not justify are the demands of the law that are not met, not those observed for the wrong reasons by Jews.'[12]

Our second response to Professor Dunn's thesis relates to the question why Paul is so negative about 'works'. There is no doubt, we agree, that Paul is opposing Jewish exclusivism, especially the notion that the Jews' favoured status automatically exempted them from judgment. But the whole context suggests that he was attacking merit also, that is, Jewish reliance on moral (and not merely ceremonial) works. For the law by whose works no-one can be justified (20a) is surely the same law which declares all human beings to be sinful (19a), so that the whole world is guilty before God (19b). Indeed, the reason the law cannot justify sinners is precisely that its function is to expose and to condemn their sin (20b). And the reason the law condemns us is that we break it.

If, then, Paul was opposing the concept of salvation by good works, who were his opponents? And how shall we respond to Professor Sanders' thesis that this was not the stance of Palestinian Judaism? In general, I think Douglas Moo is correct, as indeed I

[11] *Ibid.*, pp. 152ff.
[12] Westerholm, p. 119. Professor Fitzmyer also disagrees with Professor Dunn's 'restricted sense' of the expression 'works of the law' (p. 338).

have tried to argue in the Preliminary Essay (pp. 27ff.), 'that Palestinian Judaism was more legalistic than Sanders has found ... Even in Sanders' proposal, works play such a prominent role that it is fair to speak of a synergism of faith and works that elevates works to a crucial salvific role.' Since good works, according to E. P. Sanders, were essential if Jews were to 'stay in' the covenant, they played 'a necessary and instrumental role in salvation'.[13] The alternative possibility, which John Ziesler suggests, is that Paul was 'opposing a perversion of Judaism, arising out of official Judaism but in spite of it, a popular perversion which *did* think of earning God's favour'.[14] That some doctrine of self-salvation was widespread in Judaism in surely evident not only from Paul's polemic but also from the teaching of Jesus himself, for example in the parable of the Pharisee and the publican, and above all from our own knowledge of the proud human heart.

Returning to verse 20, we should see it as the climax of Paul's argument not just against Jewish self-confidence, but against every attempt at self-salvation. For, Paul continues, *through the law we become conscious of sin* (20b). That is, what the law brings is the knowledge of sin, not the forgiveness of sin. In spite of the contemporary fashion of saying that Luther got it wrong, I think he got it right:

> The principal point ... of the law ... is to make men not better but worse; that is to say, it sheweth unto them their sin, that by the knowledge thereof they may be humbled, terrified, bruised and broken, and by this means may be driven to seek grace, and so come to that blessed Seed [*sc.* Christ].[15]

In conclusion, how should we respond to Paul's devastating exposure of universal sin and guilt, as we read it at the end of the twentieth century? We should not try to evade it by changing the subject and talking instead of the need for self-esteem, or by blaming our behaviour on our genes, nurturing, education or society. It is an essential part of our dignity as human beings that, however much we may have been affected by negative influences, we are not their helpless victims, but rather responsible for our conduct. Our first response to Paul's indictment, then, should be to make it as certain as we possibly can that we have ourselves accepted this divine diagnosis of our human condition as true, and that we have fled from the just judgment of God on our sins to the only refuge there is, namely Jesus Christ who died for our sins. For we have no merit to plead and no excuse to make. We too stand before

---

[13] Moo, p. 216.   [14] Ziesler (1989), p. 105.
[15] Luther, *Commentary on St Paul's Epistle to the Galatians* (1531; James Clarke, 1953), p. 316.

God speechless and condemned. Only then shall we be ready to hear the great 'But now' of verse 21, as Paul begins to explain how God has intervened through Christ and his cross for our salvation.

Secondly, these chapters challenge us to share Christ with others. We cannot monopolize the good news. All around us are men and women who know enough of God's glory and holiness to make their rejection of him inexcusable. They too, like us, stand condemned. Their knowledge, their religion and their righteousness cannot save them. Only Christ can. Their mouth is closed in guilt; let our mouth be opened in testimony!

B.   The grace of God in the gospel
Romans 3:21 – 8:39

3:21 – 4:25
8. God's righteousness revealed and illustrated

All human beings, of every race and rank, of every creed and culture, Jews and Gentiles, the immoral and the moralizing, the religious and the irreligious, are without any exception sinful, guilty, inexcusable and speechless before God. That was the terrible human predicament described in Romans 1:18 – 3:20. There was no ray of light, no flicker of hope, no prospect of rescue.

'But now', Paul suddenly breaks in, God himself has intervened. 'Now' seems to have a threefold reference – logical (the developing argument), chronological (the present time) and eschatological (the new age has arrived).[1] After the long dark night the sun has risen, a new day has dawned, and the world is flooded with light. 'But now a righteousness from God, apart from law, has been made known . . .' (21a). It is a fresh revelation, focusing on Christ and his cross, although 'the Law and the Prophets testify' to it (21b) in their partial foretellings and foreshadowings. So then, over against the unrighteousness of some and the self-righteousness of others, Paul sets the righteousness of God. Over against God's wrath resting on evil-doers (1:18; 2:5; 3:5), he sets God's grace to sinners who believe. Over against judgment, he sets justification.

He begins, first, by portraying the revelation of God's righteousness in Christ's cross, and lays the foundations of the gospel of justification (3:21–26). Secondly, he defends this gospel against Jewish critics (3:27–31). Thirdly, he illustrates it in the life of Abraham, who was himself justified by faith and is in consequence the spiritual father of all who believe (4:1–25).

1. God's righteousness revealed in Christ's cross (3:21–26)

Verses 21–26 are six tightly packed verses, which Professor Cranfield rightly calls 'the centre and heart' of the whole main section of

[1] 2 Cor. 6:2.

the letter,[2] and which Dr Leon Morris suggests may be 'possibly the most important single paragraph ever written'.[3] Its key expression is 'the righteousness of God', which we considered when it first occurred, namely in 1:17. In both verses NIV renders the phrase *a righteousness from God*, thus stressing the saving initiative which he has taken to give sinners a righteous status in his sight. Both speak of his righteousness as being 'revealed' or 'made known'. Both indicate its newness by declaring that it is made known either 'in the gospel' (1:17) or *apart from law* (3:21). Yet both represent it as a fulfilment of Old Testament Scripture, which shows that it was not a divine afterthought. And both state that it is available to us through faith. The only significant difference between these two texts lies in the tense of their main verbs. According to 3:21 a righteousness from God *has been made known*, a perfect tense which must refer to the historical death of Christ and its abiding consequences, whereas in 1:17 a righteousness from God is being revealed (a present tense) in the gospel, which presumably means whenever it is preached.

In verse 22 Paul resumes his announcement of the gospel by repeating the expression *righteousness from God*, and now adds two more truths about it. The first is that it *comes through faith in Jesus Christ to all who believe*. Moreover, it is offered to all because it is needed by all. *There is no difference* between Jews and Gentiles in this respect, as Paul has been arguing in 1:18 – 3:20, or between any other human groupings, *for all have sinned* (*hēmarton*, everybody's cumulative past being summed up by an aorist tense) *and fall short* (a continuing present) *of the glory of God* (23). God's *doxa* ('glory') could mean his approval or praise, which all have forfeited,[4] but probably refers to his image or glory in which all were made[5] but which all fail to live up to. Of course there are degrees of sinning, and therefore differences, yet nobody even approaches God's standard. Bishop Handley Moule put it dramatically: 'The harlot, the liar, the murderer, are short of it [*sc.* God's glory]; but so are you. Perhaps they stand at the bottom of a mine, and you on the crest of an Alp; but you are as little able to touch the stars as they.'[6]

The second novelty in these verses is that now for the first time 'a righteousness from God' is identified with justification: *and are justified freely by his grace . . .* (24a). The righteousness of (or from) God is a combination of his righteous character, his saving initiative and his gift of a righteous standing before him. It is his just justification of the unjust, his righteous way of 'righteoussing' the unrighteous.

[2] Cranfield, vol. I, p. 199.   [3] Morris (1988), p. 173.   [4] *Cf.* Jn. 12:43.
[5] *Cf.* 1 Cor. 11:7.   [6] Moule (1894), p. 97.

Justification is a legal or forensic term, belonging to the law courts. Its opposite is condemnation. Both are the pronouncements of a judge. In a Christian context they are the alternative eschatological verdicts which God the judge may pass on judgment day. So when God justifies sinners today, he anticipates his own final judgment by bringing into the present what belongs properly to the last day.

Some scholars maintain that 'justification' and 'pardon' are synonymous. For example, Sanday and Headlam wrote that justification 'is simply Forgiveness, Free Forgiveness',[7] while more recently Professor Jeremias has insisted that 'justification is forgiveness, nothing but forgiveness'.[8] But surely this cannot be so. Pardon is negative, the remission of a penalty or debt; justification is positive, the bestowal of a righteous status, the sinner's reinstatement in the favour and fellowship of God. Sir Marcus Loane has written: 'The voice that spells forgiveness will say: "You may go; you have been let off the penalty which your sin deserves." But the verdict which means acceptance [sc. justification] will say: "You may come; you are welcome to all my love and my presence." '[9] C. H. Hodge clarifies the difference further by developing the antithesis between condemnation and justification. 'To condemn is not merely to punish, but to declare the accused guilty or worthy of punishment; and justification is not merely to remit that punishment, but to declare that punishment cannot be justly inflicted ... Pardon and Justification therefore are essentially distinct. The one is the remission of punishment, the other is a declaration that no ground for the infliction of punishment exists.'[10]

If justification is not pardon, neither is it sanctification. To justify is to declare or pronounce righteous, not to make righteous. This was the nub of the sixteenth-century debate over justification. The Roman Catholic view, as expressed at the Council of Trent (1545–64), was that justification takes place at baptism, and that the baptized person is not only cleansed from sins but simultaneously infused with a new, supernatural righteousness.[11] One can understand the motive which led to this insistence. It was the fear that a mere declaration of righteousness would leave the person concerned unrenewed and unrighteous, and might even encourage persistence in sinning (antinomianism). This was, of course, the precise criticism which was levelled at Paul (6:1, 15). It led him to expostulate in the

---

[7] Sanday and Headlam, p. 36.   [8] Jeremias, p. 66.

[9] Marcus Loane, *This Surpassing Excellence: Textual Studies in the Epistles to the Churches of Galatia and Philippi* (Angus and Robertson, 1969), p. 94.

[10] Hodge, p. 82.

[11] See the Council of Trent, Session VI, and its decrees on original sin and justification.

most vigorous manner that baptized Christians have both died to sin (so that they cannot possibly live in it any longer) and risen to a new life in Christ. Put a little differently, justification (a new status) and regeneration (a new heart), although not identical, are simultaneous. Every justified believer has also been regenerated by the Holy Spirit and so put on the road to progressive holiness. To quote Calvin, 'no one can put on the righteousness of Christ without regeneration'.[12] Again, 'the apostle maintains that those who imagine that Christ bestows free justification upon us without imparting newness of life shamefully rend Christ asunder'.[13]

An important fresh turn in this Roman Catholic–Protestant debate was taken by Professor Hans Küng in 1957, when his dialogue with Karl Barth entitled *Justification* was published. He agreed both that justification is a divine declaration and that we are justified by faith alone. But he also insisted that God's words are always efficacious, so that whatever he pronounces comes immediately into being. Therefore, when God says to somebody, 'You are just,' 'the sinner *is* just, really and truly, outwardly and inwardly, wholly and completely . . . In brief, God's *declaration* of justice is . . . at the same time and in the same act a *making just*'.[14] Thus justification is 'the single act which simultaneously declares just and makes just'.[15] There is a dangerous ambiguity here, however. What does Hans Küng mean by 'just'? If he means *legally* just, put right with God, then indeed we become immediately what God declares us to be. But if he means *morally* just, renewed, holy, then God's declaration does not immediately secure this, but only initiates it. For this is not justification but sanctification, which is a continuous lifelong process.[16] This is the point which C. K. Barrett is making when he claims that to justify does signify to make righteous, but that ' "righteous" does not mean "virtuous", but "right", "clear", "acquitted" in God's court'.[17]

Reverting now to the text of Romans, and in particular to verses 24–26, Paul teaches three basic truths about justification – first its source, where it originates; secondly its ground, on what it rests; and thirdly its means, how it is received.

a.   The source of our justification: God and his grace

We *are justified freely by his grace* (24). Fundamental to the gospel of salvation is the truth that the saving initiative from beginning to end belongs to God the Father. No formulation of the gospel is biblical which removes the initiative from God and attributes it

---

[12] Calvin, p. 8.   [13] *Ibid.*, p. 121.   [14] Küng, p. 204.   [15] *Ibid.*, p. 210.
[16] See my section on 'justification' in *The Cross of Christ* (Inter-Varsity Press, 1986), pp. 182ff.   [17] Barrett, pp. 75f.

either to us or even to Christ. It is certain that we did not take the initiative, for we were sinful, guilty and condemned, helpless and hopeless. Nor was the initiative taken by Jesus Christ in the sense that he did something which the Father was reluctant or unwilling to do. To be sure, Christ came voluntarily and gave himself freely. Yet he did it in submissive response to the Father's initiative. 'Here I am . . . I have come to do your will, O God.'[18] So the first move was God the Father's, and our justification is *freely* (*dōrean*, 'as a gift', RSV, or 'gift-wise, gratuitously')[19] *by his grace*, his absolutely free and utterly undeserved favour. Grace is God loving, God stooping, God coming to the rescue, God giving himself generously in and through Jesus Christ.

b. The ground of our justification: Christ and his cross

If God justifies sinners freely by his grace, on what ground does he do so? How is it possible for the righteous God to declare the unrighteous to be righteous without either compromising his righteousness or condoning their unrighteousness? That is our question. God's answer is the cross.

No expression in Romans is more startling than the statement that 'God . . . justifies the wicked' (4:5). Although it does not occur until the next chapter, it will help us to follow Paul's reasoning if we take it now. How can God justify the wicked? In the Old Testament he repeatedly told the Israelite judges that they must justify the righteous and condemn the wicked.[20] But of course! An innocent person must be declared innocent, and a guilty person guilty. What more elementary principle of justice could be enunciated? God then added: 'Acquitting the guilty and condemning the innocent – the LORD detests them both.'[21] He also pronounced a solemn 'woe' against those who 'acquit the guilty for a bribe, but deny justice to the innocent'.[22] For, he declared of himself, 'I will not acquit the guilty',[23] or 'I will not justify the wicked' (AV). But of course! we say again. God would not dream of doing such a thing.

Then how on earth can Paul affirm that God does what he forbids others to do; that he does what he says he will himself never do; that he does it habitually, and that he even designates himself 'the God who justifies the wicked' or (we might say) 'who "righteousses" the unrighteous'? It is preposterous! How can the righteous God act unrighteously, and so overthrow the moral order, turning it upside down? It is unbelievable! Or rather it would be, if it were not for the cross of Christ. Without the cross the justification of the

---

[18] Heb. 10:7.   [19] Moule (1894), p. 92.   [20] Dt. 25:1.   [21] Pr. 17:15.
[22] Is. 5:23.   [23] Ex. 23:7.

unjust would be unjustified, immoral, and therefore impossible. The only reason God 'justifies the wicked' (4:5) is that 'Christ died for the wicked' (5:6, REB). Because he shed his blood (25) in a sacrificial death for us sinners, God is able justly to justify the unjust.

What God did through the cross, that is, through the death of his Son in our place, Paul explains by three notable expressions. First, God justifies us *through the redemption that came by Christ Jesus* (24b). Secondly, *God presented him as a sacrifice of atonement, through faith in his blood* (25a). Thirdly, *he did this to demonstrate his justice . . .* (25b), *so as to be just and the one who justifies those who have faith in Jesus* (26). The key words are *redemption* (*apolytrōsis*), *atonement* or better 'propitiation' (*hilastērion*), and *demonstration* (*endeixis*). All three refer not to what is happening now when the gospel is preached, but to what happened once for all in and through Christ on the cross, *his blood* being a clear reference to his sacrificial death. Associated with the cross, therefore, there is a redemption of sinners, a propitiation of God's wrath and a demonstration of his justice.

(i) Redemption

The first word is *apolytrōsis*, that is, *redemption*. It is a commercial term borrowed from the marketplace, as 'justification' is a legal term borrowed from the lawcourt. In the Old Testament it was used of slaves, who were purchased in order to be set free; they were said to be 'redeemed'.[24] It was also used metaphorically of the people of Israel who were 'redeemed' from captivity first in Egypt,[25] then in Babylon,[26] and restored to their own land. Just so, we were slaves or captives, in bondage to our sin and guilt, and utterly unable to liberate ourselves. But Jesus Christ 'redeemed' us, bought us out of captivity, shedding his blood as the ransom price. He himself had spoken of his coming 'to give his life as a ransom for many'.[27] In consequence of this purchase or 'ransom-rescue',[28] we now belong to him.

(ii) Propitiation

The second word is *hilastērion*, which AV renders 'propitiation'. Many Christian people are embarrassed and even shocked by this word, however, because to 'propitiate' somebody means to placate his or her anger, and it seems to them an unworthy concept of God (more heathen than Christian) to suppose that he gets angry and needs to be appeased. Two other possible ways of understanding *hilastērion*

[24] *E.g.* Lv. 25:47ff.   [25] Ex. 15:13.   [26] Is. 43:1.   [27] Mk. 10:45.
[28] Moule (1894), p. 92.

are therefore proposed. The first is to translate it 'mercy-seat' referring to the golden lid of the ark within the temple's inner sanctuary. This is what the word nearly always means in LXX and also what it means in its only other occurrence in the New Testament.[29] Since sacrificial blood was sprinkled on the mercy-seat on the Day of Atonement, it is suggested that Jesus is himself now the mercy-seat where God and sinners are reconciled.[30] Those who hold this view tend to render the verb *protithēmi* (*presented*) as to 'set forth' (AV) or 'display publicly' (BAGD), in order to indicate that, although the mercy-seat was hidden from human eyes by the veil, 'God has publicly set forth the Lord Jesus Christ, in the sight of the intelligent universe . . .'[31] as the way of salvation. Luther and Calvin both believed that 'mercy-seat' was the right translation, and others have followed them.

But the contrary arguments seem conclusive. First, if Paul meant 'mercy-seat' by *hilastērion*, he would inevitably have added the definite article. Secondly, the concept is incongruous in Romans which, unlike Hebrews, does not move 'in the sphere of Levitical symbolism'.[32] Thirdly, the metaphor would be confusing and even contradictory, since it would represent Jesus as being simultaneously the victim whose blood was shed and sprinkled and the place where the sprinkling took place. Fourthly, Paul's sense of personal indebtedness to Christ crucified was so profound that he would hardly have likened him to 'an inanimate piece of temple furniture'.[33]

A second possible translation of *hilastērion* is 'an expiation by his blood' (RSV). The argument for this is that, whereas in secular Greek the verb *hilaskomai* means to 'placate' (whether a god or a human being), its object in LXX is not God but sin. It is therefore said to mean not to 'propitiate' God but to 'expiate' sin, that is, to annul guilt or remove defilement. C. H. Dodd, with whom this viewpoint is particularly associated, and who as Director of the NEB evidently influenced its translators in this direction, wrote that expiatory acts 'were felt to have the value, so to speak, of a disinfectant'.[34] Thus NEB translates: 'God designed him to be the means of expiating sin by his sacrificial death.'

The main reason these options are not satisfactory, and a reference to propitiation seems necessary, is the context. In these verses Paul is describing God's solution to the human predicament, which is not only sin but God's wrath upon sin (1:18; 2:5; 3:5). And where there is divine wrath, there is the need to avert it. We should not be shy of using the word 'propitiation' in relation to the cross, any

---

[29] Heb. 9:5.   [30] *Cf.* Ex. 25:22.   [31] Hodge, p. 93.   [32] Godet, p. 151.
[33] Cranfield, vol. I, p. 215. Nygren uses a similar expression on p. 156.
[34] Dodd, p. 54.

more than we should drop the word 'wrath' in relation to God. Instead, we should struggle to reclaim and reinstate this language by showing that the Christian doctrine of propitiation is totally different from pagan or animistic superstitions. The need, the author and the nature of the Christian propitiation are all different.

First, the need. Why is a propitiation necessary? The pagan answer is because the gods are bad-tempered, subject to moods and fits, and capricious. The Christian answer is because God's holy wrath rests on evil. There is nothing unprincipled, unpredictable or uncontrolled about God's anger; it is aroused by evil alone.

Secondly, the author. Who undertakes to do the propitiating? The pagan answer is that we do. We have offended the gods; so we must appease them. The Christian answer, by contrast, is that we cannot placate the righteous anger of God. We have no means whatever by which to do so. But God in his undeserved love has done for us what we could never do by ourselves. *God presented him* (sc. Christ) as a sacrifice of atonement. John wrote similarly: 'God ... loved us and sent his Son as an atoning sacrifice (*hilasmos*) for our sins.'[35] The love, the idea, the purpose, the initiative, the action and the gift were all God's.

Thirdly, the nature. How has the propitiation been accomplished? What is the propitiatory sacrifice? The pagan answer is that we have to bribe the gods with sweets, vegetable offerings, animals, and even human sacrifices. The Old Testament sacrificial system was entirely different, since it was recognized that God himself has 'given' the sacrifices to his people to make atonement.[36] And this is clear beyond doubt in the Christian propitiation, for God gave his own Son to die in our place, and in giving his Son he gave himself (5:8, 8:32).

In sum, it would be hard to exaggerate the differences between the pagan and the Christian views of propitiation. In the pagan perspective, human beings try to placate their bad-tempered deities with their own paltry offerings. According to the Christian revelation, God's own great love propitiated his own holy wrath through the gift of his own dear Son, who took our place, bore our sin and died our death. Thus God himself gave himself to save us from himself.

This is the righteous basis on which the righteous God can 'righteous' the unrighteous without compromising his righteousness. Charles Cranfield has expressed it with care and eloquence:

> God, because in his mercy he willed to forgive sinful men, and being truly merciful, willed to forgive them righteously, that is, without in any way condoning their sin, purposed to direct against

[35] 1 Jn. 4:10.   [36] E.g. Lv. 17:11.

his own very Self in the person of his Son the full weight of that righteous wrath which they deserved.[37]

Professor Cranfield returns to the theme in his final essay on 'The Death and Resurrection of Jesus Christ'. He argues that God purposed Jesus Christ to be a propitiatory sacrifice in order 'that he might justify sinners righteously, that is, in a way that is altogether worthy of himself as the truly loving and merciful eternal God'. For God to have forgiven their sin lightly would have been 'to have compromised with the lie that moral evil does not matter and so to have violated his own truth and mocked men with an empty, lying reassurance, which, at their most human, they must have recognized as the squalid falsehood which it would have been.'[38]

(iii)   Demonstration

So far we have looked at two of the words Paul uses to describe the cross, namely *apolytrōsis* ('redemption') and *hilastērion* ('propitiatory sacrifice'). We come now to the third, *endeixis* ('demonstration'). For the cross was a demonstration or public revelation as well as an achievement. It not only accomplished the propitiation of God and the redemption of sinners; it also vindicated the justice of God: *He did this to demonstrate his justice . . .* (25b); *. . . he did it to demonstrate his justice . . .* (26a). In order to understand the form which this demonstration of God's justice took, we need to note the deliberate contrast which Paul makes between *the sins committed beforehand* or previously, which *in his forbearance he had left . . . unpunished* (25b), and *the present time* in which God has acted *to demonstrate his justice* (26a). It is a contrast between the past and the present, between the divine forbearance which postponed judgment and the divine justice which exacted it, between the leaving unpunished or 'passing over' (rsv) of former sins (which made God appear unjust) and their punishment on the cross (by which God demonstrated his justice).

That is, God left unpunished the sins of former generations, letting the nations go their own way and overlooking their ignorance,[39] not because of any injustice on his part, or with any thought of condoning evil, but in his forbearance (*cf.* 2:4), and only because it was his fixed intention in the fulness of time to punish these sins in the death of his Son. This was the only way in which he could both himself *be just*, indeed *demonstrate his justice*, and simultaneously be *the one who justifies those who have faith in Jesus* (26b). Both justice (the divine attribute) and justification (the divine activity) would be impossible without the cross.

[37] Cranfield, vol. I, p. 217; *cf.* vol. II, p. 828.   [38] Cranfield, vol. II, p. 827.
[39] Acts 14:16; 17:30.

Here, then, are the three technical terms which Paul uses (*apo-lytrōsis, hilastērion* and *endeixis*) to explain what God has done in and through Christ's cross. He has redeemed his people. He has propitiated his wrath. He has demonstrated his justice. Indeed, these three achievements belong together. Through the sin-bearing, substitutionary death of his Son, God has propitiated his own wrath in such a way as to redeem and justify us, and at the same time demonstrate his justice. We can only marvel at the wisdom, holiness, love and mercy of God, and fall down before him in humble worship. The cross should be enough to break the hardest heart, and melt the iciest.

We have considered that the source of our justification is God's grace and its ground Christ's cross. Now we turn to the means by which we are justified.

c. *The means of our justification: faith*

Three times in this paragraph Paul underlines the necessity of faith: *through faith in Jesus Christ to all who believe* (22); *through faith in his blood* (25) or, more probably, 'by his blood, to be received by faith' (RSV); and God *justifies those who have faith in Jesus* (26). Indeed, justification is 'by faith alone', *sola fide*, one of the great watchwords of the Reformation. True, the word 'alone' does not occur in Paul's text of verse 28, where Luther added it. It is not altogether surprising, therefore, that the Roman Catholic Church accused Luther of perverting the text of Holy Scripture. But Luther was following Origen and other early Church Fathers, who had similarly introduced the word 'alone'. A true instinct led them to do so. Far from falsifying or distorting Paul's meaning, they were clarifying and emphasizing it. It was similar with John Wesley who wrote that he felt he 'did trust in Christ, in Christ alone, for salvation'. Justification is by grace alone, in Christ alone, through faith alone.

Further, it is vital to affirm that there is nothing meritorious about faith, and that, when we say that salvation is 'by faith, not by works', we are not substituting one kind of merit ('faith') for another ('works'). Nor is salvation a sort of cooperative enterprise between God and us, in which he contributes the cross and we contribute faith. No, grace is non-contributory, and faith is the opposite of self-regarding. The value of faith is not to be found in itself, but entirely and exclusively in its object, namely Jesus Christ and him crucified. To say 'justification by faith alone' is another way of saying 'justification by Christ alone'. Faith is the eye that looks to him, the hand that receives his free gift, the mouth that drinks the living water. 'Faith ... apprehendeth nothing else but that precious jewel Christ Jesus.'[40] As Richard Hooker, the late-sixteenth-century Anglican divine, wrote: 'God justifies the believer – not because of the worthiness of his belief, but because of his (*sc.* Christ's) worthiness who is believed.'[41]

Justification (its source God and his grace, its ground Christ and his cross, and its means faith alone, altogether apart from works) is the heart of the gospel and unique to Christianity. No other system, ideology or religion proclaims a free forgiveness and a new life to those who have done nothing to deserve it but a lot to deserve judgment instead. On the contrary, all other systems teach some form of self-salvation through good works of religion, righteousness or philanthropy. Christianity, by contrast, is not in its essence a religion at all; it is a gospel, the gospel, good news that God's grace has turned away his wrath, that God's Son has died our death and borne our judgment, that God has mercy on the undeserving, and that there is nothing left for us to do, or even contribute. Faith's only function is to receive what grace offers.

The antithesis between grace and law, mercy and merit, faith and works, God's salvation and self-salvation, is absolute. No compromising mishmash is possible. We are obliged to choose. Emil Brunner illustrated it vividly in terms of the difference between 'ascent' and 'descent'. The really 'decisive question', he wrote, is 'the direction of the movement'. Non-Christian systems think of 'the self-movement of man' towards God. Luther called speculation 'climbing up to the majesty on high'. Similarly, mysticism imagines that the human spirit can 'soar aloft towards God'. So does moralism. So does philosophy. Very similar is 'the self-confident optimism of all non-Christian religion'. None of these has seen or felt the gulf which yawns between the holy God and sinful, guilty human beings. Only when we have glimpsed this do we grasp the necessity of what the gospel proclaims, namely 'the self-movement of God', his free initiative of grace, his 'descent', his amazing 'act of condescension'. To stand on the rim of the abyss, to despair utterly of ever crossing over, this is the indispensable 'antechamber of faith'.[42]

2. God's righteousness defended against criticism (3:27–31)

Paul now re-opens his 'diatribe', which he continued throughout chapter 2 and which was clearly articulated in the four questions of

[40] Luther, *Commentary on St Paul's Epistle to the Galatians* (1531; James Clarke, 1953), p. 100.

[41] From Hooker's 'Definition of Justification', being chapter xxxiii of his *Ecclesiastical Polity* (1593).

[42] Emil Brunner, *The Mediator* (1927; Westminster, 1947), pp. 291ff.

3:1–8. These related to his indictment that all human beings are under the judgment of God and that Jews are not shielded from it. Now he anticipates a fresh set of Jewish questions, related this time not to judgment but to justification, and in particular to justification by faith only.

Question 1: Where, then, is boasting? (27–28).

In the post-Sanders era, in which many scholars accept his thesis that first-century Palestinian Judaism was not a religion of works-righteousness, it has seemed to them necessary to reinterpret Paul's rejection of 'boasting'. If Judaism was not a system of merit, it cannot be this kind of boasting that Paul has in mind. It must rather be Judaism's self-confident assumption of national, cultural and religious superiority. And indeed the Jews were immensely proud of their privileged status as the chosen people of God. They imagined that they were heaven's protected favourites, which is why Paul characterized them as 'relying' on their possession of the law and 'bragging' about their relationship to God (2:17, 23 where the verb in both cases is *kauchaomai*, to boast).

But these external privileges were not the only object of Jewish boasting. Jewish people were also proud of their personal righteousness. Thus Paul himself, reflecting on his own pre-conversion career in Judaism, bracketed his Jewish inheritance ('a Hebrew of Hebrews') with his individual attainment (his zeal in persecuting the church and being faultless in 'legalistic righteousness') as together constituting the 'flesh' in which he put his confidence until as a Christian he began to 'boast in Christ Jesus' (*kauchaomai* again).[43]

Boastfulness was not limited to the Jews, however. The Gentile world also was 'insolent, arrogant and boastful' (1:30). In fact, all human beings are inveterate boasters. Boasting is the language of our fallen self-centredness. But in those who have been justified by faith, *boasting* is altogether *excluded*. This is not on the principle *of observing the law*, which might give grounds for boasting, *but on that of faith* (27), which attributes salvation entirely to Christ and so eliminates all boasting. For our Christian conviction is that a sinner *is justified by faith*, indeed by faith alone, *apart from observing the law* (28). Whether these 'works of the law', which Paul has in mind, are ceremonial (observing rules for diet and the sabbath) or moral (obeying God's commandments), they cannot gain the favour or forgiveness of God. For salvation is 'not by works, so that no-one can boast'.[44] It is only by faith in Christ, which is why we should boast in him, not in ourselves. There is, indeed, something fundamentally anomalous about Christians who boast in themselves, as there is something essentially authentic, appropriate and attractive

---

[43] Phil. 3:3ff.   [44] Eph. 2:9.

119

about their boasting in Christ. All boasting is excluded except boasting in Christ. Praising, not boasting, is the characteristic activity of justified believers, and will be throughout eternity.[45] So 'let him who boasts boast in the Lord', and 'May I never boast except in the cross of our Lord Jesus Christ.'[46]

Question 2: Is God the God of Jews only? Is he not the God of Gentiles too? (29–30).

Jewish people were extremely conscious of their special covenant relationship with God, in which Gentiles did not share. It was to the Jews that God had entrusted his special revelation (3:2). Theirs too, as Paul will soon write, are 'the adoption as sons . . . the divine glory, the covenants, the receiving of the law, the temple worship and the promises', not to mention 'the patriarchs' and 'the human ancestry of Christ' (9:4f.). What the Jews forgot, however, was that their privileges were not intended for the exclusion of the Gentiles, but for their ultimate inclusion when through Abraham's posterity 'all peoples on earth' would be blessed.[47]

This covenant with Abraham has been fulfilled in Christ. He is Abraham's 'seed', and through him the blessing of salvation now extends to everyone who believes, without exception or distinction. If the gospel of justification by faith alone excludes all boasting, it excludes all élitism and discrimination also. God is not *the God of Jews only*; he is *the God of Gentiles too* (29), *since there is only one God* (it is the truth of monotheism which unites us), who has only one way of salvation. He *will justify the circumcised* (Jews) *by faith and the uncircumcised* (Gentiles) *through that same faith* (30).

This identical truth applies to all other distinctions, whether of race, nationality, class, sex or age. Not that all such distinctions are actually obliterated, for men remain men and women women, Jews are still circumcised and Gentiles uncircumcised, our skin pigmentation does not change, and we still have the same passport. But these continuing distinctions are rendered of no significant account. They neither affect our relationship with God, nor hinder our fellowship with one another. At the foot of Christ's cross and through faith in him, we are all on exactly the same level, indeed sisters and brothers in Christ. 'The message', writes Dr Tom Wright, '. . . is simple: all who believe in Jesus belong to the same family and should be eating at the same table. That is what Paul's doctrine of justification is all about.'[48]

Question 3: Do we, then, nullify the law by this faith? (31).

The law was the Jews' most treasured possession. By 'the law'

---

[45] *E.g.* Rev. 7:10.   [46] 1 Cor. 1:31; Gal. 6:14.   [47] Gn. 12:2f.
[48] N. T. Wright, *New Tasks for a Renewed Church* (Hodder and Stoughton, 1992), p. 168.

(Torah) they usually meant the Mosaic legislation, that is, the Pentateuch. Sometimes, however, because the word *torah* was derived from the verb 'to instruct', they extended its meaning to embrace the whole of Old Testament Scripture, conceived as divine instruction. How, then, would they react to Paul's unremitting insistence that justification was by faith only, and that 'the works of the law' could not possibly provide a satisfactory basis for God's acceptance? Paul seemed to them to set 'law' and 'faith' in opposition to each other, to exalt faith at the expense of law, and even to nullify the law altogether.

Paul denies this conclusion. Indeed, he affirms the contrary. *Do we, then, nullify the law by this faith?* he asks, and replies: *Not at all! Rather, we uphold the law* (31), or 'establish' it (AV). What does he mean? Our answer will depend on what connotation he is giving to 'the law' in this context. If he is referring to the Old Testament in general, then his gospel of justification by faith upholds rather than undermines it, by showing that the Old Testament itself taught the truth of justifying faith (*cf.* 3:21). If this interpretation is correct, verse 31 becomes a transition to Romans 4 in which the apostle argues that both Abraham and David were, in fact, justified by faith.

If, on the other hand, Paul is using 'the law' in its more restricted sense of the Mosaic law, then his assertion that faith upholds rather than nullifies the law may be understood in two ways. First, faith upholds the law by assigning to it its proper place in God's purpose. In his scheme of salvation the function of the law is to expose and condemn sin, and so to keep sinners locked up in their guilt until Christ comes to liberate them through faith.[49] In this way the gospel and the law dovetail with each other, since the gospel justifies those whom the law condemns.

The alternative explanation of Paul's statement sees it as his response to a different set of critics. These held that, by declaring justification to be by faith, not obedience, Paul was actively encouraging disobedience. This charge of antinomianism Paul will decisively refute in Romans 6 – 8. But he anticipates these chapters here by the simple affirmation that faith upholds the law. What he means, and will later elaborate, is that justified believers who live according to the Spirit fulfil the righteous requirements of the law (8:4; *cf.* 13:8, 10). It seems to me that this is the most likely explanation.

Here, then, are three implications – positive and negative – of the gospel of justification by faith alone. First, it humbles sinners and excludes boasting. Secondly, it unites believers and excludes discrimination. Thirdly, it upholds the law and excludes antinomianism. No boasting. No discrimination. No antinomianism.

---

[49] See Gal. 3:21ff.

This is the apostle's effective defence of the gospel against current criticisms.

3. God's righteousness illustrated in Abraham (4:1–25)

Paul has both expounded his gospel of God's righteousness, that is, of justification by faith (3:21–26), and defended it against its critics (3:27–31). In doing so, he has also insisted that it is attested by Old Testament Scripture (1:2; 3:21, 31). So the next step in his argument is to supply an Old Testament precedent and example. He chooses Abraham, Israel's most illustrious patriarch, supplemented by David, Israel's most illustrious king. Similarly, when Matthew introduced his gospel with Jesus' genealogy, he named him 'the son of David, the son of Abraham'.[50]

Some modern commentators make no attempt to disguise their impatience. They find both the substance and the form of Paul's reasoning equally irrelevant. His rebuttal of Jewish objections was doubtless necessary at the time, they concede, reflecting the debates going on in the rabbinical schools. But these things 'have little interest and no weight for us', wrote C. H. Dodd, and Paul's 'scholastic and rabbinic' argumentation 'makes the whole exposition seem remote and unenlightening'.[51] But on the contrary, Romans 4 occupies a very important place in the letter for at least two reasons.

First, Paul further clarifies the meaning of justification by faith. He uses what Scripture says about Abraham and David to elaborate the significance of both words, 'justification' in terms of the reckoning of righteousness to the unrighteous and 'faith' in terms of trusting the God of creation and resurrection.

Secondly, Paul wants Jewish Christians to grasp that his gospel of justification by faith is no novelty, having been proclaimed beforehand in the Old Testament,[52] and he wants Gentile Christians to appreciate the rich spiritual heritage they have entered by faith in Jesus, in continuity with the Old Testament people of God. Abraham and David show that justification by faith is God's one and only way of salvation, first in the Old Testament as well as in the New, and, secondly for Jews as well as for Gentiles. It is therefore a mistake to suppose either that in the Old Testament people were saved by works and in the New Testament by faith, or that today the Christian mission should be limited to Gentiles on the ground that Jews have their own distinctive way of salvation. I shall have more to say about the evangelization of Jewish people in chapter 14.

---

[50] Mt. 1:1.   [51] Dodd, pp. 64, 71.   [52] Gal. 3:8.

There seem to have been two reasons for Paul's choosing Abraham as his main example. The first is that he was the founding father of Israel, 'the rock from which [they] were cut',[53] the favoured recipient of God's covenant and promises.[54] The second reason is doubtless that Abraham was held in the highest esteem by the Rabbis as the epitome of righteousness and even the special 'friend' of God.[55] They took it for granted that he had been justified by works of righteousness. For instance, 'Abraham was perfect in all his dealings with the Lord and gained favour by his righteousness throughout his life.'[56] They quoted the Scriptures in which God promised to bless Abraham *because* he had obeyed him,[57] without observing that these verses referred to Abraham's life of obedience *after* his justification. They even quoted Genesis 15:6 (Paul's text in this chapter, verse 3), in such a way as to represent Abraham's faith as meaning his fidelity or faithfulness, which was therefore meritorious. For example, 'was not Abraham found faithful in temptation, and it was reckoned unto him for righteousness?'[58]

Moreover, an echo of the Jewish belief that Abraham was justified by works is heard in the letter of James.[59] True, what James is asserting is not that we can be justified by works, any more than Abraham was, but rather that the authenticity of justifying faith is seen in the good works to which it gives rise. 'I will show you my faith by my works', says the genuine believer,[60] because without resulting good works faith is dead.[61] Nevertheless, behind James's argument lies the Jewish tradition (which he rejects) that Abraham was justified by works.

Romans 4 presupposes familiarity with the biblical story of Abraham, and in particular with four of its chief episodes. First, God called Abraham to leave his home and people in Ur, and promised to show him another land, to give him a large posterity, and through him to bless all peoples on earth.[62] Secondly, God made his promises more specific, identifying the land as Canaan[63] and declaring that his posterity, though he was still childless, would be as numerous as the dust of the earth and the stars in the sky.[64] It was by believing this latter promise that Abraham was justified.[65] Thirdly, when Abraham was ninety-nine and Sarah ninety,[66] God confirmed his promise of a son, changed his name from Abram to Abraham to signify that he would be 'the father of many nations', and gave him circumcision as the sign of his covenant.[67] Fourthly,

---

[53] Is. 51:1f.   [54] *E.g.* Gn. 12:1ff.; 15:1ff.; 17:1ff.
[55] 2 Ch. 20:7; Is. 41:8; Jas. 2:23.   [56] Jubilees 23:10.   [57] Gn. 22:15ff.; 26:2ff.
[58] 1 Macc. 2:52. For other rabbinic quotations see Cranfield, vol. I, p. 229.
[59] Jas. 2:21ff.   [60] Jas. 2:18.   [61] Jas. 2:17, 21.   [62] Gn. 11:27ff.; 12:1ff.
[63] Gn. 13:14f.   [64] Gn. 14:16; 15:5.   [65] Gn. 15:6; Rom. 4:3.
[66] Gn. 17:1, 17.   [67] Gn. 17:1ff.

although Paul only hints at this indirectly, God tested Abraham by asking him to sacrifice Isaac, the subject of the promise, and, when he showed his willingness to obey, re-confirmed his covenant.[68]

Moreover, these four episodes correspond to the four occasions on which Hebrews 11 says that Abraham took action 'by faith' (verses 8, 9, 11 and 17–18). He obeyed God because he trusted God.

We now consider four assertions which Paul makes about Abraham's justification, the first three of which develop the three questions and answers of his diatribe at the end of chapter 3. Verses 1–8 affirm that boasting is excluded (cf. 3:27f.), verses 9–12 that circumcision makes no difference (cf. 3:29f.), and verses 13–17 that the law has its proper, God-assigned place (cf. 3:31).

a.   Abraham was not justified by works (1–8)

Paul begins with a question: 'What then shall we say about Abraham, our forefather according to the flesh?' 1, RSV). The NIV omits the two words kata sarka, 'according to the flesh'. And it is uncertain in the Greek text whether they are intended to qualify the verb 'discovered' or the noun 'our forefather'. If the former is correct, Paul's question is: 'What shall we say that Abraham has gained by his natural powers unaided by the grace of God?'[69] But the best manuscripts support a different order of words, by which kata sarka qualifies Abraham himself as 'our ancestor by natural descent' (REB). This seems to be right and may well be intended to prepare the way for Paul's later statements that Abraham is 'the father of us all' (16) and 'our father' (17) if we share his faith.

Responding to his own question about Abraham (1), Paul immediately sets in antithesis the wrong answer (2), namely that he was *justified by works*, and the correct answer (3), namely that he *believed God, and it was credited to him as righteousness*. The first reason the very concept of Abraham having been justified by works is so fiercely repudiated by Paul is that this would have given him *something to boast about*, or might have appeared to. But Paul will allow his imaginary interlocutor to go no further. He interrupts indignantly: *but not before God* (2). Some may boast before their fellows, and others may entertain boastful thoughts in secret. But Paul rejects any possibility of human beings boasting before God, either creatures before their Creator or sinners before their Saviour. Whether the object of boasting is national privilege or personal piety makes no difference. Both forms of boasting are expressions of self-righteousness, and to suppose that the unrighteous can

[68] Gn. 22:1ff.
[69] This is the paraphrase given by Sanday and Headlam (p. 98), although they reject this interpretation.

establish their own righteousness before God is to think the unthinkable.

Then there is a second reason for Paul's denial that Abraham was justified by works, and that is the text of Scripture. *What does the Scripture say?* he asks (3). Consider the implications of this apparently innocent question. First, the singular form ('the Scripture'), like our 'the Bible', indicates that Paul recognizes the existence of this entity, not just a library of books but a unified body of inspired writings. Secondly, his quasi-personification of Scripture as being able to speak indicates that he draws no distinction between what Scripture says and what God says through it. Indeed, throughout the New Testament we seldom know whether to translate *legei*, when it has no subject, as 'he says' or 'it says'. Thirdly, instead of the present tense, 'What does the Scripture say?' Paul could have used the perfect tense and asked, 'What was written?' or 'What stands written?' (*gegraptai*). For 'the Scripture' means 'what is written', and in asking what it 'says', the apostle indicates that through the written text the living voice of God may be heard. Fourthly, to ask the question is to turn to Scripture for authoritative guidance. It implies that, as with Jesus and his critics, so with Paul and his, in every controversy Scripture was acknowledged as the final court of appeal.

In answer to his query as to what Scripture says, Paul quotes Genesis 15:6: *'Abraham believed God, and it was credited to him as righteousness'* (3). He then proceeds in verses 4–5 to draw out the significance of the verb 'credited' (*logizomai*), which he here uses for the first time, and uses five times in six verses (3–8). It means to 'credit' or 'reckon', and when used in a financial or commercial context, it signifies to put something to somebody's account, as when Paul wrote to Philemon about Onesimus: 'If he has done you any wrong or owes you anything, charge it to me.'[70] There are, however, two different ways in which money can be credited to our account, namely as wages (which are earned) or as a gift (which is free and unearned), and the two are necessarily incompatible. *Now when a man works, his wages are not credited to him as a gift, but as an obligation* (4), literally, 'not according to grace [*charis*] but according to debt [*opheilēma*]'. This is emphatically not so with our justification, however. In this case, talk of 'work', 'wages', 'debt' or 'obligation' is entirely inappropriate. Instead, *to the man who does not work but trusts God who justifies the wicked, his faith is credited as righteousness* (5).

The contrast between these two kinds of 'crediting' should now be clear. In the context of business, those who work have their

---

[70] Phm. 18.

wages credited to them as a right, a debt, an obligation, for they have earned them. In the context of justification, however, to those who do not work, and therefore have no right to payment, but who instead put their trust in God who justifies the ungodly (a marvellous phrase we have already considered on pages 112f.), their *faith is credited* to them *as righteousness*, that is, they are given righteousness as a free and unearned gift of grace by faith. Paul cannot be teaching that faith and righteousness are equivalents, and that when righteousness is lacking faith is acceptable as a substitute. For that would make faith a meritorious work and play into the hands of the Rabbis, who thought of Abraham's 'faith' as his 'faithfulness'. If anything is clear in the antithesis between verse 4 and verse 5, it is that the crediting of faith as righteousness is a free gift, not an earned wage, and that it happens not to those who work but to those who trust, and indeed who trust the God who, far from justifying people because they are godly, actually justifies them when they are ungodly. This emphasis on faith (*Abraham believed God*) plainly shows, then, that God's 'crediting faith as righteousness' is 'not a rewarding of merit but a free and unmerited decision of divine grace'.[71] Faith is not an alternative to righteousness, but the means by which we are declared righteous.

Paul now moves on from Abraham to David, and so from Genesis 15:6 to Psalm 32:1–2. He finds a fundamental agreement between the two texts. *David says the same thing* when he describes *the blessedness of the man to whom God credits righteousness apart from works* (6). We notice at once how the language of 'crediting' has changed. God is still the person who in sheer grace does the crediting, but now what he puts to our account is not 'faith as righteousness' but 'righteousness' itself. This is what David's Old Testament beatitude teaches. Three times, in Hebrew parallelism, he refers to evil deeds, once as *transgressions* (*anomiai*, 'lawlessnesses') and twice as *sins* (*harmartiai*, 'failures'), for sin is both the stepping over a known boundary and the falling short of a known standard. And three times he tells us what God has done with them. Our *transgressions are forgiven*, our *sins are covered*, and our *sin the Lord will never count against* us (7–8). Instead of putting our sins into account against us, God pardons and covers them.

We are now in a position to bring all this rich vocabulary together. Paul's mind is not limited to one expression or to a single imagery. He has made it clear that the righteousness of (or from) God, which is revealed in the gospel (1:17; 3:21f.), is his just justification of the unjust. So in the second half of chapter 3 he keeps on using the verb 'to justify' (*e.g.* 3:24, 26, 28, 30). He also

[71] Cranfield, vol. I, p. 231.

continues to use it in chapter 4 (4:2, 5, 25), as he will in chapter 5 (5:1, 9, 16, 18). He dismisses out of hand the possibility that Abraham could have been *justified by works* (2). But when he affirms positively how God *justifies the wicked* (5), he uses new expressions. First, God credits to us faith as righteousness (3, 5, 9, 22f.). Secondly, he credits to us righteousness apart from works (6, 11, 13, 24). And thirdly, he refuses to credit our sins against us, but pardons and covers them instead (7–8). One cannot claim that these three expressions are precise synonyms, but they belong together in justification. Justification involves a double counting, crediting, or reckoning. On the one hand, negatively, God will never count our sins against us. On the other hand, positively, God credits our account with righteousness, as a free gift, by faith, altogether apart from our works.

One is reminded of another, somewhat similar, double statement of Paul's, namely that in his work of reconciliation God was 'not counting men's sins against them', but instead 'made him who had no sin to be sin for us, so that in him we might become the righteousness of God'.[72] Christ became sin with our sins, in order that we might become righteous with God's righteousness.

We may recall that in AV the verb *logizomai* is sometimes translated not to 'credit, count or reckon' but to 'impute'. For example, 'Blessed is the man to whom the Lord will not impute sin' (8), indeed the person 'unto whom God imputeth righteousness apart from works' (6). The imagery of counting and crediting is financial, but that of imputation is legal. Both mean to 'reckon something as belonging to someone', but in the former case this is money, in the latter innocence or guilt.[73] This language became prominent in the sixteenth-century debate whether in the act of justification God 'infuses' righteousness into us (as the Roman Catholic Church taught) or 'imputes' it to us (as the Protestant Reformers insisted). The Reformers were surely right that when God justifies sinners he does not make them righteous (for that is the consequent process of sanctification), but he pronounces them righteous or imputes righteousness to them, reckoning them to be, and treating them as, (legally) righteous. C. H. Hodge clarifies this for us. 'To impute sin is to lay sin to the charge of anyone, and to treat him accordingly.' Similarly, 'to impute righteousness is to set righteousness to one's account, and to treat him accordingly'.[74] Thus Paul writes in Romans 4 both of God not imputing sin to sinners, although it actually belongs to them, and of his imputing righteousness to us, although it does not belong to us.[75] What Paul affirms is 'that it was

---

[72] 2 Cor. 5:19, 21.   [73] *Cf.* 2 Sa. 19:19; Acts 7:60; 2 Tim. 4:16.
[74] Hodge, p. 115.   [75] *Ibid.*, p. 107.

by means of faith that Abraham came to be treated as righteous, and not that faith was taken in lieu of perfect obedience.'[76]

A further question is whether the righteousness which God graciously imputes to us may be said to be the righteousness of Christ, whether we may legitimately speak of being 'clothed in the spotless robe of Christ's righteousness', and whether Zinzendorf was correct to write (in John Wesley's translation):

> Jesu, thy blood and righteousness
> My beauty are, my glorious dress;
> Midst flaming worlds, in these arrayed,
> With joy shall I lift up my head.

This kind of language, even in devotional hymns, is unfashionable today, and is declared by some to be theologically inadmissible. Indeed, we must agree that the precise imagery does not occur in the New Testament. We are certainly told in this very letter to clothe ourselves with the Lord Jesus Christ,[77] but his righteousness is not mentioned as the garment we are to put on. Nevertheless, on at least three occasions Paul comes so close to this picture that I for one believe it is biblically permissible to use it. We are told that he was made sin for us, 'so that in him we might become the righteousness of God';[78] that 'he has become for us . . . our righteousness';[79] and that if we 'gain Christ' and are 'found in him', then the righteousness we have is not our own but 'the righteousness that comes from God' through faith in Christ.[80] In each case, either Christ is our righteousness, or God's righteousness becomes ours when we are in Christ. 'Being clothed' with the righteousness of God or of Christ is not mentioned; we are given the even greater privilege of 'having' it and even 'becoming' it. Once the reality of imputed righteousness is accepted, there can be little objection to the 'clothing' metaphor.

b. Abraham was not justified by circumcision (9–12)

Paul's first question has been whether Abraham was justified by works or by faith (1–3). His second is whether *this blessedness* of justification is available *only for the circumcised* (the Jews) or is *also for the uncircumcised* (9a). This question prompts a supplementary one, concerning the *circumstances* in which Abraham was justified. Was he justified *after he was circumcised, or before*? (10a). In other words, did he submit to circumcision first, and so achieve righteousness, as the Rabbis taught? Or was he already justified when he was circumcised? What was the order of events? In

---

[76] *Ibid.*, p. 110.   [77] Ro. 13:14; *cf.* Gal. 3:27.   [78] 2 Cor. 5:21.
[79] 1 Cor. 1:30; *cf.* Je. 23:6.   [80] Phil. 3:9.

particular, did his justification come before or after his circumcision? Paul's answer to his own question is brief and blunt: *It was not after, but before!* (10b). In fact it happened long before. For his justification is recorded in Genesis 15 and his circumcision in Genesis 17, and at least fourteen years (even twenty-nine years according to the Rabbis) separated the two events.

Although they were separated, they were not unrelated, however. Abraham's circumcision, though not the ground of his justification, was its sign and seal. For Abraham *received the sign of circumcision, a seal of the righteousness that he had by faith while he was still uncircumcised* (11a). God himself had called circumcision 'the sign of the covenant' which he had established with Abraham.[81] Similarly, Paul now calls it a sign of his justification. As a 'sign' it was a distinguishing mark, setting Abraham and his descendants apart as God's covenant people. Indeed, it was not only a *sign* to identify them; it was also a *seal* to authenticate them, as the justified people of God.

Thus Abraham received two distinct gifts of God, justification and circumcision, and in that order. First he received justification by faith while he was still uncircumcised. Secondly, he received circumcision as a visible sign and seal of the justification which was already his. It is the same with baptism. Leaving aside the debatable question whether an analogy between baptism and circumcision legitimizes the baptism of the infant children of believing parents, the order of events for adult converts is plain. First, we are justified by faith, and then we are baptized as a sign or seal of our justification. But we must get the order right, and we must also clearly distinguish between the sign (baptism) and the thing signified (justification)' As Hodge wrote, 'what answers well as a sign, is a miserable substitute for the thing signified'.[82]

So then, Paul continues, there was a purpose in the fact that Abraham was justified by faith, and circumcised only later. Indeed, there was a double purpose. It was first that Abraham might be (as he is) *the father of all who believe*, and so have been justified, *but have not been circumcised* (11b). In other words, Abraham is the father of Gentile believers. Circumcision is no more necessary to their justification than it was to his. The second purpose of this combination of faith, justification and circumcision was that Abraham might *also* be (as he is) *the father of the circumcised who* in addition to their circumcision *also walk in the footsteps of the faith that our father Abraham had before he was circumcised* (12). Thus he is the father of all believers, irrespective of whether they are circumcised or uncircumcised. In fact circumcision, which was of

[81] Gn. 17:11.　　[82] Hodge, p. 125.

supreme importance to the Jews, must not be allowed to undermine or disrupt the unity of believers in Christ. Although according to the Jews Abraham was 'the great dividing point in the history of mankind', according to Paul Abraham through his faith became 'the great rallying point for all who believe, whether circumcised or uncircumcised'.[83] For where circumcision divides, faith unites.

c. Abraham was not justified by the law (13–17a)

Paul begins this new paragraph with a sharp *not . . . but* antithesis, in which the negative is emphatic. There are no questions and answers now, as there have been in the continuing diatribe. There is just an uncompromising assertion that if justification is neither by works nor by circumcision, it is not by law either. For how did God's promise come to *Abraham and his offspring?* Answer: *not through law . . . but through the righteousness that comes by faith* (13). The promise in mind must still be Genesis 15:5, that Abraham's posterity would be as numerous as the stars. It was a promise without any conditions or requirements attached to it. God's word came to Abraham as gratuitous promise, not as law. He simply believed God and was justified.

To our initial astonishment, Paul portrays God's promise as being that Abraham *would be heir of the world* (13). Yet in the Genesis text Abraham was promised Canaan, 'north, south, east and west' of where he was standing,[84] whose boundaries were later delineated. How then did 'the land' become 'the world'? It is partly that, as a general principle, the fulfilment of biblical prophecy has always transcended the categories in which it was originally given. It is partly that God made the subsidiary promise that through Abraham's innumerable posterity 'all nations on earth' would be blessed.[85] This promised multiplication of Abraham's descendants led the Rabbis to the conclusion that God would 'cause them to inherit from sea to sea, and from the River unto the utmost part of the earth'.[86] The third reason for Paul's statement that Abraham would inherit 'the world' is surely messianic. As soon as Abraham's seed was identified as the Messiah,[87] it was further acknowledged that he would exercise a universal dominion.[88] Further, his people are his fellow heirs, which is why the meek will inherit the earth[89] and why in and through Christ 'all things are ours', including 'the world'.[90]

Having clarified what the promise is, why does Paul assert so

---

[83] Nygren, p. 175. [84] Gn. 13:12, 14, 17. [85] *E.g.* Gn. 12:3; 18:18; 22:18.
[86] Ecclus. 44:21. See also Jubilees 17:3; 22:14.
[87] Gal. 3:16; *cf.* Jn. 8:56. [88] *E.g.* Ps. 2:8; Is. 9:7. [89] Mt. 5:5.
[90] 1 Cor. 3:21f.

strongly that it is received and inherited by faith, not law? He gives three reasons. The first is an argument from history. He has already stated it clearly in Galatians 3:17, namely that 'the covenant previously established by God' could not possibly be annulled by the law which was given 430 years later. The same truth is implicit in Romans 4, even though it is not developed. Secondly, there is the argument from language. In these verses the apostle uses a profusion of words – law, promise, faith, wrath, transgression and grace. These terms all have their own logic, and we must not be guilty of a confusion of categories. Thus, *if those who live by law are heirs*, that is, if the inheritance depends on our obedience, then *faith has no value* (*kekenōtai*; literally, 'has been emptied', *i.e.* of its validity) *and the promise is worthless* (*katērgētai*; literally, 'has been destroyed' or 'rendered ineffective'; 14). Something can be given to us either by law or by promise, since God is the author of both, but they cannot be in operation simultaneously. As Paul has written in Galatians, 'if the inheritance depends on the law, then it no longer depends on a promise'.[91] Law and promise belong to different categories of thought, which are incompatible. Law-language ('you shall') demands our obedience, but promise-language ('I will') demands our faith.[92] What God said to Abraham was not 'Obey this law and I will bless you', but 'I will bless you; believe my promise'.

Verse 15 develops this rationale, showing why law and promise exclude each other. It is *because law brings wrath*, and because *where there is no law there is no transgression*. The words 'law', 'transgression' and 'wrath' belong to the same category of thought and language. For the law turns sin into transgression (a deliberate trespass), and transgression provokes God's wrath. Conversely, 'where there is no law there can be no breach of law' (REB), and so no wrath.

Verses 16 is a further example of the logic of language, as it brings together *grace* and *faith*. The Greek sentence is much more dramatic than the English, since in the original there are neither verbs nor the noun 'promise'. It reads literally: 'therefore by faith in order that according to grace'. The fixed point is that God is gracious, and that salvation originates in his sheer grace alone. But in order that this may be so, our human response can only be faith. For grace gives and faith takes. Faith's exclusive function is humbly to receive what grace offers. Otherwise 'grace would no longer be grace' (11:6).

Paul's antithesis in verses 13–16 is similar to his work–trust and wage–gift antithesis of verses 4–5. It may be summarized as follows: God's law makes demands which we transgress, and so we incur wrath (15); God's grace makes promises which we believe, and so

[91] Gal. 3:18.   [92] *Cf.* Gal. 3:12.

we receive blessing (14, 16). Thus law, obedience, transgression and wrath belong to one category of thinking, while grace, promise, faith and blessing belong to another. This is the argument from language and logic.

In addition to his arguments from history and language, Paul now develops an argument from theology, especially the doctrine of Jewish–Gentile unity in the family of Abraham. The reason justification is by grace through faith, or by faith according to grace (16a), is not only to preserve linguistic and logical consistency, but also so that *the promise ... may be guaranteed to all Abraham's offspring – not only to those who are of the law* (meaning Jews who trace their physical descent from Abraham) *but also to those who are of the faith of Abraham*, that is, all believers, whether Jews or Gentiles, who belong to the spiritual lineage of faith (16b; *cf.* 11b–12). The law (not least its cultural and ceremonial provisions) divides. Only the gospel of grace and faith can unite, by opening the door to the Gentiles and levelling everybody at the foot of Christ's cross (*cf.* 3:29f.). Hence the importance of faith. All believers belong to Abraham's seed and so inherit Abraham's promise. The fatherhood of Abraham is a theme which runs right through this chapter. In the first verse Paul calls him 'our forefather according to the flesh', that is, Israel's national ancestor. But after this he makes three affirmations: 'he is the father of all who believe', whether circumcised or uncircumcised (11–12); *he is the father of us all* (16); and *he is our father in the sight of God* (17). Thus the Scripture has been fulfilled which says: '*I have made you a father of many nations*' (17a). Only justification by faith could have secured this.

Much of Romans 4 has so far been negative. It has been necessary for Paul to demonstrate that Abraham was justified neither by works (since it is written that he believed God and was justified), nor by circumcision (since he was justified first and circumcised later), nor by law (since the law was given centuries later, and in any case Abraham was responding to a promise, not a law). In each case, Paul has affirmed the priority of Abraham's faith. His faith came first; works, circumcision and law all came later. It has been a process of systematic elimination. But now at last the apostle reaches his positive conclusion.

d. Abraham was justified by faith (17b–22)

Paul moves on from the priority of Abraham's faith to its reasonableness. The description of faith as 'reasonable' comes as a surprise to many people, since they have always supposed that faith and reason were alternative means of grasping reality, and mutually incompatible. Is not faith a synonym for credulity and even superstition? Is it not an excuse for irrationality, for what Bertrand Russell called 'a conviction which cannot be shaken by contrary evidence'?[93]

No. Although, to be sure, faith goes beyond reason, it always has a firmly rational basis. In particular, faith is believing or trusting a person, and its reasonableness depends on the reliability of the person being trusted. It is always reasonable to trust the trustworthy. And there is nobody more trustworthy than God, as Abraham knew, and as we are privileged to know more confidently than Abraham because we live after the death and resurrection of Jesus through which God has fully disclosed himself and his dependability. In particular, before we are in a position to believe God's promises, we need to be sure both of his power (that he is able to keep them) and of his faithfulness (that he can be relied on to do so). It is these two attributes of God which were the foundations of Abraham's faith, and on which Paul reflects in this passage.

Take God's power first. Two evidences of it are brought together at the end of verse 17, where God, the object of Abraham's (and our) faith, is called *the God who gives life to the dead*, which is resurrection, *and calls things that are not as though they were*, or, perhaps better, 'calls into being things that are not' (REB), which is creation. Nothing baffles us human beings more than nothingness and death. The 'angst' of twentieth-century existentialists, is, at its most acute, their dread of the abyss of nothingness. And death is the one event over which (in the end) we have no control, and from which we cannot escape. Woody Allen epitomizes for many modern people this inability to cope with the prospect of death. 'It's not that I'm afraid to die,' he quips; 'I just don't want to be there when it happens.'[94] But nothingness and death are no problem to God. On the contrary, it is out of nothing that he created the universe, and out of death that he raised Jesus. The creation and the resurrection were and remain the two major manifestations of the power of God. It was in prayer to the sovereign Creator, who had made the world by his 'great power and outstretched arm', that Jeremiah added, 'Nothing is too hard for you.'[95] It was also in prayer that Paul asked that the Ephesians might know God's 'incomparably great power' which he had displayed in Christ 'when he raised him from the dead'.[96]

This firm conviction about the power of God was what enabled Abraham to believe, both *against all hope* and *in hope* (18a) at the

---

[93] From the preface to the collection of his essays published under the title *Why I am Not a Christian*, ed. Paul Edwards (George Allen and Unwin, 1957), p. xii.

[94] Graham McCann, *Woody Allen, New Yorker* (Polity Press, 1990), pp. 43, 83.

[95] Je. 32:17.   [96] Eph. 1:17ff.

same time, when God promised him that his descendants would be as many as the stars, although at that time he and Sarah did not have even a single child.[97] He *became the father of many nations, just as it had been said to him, 'So shall your offspring be'* (18b). It is not that he ran away from the realities of his situation into a world of fantasy. On the contrary, *without weakening in his faith, he faced the fact*, indeed the two painful, stubborn facts, that he could not beget a child and that Sarah could not conceive one. For the facts were *that his body was as good as dead – since he was about a hundred years old – and that Sarah's womb was also dead* (19).[98] Yet out of that double death God brought a new life. It was at one and the same time an act of creation and of resurrection. For this is the kind of God Abraham believed in. Indeed later, when facing the supreme test of his faith, whether to sacrifice his one and only son Isaac, through whom God had said his promises would be fulfilled, Abraham even 'reasoned that God could raise the dead, and figuratively speaking, he did receive Isaac back from death'.[99] Hence Abraham *did not waver through unbelief regarding the promise of God, but was strengthened in* (or, better, 'by') *his faith and gave glory to God* (20). The alternative responses to God's promise are here contrasted: *unbelief (apistia)* and *faith (pistis)*. If Abraham had given in to unbelief, he would have 'wavered' or been 'at odds with himself' *(diakrinō, BAGD)*. Instead, he strengthened himself by means of his faith. In this way *he gave glory to God* (20). That is to say, he glorified God by letting God be God, and by trusting him to be true to himself as the God of creation and resurrection.

It is this concept of 'letting God be God' which forms a natural transition from his power to his faithfulness. There is a fundamental correspondence between our faith and God's faithfulness, so much so that Jesus' command, 'Have faith in God,'[100] has sometimes been roughly but justly paraphrased, 'Reckon on the faithfulness of God.' For whether people keep their promises or not depends not only on their power, but also on their will, to do so. Put differently, behind all promises lies the character of the person who makes them. Abraham knew this. As he contemplated his own senility and Sarah's barrenness, he neither turned a blind eye to these problems, nor underestimated them. But he reminded himself of God's power and faithfulness. Faith always looks at the problems in the light of the promises. 'By faith Abraham, even though he was past age – and Sarah herself was barren – was enabled to become a father because he considered him faithful who had made the promise.'[101] He knew that God could keep his promises (because of his power) and he

---

[97] Gn. 15:4f. [98] See Gn. 17:17 and 18:11. [99] Heb. 11:17ff.
[100] Mk. 11:22. [101] Heb. 11:11.

knew that he would do so (became of his faithfulness). He was *fully persuaded that God had power to do what he had promised* (21). *This is why*, Paul adds, namely because he believed God's promise, '*it* (sc. his faith) *was credited to him as righteousness*' (22).

e. Conclusion: Abraham's faith and ours (23–25)

Paul concludes this chapter by applying lessons from Abraham's faith to us, his readers. He writes that the biblical words '*it was credited to him*' *were written not for him alone* (23), *but also for us* today. For the whole Abraham story, like the rest of Scripture, was written for our instruction (15:4).[102] So the same God, who credited faith to Abraham as righteousness, *will credit righteousness* to us also if we *believe in him who raised Jesus our Lord from the dead* (24). Abraham was not unique in his experience of being justified by faith. For this is God's way of salvation for everybody.

But the God we are to trust in is not only the God of Abraham, Isaac and Jacob; he is also the God and Father of our Lord Jesus Christ, who *was delivered over to death for our sins and was raised to life for our justification* (25). 'This verse', writes Hodge, 'is a comprehensive statement of the gospel.'[103] It is indeed. Its parallelism is so well honed that some think it was an early Christian aphorism or credal fragment. The verb *delivered over* (*paradidōmi*), although it is used in the gospels of Jesus being 'handed over' by Judas, the priests and Pilate, here evidently refers to the Father who 'did not spare his own Son, but gave him up for us all' (8:32). Thus both the death and the resurrection of Jesus are attributed to the Father's initiative: he 'delivered him over to death', and he 'raised him up to life'.

Although there is little difficulty in understanding these references to the death and resurrection of Jesus, the second part of each clause presents a problem: *for our sins* and *for our justification*. The preposition *dia* with the accusative normally means 'because of' or 'on account of'. It gives a reason for something having happened, and so has a retrospective look. In this case the meaning would be that Jesus was delivered to death 'because of our sins', dying the death which we deserved, and then was resurrected 'because of our justification', which he had accomplished by his death. More briefly, in the words of Bishop Handley Moule, 'we sinned, therefore he suffered: we were justified, therefore he rose'.[104] The difficulty with this rendering is with the second clause, for Paul regards justification as happening when we believe, not as having taken place before the resurrection.

---

[102] *Cf.* 1 Cor. 10:11.   [103] Hodge, p. 129.   [104] Moule (1884), p. 98.

So other commentators understand *dia* as meaning 'for the sake of' and having a prospective reference. Thus John Murray translates: 'He was delivered up in order to atone for our sins and was raised in order that we might be justified.'[105] The difficulty here is with the first clause. 'In order to atone for' is an elaborate paraphrase of the simple preposition 'for'.

The third possibility is to abandon the consistency which insists that *dia* must have the same meaning in both clauses. It could be causal or retrospective in the first (he was delivered 'because of our sins'), and final or prospective in the second (he was raised 'with a view to our justification').[106]

In this chapter the apostle gives us instruction about the nature of faith. He indicates that there are degrees in faith. For faith can be weak (19) or strong (20). How then does it grow? Above all through the use of our minds. Faith is not burying our heads in the sand, or screwing ourselves up to believe what we know is not true, or even whistling in the dark to keep our spirits up. On the contrary, faith is a reasoning trust. There can be no believing without thinking.

On the one hand we have to think about the problems which face us. Faith is not closing our eyes to them. Abraham 'considered his own body, which was as good as dead ... and the deadness of Sarah's womb' (19, REB). Better, *he faced the fact* (NIV) that he and Sarah were both infertile. But on the other hand Abraham reflected on the promises of God, and on the character of the God who had made them, especially that he is *the God who gives life to the dead and calls things that are not as though they were* (17). And as his mind played on the promises, the problems shrank accordingly, for he was *fully persuaded that God had power to do what he had promised* (21).

We today are much more fortunate than Abraham, and have little or no excuse for unbelief. For we live on this side of the resurrection. Moreover, we have a complete Bible in which both the creation of the universe and the resurrection of Jesus are recorded. It is therefore more reasonable for us to believe than it was for Abraham. Of course we have to make sure that the promises we are seeking to inherit are neither wrenched out of their biblical context nor the product of our own subjective fancy, but truly apply to us. Then we can lay hold of them, even *against all* human *hope*, yet *in hope* (18), that is, in the confidence of God's faithfulness and power. Only so shall we prove to be genuine children of our great spiritual forefather Abraham.

---

[105] Murray, vol. I, p. 155.   [106] *Cf.* 1 Cor. 15:17.

In hope, against all human hope,
   Self-desperate, I believe . . .

Faith, mighty faith, the promise sees,
   And looks to that alone;
Laughs at impossibilities
   And cries: It shall be done![107]

---

[107] Charles Wesley.

5:1 – 6:23
9. God's people united in Christ

What is immediately noteworthy at the end of Romans 4 and the beginning of Romans 5 is Paul's change of pronoun to the first person plural, 'we'. The characteristic pronoun in the first half of Romans 1 is 'I' ('I am not ashamed of the gospel') and in the second half 'they', as Paul portrays the demoralized pagan world. With chapter 2 the pronoun changes to 'you' as he addresses first the moralizer ('You have no excuse') and then the Jew ('Now you, if you call yourself a Jew'). In Romans 3 Paul reverts to 'they', describing first 'the whole world held accountable to God' and then 'all who believe', who in the first half of chapter 4 are called the offspring of Abraham. But suddenly, in the last phrase of Romans 4:16, Paul introduces the first person plural by designating Abraham 'the father of us all' and (in verse 17) 'our father'.

The first person plural is maintained for the rest of chapter 4, and then Paul begins chapter 5 with a sequence of 'we' affirmations: 'we have peace with God', 'we have gained access . . . into grace', 'we rejoice in hope of the glory of God', 'we also rejoice in our sufferings', 'we shall be saved', and 'we also rejoice in God'. By these magnificent statements of faith the apostle identifies himself with all who have been justified by faith, whether Jewish or Gentile, and expresses the solidarity of the people of God, the new community of Messiah Jesus. Hence the title I have given this chapter. Emphasis on the unity of the people of God continues in the second half of chapter 5, as Paul contrasts Adam and Christ, and their respective communities, and in chapter 6 where 'we' are characterized first as having died and risen with Christ and then as slaves of God through Christ.

1. The results of justification (5:1–11)

Having expounded the need for justification (1:18 – 3:20) and the way of justification (3:21 – 4:25) the apostle now describes its fruits or 'blissful consequences'.[1] It is as if he is enlarging on what he has called 'the blessedness' of those whom God justifies (4:6).

The whole paragraph (verses 1–11) depends on the opening words: *Therefore, since we have been justified through faith* . . . . Paul utters six bold assertions in the name of all whom God has justified.

a.   We have peace with God (1)

The pursuit of peace is a universal human obsession, whether it is international, industrial, domestic or personal peace. Yet more fundamental than all these is *peace with God*, the reconciled relationship with him which is the first blessing of justification. Thus 'justification' and 'reconciliation' belong together, for 'God does not confer the status of righteousness upon us without at the same time giving himself to us in friendship and establishing peace between himself and us'.[2] And this peace becomes ours *through our Lord Jesus Christ* (1), who was both delivered to death and raised from death (4:25), in order to make it possible. This is the heart of the peace which the prophets foretold as the supreme blessing of the messianic age, the shalom of the kingdom of God, inaugurated by Jesus Christ, the prince of peace.

Moreover, *we have peace with God* now, Paul writes, as a present possession. But is this the correct reading? In the great majority of manuscripts the verb is in the subjunctive (*echōmen*, 'let us have', RV and RSV mg.), not in the indicative (*echomen*, 'we have', NIV and REB). In the Greek text the difference is only a single letter, and the pronunciation of the two words will have been almost identical. If *echōmen* is right, then 'let us have peace' would have to be understood as an exhortation to 'enjoy it to the full'.[3] Yet, in spite of its strong manuscript support, most commentators reject this reading. It seems to be one of those rare cases in which the context must be allowed to take precedence over the text, the internal evidence over the external, theology over grammar. For the paragraph consists of a series of affirmations, and contains not even one exhortation. 'Only the indicative is consonant with the apostle's argument.'[4]

b.   We are standing in grace (2a)

Literally, 'through him [*sc.* Christ] we have obtained our introduction into this grace in which we have taken our stand'.

'Grace' is normally God's free and unmerited favour, his undeserved, unsolicited and unconditional love. But here it is not so

---

[1] Sanday and Headlam, p. 118.   [2] Cranfield, vol. I, p. 258.
[3] Sanday and Headlam, p. 118.   [4] Metzger (1976), p. 511.

much his quality of graciousness as 'the sphere of God's grace' (NEB), our privileged position of acceptance by him.

Two verbs are used in relation to *this grace*, denoting respectively our entry into it, and our continuance in it. Both are in the perfect tense. First, *we have gained access* into this grace. *Prosagōgē* occurs elsewhere in the New Testament only in Ephesians 2:18 and 3:12. A better translation than 'access' (which might suggest that we take the initiative to enter) would be 'introduction' (which acknowledges our unfitness to enter, and our need for someone to bring us in). The Greek word has 'a certain touch of formality' about it,[5] although it is uncertain whether the imagery is of a person being brought into God's sanctuary to worship[6] or into a king's audience chamber to be presented to him.

Secondly, we have taken our stand firmly in or on this grace into which we have been introduced.[7] Justified believers enjoy a blessing far greater than a periodic approach to God or an occasional audience with the king. We are privileged to live in the temple and in the palace. The perfect tenses express this. Our relationship with God, into which justification has brought us, is not sporadic but continuous, not precarious but secure. We do not fall in and out of grace like courtiers who may find themselves in and out of favour with their sovereign, or politicians with the public. No, we stand in it, for that is the nature of grace. Nothing can separate us from God's love (8:38f.).

c. We rejoice in [our] hope of the glory of God (2b)

Christian hope (*elpis*) is not uncertain, like our ordinary everyday hopes about the weather or our health; it is a joyful and confident expectation which rests on the promises of God, as we saw in the case of Abraham. And the object of our hope is *the glory of God* (2), namely his radiant splendour which will in the end be fully displayed. Already his glory is being continuously revealed in the heavens and the earth.[8] Already it has been uniquely made manifest in Jesus Christ, the incarnate Word,[9] most notably in his death and resurrection.[10] One day, however, the curtain will be raised and the glory of God will be fully disclosed. First, Jesus Christ himself will appear 'with great power and glory'.[11] Secondly, we will not only see his glory, but be changed into it,[12] so that he will 'be glorified in his holy people'.[13] Then redeemed human beings, who were created to be 'the image and glory of

---

[5] Denney, p. 623.   [6] *Cf.* Heb. 10:19ff.   [7] *Cf.* 1 Pet. 5:12.
[8] Ps. 19:1; Is. 6:3.   [9] *E.g.* Jn. 1:14; 2:11.   [10] *E.g.* Jn. 12:23f.; 17:1ff.
[11] Mk. 13:26; *cf.* Tit. 2:13.   [12] 1 Jn. 3:2; *cf.* Col. 3:4.   [13] 2 Thes. 1:10.

God',[14] but now through sin 'fall short of the glory of God' (3:23), will again and in full measure share in his glory (8:17). Thirdly, even the groaning creation 'will be liberated from its bondage to decay and brought into the glorious freedom of the children of God' (8:21). The renewed universe will be suffused with its Creator's glory. All this is included in *the glory of God* and is therefore the object of our sure hope. We exult in it. And our vision of future glory is a powerful stimulus to present duty.

We pause, after Paul's first three affirmations about the 'blessedness' of the justified, and reflect. The fruits of justification relate to the past, present and future. 'We have peace with God' (as a result of our past forgiveness). 'We are standing in grace' (our present privilege). 'We rejoice in the hope of glory' (our future inheritance). Peace, grace, joy, hope and glory. It sounds idyllic. It is – except for Paul's fourth affirmation.

d. We also rejoice in our sufferings (3–8)

The 'sufferings' in mind are usually translated 'tribulations'. These are not what we sometimes call 'the trials and tribulations' of our earthly existence, meaning our aches and pains, fears and frustrations, deprivations and disappointments, but rather *thlipseis* (literally, 'pressures'), referring in particular to the opposition and persecution of a hostile world. *Thlipsis* was almost a technical term for the suffering which God's people must expect in the last days before the end.[15] So Jesus warned his disciples that 'in this world' they would 'have trouble',[16] and Paul similarly warned his converts that they 'must go through many hardships to enter the kingdom of God'.[17]

What attitude should Christians adopt to these 'tribulations'? Far from merely enduring them with stoic fortitude, we are to *rejoice* in them. This is not masochism, however, the sickness of finding pleasure in pain. It is rather the recognition that there is a divine rationale behind suffering. First, suffering is the one and only path to glory. It was so for Christ; it is so for Christians. As Paul will soon express it, we are 'co-heirs with Christ, if indeed we share in his sufferings in order that we may also share in his glory' (8:17). That is why we are to rejoice in them both.

Secondly, if suffering leads to glory in the end, it leads to maturity meanwhile. Suffering can be productive, if we respond to it positively, and not with anger or bitterness. *We know* this, especially from the experience of God's people in every generation.

---

[14] 1 Cor. 11:7; Gn. 1:26f.; 9:6; Jas. 3:9. [15] *Cf.* Mk. 13:19, 24; *cf.* Rev. 7:14.
[16] Jn. 16:33, *thlipsis* again. [17] Acts 14:22, same word.

Suffering produces perseverance (3, *hypomonē*, endurance). We could not learn endurance without suffering, because without suffering there would be nothing to endure. Next, *perseverance* produces *character*. *Dokimē* is the quality of a person who has been tested and has passed the test. It is 'a mature character' (JBP), 'the temper of the veteran as opposed to that of the raw recruit'.[18] Then the last link in the chain is that *character* produces *hope* (4), perhaps because the God who is developing our character in the present can be relied on for the future too.

Thirdly, suffering is the best context in which to become assured of God's love. Of course many people will immediately assert the contrary, since it is suffering which makes them doubt God's love. But consider Paul's argument. He has traced the sequence of chain reactions from tribulation to perseverance, from perseverance to character, and from character to hope. Now he adds that *hope does not disappoint us* (5a), and never will. It will never betray us by proving to be an illusion after all. 'Such hope is no fantasy' (REB). But how do we know this? What is the ultimate ground on which our Christian hope rests, our hope of glory? It is the steadfast love of God. The reason our hope will never let us down is that God will never let us down. His love will never give us up.

But how can we be sure of God's love? To be sure of the love of his or her parents is almost indispensable to the healthy emotional development of a child. To be sure of the love of spouse or friend is marvellously conducive to human fulfilment. To be sure of God's love brings even richer blessings. It is the major secret of joy, peace, freedom, confidence and self-respect.

The apostle spells out two major means by which we come to be sure that God loves us. The first is that *God has poured out his love into our hearts by the Holy Spirit, whom he has given us* (5b). This is the first mention in Romans of the work of the Holy Spirit in the life of the Christian, and it teaches us some important lessons.

The first is that the Holy Spirit is God's gift to all believers (since Paul is listing the consequences of justification), so that it is not possible to be justified by faith without at the same time being regenerated and indwelt by the Spirit. Secondly, it teaches us that the Holy Spirit was given to us at a particular time (*dothentos*, an aorist tense), namely at what is popularly called our 'conversion', or when we were justified. Thirdly, having been given to us, one of the Holy Spirit's distinctive ministries is to pour God's love into our hearts. Indeed, he has done this in such a way that the initial outpouring remains a permanent flood (*ekkechytai*, a perfect tense). It is understandable that many see here a reference to the effusion of

18 Sanday and Headlam, p. 125.

142

the Spirit at Pentecost, since the same verb is used (*ekcheō*, 'pour out').[19] But to be strictly accurate the apostle writes here not of the outpouring of the Spirit but of the outpouring of God's love by the ministry of the Spirit in our hearts. The genitive in the expression 'love of God' must surely be subjective, not objective, in that it is God's love for us, not ours for him, which is in mind. 'Under the vivid metaphor of a cloudburst on a parched countryside',[20] what the Holy Spirit does is to make us deeply and refreshingly aware that God loves us. It is very similar to Paul's later statement that 'the Spirit himself testifies with our spirit that we are God's children' (8:16). There is little if any appreciable difference between being assured of God's fatherhood and of his love.

It may be appropriate at this point to refer to the teaching of some Puritan theologians, popularized in this century by Dr Martyn Lloyd-Jones, that this outpouring of God's love in the heart, which they also identified as the 'sealing' of the Spirit, is an experience subsequent to regeneration and given only to some. 'You cannot be a Christian without the Holy Spirit, but you can be a Christian without having the love of God shed abroad in your heart ... All Christians have not had this experience, but it is open to all; and all Christians should have it.'[21] Dr Lloyd-Jones goes on to cite examples from the eighteenth and nineteenth centuries of well-known evangelical leaders who described how God's love 'seemed to come in wave after wave until they were melted under the glory of it'.[22]

Now it is not my purpose to deny that such post conversion deeper, richer, fuller experiences of God's love are authentic, for they are well documented in Christian biographies, and indeed I think I myself know from experience what it is on occasion to be 'filled with an inexpressible and glorious joy'.[23] My question is whether Romans 5:5 is primarily intended to describe unusual and overpowering experiences which are given only to some, even if they are 'open to all'. I think not. For Paul applies both his statements (that 'the Holy Spirit was given us' and that 'the love of God has been poured out into our hearts') to the same 'us' whom he has in mind throughout this paragraph, namely all justified believers. Must we not say, therefore, from both Scripture and experience, that all Christian people are given by the Holy Spirit some measure of assurance of God's love (5:5) and fatherhood (8:16)? At the same time we recognize that there are differing degrees in which this assurance is given, and that some of God's children sometimes are simply overcome by love and joy, until they cry to him to stay his

[19] Joel 2:28f. = Acts 2:17f.   [20] Dunn, vol. 38A, p. 253.
[21] Lloyd-Jones, vol. 4, pp. 84f.   [22] *Ibid.*, p. 89.   [23] 1 Pet. 1:8.

hand, lest they should collapse under the strain. Indeed, it may well be that many contemporary 'charismatic' experiences are precisely this – a vivid, heightened, intense, even overwhelming assurance of God's presence and love.

But God has a second and objective way of assuring us of his love. It is that he has proved his love by Christ's death on the cross. Previously Paul has written that God demonstrated his justice on the cross (3:25f.). Now he sees the cross as a demonstration of God's love. Indeed, 'demonstrate' is really too weak a word; 'prove' would be better. For 'Christ died for us while we were yet sinners, and that is God's proof of his love towards us' (8, REB).

In order to grasp this, we need to remember that the essence of loving is giving. 'God so loved the world that he gave his one and only Son . . . .'[24] 'The Son of God . . . loved me and gave himself for me.'[25] Moreover, the degree of love is measured partly by the costliness of the gift to the giver, and partly by the worthiness or unworthiness of the beneficiary. The more the gift costs the giver, and the less the recipient deserves it, the greater the love is seen to be. Measured by these standards, God's love in Christ is absolutely unique. For in sending his Son to die for sinners, he was giving everything, his very self, to those who deserved nothing from him except judgment.

The costliness of the gift is clear. Verses 6 and 8 say only that '*Christ* died'. But verse 10 clarifies who 'Christ' is by saying that God reconciled us to himself 'through the death of his Son'. Formerly God had sent prophets, and sometimes angels. But now he sent his only Son, and in giving his Son he was giving himself. Further, he gave his Son to die for us. Some commentators seem anxious to add that there is no doctrine of atonement here, and certainly no substitutionary doctrine, since the preposition in the expression 'for us' is *hyper* ('on behalf of'), not *anti* ('instead of'). This is a superficial judgment, however. For what is written is that *while we were still sinners, Christ died for us* (8), and whenever sin and death are coupled in Scripture, death is the penalty or 'wage' of sin (6:23; *cf.* 5:12). This being so, the statement that 'Christ died for sinners', that though the sins were ours the death was his, can mean only that he died as a sin offering, bearing in our place the penalty our sins had deserved. This helps us to understand the costliness of the gift.

What about the worthiness of the recipients? We for whom God made this costly sacrifice are portrayed by four epithets. First, we are *sinners* (8), that is, we have departed from the way of righteousness, fallen short of God's standards and missed the target.

[24] Jn. 3:16; *cf.* 1 Jn. 4:10.   [25] Gal. 2:20.

Secondly, *at just the right time . . . Christ died for the ungodly* (6b).
Instead of loving God with all our being, we have rebelled against
him. Thirdly, 'we were God's enemies' (10). This certainly means
that we cherished a deep-seated hostility to God ('the sinful mind is
hostile to God', 8:7), a resentment of his authority. But we cannot
be satisfied with the notion that the hostility was entirely on our
side and not at all on God's. For in 11:28 the opposite of 'enemies' is
'loved', so that the word 'enemies' must be passive too. The context
contains references to God's wrath (*e.g.* verse 9), which is God's
holy hatred of sin; and since the reconciliation between God and us
is said to have been 'received' (11), it cannot mean our turning from
our hostility, but must refer to God's reconciling himself to us.
Sanday and Headlam are surely correct in their conclusion: 'We
infer that the natural explanation of the passages which speak of
enmity and reconciliation between God and man is that they are not
on one side only, but are mutual.'[26] 'There is not only a wicked
opposition of the sinner to God, but a holy opposition of God to
the sinner.'[27]

Paul's fourth descriptive epithet is that *we were still powerless*
(6a), meaning that we were helpless to rescue ourselves. 'Sinners',
'ungodly', 'enemies' and 'powerless'. This is the apostle's ugly,
fourfold portrayal of us. Yet it is for us that God's Son died. Why,
he adds, *very rarely will anyone die for a righteous man* (probably
referring to somebody whose uprightness is rather cold, clinical and
unattractive), *though for a good man* (whose goodness is warm,
generous and appealing) *someone might possibly dare to die* (7). *But
God* (the stark contrast is underlined) 'commendeth' (av), demonstrates (niv), even 'proves' (reb) *his own love for us* (a love distinct
from every other love, a love uniquely God's own) *in this: While we
were still sinners* (neither good nor righteous, but ungodly, enemies
and powerless), *Christ died for us* (8).

Human beings can be very generous in giving to those they
consider worthy of their affection and respect. The unique majesty
of God's love lies in the combination of three factors, namely that
when Christ died for us, God (a) was giving himself, (b) even to the
horrors of a sin-bearing death on the cross, and (c) doing so for his
undeserving enemies.

How, then, can we doubt the love of God? To be sure, we are
often profoundly perplexed by the tragedies and calamities of life.
Indeed, Paul has been giving his teaching about God's love within
the context of 'tribulation', which can be very painful. But then we
remember that God has both proved his love for us in the death of
his Son (8) and poured his love into us by the gift of his Spirit (5).

[26] Sanday and Headlam, p. 130.   [27] Hodge, p. 138.

Objectively in history and subjectively in experience, God has given us good grounds for believing in his love. The integration of the historical ministry of God's Son (on the cross) with the contemporary ministry of his Spirit (in our hearts) is one of the most wholesome and satisfying features of the gospel.

e.   We shall be saved through Christ (9–10)

So far the apostle has concentrated on what God has already done for us through Christ. We have been justified. We have peace with God. We are standing in grace. We rejoice in our hope and in our sufferings. Yet there is more – much more – still to come, which is not yet ours. In fact, verses 9 and 10 are notable examples of the familiar New Testament tension between the 'already' and the 'not yet', between what Christ has accomplished at his first coming and what remains to be done at his second, between our past and our future salvation. For salvation has a future tense as well as past and present tenses, and the words common to these two verses are the statement that we shall be saved. If, therefore, we are asked by some brash evangelist whether we have been saved, it would be just as biblical to say 'No' as 'Yes', although the correct answer would be 'Yes and no.' For yes, we have been saved through Christ from the guilt of our sins and from the judgment of God upon them, but no, we have not yet been delivered from indwelling sin or been given new bodies in the new world.

What, then, is the future salvation which Paul has in mind here? He uses two expressions, the first negative and the second positive. First and negatively, we shall *be saved from God's wrath* through Christ (9). Of course we have already been rescued from it in the sense that through the cross God has himself turned it away from us, so that now we have peace with him and are standing in his grace. But at the end of history there is going to be a day of reckoning which Paul has called 'the day of God's wrath, when his righteous judgment will be revealed' (2:5) and his wrath will be poured out on those who have rejected Christ (2:8).[28] From that fearful coming wrath we shall be saved,[29] for, as Jesus put it, the believer 'will not be condemned; he has [*sc.* already] crossed over from death to life'.[30]

Secondly and positively, we shall *be saved through his life* (10). For the Jesus who died for our sins was raised from death and lives, and means his people to experience for themselves the power of his resurrection. We can share his life now, and will share his resurrection on the last day. Paul will elaborate these truths in Romans 8; he

---

[28] *Cf.* Eph. 5:6; Col. 3:6.   [29] 1 Thes. 1:10; 5:9.   [30] Jn. 5:24.

does no more than sketch them here in promising that we shall be saved through Christ's life.

So the best is yet to be! In our present 'half-saved' condition we are eagerly looking forward to our full and final salvation. But how can we be sure of it? It is mainly to answer this question that Paul pens verses 9 and 10. Both are *a fortiori* or 'how much more' arguments. The basic structure of both is identical, namely that 'if one thing has happened, *much more* will something else take place'. What, then, has happened to us? The answer is that we have been *justified* (9) and *reconciled* (10), both of which are attributed to the cross. On the one hand, *we have now been justified by his blood* (9a), and on the other, *we were reconciled to him* (sc. God) *through the death of his Son* (10a). So the Judge has pronounced us righteous, and the Father has welcomed us home.

In addition, it is essential to Paul's argument that he stresses the costliness of these things. It was *by his blood* (9a), shed in a sacrificial death on the cross, that we have been justified, and it was *when we were God's enemies* (10a) that we were reconciled to him. Here then is the logic. If God has already done the difficult thing, can we not trust him to do the comparatively simple thing of completing the task? If God has accomplished our justification at the cost of Christ's blood, *much more* will he save his justified people from his final wrath (9)! Again, if he reconciled us to himself when we were his enemies, *much more* will he finish our salvation now that we are his reconciled friends (10)! These are the grounds on which we dare to affirm that we *shall . . . be saved*.

f. We also rejoice in God (11)

What is extraordinary about this sixth and last affirmation is that, verbally speaking, it is identical with the Jewish attitude which Paul has condemned in 2:17, which NIV paraphrases, 'You . . . brag about your relationship to God.' Literally, however, 2:17 reads 'you boast in God', and 5:11 reads 'we boast in God'. The verb, the noun and the preposition are all the same. Yet by a true instinct most translators have rendered the verbs differently, 'boasting' or 'bragging' there, 'rejoicing' or 'exulting' here. For Christian exulting in God, according to Paul, is quite different from Jewish bragging about him. The latter was a boast in God as if he were their exclusive property and they had a monopoly interest in him, whereas the former is the opposite. Christian exultation in God begins with the shamefaced recognition that we have no claim on him at all, continues with wondering worship that while we were still sinners and enemies Christ died for us, and ends with the humble confidence that he will complete the work he has begun. So to exult in God is to rejoice not in our privileges but in his mercies, not in our possession of him but in his of us.

In spite of our knowledge that for Christian people all boasting is excluded (3:27), we nevertheless boast or rejoice in our hope of sharing God's glory (2), in our tribulations (3) and above all in God himself (11). This exulting is *through our Lord Jesus Christ*, because it is through him that *we have now received* ('the' or 'our') *reconciliation* (11).

It seems clear from this paragraph, then, that the major mark of justified believers is joy, especially joy in God himself. We should be the most positive people in the world. For the new community of Jesus Christ is characterized not by a self-centred triumphalism but by a God-centred worship.

2. The two humanities, in Adam and in Christ (5:12-21)

So far Paul has surveyed both the universal extent of human sin and guilt and the glorious adequacy of God's justifying grace in and through Christ. In so doing he has led us both down into the depths of human depravity and up into the heights of divine mercy. He has also indicated his readers' involvement (whether Jews or Gentiles) in both the guilt and the grace. On the one hand, he has 'made the charge that Jews and Gentiles alike are *all* under sin' (3:9), whereas on the other he has declared that Abraham is 'the father of us *all*' through faith (4:16). Here then are two communities, one characterized by sin and guilt, the other by grace and faith. Anticipating verses 12-21 a little, we may say that the former is in Adam and the latter in Christ.

Moreover, Paul has identified himself with the new, believing community by his consistent use of the first person plural. Having been both justified (1) and reconciled (11), all of us are enjoying peace with God, standing in grace, rejoicing in present sufferings and future glory, assured of final salvation, and exulting in God through Christ by whom these blessings have become ours (1-11).

Therefore, Paul continues. The word must not be overlooked. It shows that the next verses (12-21) are not an alien intrusion into the argument, or an isolated section unconnected with what precedes or follows, or even a parenthesis, but a logical development, indeed a conclusion of his thesis thus far and a necessary transition to what comes next. Two particular links between the two halves of Romans 5 (1-11 and 12-21) may be mentioned.

The first is that Paul has attributed our reconciliation and salvation to the death of God's Son (9-10). This immediately prompts the question how one person's sacrifice could have brought such blessings to so many. It is not that (in Winston Churchill's famous saying) so many owe so much to so few; it is rather that so many owe so much to only one person. How can that be? Paul's answer is contained in his analogy between Adam and Christ. For both demonstrate the principle that many can be affected, for good or ill, by one person's action.

A second possible clue to the link between the two halves of Romans 5 is that both conclude with the expression 'through our Lord Jesus Christ' (11 and 21). Determined as he is to honour Jesus Christ as the only mediator of all our blessings, Paul presents Adam and Christ, the respective heads of the old and new humanities, in such a way as to demonstrate the overwhelming superiority of the work of Christ.

All students of verses 12–21 have found it extremely condensed. Some have mistaken compression for confusion. But most have marvelled at the almost 'mathematical precision'[31] of Paul's writing, and have admired its craftsmanship. It may be likened to a well-chiselled carving or a carefully constructed musical composition.

The text divides itself naturally into three short paragraphs, in each of which Adam and Christ are related to each other, although with significant differences. First (12–14), Adam and Christ are *introduced*, Adam as responsible for sin and death, and as 'a pattern of the one to come' (14), who is Christ. Secondly (15–17), Adam and Christ are *contrasted*. In each of these three verses the work of Christ is said to be either 'not like' Adam's or 'much more' success-ful than his. Thirdly (18–21), Adam and Christ are *compared*. The structure now (in 18, 19 and 21) is 'just as . . . so also'. For through the one man's one deed (Adam's disobedience or Christ's obedi-ence) the many have been either cursed or blessed.

a. Adam and Christ are introduced (12–14)

Paul begins with a sentence he never completes. His opening words are *Therefore, just as sin entered . . .*, but the corresponding words we expect ('so also . . .', as in the sentence structure of verses 18, 19 and 21) never come. What he was intending to write we can only guess. But the symmetry would require something like this: 'Just as through one man sin entered the world, and death through sin, and so death came to all because all shared his sin, so also through one man righteousness entered the world, and life through righteous-ness, and so life came to all because all shared his righteousness.' Indeed, this is more or less what Paul does write later. Verses 18–19 may be regarded as completing the sentence which he began in verse 12. Instead, however, he breaks off his argument in order to explain

[31] Godet, p. 213.

and justify (in verses 13–14) what he has just written (in verse 12).

The topic of verse 12 is sin and death, and in it Paul describes three downward steps or deteriorating stages in human history, from one man sinning to all men dying.

First, *sin entered the world through one man*. Adam is not named but is obviously meant. Paul is not concerned with the origin of evil in general, but only with how it invaded the world of human beings. It entered through one man, that is, through his disobedience. Eve was also implicated,[32] although Paul leaves her out of the picture here, because he holds Adam responsible.

Secondly, *death* then entered the world *through sin*. As Adam was the door through which sin entered, so sin was the door through which death entered. This is an allusion to Genesis 2:17 and 3:19, where death (both physical and spiritual) is said to have been the penalty for disobedience (*cf.* 1:32; 6:23). I will come back later to modern questions about the historicity of Adam and the origin of death.

Thirdly, *in this way death came to all men, because all sinned* (12). The apostle is still handling the relation between sin and death, but now he moves on from their presence in *one man* to their presence in *all men* (the human race). Moreover, he sees a similarity between these two situations (*houtōs, in this way*). This may refer to the essential connection between sin and death: as death came to one man because he sinned, so death came to all men because they sinned. Or it may refer to the agency through which both happened: as through one man sin and death 'entered' the world (*eisēlthen*), so through one man they 'spread' throughout the world (*diēlthen*).

Here then are the three stages – from Adam's sin to Adam's death, to universal death due to universal sin. But what is the meaning of the third statement that *death came to all men, because all sinned?* In what sense have all sinned so that all die?

Grammatically speaking, there are two possible answers to this question. Either *all sinned* by copying and so repeating Adam's sin, or *all sinned* when Adam sinned and were included in his sinning. The first would be a case of imitation (all sinned *like* Adam), and the second a case of participation (all sinned *in and with* Adam). The first explanation is usually associated with the name of Pelagius, the early fifth-century British monk, who denied original sin, taught a form of self-salvation, and was opposed by Augustine. In Pelagius' view Adam was simply the first sinner, and everybody ever since has followed his bad example. Moreover, Paul's actual language could justly be understood in this way. His two words *all sinned*

---

[32] 2 Cor. 11:3; 1 Tim. 2:13f.; *cf.* Ecclus. 25:24.

(*pantes hēmarton*) are precisely those which he has used in 3:23 when affirming that 'all have sinned and fall short of the glory of God'. As John Murray has written, 'verse 12 of itself is compatible with a Pelagian interpretation, and if Paul had entertained the Pelagian view he could have stated it admirably well in these terms . . . If Paul meant that death passed upon all because all men were guilty of actual transgression, this is the way he would have said it. At least no more suitable way could be considered.'[33] Consequently, many have held this position, not least because of the difficulties inherent in the alternative view. For example, C. K. Barrett writes straightforwardly: 'That is, all men sin (3:23), and all men die because they sin.'[34] Other scholars make much of the use of Adam in the literature of Judaism at that time. Take 2 Esdras: 'A grain of evil seed was sown in the heart of Adam from the beginning, and how much wickedness hath it brought forth unto this time!'[35] 'O thou Adam, what hast thou done? for though it was thou that sinned, the evil is not fallen on thee alone, but upon all of us that come of thee.'[36] 'In the light of contemporary and near-contemporary Jewish thought,' writes John Ziesler, 'it is more likely that Adam is Everyman (and Everywoman), so that to say that Adam sinned is a way of saying that everybody sins. Everyone is his or her own Adam.'[37] Others, wanting to preserve a stronger link between Adam's sin and the sinning of his posterity, have stressed the transmission of his depraved nature to them: 'If they sinned, their sin was due in part to tendencies inherited from Adam.'[38]

Inheriting Adam's nature, following Adam's example, and recapitulating Adam's story: I am not wishing to deny these truths. But is this what Paul meant by writing *because all sinned*? That is the primary question. And in seeking to answer it, context as well as grammar must be taken into consideration.

That Paul meant 'all sinned in and through Adam and therefore all died', although theologically difficult, is surely exegetically correct. There are three main arguments.[39] The first concerns *the addition of verses 13–14*, in which Paul makes three points. First, *before the* (Mosaic) *law was given, sin was in the world* (13a). There is nothing controversial here. It is a fact that sin long antedated the law, as Adam antedated Moses. Secondly, *but sin is not taken into account (i.e.* punished) *when there is no law* (13b). For 'where there is no law there is no law to break'.[40] So, until the Mosaic law was

---

[33] Murray, vol. I, pp. 182f.   [34] Barrett, p. 111.   [35] 2 Esdras 4:30.
[36] 2 Esdras 7:118.   [37] Ziesler (1989), p. 147.
[38] Sanday and Headlam, p. 134.
[39] See the full statements by Hodge (pp. 142ff.) and by Murray, vol. I (pp. 178ff.).
[40] Morris (1988), p. 233.

given and could exercise its role of defining and identifying sin (*cf.* 3:20), sin was not reckoned against sinners. *Nevertheless* (this is Paul's third point), *death reigned from the time of Adam to the time of Moses*, that is, throughout the period before the law was given, *even over those who did not sin by breaking* a (specific, explicit) *command, as did Adam* (14). Of course some did flagrantly disobey God's moral law, which was written in their hearts (2:14f.), and were punished, as in the flood, the judgment of those who built the tower of Babel, and the destruction of Sodom and Gomorrah. But Paul's point is that there were others who did not sin 'by disobeying a direct command' (REB), as Adam did, and as the people of the flood, Babel and Sodom did. These others 'did not voluntarily and overtly violate an expressly revealed ordinance of God'.[41] Perhaps we should include among them, as is sometimes suggested, 'the heathen, and the infant, and the imbecile'.[42] Yet all died (the reference is clearly to physical death), and death is the penalty for sin. There can be only one explanation. All died *because all sinned* in and through Adam, the representative or federal head of the human race.

The second argument for this interpretation is *the wider context*, especially verses 15–19. Five times in these five verses, once in every verse, Paul states that the trespass or disobedience of one man brought death, judgment or condemnation to all men. The language varies slightly from verse to verse, but the meaning is the same. Verse 15 clinches the matter: *the many died by the trespass of the one man*. That is, universal death is attributed to a single, solitary sin.

The third argument relates to *the analogy between Adam and Christ*, and between those who are in Adam and those who are in Christ. If death comes to all because they sin like Adam, then by analogy we would have to say that life comes to all because they are righteous like Christ. But that would turn the way of salvation on its head. Hodge was right to say that 'Paul has been engaged from the beginning of the Epistle in inculcating one main idea, viz. that the ground of the sinner's acceptance with God is not in himself, but the merit of Christ'. And the correspondence between Christ and Adam must preserve, not destroy, this truth. It should read, therefore: 'As we are condemned on account of what Adam did, (so) we are justified on account of what Christ did.'[43]

These three arguments (from the text, the context and the analogy) seem decisively to support the view that 'all sinned in and through Adam'. Dr Martyn Lloyd-Jones summed up the rationale in these words: 'God has always dealt with mankind through a head

---

[41] Murray, vol. I, p. 187.   [42] Moule (1894), p. 147   [43] Hodge, p. 142.

and representative. The whole story of the human race can be summed up in terms of what has happened because of Adam, and what has happened and will yet happen because of Christ.'[44] But can we accept this teaching? It may be exegetically correct, but is it theologically and personally meaningful? Paul evidently believed it; can we?

The concept of our having sinned in Adam is certainly foreign to the mindset of western individualism. But are we to subordinate Scripture to our own cultural perspective? Africans and Asians, who take for granted the collective solidarity of the extended family, tribe, nation and race, do not have the difficulty which western people experience.

More important even than African and Asian models, however, is that Scripture itself contains a number of significant variations on the theme of human solidarity. The first takes us back to Abraham's day and to the use which the author of Hebrews makes of that mysterious king-priest Melchizedek. He not only blessed Abraham, the ancestor of Levi, but accepted from him a tithe of the battle spoils. 'One might even say', the writer concludes, 'that Levi himself, who receives tithes, paid tithes through Abraham, for he [Levi, long before his birth] was still in the loins of his ancestor [*sc.* Abraham] when Melchizedek met him.'[45]

Secondly, when Achan stole some Jericho treasure, which by God's decree had been devoted to destruction, we read that 'the Israelites acted unfaithfully' and 'the LORD's anger burned against Israel'. That is, the nation was regarded as implicated in Achan's sin. 'Israel has sinned,' God said; 'they have violated my covenant.'[46]

My third example takes us to the cross. We like to identify with Pilate, who washed his hands and declared his innocence. We were not guilty, we say; it had nothing to do with us. The apostles disagree. Not only did Herod and Pilate, Gentiles and Jews 'conspire' against Jesus,[47] but the sins which led to his death are our sins too. Moreover, if we turn away from God, we 'are crucifying the Son of God all over again'.[48] 'Were you there', the negro spiritual asks, 'when they crucified my Lord?' The only possible answer is that we *were* there, and not merely as spectators, but as guilty participants. Horatius Bonar, the nineteenth-century Scottish hymn-writer, expressed it well:

> 'Twas I that shed the sacred blood;
> I nailed him to the tree;
> I crucified the Christ of God;
> I joined the mockery.

---

[44] Lloyd-Jones, vol. 4, p. 178. [45] Heb. 7:9f., RSV. [46] Jos. 7:1, 11.
[47] Acts 4:27. [48] Heb. 6:6.

153

My fourth and final example also relates to the cross, but sees it now not as a deed done by us but as a sacrifice offered for us. How can his death of long ago benefit us? One answer, specially developed by Paul, is that believers have become identified with Christ in his death and resurrection, and so have died and risen with him: 'We are convinced that one died for all, and therefore all died [*sc.* by union with him]' and 'live . . . for him who died for them and was raised again.'[49] When we reach Romans 6 we shall encounter the same truth.

Thus, Levi paid tithes in and through his ancestor Abraham; Israel sinned in and through Achan; we hounded Christ to the cross in and through his enemies; and in particular, if it is true that we sinned in and with Adam, it is yet more gloriously true that we died and rose again in and with Christ. It is in this way that Adam's sin and Christ's righteousness have been imputed to us or reckoned as ours.

Paul ends this paragraph (12–14), in which he has concentrated on Adam's sin and death, with the briefest possible allusion to the corresponding figure of Christ. *Adam*, he writes, . . . *was a pattern of the one to come* (14b), the Coming One, the Messiah. He will develop the analogy in the next paragraphs. For now, it is enough to call Adam the *typos* of Christ, because he 'prefigured' (jb) and 'foreshadows' (reb) him. Like Adam, Christ is the head of a whole humanity.

b. Adam and Christ are contrasted (15–17)

Paul has called Adam the type or prototype of Christ (14). But he has no sooner made this statement than he feels embarrassed by the anomaly, the impropriety, of what he has said. To be sure, there is a superficial similarity between them in that each is one man through whose one deed enormous numbers of people have been affected. But there indubitably the likeness between them ends. How can the Lord of glory be likened to the man of shame, the Saviour to the sinner, the giver of life to the broker of death? The correspondence is not a parallel, but an antithesis. So before returning to the solitary similarity between them (18–21), Paul elaborates their dis-similarities. 'Adam and Christ stand there', writes Anders Nygren, 'as the respective heads of the two aeons. Adam is the head of the old aeon, the age of *death*; Christ is the head of the new aeon, the age of *life*.'[50] So the structure of each of verses 15–17 embodies a statement that Christ's gift is either *not like* Adam's trespass (15–16) or *much more* effective than it (15–17). The differences concern

---

[49] 2 Cor. 5:14ff.   [50] Nygren, p. 210.

the nature of the two actions (15), their immediate results (16), and their ultimate effects (17).

First, the nature of their actions was different. *But the gift is not like the trespass* (15a). This succinct assertion is almost a text for the rest of the paragraph. Adam's *trespass* was a fall (*paraptōma*), indeed 'the fall', as we call it, a deviation from the path which God had clearly shown him. He insisted on going his own way. With it Paul contrasts Christ's *gift* (*charisma*), an act of self-sacrifice which bears no resemblance to Adam's act of self-assertion. It is this enormous disparity which Paul elaborates in the rest of the verse: *if the many died by the trespass of the one man, how much more did God's grace and* consequent *gift* (presumably of eternal life, 6:23) . . . *overflow* in rich, undeserved abundance *to the many!* (15b).

Secondly, the immediate effect of their actions was different. *Again, the gift of God is not like the result of the one man's sin* (16a). The words are almost identical with those which introduced the previous verse. But now the emphasis is on the consequence of each action. In the case of Adam God's *judgment brought condemnation*; in the case of Christ God's *gift brought justification* (16b). The contrast is absolute. Yet there is more to the antithesis than the two words 'condemnation' and 'justification'. It is that God's judgment *followed* only *one sin*, whereas God's gift *followed many trespasses*. The secular mind would have expected many sins to attract more judgment than one sin. But grace operates a different arithmetic. 'That one single misdeed should be answered by judgment,' writes Charles Cranfield, 'this is perfectly understandable: that the accumulated sins and guilt of all the ages should be answered by God's free gift, this is the miracle of miracles, utterly beyond human comprehension.'[51]

Thirdly, the ultimate effect of the two actions is also different (17). Once more *the one man* Adam and *the one man Jesus Christ* are juxtaposed, and so are the end results of their actions, which now are said to be *death* and *life*. But this time the contrast is subtly modulated in order to highlight the superiority of the work of Christ. On the one hand, we are given the stark information that *death reigned*, not now temporarily from Adam to Moses (14), but permanently. 'The world is a place of cemeteries.'[52] On the other hand, we are not told that through Christ 'life reigned'. The words *how much more*, together with the reference to *God's abundant provision of grace and of the gift of righteousness*, alert us to expect a greater blessing. Even so we are not prepared for what follows, namely that the recipients of God's abundant grace will themselves *reign in life*. Formerly death was our king, and we were slaves under

---

[51] Cranfield, vol. I, p. 286.   [52] Lloyd-Jones, vol. 4, p. 261.

its totalitarian tyranny. What Christ has done for us is not just to exchange death's kingdom for the much more gentle kingdom of life, while leaving us in the position of subjects. Instead, he delivers us from the rule of death so radically as to enable us to change places with it and rule over it, or *reign in life*. We become kings, sharing the kingship of Christ, with even death under our feet now, and one day to be destroyed.

c. Adam and Christ are compared (18–21)

Having completed his contrast between Adam and Christ, Paul now develops the comparison. His sentence structure is no longer either 'not like' or 'how much more' (as in verse 15–17), but 'just as . . . so also' (as in verses 18, 19 and 21). Not that contrast and comparison are mutually exclusive. Even while painting the contrasts in verses 15–17 (between trespass and gift, condemnation and justification, death and life), Paul did not forget the comparison (the one affecting the many). So now in verses 18–21, while emphasizing the parallel, he will not overlook the contrasts. Yet his 'just as . . . so also' structure in each verse is intended to highlight the similarity between Adam and Christ: the one act of the one man determined the destiny of the many.

Verse 18 takes up the immediate results of the work of Adam and Christ, as in verse 16, namely condemnation and justification. Yet the emphasis is on the parallel: *just as the result of one trespass was condemnation for all men, so also the result of one act of righteousness was justification that brings life for all men.*

Verse 19 takes up the nature of their actions, as in verse 15, though using different language. There it was trespass and gift; here it is disobedience and obedience. Yet again the emphasis is on the parallel that *just as through the disobedience of the one man the many were made sinners, so also through the obedience of the one man* (obedience 'to death – even death on a cross!')[53] *the many will be made righteous.* The expressions 'made sinners' and 'made righteous' cannot mean that these people actually became morally good or evil, but rather that they were 'constituted' legally righteous or unrighteous in God's sight. Hodge writes: 'The disobedience of Adam . . . was the ground of their being placed in the category of sinners' and 'the obedience of Christ was the ground on which the many are to be placed in the category of the righteous'.[54] Dr Lloyd-Jones clarifies the situation further for us: 'Look at yourself in Adam; though you had done nothing you were declared a sinner. Look at yourself in Christ; and see that, though you have done

---

[53] Phil. 2:8.   [54] Hodge, pp. 173f.

nothing, you are declared to be righteous. That is the parallel.'[55] Professor Dunn adds that, since 'righteous' (*dikaios*) was 'such a favourite self-description of devout Jews', Paul may be emphasizing that 'the many' who will be finally acquitted will include Gentiles as well. He is 'denying the limited nationalism of the normal Jewish hope'.[56]

Verse 20 is a digression, but a necessary one. Paul has been developing his analogy between Adam and Christ. His Jewish readers may have been asking if there was any room in his scheme for Moses. 'Ought we not to distinguish three ages, ruled by the names of Adam, Moses and Christ?' But no, that would be 'a complete misunderstanding of the role of the law. Adam and Christ are . . . such total opposites that they leave place for no third.'[57]

What then was the purpose of the law? It *was added so that the trespass might increase* (20a). Part of what Paul meant by this he has already explained in previous places. The law reveals sin (3:20; *cf.* 7:7, 13), defining and displaying it. The law turns sin into transgression, since 'where there is no law there is no transgression' (4:15; *cf.* 5:13; Gal. 3:19). In Romans 7:8 Paul will add that the law even provokes sin. These statements must have been shocking to Jewish people, who thought of the Mosaic law as having been given to increase righteousness, not to increase sin. Yet Paul says that the law increased sin rather than diminishing it, and provoked sin rather than preventing it.

God, however, had made ample provision for the increase of sin by the increase of his grace, for *where sin increased, grace increased all the more* (20b). If, as some exegetes believe, the 'trespass' (20a) is an allusion to the specific sin of Adam, and if its 'increase' is its spread and intensification across history, reaching a 'hideous climax' in the rejection of Christ at the cross, then God's abounding grace will refer to 'the divine self-giving of the cross'.[58] This allusion to grace introduces Paul's third comparison between Adam and Christ, in which he takes up the alternative ultimate issues of life and death. It is true that verse 21 contains no explicit mention of Adam, but he lurks behind it all the same in the reference to sin and death. Once more the contrasts are not forgotten, as grace and life are set in antithesis to sin and death. But the emphasis is again on the parallel which compares two kinds of 'reign'. God's purpose is that *just as sin reigned in death, so also grace might reign through righteousness to bring eternal life* (21).

Nothing could sum up better the blessings of being in Christ than the expression 'the reign of grace'. For grace forgives sins through the

[55] Lloyd-Jones, vol. 4, p. 274.   [56] Dunn, vol. 38A, p. 285.
[57] Nygren, pp. 224f.   [58] Cranfield, vol. II, p. 830.

cross, and bestows on the sinner both righteousness and eternal life. Grace satisfies the thirsty soul and fills the hungry with good things. Grace sanctifies sinners, shaping them into the image of Christ. Grace perseveres even with the recalcitrant, determining to complete what it has begun. And one day grace will destroy death and consummate the kingdom. So when we are convinced that 'grace reigns', we will remember that God's throne is a 'throne of grace', and will come to it boldly to receive mercy and to find grace for every need.[59] And all this is *through Jesus Christ our Lord*, that is, through his death and resurrection. The same reference to the mediation of Jesus Christ also concluded the previous paragraph (verse 11) and will conclude the next three chapters (6, 7 and 8) as well as this one.

d. The scope of the work of Christ

The parallel between Adam and Christ, on which we have been reflecting, has led a number of students to conclude that Paul is teaching 'universalism', namely that the life won by Christ will be as universal as the death caused by Adam. Is this so? According to verse 18, one trespass brought condemnation *for all men*, while one act of righteousness brought justification *for all men*. Similarly, according to verse 19, through one man's disobedience *the many* were constituted sinners, while through one man's obedience *the many* will be constituted righteous. With these verses it is natural to associate Paul's statement in 1 Corinthians: 'For as in Adam all die, so in Christ all will be made alive.'[60] For example, Professor Cranfield comments (although on another verse): 'Something has been accomplished by Christ which is as universal in its effectiveness as was the sin of the first man. Paul is no longer speaking just about the church: his vision now includes the whole of humanity.'[61]

One of the arguments which universalists use is that (as in verses 18–19 quoted above) the expressions 'the many' and 'all men' appear to be synonymous and therefore interchangeable. In an often quoted article on *polloi* ('many') in *TDNT*,[62] Joachim Jeremias shows that in Greek writing *polloi* is 'exclusive', referring to the many or the majority as opposed to all, whereas in Hebrew and Jewish Greek literature *polloi* is 'inclusive', meaning 'the many who cannot be counted', 'the great multitude', indeed 'all'. He draws special attention to Isaiah 52:13 – 53:12, where 'many' or 'the many' occurs five times, apparently meaning 'all'. He also points out that

---

[59] Heb. 4:16.   [60] 1 Cor. 15:22.   [61] Cranfield, vol. I, p. 271; *cf.* vol. II, p. 830.
[62] *TDNT*, vol. VI, pp. 536ff.

the expression *the many died* in verse 15 means the same as *death came to all men* in verse 12. Professor Jeremias' case is not conclusive, however. As he himself concedes, *hoi polloi* could mean 'a very large number' in contrast to 'one', rather than 'all' as opposed to only 'some'.

We certainly have no liberty to insist that the word 'all' is invariably absolute and can never admit any qualification, for Scripture itself often uses it relatively of all within a certain category or context, or from a particular perspective. For example, on the day of Pentecost the statement that God poured out his Spirit 'on all people'[63] does not mean every single human being in the world, but people of all categories, of all nations, ages and social strata, and of both sexes. When Luke later declares that 'all . . . who lived in the province of Asia heard the word of the Lord' through Paul in Ephesus,[64] he evidently means representatives from every part of the province.

So in Romans 5 the 'all men' who are affected by the work of Christ cannot refer to absolutely everybody, for a number of reasons. First, the two communities of people related to Adam and Christ are related to them in different ways. We are 'in Adam' by birth, but 'in Christ' only by new birth and by faith. So, although the phrase in a related passage, 'as in Adam all die', means literally everybody without exception, the 'all' who in Christ are made alive are identified as 'those who belong to him'.[65] Secondly, this is made clear in Romans 5:17, where those who *reign in life* through Christ are not everybody, but 'those who receive God's abundant provision of grace'. Thirdly, Paul emphasizes throughout Romans that justification is 'by faith' (*e.g.* 1:16f.; 3:21ff.; 4:1ff.); therefore not all people are justified, irrespective of whether they believe or not. Fourthly, Romans also contains solemn warnings that on the last day God's wrath will be poured out (2:5, 8), and that those who persist in their sinful self-seeking will perish (2:12). This cumulative evidence makes it difficult, if not impossible, to interpret Paul's 'all' as 'everybody without exception' and to believe in universal salvation.

Nevertheless, Romans 5:12–21 gives us solid grounds for confidence that a very large number will be saved and that the scope of Christ's redeeming work, although not universal, will be extremely extensive. There are three indications of this in the language Paul uses in the text.

First, he employs *kingdom language*. Five times the verb *basileuō* occurs, meaning to reign as *basileus* (king), to wield kingly rule, to exercise authority. Three times it is used of the reign of sin and

---

[63] Acts 2:17.   [64] Acts 19:10.   [65] 1 Cor. 15:22f.

death (14, 17, 21), and twice of God's people reigning in life through Christ and of grace reigning unto life. This cannot be taken to teach that both reigns will involve a universal jurisdiction, since all kings in history have ruled over particular kingdoms with limited territories. Nevertheless, Paul's use of the same metaphorical language in relation to both kingdoms surely implies that the reign of life will be substantially comparable to the reign of death, and the reign of grace to the reign of sin.

But the work of Christ is not merely equivalent to the work of Adam. It is more appropriate to contrast than to compare them. Hence secondly the *superlative language* which Paul presses into service, especially the verbs *perisseuō*, to 'abound', 'exist in abundance', 'surpass' or 'overflow', and *hyperperisseuō*, to 'exist in even greater abundance'. Bishop Lightfoot commented on the latter: 'St. Paul is not satisfied with *perisseuein*; he doubles the superlative.'[66] These are the words Paul uses in regard to God's grace and gift (15, 17), adding that where sin increased, grace superabounded (20). Whether he is picturing the ample provision of the harvest, or the abundance of rain, or the overflowing of a river, we must give full weight to his words. What is clear is that he uses them of Christ's work alone; it would have been wholly inappropriate to apply them to the work of Adam. Although Adam's disobedience led to universal sin and death, there has been a lavish extravagance about the grace of Christ, in both quality and quantity, which was entirely absent from Adam and all his works. 'There is nothing parsimonious about grace,' writes Dr Lloyd-Jones.[67] For 'grace is superlative generosity'.[68]

Thirdly, Paul twice employs *a fortiori* ('how much more') *language*, in both cases in order to affirm that *the gift is not like the trespass* (15a). For if through the one man's one trespass the many died (the substance of this is repeated in verses 15 and 17), *how much more* through the grace of the one man Jesus Christ did God's grace and gift overflow to the many (15b), and *how much more* will the recipients of God's abundant grace and gift reign in life (17)! Thus Adam was simply 'one man' (unnamed), whereas Jesus Christ was the special agent of God's grace. The one man committed a trespass, whereas God's grace overflowed in a gift. The trespass led to death, which (it is implied, *cf.* 6:23) was earned, whereas the gift was entirely free and unearned. Three contrasts have therefore been made relating to the actor, his action and its consequences; and all three exemplify the greater excellence of Jesus Christ. For God is superior to man, grace to sin, and life (God's free gift) to death (sin's wage).

---

[66] Lightfoot, p. 294.   [67] Lloyd-Jones, vol. 4, p. 357.
[68] Morris (1988), p. 237.

The deliberate use of these three models of speech (kingdom, superlative and *a fortiori* language) surely justifies the conclusion that the work of Christ will in the end be seen to be much more effective than the work of Adam; that Christ will raise to life many more than Adam will drag to death; and that God's grace will flow in more abundant blessings than the consequences of Adam's sin. When it is asked in what way *the gift is not like the trespass* (15), but enormously transcends it, cautious scholars tend to say that the *a fortiori* is purely logical, not numerical, and means only 'much more certainly'.[69] But this surely falls far short of what Paul's statements warrant. He is affirming that Christ's work is superior to Adam's not only in the nature of his action and achievement, but in the degree of its success. Granted that 'the many' does not mean 'all', or even 'the great mass of mankind',[70] it certainly means 'a very great multitude', in other words, a majority. As Calvin put it, the grace of Christ 'belongs to a greater number than the condemnation contracted by the first man'. For 'if the fall of Adam had the effect of producing the ruin of many, the grace of God is much more efficacious in benefiting many, since it is granted that Christ is much more powerful to save than Adam was to destroy'.[71]

C. H. Hodge, who stood in the same Reformed tradition as Calvin, goes even further than he. Commenting on verse 20, he affirms that 'the gospel of the grace of God has proved itself much more efficacious in the production of good, than sin in the production of evil'.[72] Then on verse 21 he writes: 'That the benefits of redemption shall far outweigh the evils of the fall, is here clearly asserted.' This is partly, he explains, because Christ 'exalts his people to a far higher state of being than our race, if unfallen, could ever have attained', and partly because the blessings of redemption 'are not to be confined to the human race', since through the church God's wisdom is to be revealed throughout the ages to principalities and powers,[73] but first and foremost because 'the number of the saved shall doubtless greatly exceed the number of the lost.' He concludes: 'We have reason to believe that the lost shall bear to the saved no greater proportion than the inmates of a prison do to the mass of the community.'[74]

But we do not rely only on Romans 5 for this assurance. We are also persuaded that God will fulfil his promise to make Abraham's seed as numerous as the stars in the sky, the dust of the earth and the sand on the shore. This refers of course to his spiritual family, and that includes all who believe. Abraham is our father now, not Adam, and Abraham's children will far outnumber Adam's. For

---

[69] Godet, pp. 216, 223.   [70] Bruce, p. 124.   [71] Calvin, pp. 114f.
[72] Hodge, p. 177.   [73] *Cf.* Eph. 3:10.   [74] Hodge, p. 178.

when the redeemed are all gathered before God's throne, they will be 'a great multitude that no-one could count', from all the world's nations, peoples and languages.[75]

This expectation should be a great spur to world evangelization. For God's promise assures us that the church's mission will be attended by great blessing, and that a mighty harvest is yet to be reaped. Exactly how God will achieve this result we are not told. All we know is that we are to preach the gospel to all nations, and that God's grace will triumph in the end.

Ultimately our confidence is in the grace of God. 'Grace' is the key word in the three 'languages' mentioned above. Grace will 'reign' (21), grace 'overflows' (15), and much more will those who receive God's grace reign in life (17). This repetition challenges our perspective. Who reigns today? Who is on the throne? Before Christ came, the throne was occupied by sin and death (14, 17), and the world was strewn with corpses. But since Christ came, the throne has been occupied by grace and by those who have received grace, and their reign is characterized by life (17, 21). Verse 21 sums up God's purpose *that (hina), just as sin reigned in death, so also grace might reign through righteousness to bring eternal life through Jesus Christ our Lord.* Is this our vision? In our view of ultimate reality, who is occupying the throne today? Are we still living in the Old Testament, with the whole scene dominated by Adam, as if he remained unchallenged and Christ had never come? Or are we authentic New Testament Christians, whose vision is filled with Christ crucified, risen and reigning? Is guilt still reigning, and death? Or is grace reigning, and life? To be sure, sin and Satan may seem to be reigning still, since many continue to bow down to them. But their reign is an illusion, a bluff. For at the cross they were decisively defeated, dethroned and disarmed.[76] Now Christ reigns, exalted to the Father's right hand, with all things under his feet, welcoming the nations, and waiting for his remaining enemies to be made his footstool.[77]

e. The historicity and death of Adam

It is fashionable nowadays to regard the biblical story of Adam and Eve as 'myth' (whose truth is theological but not historical), rather than 'significant event' (whose truth is both). Many people assume that evolution has disproved and discarded the Genesis story as having no basis in history. Since 'Adam' is the Hebrew word for 'man', they consider that the author of Genesis was deliberately giving a mythical account of human origins, evil and death.

[75] Rev. 7:9.　　[76] Cf. Col. 2:15.　　[77] Ps. 110:1 and e.g. Eph. 1:20ff.

We should certainly be open to the probability that there are symbolical elements in the Bible's first three chapters. The narrative itself warrants no dogmatism about the six days of creation, since its form and style suggest that it is meant as literary art, not scientific description. As for the identity of the snake and the trees in the garden, since 'that old serpent' and 'the tree of life' reappear in the book of Revelation, where they are evidently symbolic,[78] it seems likely that they are meant to be understood symbolically in Genesis as well.

But the case with Adam and Eve is different. Scripture clearly intends us to accept their historicity as the original human pair. For the biblical genealogies trace the human race back to Adam;[79] Jesus himself taught that 'at the beginning the Creator "made them male and female"' and then instituted marriage;[80] Paul told the Athenian philosophers that God had made every nation 'from one man';[81] and in particular Paul's carefully constructed analogy between Adam and Christ depends for its validity on the equal historicity of both. He affirmed that Adam's disobedience led to condemnation for all, as Christ's obedience led to justification for all (5:18).[82]

Moreover, nothing in modern science contradicts this. Rather the reverse. All human beings share the same anatomy, physiology and chemistry, and the same genes. Athough we belong to different so-called 'races' (Caucasoid, Negroid, Mongoloid and Australoid), each of which has adjusted to its own physical environment, we nevertheless constitute a single species, and people of different races can intermarry and interbreed. This homogeneity of the human species is best explained by positing our descent from a common ancestor. 'Genetic evidence indicates', writes Dr Christopher Stringer of London's Natural History Museum, 'that all living people are closely related and share a recent common ancestor.' He goes on to express the view that this common ancestor 'probably lived in Africa' (though this is not proved) and that from this ancestral group 'all the living peoples of the world originated'.[83]

But how 'recent' was our 'common ancestor'? The evidence of Genesis 2 – 4 is that Adam was a Neolithic farmer. The New Stone Age ran from about 10000 to 6000 BC, and its beginning was marked by the introduction of agriculture, the original 'green revolution', which seems to have begun in the region of Eastern Turkey, near the head waters of the Euphrates and Tigris rivers (*cf*. Gn. 2:10,

---

[78] *E.g.* 12:9; 22:2ff.   [79] Gn. 5:3ff.; 1 Ch. 1:1ff.; Lk. 3:38.
[80] Mt. 19:4ff., quoting Gn. 1:27.
[81] Acts 17:26.   [82] *Cf.* 1 Cor. 15:22, 45ff.
[83] From his article 'Evolution of Early Humans', in *The Cambridge Encyclopedia of Human Evolution*, ed. Steve Jones, Robert Martin and David Pilbeam (Cambridge University Press, 1992), p. 249.

14), and which has been described as the most important cultural development in all human history. So Adam cultivated the garden of Eden,[84] and he and Eve made clothing for themselves.[85] Then the next generations, we read, domesticated and reared stock, as well as working the soil and cultivating crops;[86] built a protected settlement, which Genesis graces with the word 'city';[87] made and played musical instruments;[88] and 'forged all kinds of tools out of bronze and iron'.[89]

But surely the human fossil and skeleton record indicates that the genus *homo* existed hundreds of thousands of years before the New Stone Age? Yes. *Homo sapiens* (modern) is usually traced back to about 100,000 years ago, and *homo sapiens* (archaic) to about half a million years ago, *homo erectus* to about 1.8 million years ago, and *homo habilis* even to two million years ago. Moreover, *homo habilis* was already making stone tools in East and South Africa; *homo erectus* was making wooden tools as well and living in caves and camps, while *homo sapiens* (especially the European Stone Age sub-species Neanderthal man), although still a hunter-gatherer, was beginning to paint, carve and sculpt, and even to care for the sick and bury the dead. But were these species of *homo* 'human' in the *biblical* sense, created in the image of God, endowed with rational, moral and spiritual faculties which enabled them to know and love their Creator? Ancient skeletons cannot answer this question; the evidence they supply is anatomical rather than behavioural. Even signs of cultural development do not prove that those involved were authentically human, that is, God-like. The likelihood is that they were all pre-Adamic hominids, still *homo sapiens* and not yet *homo divinus*, if we may so style Adam.

Adam, then, was a special creation of God, whether God formed him literally 'from the dust of the ground' and then 'breathed into his nostrils the breath of life',[90] or whether this is the biblical way of saying that he was created out of an already existing hominid. The vital truth we cannot surrender is that, though our bodies are related to the primates, we ourselves in our fundamental identity are related to God.

What then about those pre-Adamic hominids which had survived natural calamity and disaster (as large numbers did not), had dispersed to other continents, and were now Adam's contemporaries? How did Adam's special creation and subsequent fall relate to them? Derek Kidner suggests that, once it became clear that there was 'no natural bridge from animal to man, God may have now conferred his image on Adam's collaterals, to bring them into the

---

[84] Gn. 2:15.   [85] Gn. 3:7; *cf.* 21.   [86] Gn. 4:2ff.   [87] Gn. 4:17.
[88] Gn. 4:21.   [89] Gn. 4:22.   [90] Gn. 2:7.

same realm of being. Adam's "federal" headship of humanity extended, if that was the case, outwards to his contemporaries as well as onwards to his offspring, and his disobedience disinherited both alike.'[91]

Having thought about Adam's creation and fall, we are ready to ask about his death. 'Adam . . . died.'[92] Why did he die? What was the origin of death? Was it there from the beginning? Certainly vegetable death was. God created 'seed-bearing plants . . . that bear fruit with seed in it.'[93] That is, the cycle of blossom, fruit, seed, death and new life was established in the created order. Animal death existed too, for many fossils of predators have been found with their prey in their stomach. But what about human beings? Paul wrote that death entered the world through sin (5:12). Does that mean that, if he had not sinned, he would not have died? Many ridicule this notion. 'Obviously', writes C. H. Dodd with great self-confidence, 'we cannot accept such a speculation as an account of the origin of death, which is a natural process inseparable from organic existence in the world we know . . . .'[94]

We have already agreed that death is 'a natural process' in the vegetable and animal kingdoms. But we must not think of human beings as merely rather superior animals, who on that account die like animals. On the contrary, it is because we are not animals that Scripture regards human death as unnatural, an alien intrusion, the penalty for sin, and not God's original intention for his human creation. Only if Adam disobeyed, God warned him, would he 'surely die'.[95] Since, however, he did not immediately die, some conclude that it was spiritual death, or separation from God, which was meant. But when God later pronounced his judgment on Adam, he said to him, 'Dust you are, and to dust you will return.'[96] So physical death was included in the curse, and Adam became mortal when he disobeyed. Certainly the Rabbis understood Genesis in this way. For example, 'God created man for incorruption, and made him an image of his own proper being; but by the envy of the devil death entered into the world . . . .'[97] This is why the biblical authors lament death, and are outraged by it. They see it as demoting us, levelling us down to the animal creation, so that we (God's special creation) have become 'like the beasts that perish'.[98] The author of Ecclesiastes feels the indignity of it too: 'Man's fate is like that of the animals; the same fate awaits them both: As one dies, so dies the other. All have the same

---

[91] Derek Kidner, *Genesis*, *Tyndale Old Testament Commentaries* (Inter-Varsity Press, 1967), p. 29.
[92] Gn. 5:5.   [93] Gn. 1:11ff.   [94] Dodd, p. 81.   [95] Gn. 2:17.
[96] Gn. 3:19.   [97] Wisdom 2:23f.   [98] Ps. 49:12.

breath; man has no advantage over the animal.'[99]

It appears, therefore, that for his unique image-bearers God originally had something better in mind, something less degrading and squalid than death, decay and decomposition, something which acknowledged that human beings are not animals. Perhaps he would have 'translated' them like Enoch and Elijah,[100] without the necessity of death. Perhaps he would have 'changed' them 'in a flash, in the twinkling of an eye', like those believers who will be alive when Jesus comes.[101] Perhaps too we should think of the transfiguration of Jesus in this light. His face shone, his clothing became dazzling white, and his body translucent like the resurrection body he would later have.[102] Because he had no sin, he did not need to die. He could have stepped straight into heaven without dying. But he deliberately came back in order of his own free and loving will to die for us.

All this evidence confirms the straightforward statement of the apostle Paul: . . . *sin entered the world through one man, and death through sin . . .* (5:12).

3. United to Christ and enslaved to God (6:1–23)

The apostle has been painting an idyllic picture of the people of God. Having been justified by faith, they are standing in grace and rejoicing in glory. Having formerly belonged to Adam, the author of sin and death, they now belong to Christ, the author of salvation and life. Although at one point in the history of Israel the law was added to increase sin (5:20a), yet 'grace increased all the more' (5:20b), so that 'grace might reign' (5:21). It is a splendid vision of the triumph of grace. Against the grim background of human guilt, Paul depicts grace increasing and grace reigning.

But is his picture not unbalanced? In his concentration on the secure status of the people of God, he has said little or nothing about Christian life or growth or discipleship. He seems to have jumped straight from justification to glorification, without any intervening stage of sanctification. By this omission (so far) he has exposed himself to misrepresentation by his critics. Already they have 'slanderously' misquoted him as saying, 'Let us do evil that good may result' (3:8). At that point he dismissed their charge, but he did not answer it. Now, however, as they rally to the attack, he refutes their slander. This is the topic of Romans 6.

What was their criticism? It was not just that Paul's gospel of justification by grace through faith without works seemed to make

[99] Ec. 3:19.   [100] Gn. 5:24; 2 Ki. 2:11.   [101] 1 Cor. 15:51f.
[102] Mk. 9:2ff., 9.

the doing of good works otiose. Worse than that, it seemed to stimulate people to sin more than ever. For if, in his understanding of Israel's story, the law led to an increase of sin, and sin led to an increase of grace (5:20f.), then logically, in our story too, we should increase our sinning in order to give God the chance to increase his gracious forgiving. They put it in the form of a question: *Shall we go on sinning, so that grace may increase?* (1). They were implying that Paul's gospel of free grace actually encouraged lawlessness and put a premium on sin, because it promised sinners the best of both worlds: they could indulge themselves freely in this world, without any fear of forfeiting the next.

The technical term for people who argue like this is 'anti-nomians', since they set themselves against the moral law (*nomos*) and imagine that they can dispense with it. Antinomianism has had a long history in the church. We meet it already in the New Testament, in the false teachers Jude described as 'godless men, who change the grace of our God into a licence for immorality and deny Jesus Christ our only Sovereign and Lord'.[103] While recognizing antinomianism in others, however, we must not be allowed to conceal its ugly presence in ourselves. Have we never caught ourselves making light of our failures on the ground that God will excuse and forgive them?

Incidentally, it is highly significant both that Paul's critics lodged the charge of antinomianism against him, and that he took time, trouble and space to answer them, without withdrawing or even modifying his message. For this shows conclusively that he did preach the gospel of grace without works. Otherwise, if he did not teach this, the objection would never have been raised. It is the same today. If we are proclaiming Paul's gospel, with its emphasis on the freeness of grace and the impossibility of self-salvation, we are sure to provoke the charge of antinomianism. If we do not arouse this criticism, the likelihood is that we are not preaching Paul's gospel.

Paul's answer to his critics is that God's grace not only forgives sins, but also delivers us from sinning. For grace does more than justify: it also sanctifies. It unites us to Christ (1–14), and it initiates us into a new slavery to righteousness (15–23). These two halves of Romans 6 are closely parallel to one another in at least five respects.

First, both are prompted by the same exaltation of God's grace, verses 1–14 by the statement that 'grace increased . . . so that . . . grace might reign' (5:20f.), and verses 15–23 by the statement that 'we are not under law but under grace' (15).

Secondly, both ask the same probing question about sin in relation to grace. Verse 1: 'What shall we say, then? Shall we go on

---

[103] Jude 4.

sinning, so that grace may increase?' And verse 15: 'What then? Shall we sin because we are not law but under grace?' In other words, does grace undermine ethical responsibility and promote reckless sinning?

Thirdly, both react to the question with the same indignant, outraged, even horrified, expostulation: 'God forbid!' (2, 15, AV). 'By no means!' (RSV, NIV). 'No, no!' (NEB). 'Certainly not!' (REB). 'What a ghastly thought!' (JBP).

Fourthly, both diagnose the same reason for the antinomian question. They trace it to ignorance, especially with regard to Christian beginnings. Verse 3: 'Don't you know that all of us who were baptised into Christ Jesus were baptised into his death?' Verse 16: 'Don't you know that when you offer yourselves to someone to obey him as slaves, you are slaves to the one whom you obey . . . ?' If they had understood the meaning of their baptism and their conversion, they would never have asked their question.

Fifthly, both teach the same radical discontinuity between our old, pre-conversion, pre-baptism life and our new, post-conversion, post-baptism life, and therefore the total incongruity of sin in converted and baptized believers. Both express this by a counter-question. Verse 2: 'We died to sin; how can we live in it any longer?' Verse 16 (paraphrased): 'We offered ourselves as slaves to obedience; how can we repudiate our commitment?'

Having noted these five similarities between the two halves of Romans 6 (1–14 and 15–23), we are ready to examine in greater detail the text of each.

a. United to Christ, or the logic of our baptism (1–14)

Paul begins with a vehement rejection of the notion that God's grace gives us a licence to sin. *What shall we say, then? Shall we go on sinning, so that grace may increase?* (1). *By no means!* (2a). But on what grounds can he be so categorical? At first sight, logic seems to be on the side of the antinomians, since the more we sin, the more opportunity God will have to display his grace. What counter-logic does the apostle propose? Because the first half of Romans 6 is such a tightly packed argument, it may be helpful to outline it in eight steps or stages.

1. We died to sin. This is the foundation fact of Paul's thesis. How can we live in what we have died to (2)?

2. The way in which we have died to sin is that our baptism united us with Christ in his death (3).

3. Having shared in Christ's death, God wants us also to share in his resurrection life (4–5).

4. Our former self was crucified with Christ in order that we might be freed from sin's slavery (6–7).

5. Both the death and the resurrection of Jesus were decisive events: he died to sin once for all, but he lives continuously unto God (8–10).

6. We must realize that we are now what Christ is, namely 'dead to sin but alive to God' (11).

7. Being alive from death, we must offer our bodies to God as instruments of righteousness (12–13).

8. Sin shall not be our master, because our position has radically changed from being 'under law' to being 'under grace'. Grace does not encourage sin; it outlaws it (14).

We need now to consider these eight steps in greater detail.

(i) We died to sin (2)

Paul lays down this fundamental truth as being in itself a sufficient answer to the antinomians. *They* say that believers may persist in sin; *he says* that they have died to it. So *how can we live in it any longer?* (2). The Greek verb is in the simple future tense (*zēsomen*). So the sentence could be translated: 'We died to sin [in the past]; how then *shall* we live in it [in the future]?' It is not the literal impossibility of sin in believers which Paul is declaring, but the moral incongruity of it. J. B. Phillips catches the point in his rendering: 'We, who have died to sin – how *could* we live in sin any longer?'

Paul is drawing attention to the essential anomaly of living in sin when we have died to sin. What, then, does he mean by our having *died to sin*? Let us consider first *a popular misunderstanding*.

Soon after my own conversion, I was taught the following kind of reconstruction. When we die, our five senses will cease to operate. We will no longer be able to touch, taste, see, smell or hear. We will lose all ability to feel or to respond to external stimuli. Just so, it is argued, to die to sin means to become insensitive to it. For example, if we see a dog or cat lying in the gutter, we cannot tell from a distance whether it is alive or dead. But touch it with our foot, and we will know at once. If it is alive, there will be an immediate reaction: it will jump up and run away. If it is dead, however, there will be no response at all. Just so, according to this popular view, having died to sin, we are as unresponsive to temptation as a corpse is to a physical stimulus. And the reason for this, we are assured from verse 6, is that our old nature was in some way crucified with Christ. For he bore not only our guilt but our 'flesh', our fallen nature. It was nailed to the cross and killed, and our task (however much evidence we may have to the contrary) is to reckon it dead (11).

Several commentators appear to hold this view. C. J. Vaughan, for example, wrote: 'A dead man cannot sin. And you are dead . . . Be in relation to all sin as impassive, as insensible, as immovable, as is he who has already died.'[104] Similarly, H. P. Liddon wrote: 'This *apothanein* (to have died) has presumably made the Christian as insensible to sin as a dead man is to the objects of the world of sense.'[105] Even Sanday and Headlam in their usually fine paraphrase write: 'In like manner do you Christians regard yourselves as dead, inert and motionless as a corpse, in all that relates to sin.'[106] And J. B. Phillips writes that 'a dead man can safely be said to be immune to the power of sin' (7), and that we are to look upon ourselves as 'dead to the appeal and power of sin' (11).

There are, however, at least three fatal objections to this popular view. First, it is incompatible with the meaning of the death of Christ. The expressions 'died to sin' or 'dead to sin' occur in this section twice of Christians (2, 11) and once of Christ (10). Since it is a right principle of interpretation that the same phrase recurring in the same context bears the same meaning, we must find an explanation of this death to sin which is true both of Christ and of Christians. What, then, did Paul mean when he stated that Christ 'died to sin once for all' (10)? It cannot mean that at some point he became unresponsive to it, since this would imply that previously he had been responsive to it. To be sure, his temptations were real. But was our Lord Jesus Christ earlier so continuously alive to sin that he needed on the cross to die to it decisively, once for all? That would be an intolerable slur on his character.

Secondly, this view is incompatible with Paul's concluding exhortations. If our fallen nature has effectively died, or we have died to it, so that we are no longer responsive to temptation, it would be unnecessary for the apostle to exhort us not to let sin 'reign' in our body, lest we obey its 'evil desires' (12), and not to 'offer' our faculties to sin (13). Nor later in his letter could he have urged us to 'put aside the deeds of darkness' and not to think 'how to gratify the desires of the sinful nature' (13:12, 14). How could he have written these things if our fallen nature were dead and had no desires, or if we had a 'sanctified disposition' from which the inclination to sin had been removed?

Thirdly, it is incompatible with Christian experience. It is important to note that Paul is not referring in these verses to a minority of exceptionally holy Christians. He is describing all Christians, who have believed and been baptized into Christ (2–3). So, whatever the 'death to sin' may be, it is common to all Christian people. But are

[104] Vaughan, pp. 117, 123.   [105] Liddon, pp. 108f.
[106] Sanday and Headlam, p. 155.

all God's people 'dead to sin' in the sense of being unresponsive to it? No; scriptural and historical biographies, together with our own experience, combine to deny this. Far from being dead, in the sense of quiescent, our fallen nature is so alive and active that we are urged not to obey its desires, and are given the Holy Spirit to subdue and control them.

A serious danger of this popular view is that it can easily lead to disillusion or self-deception. If we struggle to 'reckon' ourselves to be 'dead to sin' (*i.e.* unresponsive to it), when we know full well that we are not, we feel torn between Scripture and experience, and may then be tempted either to doubt God's Word or, in order to maintain our interpretation of it, to resort even to dishonesty about our experience. To sum up the objections to the popular view: Christ did not 'die to sin' in the sense of becoming insensitive to it, for he never was thus alive to it that he needed to die to it. And we have not died to sin in this sense either, because we *are* still alive to it, as Paul's exhortations and our experience demonstrate. Indeed, we are told to 'put to death' our fallen nature and its activities (*e.g.* 8:13). But how can we put to death what is already dead? There must be a better and more liberating interpretation of the death to sin which is true of Christ and of Christians – *all* Christians. So we turn now to *Paul's true meaning*.

The popular misunderstanding well illustrates the danger of arguing from an analogy. In every analogy we need to consider at what point the parallel or similarity is being drawn; we must not press a resemblance at every point. For instance, when Jesus told us to become like little children, he did not mean that we were to copy every characteristic of children (including their immaturity, waywardness and selfishness), but only one, namely their humble dependence. In the same way, to say that we have 'died' to sin does not mean that we must exhibit every characteristic of dead people, including their insensibility to stimuli. We have to ask ourselves: at what point is the analogy of death being made?

If we answer these questions from Scripture rather than from analogy, from biblical teaching about death rather than from the properties of dead people, we shall find immediate help. Death is represented in Scripture more in legal than in physical terms; not so much as a state of lying motionless but as the grim though just penalty for sin. Whenever sin and death are coupled in the Bible, from its second chapter ('when you eat . . . [*i.e.* sin], you will surely die')[107] to its last two chapters (where the fate of the impenitent is called 'the second death'),[108] the essential nexus between them is that death is sin's penalty. This is plain also in Romans, in which we

[107] Gn. 2:17.   [108] Rev. 21 – 22.

read that those who sin 'deserve death' (1:32), that death entered the world through sin (5:12), and that 'the wages of sin is death' (6:23).

Take Christ first: 'the death he died, he died to sin once for all' (10). The natural and obvious meaning of this is that Christ bore sin's condemnation, namely death. He met its claim, he paid its penalty, he accepted its reward, and he did it 'once for all' (*ephapax*), an adverb which is many times applied to his atoning death in the New Testament.[109] In consequence, sin has no more claim or demand on him. So God raised him from the dead, in order to demonstrate the satisfactoriness of his sin-bearing, and he now lives for ever to God.

What is true of Christ is equally true of Christians who are united to Christ. We too have 'died to sin', in the sense that through union with Christ we may be said to have borne its penalty. Some may object that we surely cannot speak of our bearing the penalty of our sins, even in Christ, since we cannot die for our own sins; he alone has done that. Is not the suggestion that we could a veiled form of justification by works? But no, it is nothing of the kind. Of course Christ's sin-bearing sacrifice was altogether unique, and we cannot share in its offering. But we can and do share in its benefits by being united to Christ. So the New Testament tells us not only that Christ died instead of us, as our substitute, so that we will never need to die for our sins, but also that he died for us, as our representative, so that we may be said to have died in and through him. As Paul wrote elsewhere, for example, 'we are convinced that one died for all, and therefore all died'.[110] That is, by being united to him, his death became their death.[111]

Among the commentators only Robert Haldane appears to understand Paul in this way. 'To explain the expression "dead to sin" as meaning dead to the influence and love of sin', he writes, 'is entirely erroneous.' Paul is referring not to a death to the *power* of sin, but to a death to its *guilt*, that is to our justification.[112]

---

[109] *E.g.* Heb. 7:27; 9:12, 26, 28; 10:10; 1 Pet. 3:18.   [110] 2 Cor. 5:14.

[111] Other commentators argue that by his incarnation Christ so completely identified with the old era that sin had authority over him, although he never succumbed to it; and that by his death he gained freedom from its rule (*e.g.* Moo, pp. 396f.). Similarly, Martyn Lloyd-Jones urges that Christ 'died to the realm and to the rule and to the reign of sin' (vol. 5, pp. 103, 121); and that we are 'dead to sin' in the sense that we are 'no longer under its rule', being 'out of the territory and the jurisdiction of sin' (p. 290). This does not seem, however, to be the most natural way to explain the link between sin and death in the expression 'died to sin'. Nor in fact do Christian people seem to be altogether beyond the reign of sin, since we still need to be urged not to let it reign over us (12).

[112] Haldane, pp. 239ff.

Paul's next step is to explain how we may be said to have *died to sin*, namely through our baptism by which we were united to Christ in his death.

(ii) We were baptized into Christ's death (3)

Or don't you know, the apostle asks incredulously, *that all of us who were baptised into Christ Jesus were baptised into his death?* (3). Those who ask whether Christian people are free to sin betray their complete ignorance of what their baptism meant. In order to grasp Paul's argument, three clarifications need to be made about baptism.

First, baptism means water baptism unless in the context it is stated to the contrary. It is true that the New Testament speaks of other kinds of baptism, for example a baptism 'with fire'[113] and a baptism 'with the Spirit'.[114] Some commentators have suggested that Paul here is referring to baptism with the Spirit as uniting us with Christ, and have quoted 1 Corinthians 12:13 as a parallel. But it is safe to say that whenever the terms 'baptism' and 'being baptized' occur, without mention of the element in which the baptism takes place, the reference is to water baptism.[115] Whenever water baptism is not meant, however, the alternative baptismal element is mentioned; for instance, 'with the Spirit'. The reason some have been hesitant to understand Romans 6 as referring to water baptism is usually plain. They fear that Paul will then be held to teach 'baptismal regeneration', namely that the mere administration of water in the name of the Trinity automatically bestows salvation. But the apostle neither believed nor taught this.

Secondly, baptism signifies our union with Christ, especially with Christ crucified and risen. It has other meanings, including cleansing from sin and the gift of the Holy Spirit, but its essential significance is that it unites us with Christ. Hence the use of the preposition *eis*, 'into'. True, at its institution, baptism was said to be into the single name of Father, Son and Holy Spirit.[116] Elsewhere, however, it is 'into the name of the Lord Jesus'[117] or simply 'into Christ'.[118] And to be baptized into Christ means to enter into relationship with him, much as the Israelites were 'baptised into Moses in the cloud and in the sea', that is, into allegiance to him as their leader.[119]

Thirdly, baptism does not by itself secure what it signifies. To be sure, the New Testament speaks of baptism in terms of our washing away our sins,[120] our clothing ourselves with Christ,[121] and even of

---

[113] Mt. 3:11.   [114] *E.g.* Jn. 1:33; Acts 1:5.
[115] *E.g.* Acts 2:38, 'Repent and be baptised . . . .'
[116] Mt. 28:19.   [117] Acts 8:16; 19:5; contrast 1 Cor. 1:13, 'into the name of Paul'.
[118] Gal. 3:27; Rom. 6:3.   [119] 1 Cor. 10:2.   [120] Acts 22:16.   [121] Gal. 3:27.

our being saved by it,[122] but these are examples of dynamic language which attributes to the visible sign the blessing of the reality signified. It is inconceivable that the apostle Paul, having spent three chapters arguing that justification is by faith alone, should now shift his ground, contradict himself, and declare that after all salvation is by baptism. No, we must give the apostle credit for consistency of thought. 'The baptized's faith is, of course, taken for granted . . . not forgotten, nor denied.'[123] So union with Christ by faith, which is invisibly effected by the Holy Spirit, is visibly signified and sealed by baptism. The essential point Paul is making is that being a Christian involves a personal, vital identification with Jesus Christ, and that this union with him is dramatically set forth in our baptism. That is step two.

(iii)   God intends us to share also in Christ's resurrection (4–5)
Verses 3–5 contain references to the death, burial and resurrection of Christ, and to our participation with him in all three events. For the basic theme of the first half of Romans 6 is that the death and resurrection of Jesus Christ are not only historical facts and significant doctrines, but also personal experiences, since through faith-baptism we have come to share in them ourselves. So we read that we *were baptised into his death* (3b) and that *we were therefore buried with him through baptism into death* (4a), *in order that, just as Christ was raised from the dead through the glory of the Father*, that is, through a glorious display of his mighty power,[124] *we too may live a new life* (4b), in fact 'the new resurrection life' of Christ,[125] which begins now and will be completed on the day of resurrection.

Verse 5 seems to endorse this emphasis on our sharing in Christ's death and resurrection, for *if we have been united with him like this in his death*, more literally 'with him in the likeness of his death', *we will certainly also be united with him in his resurrection* or probably 'with him in the likeness of his resurrection'. Exactly what the 'likeness' (*homoiōma*) of Christ's death and resurrection is has puzzled all commentators. It seems to refer either to baptism as representing death and resurrection, or to the fact that our death and resurrection with Christ are very similar to his, though not identical with them. Or it may be better to translate the verse in more general terms: 'For if (in baptism) we have become conformed to his death, we shall certainly also . . . be conformed (in our moral life) to his resurrection.'[126]

These verses seem to allude to the pictorial symbolism of baptism, although its significance stands firm (our sharing in Christ's

---

[122] 1 Pet. 3:21.   [123] Dunn, vol. 38A, p. 314.   [124] *Cf.* Eph. 1:19ff.
[125] Barrett, pp. 119, 123.   [126] Cranfield, vol. I, p. 308.

death, burial and resurrection), even if the symbolism should not be pressed. Sanday and Headlam put it graphically: 'That plunge beneath the running waters was like a death; the moment's pause while they swept on overhead was like a burial; the standing erect once more in air and sunlight was a species of resurrection.'[127] It is far from certain whether the first baptisms were by total immersion, for some early pictures of, for example, Jesus' baptism portrayed him wading in the river up to his waist, while John poured water over him. But the symbolic truth of dying to the old life and rising to the new remains, whatever mode of baptism is used. 'In other words,' wrote C. J. Vaughan, 'our baptism was a sort of funeral.'[128] A funeral, yes, and a resurrection from the grave as well. For by faith inwardly and baptism outwardly we have been united with Christ in his death and resurrection, and have thus come to share in their blessings. What these are Paul now enlarges on, elaborating the significance of his death in verses 6–7 and of his resurrection in verses 8–9, bringing them together in verse 10.

(iv) We know that our old self was crucified with Christ (6–7)

Verses 6 contains three closely related clauses. We are told that something happened, in order that something else might happen, in order that a third thing might happen. *We know that our old self was crucified with him* (sc. Christ), *so that the body of sin might be done away with, that we should no longer be slaves to sin* (6). Perhaps the best way to grasp Paul's logic is to take these three stages in the opposite order. God's end-purpose, he tells us, is our freedom from sin's tyranny: *that we should no longer be slaves to sin.* That is plain.

But before our rescue is possible, *the body of sin* must be *done away with.* This conquest must precede our deliverance. What is it? The 'body of sin' should certainly not be rendered 'the sinful body' (rsv), implying that the human body itself is contaminated or corrupt. That was a gnostic notion. The biblical doctrines of creation, incarnation and resurrection all give us a high view of our body as the God-intended vehicle through which we express ourselves. Perhaps then *the body of sin* means 'our sin-dominated body'[129] or 'the body as conditioned and controlled by sin',[130] because sin uses our body for its own evil purposes, perverting our natural instincts, degrading sleepiness into sloth, hunger into greed, and sexual desire into lust. Others suggest that 'the body of sin' means 'the sinful self' (reb), our fallen, self-centred nature, *sōma* (body) being used here as a synonym for *sarx* (flesh). This seems to suit the context best.

---

[127] Sanday and Headlam, pp. 162f.   [128] Vaughan, p. 118.
[129] Barrett, pp. 120, 124.   [130] Murray, vol. I, p. 220.

Now God's purpose is that this sinful self should be 'destroyed' (RSV) or better *done away with* (NIV). The verb *katargeō* has a wide range of meanings from 'nullify' to 'abolish'. Since it is used in this verse of our sinful nature, and in Hebrews 2:14 of the devil, and since both are alive and active, it cannot here mean 'eliminate' or 'eradicate'. It must mean rather that our selfish nature has been defeated, disabled, deprived of power.

To understand how this has happened we come to the first clause of verse 6, which says that *our old self* (AV 'our old man') *was crucified with him* (*sc.* Christ). This cannot refer to our sinful self or old nature, if that is what *the body of sin* means. The two expressions cannot mean the same thing, or the sentence makes nonsense. No, *our old self* denotes not our lower self but our former self, 'the man we once were' (NEB), 'our old humanity' (REB), the person we used to be in Adam. So what was crucified with Christ was not a part of us called our old nature, but the whole of us as we were in our pre-conversion state. This should be clear because the phrase *our old self was crucified* (6) is equivalent to *we died to sin* (2).

One of the causes of confusion in understanding verse 6 is Paul's use of the verb *crucified*. For many people associate it with Galatians 5:24, where 'those who belong to Christ Jesus' are said to 'have crucified the sinful nature with its passions and desires'. A mental link between these two verses would naturally suggest that here too in verse 6 Paul is alluding to the crucifixion of our old nature. But the two verses are entirely different, since Romans 6:6 describes something which has happened to us (*our old self was crucified with him*), whereas Galatians 5:24 refers to something which we ourselves have done (we 'have crucified the sinful nature'). There are, in fact, two quite distinct ways in which the New Testament speaks of crucifixion in relation to holiness. The first is our death to sin through identification with Christ; the second is our death to self through imitation of Christ. On the one hand, we have been crucified with Christ. But on the other we have crucified (decisively repudiated) our sinful nature with all its desires, so that every day we renew this attitude by taking up our cross and following Christ to crucifixion.[131] The first is a legal death, a death to the penalty of sin; the second is a moral death, a death to the power of sin. The first belongs to the past, and is unique and unrepeatable; the second belongs to the present, and is repeatable, even continuous. I died to sin (in Christ) once; I die to self (like Christ) daily. It is with the first of these two deaths that Romans 6 is chiefly concerned, although the first is with a view to the second, and the second cannot take place without the first.

[131] Lk. 9:23.

But how has the fact that our former self was crucified with Christ resulted in the disabling of our sinful self and so in our rescue from sin's slavery? Verse 7 supplies the answer. It is *because anyone who has died has been freed from sin.* At least that is the AV, RSV and NIV rendering. It seems to lack adequate warrant, however, since *freed* translates *dedikaiōtai* which means 'has been justified'. True, there is some slight evidence from early Jewish literature that *dikaioō* could mean to 'make free or pure' (BAGD). But there is a perfectly good word in Greek for to 'set free', namely *eleutheroō*, which in fact Paul uses in verses 18 and 22, whereas *dikaioō* comes fifteen times in Romans, and twenty-five times in the New Testament, in all of which occurrences the natural meaning is to 'justify'. So surely the verse should be translated 'he who has died has been justified from his sin'. But exactly how are our death and consequent justification (7) the basis of our liberation from sin (6)?

The only way to be justified from sin is that the wages of sin be paid, either by the sinner or by the God-appointed substitute. There is no way of escape but that the penalty be borne. How can a man be justified who has been convicted of a crime and sentenced to a term of imprisonment? Only by going to prison and paying the penalty of his crime. Once he has served his term, he can leave prison justified. He need have no more fear of police or magistrates, for the demands of the law have been satisfied. He has been justified from his sin.

The same principle holds good if the penalty is death. There is no way of justification except by paying the penalty. You may respond that in this case to pay the penalty is no way of escape. And you would be right if we were talking about capital punishment on earth. Once a murderer has been executed (in countries where the death penalty survives), his life on earth is finished. He cannot live again on earth justified, as can a person who has served a prison sentence. But the wonderful thing about our Christian justification is that our death is followed by a resurrection, in which we can live the life of a justified person, having paid the death penalty (in and through Christ) for our sin.

For us, then, it is like this. We deserved to die for our sins. And in fact we did die, though not in our own person, but in the person of Jesus Christ our substitute, who died in our place, and with whom we have been united by faith and baptism. And by union with the same Christ we have risen again. So the old life of sin is finished, because we died to it, and the new life of justified sinners has begun. Our death and resurrection with Christ render it inconceivable that we should go back. It is in this sense that our sinful self has been deprived of power and we have been set free.

177

(v)   We believe that we will also live with Christ (8–10)
Verses 6–7 elaborated the implication of Christ's death in relation to us, namely that our former self was crucified with him. Now verses 8–9 elaborate the implication of his resurrection, again in relation to us, namely that we will also live with him. *Now if we died with Christ, we believe that we will also live with him* (8). Commentators are divided as to whether the verb *will live* is logical (future in relation to the death which preceded it), or chronological (future in relation to the present moment). If the former, the reference will be to our sharing Christ's life now; if the latter, to our sharing his resurrection on the last day. It is doubtful, however, whether Paul would have conceived of either without the other. He will write later that, in consequence of the Holy Spirit's indwelling, 'your spirit is alive' and 'he . . . will also give life to your mortal bodies' (8:10f.). Life is resurrection anticipated; resurrection is life consummated.

The guarantee of the continuing nature of our new life, beginning now and lasting for ever, is to be found in Christ's resurrection. *For we know that since Christ was raised from the dead, he cannot die again* (9a). This is because he was not resuscitated, brought back to this life, in which case like Lazarus he would have had to die again. Instead he was resurrected, raised to an altogether new plane of living, from which there will never be any question of return. *Death no longer has mastery over him* (9b). Having been delivered from its tyranny, he has passed beyond its jurisdiction for ever. As the glorified Lord himself declares: 'I am the Living One; I was dead, and behold I am alive for ever and ever!'[132]

Next Paul summarizes in a neat epigram the death and resurrection of Jesus about which he has been writing. As he does so, although he implies that they belong together and must never be separated, he also indicates that there are radical differences between them. *The death he died, he died to sin once for all; but the life he lives, he lives to God* (10). There is a difference of time (the past event of death, the present experience of life), of nature (he died to sin, bearing its penalty, but lives to God, seeking his glory), and of quality (the death 'once for all', the resurrection life continuous). These differences are of importance for our understanding not only of the work of Christ but also of our Christian discipleship, which, by our union with Christ, begins with a once-for-all death to sin and continues with an unending life of service to God.

A homely illustration may help. Imagine an elderly believer called John Jones, who is looking back over his long life. It is divided by his conversion into two halves, the old self (John Jones before his

---

[132] Rev. 1:18.

conversion) and the new self (John Jones after his conversion). These are not his two natures, but his two consecutive lives. By faith and baptism John Jones was united to Christ. His old self died with Christ to sin, its penalty borne and finished. At the same time John Jones rose again with Christ, a new man, to live a new life unto God. John Jones is every believer. We are John Jones if we are one with Christ. We died with Christ (6–7); we have risen with Christ (8–9). Our old life terminated with the judicial death it deserved; our new life began with a resurrection.

(vi)   We must count ourselves dead to sin but alive to God (11)
We could put it in this way. If Christ's death was a death to sin (which it was), and if his resurrection was a resurrection to God (which it was), and if by faith-baptism we have been united to Christ in his death and resurrection (which we have been), then we ourselves have died to sin and risen to God. We must therefore 'reckon' (AV), 'consider' (RSV), 'regard' (NEB), 'look upon' (JBP) or *count* (NIV) ourselves *dead to sin but alive to God in*, or by reason of our union with, *Christ Jesus* (11).

This 'reckoning' is not make-believe. It is not screwing up our faith to believe what we do not believe. We are not to pretend that our old nature has died, when we know perfectly well it has not. Instead we are to realize and remember that our former self did die with Christ, thus putting an end to its career. We are to consider what in fact we are, namely *dead to sin and alive to God* (11), like Christ (10). Once we grasp this, that our old life has ended, with the score settled, the debt paid and the law satisfied, we shall want to have nothing more to do with it.

Let me revert to John Jones. We saw that his life was divided into two halves, his biography into two volumes. Volume 1 ended with the judicial death of his former self; volume 2 opened with his resurrection. He must remember these facts about himself. It is not to pretence that Paul calls him, but to reflection and recol-lection. He has to keep reminding himself: 'Volume 1 is long since closed. I am now living in volume 2. It is inconceivable that I should reopen volume 1, as if my death and resurrection with Christ had never taken place.'

Can a married woman live as though she were still single? Well, yes, I suppose she could. It is not impossible. But let her remem-ber who she is. Let her feel her wedding ring, the symbol of her new life of union with her husband, and she will want to live accordingly. Can born-again Christians live as though they were still in their sins? Well, yes, I suppose they could, at least for a while. It is not impossible. But let them remember who they are. Let them recall their baptism, the symbol of their new life of union

179

with Christ, and they will want to live accordingly.

So the major secret of holy living is in the mind. It is in knowing (6) that our former self was crucified with Christ, in knowing (3) that baptism into Christ is baptism into his death and resurrection, and in considering (11, RSV) that through Christ we are dead to sin and alive to God. We are to recall, to ponder, to grasp, to register these truths until they are so integral to our mindset that a return to the old life is unthinkable. Regenerate Christians should no more contemplate a return to unregenerate living than adults to their childhood, married people to their singleness or discharged prisoners to their prison cell. For our union with Jesus Christ has severed us from the old life and committed us to the new. Our baptism stands between the two like a door between two rooms, closing on the one and opening into the other. We have died, and we have risen. How can we possibly live again in what we have died to?

(vii)   We must therefore offer ourselves to God (12–14)
The word *therefore* introduces the conclusion of Paul's argument. Because Christ died to sin and lives to God, and because through union with Christ we are ourselves 'dead to sin but alive to God', and must 'count' or consider ourselves so, therefore our whole attitude to sin and to God must change. Do not offer yourselves *to sin* (13a), because you have died to it; but offer yourselves *to God* (13b), because you have risen to live for his glory. This is the emphasis of these verses.

Paul's exhortation has negative and positive aspects, which complement one another. The negative comes first. *Therefore do not let sin reign in your mortal body so that you obey its evil desires* (12). Paul's use of the adjective 'mortal' shows that it is our physical body to which he is referring. Not all its desires are evil, as we saw when considering the meaning of 'the body of sin' (6), but sin can use our body as a bridgehead through which to govern us. So Paul calls us to rise up in rebellion against sin. 'Precisely because we are "free from sin", we have to fight against it.'[133] The Roman Christians 'must revolt in the name of their rightful ruler, God, against sin's unsurping rule.'[134] A second negative exhortation follows: *Do not offer the parts of your body to sin, as instruments of wickedness* (13a). Since the *body* seems again to be our material frame, its *parts* (*melē*) are likely to be our various limbs or organs (eyes and ears, hands and feet), although probably including our human faculties or capacities, which can be used by sin as *instruments of wickedness*. *Hopla* is a general word for tools, implements or instruments of any kind, though some think sin is here personified as a military

---

[133] Nygren, p. 263.   [134] Cranfield, vol. I, pp. 316f.

commander to whom it would be possible to offer our organs and faculties as 'weapons'.[135]

Instead of giving in to sin, letting it rule over our bodies and surrendering them to its service, Paul now exhorts us to the positive alternative: *rather offer yourselves to God* (13b). Whereas the command not to offer ourselves to sin was in the present tense, indicating that we must not go on doing it, the exhortation to offer ourselves to God is an aorist, which is clearly significant. Although it may not be a call for a once-for-all surrender, it at least suggests 'deliberate and decisive commitment'.[136] As with the negative prohibitions, so with the positive commands, Paul looks beyond a general self-offering to the presentation of *the parts* (again both members and faculties) of our bodies to God, this time *as instruments* (or weapons) *of righteousness* (13c).

And the ground on which these exhortations are based is that we *have been brought from death to life* (13b). The logic is clear. Since we have died to sin, it is inconceivable that we should let sin reign in us or offer ourselves to it. Since we are alive to God, it is only appropriate that we should offer ourselves and our faculties to him. This theme of life and death, or rather death and life, runs right through this section. Christ died and rose. We have died and risen with him. We must therefore regard ourselves as dead to sin and alive to God. And, as those who are alive from death, we must offer ourselves to his service.

The apostle now supplies a further reason for offering ourselves not to sin but to God. It is that *sin shall not* (he is expressing an assurance, even a promise, not a command) *be your master*. Why not? *Because you are not under law, but under grace* (14). This is the ultimate secret of freedom from sin. Law and grace are the opposing principles of the old and the new orders, of Adam and of Christ. To be *under law* is to accept the obligation to keep it and so to come under its curse or condemnation.[137] To be *under grace* is to acknowledge our dependence on the work of Christ for salvation, and so to be justified rather than condemned, and thus set free. For 'those who know themselves freed from condemnation are free to resist sin's unsurped power with new strength and boldness'.[138]

Thus the first half of Romans 6 is wedged between two notable references to sin and grace. In the first verse the question is asked whether grace encourages sin; in the last verse (14) the answer is given that, on the contrary, grace discourages and even outlaws sin. It is law which provokes and increases sin (5:20); grace opposes it.

[135] *Cf.* Rom. 13:12; 2 Cor. 6:7; 10:4.   [136] Dunn, vol. 38A, p. 338.
[137] Gal. 3:10.   [138] Cranfield, vol. I, p. 320.

Grace lays upon us the responsibility of holiness. This was William Tyndale's thought as he concluded his *Prologue on ... Romans* (1526):

> Now go to, reader ... Remember that Christ made not this atonement, that thou shouldest anger God again; neither died he for thy sins, that thou shouldest live still in them; neither cleansed he thee, that thou shouldest return (as a swine) unto thine old puddle again; but that thou shouldest be a new creature and live a new life after the will of God and not of the flesh.

b.   Enslaved to God, or the logic of our conversion (15–23)

Verse 15 (*Shall we sin because we are not under law but under grace?*) is clearly parallel to verse 1 ('Shall we go on sinning, so that grace may increase?'). True, there are differences between sinning and persisting in sin, and between sinning *so that* grace may increase and sinning *because* we are under grace. But these are minor. Substantially the same question is being asked in both verses, namely whether grace sanctions sin, and even encourages it. And in both cases it calls forth from the apostle the same vehement protest: *By no means!* (2, 15).

We might say that Paul has rewound the tape, and will now replay it, although with two significant shifts of emphasis. First, although he develops the same argument that freedom to sin is fundamentally incompatible with our Christian reality, he describes this in terms of our being united to Christ in verses 3–14 and of our being enslaved to God in verses 16–23. It is not only the figure of speech which is different, however, namely 'dead to sin but alive to God' (11) and 'free from sin and ... slaves to God' (22). It is also and secondly how these radical changes came about. The emphasis of the former is on what was done to us (we were united to Christ), while the emphasis of the latter is on what we did (we offered ourselves to God to obey him). The passive statement alludes to our baptism (we were baptized), whereas the active is properly called conversion (we turned from sin to God), although of course only grace enabled us to do it.

What Paul does in the second half of Romans 6 is to draw out the logic of our conversion, as in the first half he has drawn out the logic of our baptism. In both cases his argument begins with the same astonished question, 'Don't you know?' (3, 16), and continues by probing our understanding of our Christian beginnings. Since through baptism we were united to Christ, and in consequence are dead to sin and alive to God, how can we possibly live in sin? Since through conversion we offered ourselves to God to be his slaves, and in consequence are committed to obedience, how can we possibly claim freedom to sin?

(i)   The principle: self-surrender leads to slavery (16)
The apostle's basic question to his readers is this: *Don't you know that when you offer yourselves to someone to obey him as slaves, you are slaves to the one whom you obey?* (16a). The concept may surprise us because we tend to think of Roman slaves as having been either captured in war or bought in the marketplace, not as having offered themselves. But there was such a thing as voluntary slavery. 'People in dire poverty could offer themselves as slaves to someone simply in order to be fed and housed.'[139] Paul's point is that those who thus offered themselves invariably had their offer accepted. They could not expect to give themselves to a slave-master and simultaneously retain their freedom. It is the same with spiritual slavery. Self-surrender leads inevitably to slavery, *whether* we thus become *slaves to sin, which leads to death, or to obedience, which leads to righteousness* (16b). The notion of slavery to sin is readily intelligible (not least because Jesus spoke of it),[140] and so is the fact that it leads to death (separation from God both here and hereafter), since at the end of the chapter Paul will refer to death as the 'wages' which sin pays (23). It is less easy, however, to understand his apparently inexact parallels. As the alternative to being 'slaves to sin' one might have expected 'slaves to Christ' rather than 'slaves to obedience', and as the alternative to 'death' the expectation would be 'life' rather than 'righteousness'. Yet the idea of being 'obedient to obedience' is a dramatic way of emphasizing that obedience is the very essence of slavery, and 'righteousness' in the sense of justification is almost a synonym of life (*cf.* 5:18). At least Paul's general meaning is beyond doubt. Conversion is an act of self-surrender; self-surrender leads inevitably to slavery; and slavery demands a total, radical, exclusive obedience. For no-one can be the slave of two masters, as Jesus said.[141] So, once we have offered ourselves to him as his slaves, we are permanently and unconditionally at his disposal. There is no possibility of going back on this. Having chosen our master, we have no further choice but to obey him.

(ii)   The application: conversion involves an exchange of slaveries (17–18)
Having laid down the principle that surrender leads to slavery, Paul applies it to his Roman readers, reminding them that their conversion involved an exchange of slaveries. Indeed, so complete is the change which has taken place in their lives that he breaks out into a

[139] Ziesler (1989), p. 167.   [140] Jn. 8:34.   [141] Mt. 6:24.

spontaneous doxology: *Thanks be to God!* He then sums up their experience in four stages, which concern what they used to be (*slaves to sin*), what they did (*wholeheartedly obeyed*), what happened to them (*set free from sin*) and what they had become (*slaves to righteousness*).

First, *you used to be slaves to sin* (17a). Paul does not mince his words. All human beings are slaves, and there are only two slaveries, to sin and to God. Conversion is a transfer from the one to the other. Secondly, *you wholeheartedly obeyed the form of teaching to which you were entrusted* (17b). This is a most unusual description of conversion. That they had 'obeyed' is understandable, since the proper response to the gospel is 'the obedience of faith' (1:5, RSV). But here it is not God or Christ whom they are said to have obeyed, but a certain *form* (RSV 'standard') *of teaching*. This must have been a 'pattern of sound teaching,[142] or structure of apostolic instruction, which probably included both elementary gospel doctrine[143] and elementary personal ethics.[144] Paul evidently sees conversion not only as trusting in Christ but as believing and acknowledging the truth.[145] Moreover, Paul writes not that this teaching was committed to them, but that they were committed (*entrusted*) to it. The verb he uses is *paradidōmi*, which is the regular word for passing on a tradition. 'One expects the doctrine to be handed over to the hearers,' writes C. K. Barrett, 'not the hearers to the doctrine. But Christians are not (like the Rabbis) masters of a tradition; they are themselves created by the word of God, and remain in subjection to it.'[146]

Thirdly, the Romans *have been set free from sin* (18a), emancipated from its slavery. Not that they have become perfect, for they are still capable of sinning (*e.g.* 12–13), but rather that they have been decisively rescued out of the lordship of sin into the lordship of God, out of the dominion of darkness into the kingdom of Christ.[147] In consequence, fourthly, they *have become slaves to righteousness* (18b). So decisive is this transfer by the grace and power of God from the slavery of sin to the slavery of righteousness that Paul cannot restrain himself from thanksgiving.

(iii)   The analogy: both slaveries develop (19)
Verse 19 begins with a kind of apology by Paul for the *human terms* in which he has been describing conversion. For slavery is not an altogether accurate or appropriate metaphor of the Christian life. It

---

[142] 2 Tim. 1:13.   [143] *E.g.* 1 Cor. 15:3f.   [144] *E.g.* 1 Thes. 4:1ff.

[145] For 'believing' the truth see 2 Thes. 2:12f.; 1 Tim. 4:3; for 'knowing' or 'acknowledging' it see Jn. 8:32; 1 Tim. 2:4; 2 Tim. 2:25 and Tit. 1:11; and for 'obeying' the truth see Rom. 2:8; Gal. 5:7 and 1 Pet. 1:22.

[146] Barrett, p. 132.   [147] Col. 1:13.

indicates well the exclusivity of our allegiance to the Lord Christ, but neither the easy fit of his yoke, nor the gentleness of the hand that lays it on us,[148] nor indeed the liberating nature of his service. Why then did the apostle use it? He gives his reason: *because you are weak in your natural selves* (*sarx*, 'flesh'), or 'because of your natural limitations' (19a, RSV). Their natural 'weakness' or 'limitations' must be a reference to their fallenness, either in their minds, so that they are dull of perception, or in their characters, so that they are vulnerable to temptation and need to be reminded of the obedience to which they have committed themselves.

In spite of his apologetic explanation, Paul continues to compare and contrast the two slaveries. But this time he draws an analogy between them (*Just as . . . so now*) in the way they both develop. Neither slavery is static. Both are dynamic, the one steadily deteriorating, the other steadily progressing. *Just as you used to offer the parts of your body in slavery to impurity and to ever-increasing wickedness* (literally 'and of lawlessness unto lawlessness', or 'making for moral anarchy', NEB, REB), *so now offer them* (which you have done already, but will be wise to do again) *in slavery to righteousness leading to holiness* (19b; *hagiasmos*, the process of sanctification, that is, of being changed into the likeness of Christ). Thus despite the antithesis between them, an analogy is also drawn between the grim process of moral deterioration and the glorious process of moral transformation.

(iv)   The paradox: slavery is freedom and freedom is slavery (20–22)
Still the comparison and contrast between the two slaveries continue. This time the apostle points out that each slavery is also a kind of freedom, although the one is authentic and the other spurious. Similarly, each freedom is a kind of slavery, although the one is degrading and the other ennobling. On the one hand, he writes, *When you were slaves to sin, you were free from the control of righteousness* (20), although that sort of freedom is better called licence. On the other hand, he writes: *But now . . . you have been set free from sin and have become slaves to God* (22a), although that sort of slavery is better called liberty. Moreover, the way to assess the rival claims of these two slaveries or freedoms is by evaluating their *benefit*, literally their 'fruit'. The negative benefits of slavery to sin and freedom from righteousness are remorse in the present (a sense of guilt over *the things you are now ashamed of*, or 'blush to remember', JBP), and in the end *death* (21), here surely meaning the eternal death of separation from God in hell, which is called in the final chapters of the book of Revelation 'the second death'.[149] *But*

---

[148] Mt. 11:29f.   [149] *E.g.* Rev. 20:14; 21:8.

now, Paul goes on, the positive benefits of freedom from sin and slavery to God are *holiness* in the present and in the end *eternal life* (22b), surely here meaning fellowship with God in heaven. Thus there is a freedom which spells death, and a bondage which spells life.

(v)   The conclusion: the ultimate antithesis (23)

In this final verse of the chapter Paul continues his stark antithesis between sin (personified) and God, whom he has characterized throughout as the alternative slave-masters, to one or other of whom all human beings are in bondage. Those who are in Adam serve sin, while those who are in Christ serve God. He also repeats the warning that these two slaveries are so diametrically opposed to each other that the ultimate destinies to which they lead are either *death* or *eternal life*. What is new is the third contrast, which concerns the terms of service on which the two slave-owners operate. *For the wages of sin is death, but the gift of God is eternal life in Christ Jesus our Lord* (23). Thus sin pays *wages* (you get what you deserve), but God gives a free *gift* (you are given what you do not deserve). *Opsōnia* normally refers to 'ration [money] paid to a soldier' (BAGD), but in this context perhaps to 'the pocket money allowed to slaves'.[150] *Charisma*, on the other hand, is a gift of God's grace. If, then, we are determined to get what we deserve, it can only be death; by contrast, eternal life is God's gift, wholly free and utterly undeserved. The only ground on which this gift is bestowed is the atoning death of Christ, and the only condition of receiving it is that we are *in Christ Jesus our Lord*, that is, personally united to him by faith.

Here, then, are two lives which are totally opposed to each other. Jesus portrayed them as the broad road which leads to destruction and the narrow road which leads to life.[151] Paul calls them two slaveries. By birth we are in Adam, the slaves of sin; by grace and faith we are in Christ, the slaves of God. Bondage to sin yields no return except shame and ongoing moral deterioration, culminating in the death we deserve. Bondage to God, however, yields the precious fruit of progressive holiness, culminating in the free gift of life.

Looking back over Romans 6, we recall that both its halves begin with an almost identical question: 'Shall we go on sinning?' (1) and 'Shall we sin?' (15). This question was posed by Paul's detractors, who intended by it to discredit his gospel; it has been asked ever

---

[150] Ziesler (1989), p. 171.   [151] Mt. 7:13.

since by the enemies of the gospel; and it is often whispered in our ears today by that most venomous of all the gospel's enemies, the devil himself. As in the Garden of Eden he asked Eve, 'Did God really say, "You must not . . ."?'[152] so he insinuates into our minds the thought, 'Why not continue in sin? Go on! Feel free! You are under grace. God will forgive you.'

Our first response must be the outraged negative, 'God forbid!' 'By no means!' But then we need to go further and confirm this negative with a reason. For there is a reason (solid, logical, irrefutable) with which to rebut the devil's devious arguments and with which at the same time Paul brings his high theology down to the level of practical everyday experience. It is the necessity of remembering who we are, on account of our conversion (inwardly) and our baptism (outwardly). We are one with Christ (1–14), and we are slaves of God (15–23). We became united to Christ by baptism and enslaved to God by the self-surrender of conversion. But whether we emphasize baptism or faith, the point is the same. Being united to Christ, we are 'dead to sin but alive to God' (11), and being enslaved to God we are *ipso facto* committed to obedience (16), pledged to 'the total belongingness, the total obligation, the total commitment and the total accountability which characterize the life under grace'.[153] It is inconceivable that we should go back on this by wilfully persisting in sin and presuming on grace. The very thought is intolerable, and a complete contradiction in terms.

So, in practice, we should constantly be reminding ourselves who we are. We need to learn to talk to ourselves, and ask ourselves questions: 'Don't you know? Don't you know the meaning of your conversion and baptism? Don't you know that you have been united to Christ in his death and resurrection? Don't you know that you have been enslaved to God and have committed yourself to his obedience? Don't you know these things? Don't you know who you are?' We must go on pressing ourselves with such questions, until we reply to ourselves: 'Yes, I *do* know who I am, a new person in Christ, and by the grace of God I shall live accordingly.'

On 28 May 1972 the Duke of Windsor, the uncrowned King Edward VIII, died in Paris. The same evening a television programme rehearsed the main events of his life. Extracts from earlier films were shown, in which he answered questions about his upbringing, brief reign and abdication. Recalling his boyhood as Prince of Wales, he said: 'My father [King George V] was a strict disciplinarian. Sometimes when I had done something wrong, he would admonish me saying, "My dear boy, you must always

[152] Gn. 3:1.   [153] Cranfield, vol. I, p. 326.

remember who you are."' It is my conviction that our heavenly Father says the same to us every day: 'My dear child, you must always remember who you are.'

7:1–25
10. God's law and Christian discipleship

Romans 7 is well known to most Christian people because of the debate it has provoked about holiness. Who is the 'wretched man' or 'miserable creature' (NEB) of verse 24, who gives us a graphic account of his inner moral turmoil (15ff.), cries out for deliverance, and then immediately appears to thank God for it (25)? Is this person regenerate or unregenerate? And if the former, is he or she normal or abnormal, mature, immature or backsliding? The different schools of holiness teaching are obliged to come to terms with this chapter.

But it is never wise to bring to a passage of Scripture our own ready-made agenda, insisting that it answers our questions and addresses our concerns. For that is to dictate to Scripture instead of listening to it. We have to lay aside our presuppositions, so that we can conscientiously think ourselves back into the historical and cultural setting of the text. Then we shall be in a better position to let the author say what he does say and not force him to say what we want him to say. It is of course legitimate to seek secondary applications to contemporary questions, but only after the primary task of 'grammatico-historical exegesis' has been diligently done.

If we come to Romans 7 in such a mood of meekness and receptivity, it becomes evident at once that Paul's preoccupation is more historical than personal. He is not answering questions put to him in a Christian holiness convention, but rather struggling with the place of the law in God's purpose. For the 'law' or the 'commandment' or the 'written code' is mentioned in every one of the chapter's first fourteen verses, and some thirty-five times in the whole passage which runs from 7:1 to 8:4. What is the place of the law in Christian discipleship, now that Christ has come and inaugurated the new era?

Before coming to Romans 7, however, we need to ask what Paul has written thus far about God's purpose in giving the law. Paul's reply is couched in almost entirely uncomplimentary terms. To be sure, in theory the person 'who does these things will live by them'.[1] But in practice no human being has ever succeeded in obeying the law. Therefore it can never be the way of salvation.[2] Instead, the law reveals sin (3:20), condemns the sinner (3:19), defines sin as transgression (4:15; 5:13; *cf.* Gal. 3:19), 'brings wrath' (4:15), and was even 'added so that the trespass might increase' (5:20). In consequence, God's righteousness has been revealed in the gospel altogether 'apart from law' (1:17; 3:21a), although the law helped to bear witness to it (1:2; 3:21b). And sinners are justified by God, not through obeying the law but through faith in Christ (3:27). Such faith upholds the law (3:31) by assigning to it its proper function. Abraham himself illustrated this principle, since the way he received God's promise was 'not through law ... but through the righteousness that comes by faith' (4:13f.). This antithesis shows that the whole gospel vocabulary of promise, grace and faith is incompatible with law.

So far, then, almost all Paul's allusions to the law have been pejorative. The law reveals sin, not salvation; it brings wrath, not grace. And these negative references culminate in what to Jewish ears must have appeared his shocking epigram that Christian believers are 'not under law, but under grace' (6:14f.). It is the springboard into Romans 7, which begins with similar statements that we have 'died to the law' (4) and so have been 'released from the law' (6). How dare the apostle be so dismissive of God's law? One has only to read Psalms 19 and 119 to sense the enormous pleasure which godly Jews derived from the law. It was to them 'more precious than gold, than much pure gold' and 'sweeter than honey, than honey from the comb'.[3] How then could the apostle denigrate it as promoting sin rather than righteousness, and death rather than life? How could he proclaim freedom from it? What did he mean that we are 'no longer under law'? Was he declaring it to be abrogated? His words must have sounded like a clarion call to antinomianism.

Moreover, Paul's teaching is by no means of purely antiquarian interest today. For the advocates of the so-called 'new morality', which was first proclaimed in the 1960s but is still popular today, appear to be twentieth-century antinomians. They maintain that the category of 'law' has been abolished for Christians and that the only absolute left is the commandment of love. There are also contemporary holiness teachers who declare similarly that the law has no place in the Christian life. In support of their position they quote both 'Christ is the end of the law' (10:4) and 'you are not under law' (6:14f.), as if these statements meant that the moral law has been

---

[1] Rom. 10:5, quoting Lv. 18:5.   [2] Gal. 3:10f.; 21f.   [3] Ps. 19:10.

annulled. What Paul writes in Romans has direct relevance to this debate.

Whenever we come across a negative statement, however, we cannot interpret it until we discern with what it is being contrasted. For example, if you were to say to me, 'You're not a man' without adding any positive counterpart, you could be insulting me (meaning 'but you're a baby or a pig or a demon'), or you could be flattering me (meaning 'but you're an angel'). Similarly, on my return from a recent visit to the United States, I remarked to a friend, 'I haven't had a bath for a month.' Before he had time to express disgust at my lack of personal hygiene, however, I added, 'But I've had a shower every day.'

What, then, did Paul intend when he described Christians as being 'not under law'? He used this expression in two different letters and contexts, and so in two different senses. He also clarified the meaning of each by the contrasting phrases he added. In Romans 6:14f. he wrote that 'you are not under law, but under grace'. Here the antithesis between law and grace indicates that he is referring to the way of *justification*, which is not by our obedience to the law, but by God's sheer mercy alone. In Galatians 5:18, however, he wrote that 'if you are led by the Spirit, you are not under law'. Here the antithesis between law and Spirit indicates that he is referring to the way of *sanctification*, which is not by our struggling to keep the law, but by the power of the indwelling Spirit. So for justification we are not under law but under grace; for sanctification we are not under law but led by the Spirit.

It is in these two senses that we have been 'freed' or 'released' from the law. But this does not mean that we have been divorced from it altogether, in the sense that it has no more claims on us of any kind, or that we have no more obligations to it. On the contrary, the moral law remains a revelation of God's will which he still expects his people to 'fulfil' by living lives of righteousness and love (8:4; 13:8, 10). This is what the Reformers called 'the third use of the law'.

We are now ready to summarize three possible attitudes to the law, the first two of which Paul rejects, and the third of which he commends. We might call them 'legalism', 'antinomianism' and 'law-fulfilling freedom'. *Legalists* are 'under the law' and in bondage to it. They imagine that their relationship to God depends on their obedience to the law, and they are seeking to be both justified and sanctified by it. But they are crushed by the law's inability to save them. *Antinomians* (or libertines) go to the opposite extreme. Blaming the law for their problems, they reject it altogether, and claim to be rid of all obligation to its demands. They have turned liberty into licence. *Law-fulfilling free people* preserve the balance.

191

They rejoice both in their freedom from the law for justification and sanctification, and in their freedom to fulfil it. They delight in the law as the revelation of God's will (7:22), but recognize that the power to fulfil it is not in the law but in the Spirit. Thus legalists fear the law and are in bondage to it. Antinomians hate the law and repudiate it. Law-abiding free people love the law and fulfil it.

Directly or indirectly Paul alludes to these three types in Romans 7. He does not portray or address them directly one by one, but their shadowy forms are discernible throughout. In verses 1–6 he asserts that the law no longer has 'authority' over us. By dying to it with Christ we have been released from it, and we now belong to Christ instead. This is his message for legalists. In verses 7–13 he defends the law against the unjust criticism that it causes both sin and death. He attributes these instead to our fallen nature. The law itself is good (12–13). This is his message to antinomians. In verses 7:14–25 Paul describes the inner conflict of those who are still living under the regime of the law. If left to ourselves in our fallenness we cannot keep God's law, even though we delight in it. Nor can the law rescue us. But God has done what the law could not do, by giving us his Spirit (8:3–4). This is the experience of those who find their freedom in fulfilling the law.

These three paragraphs of Romans 7 may appropriately be en-titled 'Release from the Law' (1–6), in order to serve God in the Spirit, 'A Defence of the Law' (7–13), against the calumny that it causes sin and death, and 'The Weakness of the Law' (14–25), because it can neither justify nor sanctify sinners.

1. Release from the law: a marriage metaphor (1–6)

Paul begins this paragraph by addressing his readers affectionately as *brothers* and by asking them for the third time: *Do you not know?* Having questioned their understanding both of the meaning of baptism (6:3) and of the implication of slavery (6:16), he now asks if they know the limited jurisdiction of the law. There can be no doubt that the dominant theme of the paragraph concerns 'release from the law', since he uses this expression three times (2, 3, 6), and refers to the law in every verse. He assumes that they do know, since he adds in parenthesis that he is *speaking to men who know the law*, the Jewish law certainly and the Roman law probably as well.

a. The legal principle (1)

Paul lays down the principle which he assumes his readers know: *the law has authority over a man only as long as he lives* (1). Or better, 'the law is binding on a person only during his life' (rsv). The word for 'is binding on' or 'has authority over' is *kyrieuō*, which is rendered 'lord it over' in Mark 10:42, rsv. It expresses the imperious authority of law over those who are subject to it. But this authority is limited to our lifetime. The one thing which invalidates it is death. Death brings release from all contractual obligations involving the dead person. If death supervenes, relationships established and protected by law are *ipso facto* terminated. So law is for life; death annuls it. Paul states this as a legal axiom, universally accepted and unchallengeable.

b. The domestic illustration (2–3)

As an example of this general principle Paul chooses marriage, and in applying it extends it. Death changes not only the obligations of the dead person (it is obvious that these are cancelled), but also the obligations of those survivors who had a contract with the dead person. *For example, by law a married woman is bound to her husband as long as he is alive* (or 'until death parts them'), *but if her husband dies, she is released* ('discharged', rsv, neb) from her marriage vows, indeed *from the law of marriage* itself (2), literally 'from the law of her husband' (av), that is, from the law relating to him and her contract with him. The contrast is clear: the law binds her, but his death frees her. Moreover, her release is complete. The strong verb used (*katargeō*) can mean to 'annul' or 'destroy'. 'The apostle is saying that the woman's status as a wife has been abolished, completely done away. She is no longer a wife.'[4]

So then, Paul now draws a conclusion, *if she* (sc. a married woman) *marries another man while her husband is still alive, she is called an adulteress* (she 'incurs the stigma of adultery', jbp). *But if her husband dies*, and she remarries, *she is not an adulteress* (3), because she has been *released from that law* which had previously bound her. What has made the difference? How is it that one remarriage would make her an adulteress, while the other would not? The answer lies of course in her husband's death. The second marriage is morally legitimate because death has terminated the first. Only death can secure freedom from the marriage law and therefore the right to remarry. These references to death, freedom from law and remarriage already hint at the application which Paul is about to make.

c. The theological application (4)

Paul turns from human laws to the law of God. It too claims lordship over us while we live. Indeed, although without explicitly saying so,

---

[4] Morris (1988), p. 271.

the apostle implies that we were previously married to the law and so under its authority. But as death terminates a marriage contract and permits remarriage, so we *also died to the law through the body of Christ*, so that we might remarry or *belong to another* (4a).

Two questions confront us about this death which we are said to have died. First, how did it happen? It took place *through the body of Christ*. It is impossible to believe that there is any allusion here to the church as Christ's body. No, it was his physical body which died on the cross. But through our personal union with Christ we have shared in his death (as the apostle has argued in Romans 6), and we may therefore be said to have died 'through' his body. Secondly, what does it mean that we *died to the law*? The expression reminds us of the similar statement that we 'died to sin' (6:2). Indeed, they appear to mean the same thing. For if to die to sin means to bear its penalty, which is death, it is the law which prescribes this penalty. Therefore to die to sin and to die to the law are identical. Both signify that through participation in the death of Christ the law's curse or condemnation on sin has been taken away.[5] 'The death to sin . . . is necessarily also a death to the law's condemnation.'[6]

There are, in fact, many parallels between Romans 6 (freedom from sin) and Romans 7 (freedom from the law). As we died to sin (6:2), so we died to the law (7:4). As we died to sin by union with Christ's death (6:3), so we died to the law through the body of Christ (7:4). As we have been justified and freed from sin (6:7, 18), so we have been released from the law (7:6). As we have also shared in Christ's resurrection (6:4–5), so we belong to him who was raised from the dead (7:4). As we now live in newness of life (6:4), so we now serve in newness of Spirit (7:6). As the fruit we reap leads to holiness (6:22), so we bear fruit to God (7:4).

The purposes of our dying with Christ to the law are now spelled out. The immediate purpose is that we *might belong to another*, namely, *to him who was raised from the dead* (4b). Every reader notices that with this statement Paul's metaphor has undergone a shift. In the marriage metaphor the husband dies and the wife remarries; in the reality it is the wife (formerly married to the law) who does both the dying and the remarrying. Some commentators appear to enjoy poking fun at Paul for his supposed literary ineptitude. Nobody is more scathing than C. H. Dodd: 'The illustration . . . is confused from the outset . . . Paul . . . lacks the gift for sustained illustration of ideas through concrete images . . . It is probably a defect of imagination. We cannot help contrasting his laboured and blundering allegories with the masterly parables of Jesus . . . Paul flounders among the images he has tried to evoke . . .

---

[5] *Cf.* Gal. 2:19; 3:10, 13.   [6] Cranfield, vol. I, p. 336.

We are relieved when he tires of his unmanageable puppets, and talks about real things.'[7] But this kind of sarcasm is unfair, as is also the comparison with Jesus. We must allow Paul to be himself and do what he is intending to do. He is not writing a parable. But neither is he developing an allegory in which every detail of the picture corresponds exactly to something in the reality. His purpose is admirably served by the essence of his illustration, which is that death has secured our release from the law and our remarriage to Christ.

If the immediate purpose of our dying with Christ to the law is that we may now belong to Christ, the ultimate purpose is *that we might bear fruit to God* (4c). Some commentators believe that Paul is continuing his marriage metaphor, and that 'fruit' refers to the children of the marriage. 'It can hardly be doubted [*sc.* because of the context]', writes C. K. Barrett, 'that he [Paul] has in mind the birth of children.'[8] By it Paul 'unmistakably' completes his metaphor, says Godet, and he accuses those who reject it as being guilty of 'prudery'.[9] Martyn Lloyd-Jones goes further and elaborates the parallel. He refers to Ephesians 5:25ff. and to the union of the church with Christ, which he portrays as mysterious, submissive, permanent, privileged and intimate.[10] He goes on: '"Fruit" means children, the fruit of the marriage, the offspring . . . that are to be born.'[11] What is meant? It is 'the fruit of holiness', the fruit of the Spirit.[12] He concludes that the law was impotent to do this. 'But we are now married to One who has the strength and the virility and the potency to produce children even out of us', that is to say, a life which is lived 'to God's glory and to God's praise'.[13]

Other commentators have been very dismissive of this construction. James Denney and Charles Cranfield have both used the epithet 'grotesque' in relation to it,[14] and James Dunn declares that it is 'neither necessary nor appropriate'.[15] Although I do not personally feel quite so negative, I do want to register some criticisms. First, it pushes Paul's metaphor into an allegory, which his explicit development of it does not encourage. Secondly, it gives a forced interpretation of 'fruit' (*karpos*) when the word is not used in this sense in the New Testament (in spite of God's original command to be 'fruitful'),[16] when other words for 'children' could have been used, and when already in the context 'fruit' has been used for 'outcome' or 'benefit' (6:21f.). Thirdly, it depicts the individual Christian as married to Christ, whereas it is the church

---

[7] Dodd, pp. 100, 103.   [8] Barrett, p. 137.   [9] Godet, p. 267.
[10] Lloyd-Jones, vol. 6, pp. 51ff.
[11] *Ibid.*, p. 64.   [12] *Ibid.*, p. 66.   [13] *Ibid.*, p. 66.
[14] Denney, p. 638; Cranfield, vol. I, p. 337.
[15] Dunn, vol. 38A, p. 363.   [16] Gn. 1:28.

which is Christ's bride, as Israel was Yahweh's.

At all events, whether 'fruit' means 'children' or not, all are agreed that the result of being released from the law and joined to Christ is holy living, not antinomian licence. For becoming a Christian involves a radical change of allegiance. At the end of chapter 6 our two slaveries were contrasted. At the beginning of chapter 7 it is our two marriages, death dissolving the first and so permitting the second. Both metaphors speak of our new freedom to serve, which is the topic to which Paul now comes.

d. The fundamental antithesis (5–6)

In the further contrast which Paul now paints between our old and our new lives (*when we were ... But now*, reminiscent of 6:20, 22), he is particularly careful to point out the place of the law in each. In our old life, *when we were controlled by the sinful nature* (literally, 'when we were in the flesh'), our *sinful passions aroused by the law* (provoked to rebellion, as Paul will elaborate in verses 8–12) *were at work in our bodies, so that we bore fruit for death* (5). *But now, by dying to what once bound us*, that is, the law, *we have been released from the law so that* in consequence, far from being free to sin, we are free to *serve* (as slaves). And our slavery to Christ is *in the new way of the Spirit, and not in the old way of the written code* (6). Or literally and more briefly, it is 'in newness of Spirit and not in oldness of letter'.

The distinction Paul has in mind in this neat aphorism is neither between the so-called 'letter' and 'spirit' of the law, nor between the literal and the allegorical interpretations of Scripture, but between the old covenant which was one of 'letter' (*gramma*), an external code written on stone tablets, and the new covenant which is one of 'Spirit' (*pneuma*), for the new age is essentially the age of the Spirit, in which the Holy Spirit writes God's law in our hearts.[17]

We are now in a position to sum up the contrast contained in verses 5–6. It is an antithesis between the two ages, the two covenants or the two dispensations, and so, since we have been personally transferred from the old to the new, between our pre- and post-conversion lives. In our old life we were dominated by that terrible quartet – flesh, law, sin and death (5). But in our new life, having been released from the law, we are slaves of God through the power of the Spirit (6). The contrasts are striking. We were 'in the flesh', but are now 'in the Spirit'. We were aroused by the law, but are now released from it. We bore fruit for death (5), but now bear fruit for God (4). And what has caused this release from the old life

[17] *Cf.* Rom. 2:29; 2 Cor. 3:6.

and this introduction to the new? Answer: it is that radical double event called death and resurrection. We *died to the law* through the death of Christ (4a); now we belong to Christ, having been *raised from the dead* with him (4b).

So we return to the question whether the law is still binding on Christians, and whether we are expected still to obey it. Yes and no! Yes, in the sense that Christian freedom is freedom to serve, not freedom to sin. We are still slaves (6), slaves of God and of righteousness (6:18, 22). But also no, because the motives and means of our service have completely changed. Why do we serve? Not because the law is our master and we have to, but because Christ is our husband and we want to. Not because obedience leads to salvation, but because salvation leads to obedience. And how do we serve? *We serve in the new way of the Spirit* (6). For the indwelling of the Holy Spirit is the distinguishing characteristic of the new age, and so of the new life in Christ.

For our justification, then, we are 'not under law, but under grace' (6:14f.), and for our sanctification we serve 'not in oldness of letter but in newness of Spirit' (6, literally). We are still slaves, but the master we serve is Christ, not the law, and the power by which we serve is the Spirit, not the letter. The Christian life is serving the risen Christ in the power of the Spirit.

Having reached this point, Paul could have gone straight to Romans 8, which elaborates the meaning of life in the Spirit. But he knew that his insistence on liberation from the law would have been so provocative to his Jewish readers that he must take time to anticipate and answer their objections. This he does in verses 7–25, which are really a parenthesis between Romans 7:6 and 8:1. He does not mention the Holy Spirit again throughout the rest of chapter 7.

2. A defence of the law: a past experience (7–13)

We have seen how negative most of Paul's references to the law have been in the letter's early chapters. Further, verses 1–6 of Romans 7 celebrate our release from the law. These verses contain three outspoken expressions of this theme. First, we died to the law through Christ's body in order that we might belong to him (4). That is, it is impossible to give our allegiance to the law and to Christ simultaneously. Just as a first marriage must be terminated by death before a remarriage is permissible, so death to the law must precede commitment to Christ. Secondly, the law aroused our sinful passions, so that we 'bore fruit for death' (5). And this sequence of law–sin–death will have given Paul's readers the distinct impression that he thought the law responsible for both. Thirdly, we have now been released from the law in order to serve in the newness which the

Holy Spirit brings (6). And this new Spirit-controlled life was impossible until we had received our discharge from the law.

All this is strong meat and strong language. The law is apparently characterized as barring marriage to Christ, arousing sin, causing death, and impeding life in the Spirit, so that the sooner we gain freedom from it, the better. It must have sounded to some like full-blown antinomianism. Indeed, the Romans' anticipated re-action prompts Paul to ask the ultimate antinomian questions: *Is the law sin?* (7), and *Did that which is good* (*sc.* the law) ... *become death to me?* (13). That is, is the law responsible for both sin and death, and therefore so deleterious in its influence that we should repudiate it altogether? Is that what Paul is teaching? To both questions Paul immediately responds with his violent negative: *Certainly not!* (7). *By no means!* (13).

We note that this is the second objection to his teaching to which Paul responds. The first was 'Shall we go on sinning, so that grace may increase? ... Shall we sin because we are ... under grace?' (6:1, 15). The second is 'Is the law sin? ... Did the law become death to me?' (7:7, 13). The first is a question about grace, whether it encourages people to sin. The second is a question about law, whether it is the origin of sin and death. So the apostle defends both grace and law against his detractors. In Romans 6 he has argued that grace does not encourage sin; on the contrary, it renders sin inadmissible, even inconceivable. In Romans 7 he now argues that the law does not create sin and death; on the contrary, it is our fallen human nature which is to blame for them.

More fully, in his treatment of the law (to which he has at last come) he performs a skilful balancing act. For he is neither wholly positive towards the law, nor wholly negative, but ambivalent. On the one hand the law is indeed the law of God, the revelation of his righteous will. In itself it is *holy, righteous, good* and spiritual (12, 14). On the other hand, it is unable to save sinners, and its impotence is a major reason for every continuing inner conflict. This, then, is his double theme in the rest of the chapter: first our present section, 'A Defence of the Law' (7–13), followed by 'The Weakness of the Law' (14–25).

a. The identity of the 'I'

As Paul develops his thesis, we are immediately struck by the prominence of the personal pronoun. Both this paragraph (7–13) and the subsequent one (14–25) are full of the first person singular, 'I' and 'me'. Indeed, the debate about Romans 7 is reduced in essence to an enquiry into the identity of this 'I'.

Our first and natural reaction (confining ourselves now to verses

7–13) is that this is a page from Paul's pre-conversion auto-biography. What he writes seems too realistic and vivid to be either a purely rhetorical device or the impersonation of somebody else. At the same time, his references are not so personal as to apply to him exclusively. They are general enough to include others. Consequently, from the early Greek Church Fathers onwards, many commentators have interpreted Paul's experiences as being not only autobiographical but also typical, representative either of human beings in general or of the Jewish people in particular. The options are, then, that 'I' in this paragraph is Paul or Adam or Israel. And the key question is how the four events of verse 9 apply to each: (a) *Once I was alive apart from law*; (b) ... *the commandment came*, (c) *sin sprang to life* (d) *and I died.*

If Paul is describing stages of his own experience, then two reconstructions are possible. The first is that he is alluding to his boyhood. In childhood innocence he was *alive apart from law*; 'the commandment came' at his bar mitzvah when aged thirteen, in which he became a 'son of the commandment' and assumed responsibility for his own behaviour; then with his 'dawn of conscience'[18] *sin sprang to life*; and adolescent rebellion caused his separation from God. That is, he 'died'. It is a plausible scenario, except that a Jewish boy, circumcised on the eighth day and brought up as 'a Hebrew of Hebrews',[19] could hardly be described as being 'apart from law'. On the contrary, it will have been inculcated into him almost from birth. Perhaps therefore we should understand 'alive apart from law' as meaning that he had not yet come consciously under the law's condemnation.

The second possible reconstruction is that Paul is referring to his pre-conversion life as a Pharisee. In this case he was 'alive' in his own estimation, and untroubled by the law, since in regard to legalistic righteousness he was 'blameless'.[20] 'He is speaking', writes John Murray, 'of the unperturbed, self-complacent, self-righteous life which he once lived before the turbulent motions and conviction of sin ... overtook him.'[21] In order to describe what happened then, he set his pre-law and post-law situations in dramatic contrast. Apart from law sin was dead and he was alive, but when the commandment came, 'there was a complete reversal',[22] for sin sprang to life and he died (8b, 9a). It was the tenth commandment which opened his eyes to his inner sinfulness, and so brought him to conviction of sin and spiritual death. The main difficulties with this suggestion are that 'alive apart from law' is not the most obvious description of self-righteousness, and that we have no independent

---

[18] Bruce, p. 139. [19] Phil. 3:5. [20] Phil. 3:6; *cf.* Rom. 2:17ff.
[21] Murray, vol. I, p. 251. [22] Lloyd-Jones, vol. 6, p. 132.

evidence of a spiritual crisis in Paul before his Damascus road encounter with the risen Lord.

So is Paul's 'I' in reality Adam? Although many ancient commentators have understood Paul's experience as typical of human beings, it is modern scholars who have drawn out the parallels between verses 7–11 and Genesis 2–3, and so between Paul and Adam. Ernst Käsemann goes so far as to state that 'the event depicted [*sc.* in verses 9–11] can refer strictly only to Adam', that 'there is nothing in the passage which does not fit Adam' and that 'everything fits Adam alone'.[23] James Dunn makes a more moderate evaluation, although he sees the reference to Adam in verse 9 as 'all but inescapable', especially in this sense: 'before the commandment came, life; after the commandment, sin and death'.[24] And John Ziesler identifies the same pattern in Romans 7:7–13 and Genesis 2–3, namely 'innocence, command, transgression, death'.[25]

One may go even further than this and detect six parallel stages in the history of Adam and Paul. First, Paul's *once . . . alive apart from law* could correspond to the age of innocence in paradise. Second, *the commandment came* could refer to God's command to Adam and Eve not to eat from the tree in the middle of the garden.[26] Third, Paul's statements that sin *sprang to life* and seized *the opportunity afforded by the commandment* (8) could mean that 'sin (the serpent) was in the garden even before man, but had no opportunity of attacking man until the command "thou shalt not eat of it" . . . had been given'.[27] Fourth, Paul's complaint that sin had *deceived* him (11) recalls Eve's complaint that the devil had deceived her.[28] Fifth, Paul's awakening to his sin was due to the prohibition of covetousness (7f.), while the sin of Adam and Eve was similarly one of false desire.[29] Sixth, disobedience to God's commandment brought death to both Paul (9, 11) and Adam.[30] Thus the sequence of law–sin–death, so prominent in Romans, is evident in Genesis also.

These correspondences are striking. At the same time, one could also draw up a list of non-correspondences. Paul is certainly not quoting from the Genesis narrative, for the only verbal parallels are the words *commandment, deceived* and *death*. It is not even clear that Paul is consciously alluding to Adam and Eve, since he does not mention them. The most we have liberty to say is that the two biographies (Adam's and Paul's) ran parallel.

So is 'I' Israel? This alternative is attractively commended by Douglas Moo. He points out, first, that the law throughout

---

[23] Käsemann, p. 196.   [24] Dunn, vol. 38A, p. 401.   [25] Ziesler (1989), p. 182.
[26] Gn. 2:17.   [27] Barrett, p. 143; *cf.* Dunn, vol. 38A, p. 400.
[28] Gn. 3:13; *cf.* 2 Cor. 11:3; 1 Tim. 2:14.
[29] Gn. 3:6.   [30] Gn. 2:17; 3:19.

Romans 7 is the Mosaic law, Torah, so that a reference to Adam centuries previously would be an anachronism, even if 'what is true of Israel under God's law through Moses is true *ipso facto* of all people under "law".'[31] Secondly, he says, 'the coming of the commandment' (9) 'is most naturally taken as a reference to the giving of the law at Sinai',[32] including the tenth commandment against covetousness.[33] Thirdly, he suggests that the sequence of verses 9–10 (life–commandment–sin–death) could be describing Israel's history in a personal 'vivid narrative style'.[34]

At the same time, Dr Moo recognizes that only Adam and Eve before the fall could accurately be described as 'alive apart from law'; and that all others have been from birth 'dead in trespasses and sins'.[35] Conversely, Israel's pre-Sinai period could be styled 'alive without the law' only in the sense of 5:13 that 'before the law was given, sin was in the world', but that 'sin is not taken into account when there is no law'. Dr Moo concludes by reminding us that 'the individual Jew had a lively sense of corporate identity with his people's history', as when at Passover he rehearsed Israel's story as having been his own, so that Paul may well have been identifying himself with Israel in their experience of the law. In this case, '*egō* [I] is not Israel, but *egō* is Paul in solidarity with Israel'.[36]

Most commentators are understandably reluctant, when considering the identity of the 'I' in verses 7–13, to be compelled to choose between Paul, Adam and Israel, and several combinations have been proposed. For example, John Ziesler suggests that Paul's use of the tenth commandment prohibiting covetousness as a paradigm of sin's relation to the law 'enables him ... to make a fusion between the giving of the Law at Sinai and the giving of the command not to eat in the Garden of Eden'.[37] Yet it would be impossible to eliminate the autobiographical element altogether. Perhaps, therefore, Paul is both telling his own story and universalizing it. In brief, his experience (the sequence of comparative innocence, law, sin and death), though uniquely his own, is also everybody's, whether Adam's in the garden, Israel's at the mountain or, for that matter, ours today.

b. The law, sin and death

We return now to the text of verses 7–13, and to the two which Paul asks, namely whether he is teaching that the law is the cause of sin and death.

Question 1: Is the law sin? (7–12).

---

[31] Moo, p. 453.   [32] *Ibid.*, p. 454.   [33] Ex. 20:17.   [34] Moo, p. 455.
[35] Eph. 2:1.   [36] Moo, p. 456.   [37] Ziesler (1989), p. 180.

Must the law be dubbed as being in itself 'sinful' in the sense that it is responsible for creating sin? After his emphatic rejoinder (*Certainly not!*), the apostle begins to delve into the relations between the law and sin.

First, *the law reveals sin*. He has already written that 'through the law we become conscious of sin' (3:20). Now he writes: *Indeed, I would not have known what sin was except through the law* (7a). This probably means both that he had come to recognize the gravity of sin, because the law unmasks and exposes it as rebellion against God, and that he had been brought under conviction of sin by it. In his case it was the tenth commandment prohibiting covetousness which convicted him. *For I would not have known what coveting really was if the law had not said, "Do not covet"* (7b).

Ever since Bishop Krister Stendahl first used the expression, it has been fashionable to speak of Paul before his conversion as having had a 'robust conscience', in contrast to the 'introspective conscience' of the West.[38] The ground for this judgment is that he described himself when a Pharisee as having been 'blameless' in regard to righteousness under the law.[39] But is this an adequate basis for declaring Paul's pre-conversion conscience 'robust'? The 'legalistic righteousness' (NIV), in which he claimed to be blameless, was surely an external conformity to the law. But covetousness (*epithymia*) is internal – a desire, a drive, a lust. Indeed it 'includes every kind of illicit desire',[40] and is itself a form of idolatry,[41] because it puts the object of desire in the place of God. Paul could well have obeyed the other nine commandments in word and deed; but covetousness lurked hidden in his heart, as did other evil thoughts of which Jesus spoke in the Sermon on the Mount.[42] So it was the prohibition of covetousness which opened Paul's eyes to his own depravity. The rich young ruler was another case in point.[43] Paul's pre-conversion conscience, therefore, was neither 'robust' nor morbidly 'introspective'. That is a false polarization. Instead, his conscience was performing its healthy, God-intended function, especially when confirmed by the Holy Spirit. That is, it was convicting him of sin.

Secondly, *the law provokes sin*. Having already said that 'our sinful passions [were] aroused by the law' (5), Paul now writes: *But sin, seizing the opportunity afforded by the commandment, produced in me every kind of covetous desire. For apart from law, sin is dead* (8). *Aphormē* ('opportunity') was used of a military base, 'the starting-point or base of operations for an expedition' (BAGD), a springboard for further advance. So it is that sin establishes within

---

[38] Stendahl, pp. 5, 14.   [39] Phil. 3:6.   [40] Sanday and Headlam, p. 179.
[41] Col. 3:5.   [42] Mt. 5:21ff.   [43] Mk. 10:17ff.

us a base or foothold by means of the commandments which provoke us. This provocative power of the law is a matter of everyday experience. Ever since Adam and Eve, human beings have always been enticed by forbidden fruit. This strange phenomenon is apparently called 'contra-suggestibility', 'the propensity some people have to react negatively to any directive'.[44] For example, a peremptory traffic signal says 'STOP' or 'REDUCE SPEED NOW', and our instinctive is, 'Why should I?' Or we see on a door the notice 'PRIVATE – DO NOT ENTER', and we immediately want to cross the prohibited threshold.

Augustine gives us in his *Confessions* a good example of this perversity. One night at the age of sixteen, in company with 'a gang of naughty adolescents', he shook a pear tree and stole its fruit. His motive, he confesses, was not that he was hungry, for they threw the pears to the pigs. 'I stole something which I had in plenty and of much better quality. My desire was to enjoy not what I sought by stealing, but merely the excitement of thieving and the doing of what was wrong.'[45] 'Was it possible', he asked himself, 'to take pleasure in what was illicit for no reason other than that it was not allowed?'[46]

In all such cases the real culprit is not the law but sin which is hostile to God's law (8:7). Sin twists the function of the law from revealing, exposing and condemning sin into encouraging and even provoking it. We cannot blame the law for proclaiming God's will.

Thirdly, *the law condemns sin* (9–11). We have already looked at verse 9 and asked whether its four stages – *I was alive apart from law, the commandment came, sin sprang to life,* and *I died* – are intended as a description of Paul, Adam or Israel. Our conclusion was that they refer primarily to Paul, but to Paul in solidarity with both the human and the Jewish race. Through this personal experience, he continues, *I found that the very commandment that was intended to bring life actually brought death* (10). In other words, the law condemned him. To explain this further, Paul first repeats the sentence from verse 8 that *sin* seized *the opportunity afforded by the commandment* (he mentions 'the commandment' six times in these verses because it is the role of the law which he is unfolding), and adds that sin first *deceived me* (presumably by promising blessings it could not deliver) and then *through the commandment put me to death* (11). Thus, all three of these verses (9, 10 and 11) speak of the commandment in relation to death; they anticipate verse 13, in which Paul will clarify that what caused his death was not the law but sin which exploited the law.

---

[44] Ziesler (1989), p. 176.   [45] Augustine, Book II.9, p. 29.
[46] *Ibid.*, II.14, p. 32.

Here, then, are the three devastating effects of the law in relation to sin. It exposes, provokes and condemns sin. For 'the power of sin is the law'.[47] But the law is not in itself sinful, nor is it responsible for sin. Instead, it is sin itself, our sinful nature, which uses the law to cause us to sin and so to die. The law is exonerated; sin is to blame. The teaching of this paragraph is well summarized in the question of verse 7 and the affirmation of verse 12. Question: *Is the law sin?* (7). Affirmation: *So then, the law is holy, and the commandment is holy, righteous and good* (12). That is, its requirements are both holy and righteous in themselves and also good (*agathos*), meaning 'beneficent in their intention'.[48] This brings Paul to the objectors' other question about the law.

Question 2: Did the law become death to me? (13).

Certainly verse 10 seemed to implicate the law as being responsible for death, stating that the commandment which 'was intended to bring life actually brought death'. So was the law guilty of offering life with one hand and inflicting death with the other? *Did that which is good, then, become death to me?*

The apostle answers this second question as he has answered the first, with his emphatic *mē genoito*, 'God forbid!' The law does not cause sin; it exposes and condemns it. And the law does not cause death; sin does. *But in order that sin might be recognised as sin, it produced death in me through what was good* (*viz.* the law), *so that* (this was God's intention) *through the commandment sin might become utterly sinful* (13b). Indeed the extreme sinfulness of sin is seen precisely in the way it exploits a good thing (the law) for an evil purpose (death).

In answer to both questions, then, Paul has declared that the culprit is not the law (which has good designs) but sin (which misuses the law). Verses 8 and 11 are closely parallel. Both describe sin as *seizing the opportunity afforded by the commandment*, either to produce sin (8) or to inflict death (11). Take a criminal today. A man is caught red-handed breaking the law. He is arrested, brought to trial, found guilty, and sentenced to prison. He cannot blame the law for his imprisonment. True, it is the law which convicted and sentenced him. But he has no-one to blame but himself and his own criminal behaviour. In a similar way Paul exonerates the law. 'The villain of the piece is sin',[49] indwelling sin which, because of its perversity, is aroused and provoked by the law. Those antinomians, who say that our whole problem is the law, are quite wrong. Our real problem is not the law, but sin. It is indwelling sin which accounts for the weakness of the law, as the apostle will go on to show in the next paragraph. The law cannot

---

[47] 1 Cor. 15:56.   [48] Barrett, p. 145.   [49] Bruce, p. 142.

save us because we cannot keep it, and we cannot keep it because of indwelling sin.

3. The weakness of the law: an inner conflict (14–25)

Having vindicated the law in verses 7–13 as not responsible for sin or death, Paul now proceeds to show that nevertheless the law cannot be responsible for our holiness either. The law is good, but it is also weak. In itself it is holy, but it is impotent to make us holy. This important truth lies behind the whole final section of Romans 7. It depicts the hopeless struggle of people who are still 'under the law'. They are right to look to the law for moral guidance, but wrong to look to it for saving power.

As we turn to this passage, what immediately catches our attention is that, although he retains the personal 'I', Paul changes the tenses of all his verbs. He has been using the past tense: 'Once I was alive apart from law; but when the commandment came . . . I died' (9). This was his past, pre-conversion experience. But now suddenly his verbs are in the present tense: 'What I want to do I do not do, but what I hate I do' (15). It sounds like his present, post-conversion experience. This would be the natural interpretation of the personal pronouns and the present tense. But is this really the Christian apostle who is describing his own continuing painful conflict between what he wants and what he does, between desire and performance? Or is he impersonating somebody else?

Before studying the text, it is essential to probe the identity of this 'I'.

a. Is this 'I' regenerate or unregenerate?

The earliest Greek interpreters from Origen onwards repudiated the view that Paul was referring to his own moral struggles. They could not accept that a regenerate and mature believer like Paul could describe himself as *sold as a slave to sin* (14), when he has just celebrated his transfer to another slavery which in reality is freedom (6:6, 17–18, 22). Could this Paul confess that he cannot do what he wants to do, while he does do what he hates (15)? Could it be Paul who cries out in great anguish and wretchedness for deliverance (24), apparently now forgetting the peace, joy, freedom and hope of the justified people of God which he has previously portrayed (5:1ff.)? So these commentators concluded that Paul was impersonating an unregenerate person, at least until 8:1ff., and was portraying the human being in Adam, not in Christ. Some contemporary scholars who hold this position back it up with a quotation from the first-century Roman poet Ovid: 'I see and approve the better things, but I pursue the worse.'[50]

The western church, however, followed Augustine, who first espoused the view of the Greek commentators but subsequently changed his mind, and then influenced the Protestant Reformers. Their view was that Paul is writing as a truly regenerate and even mature believer. Three characteristics of his self-portrait support this. The first concerns his opinion of himself. He calls himself *unspiritual* (14; RSV 'carnal') and declares that *nothing good lives* in him, that is, in his *sinful nature* (18). But unbelievers are self-righteous and self-confident; only believers think and speak of themselves in self-disgust and self-despair.

Secondly, there is Paul's attitude to the law. He not only calls it *holy, righteous and good* (12), and *spiritual* (14), but also refers to it as *the good I want to do* (19). He states both that *in my inner being I delight in God's law* (22) and that *I myself in my mind am a slave to God's law* (25). So here is a man who not only acknowledges the intrinsic goodness of the law, but who loves it, delights in it, longs for it, and considers himself enslaved to it. This is not the language of the unregenerate. For in the next chapter Paul declares that 'the sinful mind [AV 'the carnal mind'] is hostile to God' and that 'it does not submit to God's law, nor can it do so' (8:7). Paul, however, feels love for the law, not enmity; and is submissive to it, not rebellious.

Thirdly, consider Paul's longing for final deliverance. The wretched man's cry (24) expresses desire rather than despair. He yearns to be rescued 'out of this body of death', that is, out of this present state of sinfulness and mortality into a new and glorious resurrection body. Is not this an example of the inward 'groaning' of God's people who are eagerly waiting for the redemption of their bodies (8:23)?

Such a person, deploring evil in his fallen nature, delighting himself in God's law, and longing for the promised full and final salvation, seems to provide ample evidence of being regenerate and even mature.

Commentators still range themselves on both sides of this debate. The most eloquent recent defence of the 'unregenerate' position is provided by Douglas Moo.[51] He sees Paul as 'looking back from his Christian understanding to the situation of himself, and other Jews like him living under the law of Moses'.[52] What was decisive for him in reaching his conclusion was the contrast between Paul's self-designation here as sin's slave (14) and his statements in Romans 6 and 8 of Christian freedom.

The most cogent statement of the alternative position has been

---

[50] *Metamorphoses*, vii. 19ff.   [51] Moo, pp. 474ff.   [52] *Ibid.*, p. 474.

provided by Charles Cranfield,[53] who writes that these verses in Romans 7 'depict vividly the inner conflict characteristic of the true Christian, a conflict such as is possible only in the man in whom the Holy Spirit is active, and whose mind is being renewed under the discipline of the gospel'.[54]

But neither position is wholly satisfactory. It would be as strange for unregenerate people to want ardently to do what is good as for regenerate people to confess that they cannot do it (15–19). How can a regenerate person, who has been set free from sin (6:18, 22; 8:2), describe himself as still its slave and prisoner (7:14, 23–25)? And how can an unregenerate person, who is hostile to God's law (8:7), declare that he delights in it (7:22)? There is an inherent contradiction here, which makes both extreme positions unacceptable.

Dr Martyn Lloyd-Jones rejects both. Anyone who delights in God's law 'cannot possibly be . . . unregenerate', and anyone who calls himself sin's slave cannot possibly be a 'fully regenerate' person either.[55] The wretched man's cry is entirely incompatible with the profile of a Christian in the rest of the New Testament.[56] He suggests, therefore, that the people Paul is describing are those who in times of revival are 'brought under conviction of sin by the Holy Spirit', feel themselves 'utterly condemned', struggle to keep the law in their own strength, but have not yet grasped the gospel. They are for a time 'neither unregenerate nor regenerate',[57] for they experience 'conviction but not conversion'.[58] He cites John Bunyan's intense agony of spirit portrayed in *Grace Abounding* as an example, and refers to the teaching of several Puritans, especially William Perkins.[59] My hesitation in accepting this view is that what distinguishes the people Paul is depicting, indeed impersonating, is not the unusual situation of revival, but rather their peculiar relation to the law. Their anomaly was that, although they were Christian enough to delight in God's law, they were not Christian enough to obey it. They were making the mistake of looking to the law, instead of to the Spirit, for their sanctification.

Professor Dunn lays his emphasis on 'the eschatological tension of being caught between the two epochs of Adam and Christ'.[60] He believes that Paul is giving voice to his experience as a regenerate Christian, who had indeed died in Christ to sin and the law, but who has not yet fully shared in the resurrection. So he 'is suspended (so uncomfortably) between the death and resurrection of Christ'.[61]

---

[53] Cranfield, vol. I, pp. 340ff.   [54] *Ibid.*, p. 341.
[55] Lloyd-Jones, vol. 6, p. 229.
[56] *Ibid.*, pp. 229ff.   [57] *Ibid.*, pp. 255f.   [58] *Ibid.*, p. 262.
[59] *Ibid.*, pp. 261, 357ff.   [60] Dunn, vol. 38A, p. 396.   [61] *Ibid.*, p. 404.

Consequently the believer's '"I"' is split, suspended between the epochs, divided between my belonging to Christ and my belonging to this age'.[62] This is 'the two-sidedness of the believer's experience',[63] being simultaneously in Adam and in Christ, enslaved and liberated. And the piteous cry of verse 24 is for 'escape from the tension of being suspended between the two ages'.[64]

In response to this explanation, we must certainly agree that Christians are caught in the tension between the 'already' of the kingdom's inauguration and the 'not yet' of its consummation, and that this tension can be painful. But is not the antithesis between freedom and slavery too stark for them to be combined in the same person at the same time? Can we really maintain that all Christians are simultaneously 'set free from sin' and 'sold as slaves to sin'? This is not a tension, but a contradiction.

If we go back to the beginning, and try to construct a profile of the 'I' of Romans 7:14–25, we come up against three stubborn facts which cannot be avoided. First, he is regenerate. If the unregenerate mind is hostile to God's law and refuses to submit to it (8:7), then somebody who loves God's law and longs to submit to it is regenerate. Secondly, although regenerate, he is not a normal, healthy, mature believer. For believers 'used to be slaves to sin' but now 'have been set free from sin' and have become slaves of God and righteousness (6:17ff.), whereas this believer declares himself to be still the slave and the prisoner of sin (14, 23). True, conflict between flesh and Spirit is normal Christian experience, and Reformed commentators have tended to identify Romans 7:14ff. with Galatians 5:16ff. Thus Calvin writes in his comment on verse 15: 'This is the Christian warfare between flesh and Spirit, of which Paul speaks in Gal. 5:17.'[65] But is it? Galatians 5 promises victory now to those who walk in the Spirit; Romans 7, however, while expressing assurance of ultimate deliverance (25), describes only unremitting defeat.

Thirdly, this man appears to know nothing, either in understanding or in experience, of the Holy Spirit. Many commentators have paid insufficient attention to what Bishop Handley Moule called 'this absolute and eloquent silence' in Romans 7 about the Holy Spirit.[66] He is mentioned only in verse 6. Since that verse characterizes the Christian era as the age of the Spirit, one would have expected this chapter to be full of the Spirit. Instead, Romans 7 is full of the law (mentioned , with its synonyms, thirty-one times). It is Romans 8 which is full of the Spirit (mentioned twenty-one times) and which calls the indwelling of the Spirit the authenticating

---

[62] *Ibid.*, p. 408. [63] *Ibid.*, p. 435. [64] *Ibid.*, p. 410. [65] Gal. 5:16f.
[66] Calvin, p. 149.

mark of belonging to Christ (8:9). If then we are looking for a description of the normal Christian life we will find it in Romans 8; Romans 7, with its concentration on the law and its omission of the Spirit, cannot be held to describe Christian normality.

To sum up, the three salient features of the person portrayed in Romans 7:14–25 are that he or she loves the law (and therefore is regenerate), is still a slave of sin (and therefore is not a liberated Christian) and knows nothing of the Holy Spirit (and therefore is not a New Testament believer). Who then is this extraordinary person?

If we approach the question from the perspective of 'salvation history', that is, of the story of God's unfolding purpose, the 'I' seems to be an Old Testament believer, an Israelite who is living under the law, including even the disciples of Jesus before Pentecost and probably many Jewish Christian contemporaries of Paul. Such people were regenerate. Old Testament believers were almost ecstatic about the law. 'Blessed is the man . . . [whose] delight is in the law of the LORD.'[67] The Lord's precepts give both 'joy to the heart' and 'light to the eyes'.[68] 'I delight in your commands because I love them.'[69] 'Oh, how I love your law! I meditate on it all day long.'[70] This is the language of born-again believers.

But these same Old Testament believers who loved the law lacked the Spirit. And the penitential psalms bear witness to their inability to keep the law they loved. They were born of the Spirit, but not indwelt by the Spirit. He came upon special people to anoint them for special tasks. But the prospect of the Spirit's continuous indwelling belonged to the messianic age. 'I will put my Spirit in you,' God promised through Ezekiel.[71] And Jesus confirmed this: 'He lives with you and will be in you.'[72] It seems accurate, therefore, to describe pre-Pentecost believers in terms of 'love for the law but lack of the Spirit'. And even after Pentecost it appears that many Jewish Christians took time to adjust to the transition from the old aeon to the new. To be sure, they loved the law, but they were also still 'under' it. Even those who had grasped that they were 'not under law but under grace' for justification had not all grasped that they should also be 'not under law but under the Spirit' for sanctification. They had not yet come out of the Old Testament into the New, or exchanged 'the old way of the written code' for 'the new way of the Spirit' (7:6).

Hence their painful struggle, their humiliating defeat. They were relying on the law, and had not yet come to terms with its weakness. In order to emphasize this, Paul identifies with that stage of his own

---

[67] Ps. 1:1f.   [68] Ps. 19:8.   [69] Ps. 119:47.   [70] Ps. 119:97.   [71] Ezk. 36:27.
[72] Jn. 14:17.

pilgrimage. He proclaims the impotence of the law by dramatizing it in the vivid terms of personal experience. He describes what happens to anybody who tries to live according to the law instead of the gospel, according to the flesh instead of the Spirit. The resulting defeat is not the law's fault, for the law is good, although weak. The culprit is *sin living in me* (17, 20), the power of indwelling sin which the law is powerless to control. Not until Romans 8:9ff. will the apostle bear witness to the indwelling Spirit as alone able to subdue indwelling sin. Before that, however, he will refer specifically to the law as 'weakened by the sinful nature', and will declare that God himself has done what the sin-weakened law could not do. He sent his Son to die for our sins in that the law's requirement might be fulfilled in us, provided that we live 'not according to the sinful nature but according to the Spirit' (8:3–4). Only when the gospel has replaced the law, and the Holy Spirit the written code, can defeat be replaced by victory.

If the 'wretched man' of verse 24 is typical of many Jewish Christians of Paul's day, regenerated but not liberated, under the law and not yet in or under the Spirit, does Romans 7 have any application to us today? Or must we jettison it as having historical interest only but no contemporary relevance? I want to suggest that there is both a wrong and a right way to apply this passage to ourselves. The wrong way is to regard it as a pattern of normal Christian experience, so that we all have to pass 'through Romans 7 into Romans 8'. This would create a two-stage stereotype of Christian initiation, in which the Holy Spirit first regenerates us and only later indwells us, and in which defeat is the necessary prelude to victory. But that was a once-for-all, Old Testament/New Testament, 'salvation-history' development. God does not intend it to be repeated in everybody today. For we live on this side of Pentecost, so that the indwelling of the Spirit is the birthright and hallmark of all who belong to Christ (8:9).

The right way of applying Romans 7 – 8 is to recognize that some church-goers today might be termed 'Old Testament Christians'. The contradiction implied in this expression indicates what an anomaly they are. They show signs of new birth in their love for the church and the Bible, yet their religion is law, not gospel; flesh, not Spirit; the 'oldness' of slavery to rules and regulations, not the 'newness' of freedom through Jesus Christ. They are like Lazarus when he first emerged from the tomb, alive but still bound hand and foot. They need to add to their life liberty.

As we now turn to the text (14–25), it divides itself naturally into two paragraphs (14–20 and 21–25), both of which open with a positive reference to the law. *We know that the law is spiritual* (14), and *in my inner being I delight in God's law* (22). The tragedy is, however, that the writer (or rather the half-saved person Paul is impersonating) cannot keep this law. Nor can it keep (or save) him. So both paragraphs elaborate the weakness of the law, which is attributed to sin.

b.   The law and the 'flesh' in believers (14–20)

In this paragraph the apostle writes almost exactly the same things twice, presumably for emphasis, first in verses 14–17 and then in verses 18–20. It may therefore be helpful if we consider them together. Each of the two sections begins, continues and ends in the same way.

First, each begins with a frank acknowledgment of innate sinfulness. It is a question of self-knowledge. *We know* (14) and *I know* (18). And in both cases the self-knowledge concerns the flesh (*sarx*). Although *the law is spiritual*, the writer himself is *unspiritual*, 'fleshly' (*sarkinos*), still possessing and being oppressed by his twisted, self-centred nature (*sarx*), on account of which he can also describe himself as *sold as a slave to sin* (14), or 'the purchased slave of sin' (NEB). Literally translated, the expression would be 'sold under sin'. But because the verb *pipraskō* was used of selling slaves,[73] and because of the preposition 'under' (suggesting the slave-master's authority over his slaves), it seems legitimate to add the word 'slave'. We have already noted the difficulty of reconciling this admitted slavery to sin with the freedom from sin, and slavery to God and righteousness, which Paul claimed for Christians in the previous chapter (6:18, 22). The continuing slavery to sin is easier to understand if the 'I' is a believer who is still under the law.

The corresponding statement of verse 18a is this: *I know that nothing good lives in me, that is, in my sinful nature (sarx)*. This cannot be interpreted absolutely, meaning that there is nothing at all in fallen human beings which can be labelled 'good', since God's image in which we are still made,[74] although defaced, has not been destroyed, and since Jesus himself spoke of the possibility of even pagans doing good.[75] Since the person Paul is describing goes on in the second part of the verse to say that he has *the desire to do what is good* (18b), it seems likely that the 'nothing good' of the first part of the verse alludes to his inability to turn the desire into action. It also means that everything 'good' in human beings is tainted with evil.

Those who are still under the law, therefore, although (being regenerate) they love it, yet (being also *sarkinos*, fallen) are enslaved, and so incapable of turning good desires into good deeds.

Secondly, each of the two sections of this paragraph continues

[73] *E.g.* Mt. 18:25.   [74] Gn. 9:6; Jas. 3:9.   [75] *E.g.* Mt. 5:46f.; 7:11.

211

with a vivid description of the resulting conflict (15 and 18b–19). After confessing that he does not altogether understand his own actions (15a), and that he has desires for good which he cannot carry out (18b), the writer summarizes his inward struggle in negative and positive counterparts. On the one hand, *what I want to do I do not do*, and on the other *what I hate I do* (15b). Similarly, *what I do is not the good I want to do*. Instead, *the evil I do not want to do – this I keep on doing* (19). He is conscious of a divided 'I'. For there is an 'I' which wants the good and hates the evil, and there is an 'I' which acts perversely, doing what is hated and not doing what is wanted. The conflict is between desire and performance; the will is there, but the ability is not.

Surely this is the conflict of a regenerate person who knows, loves, chooses and longs for God's law, but finds that by himself he cannot do it. His whole being (especially his mind and will) is set upon God's law. He wants to obey it. And when he sins, it is against his reason, his desire, his consent. But the law cannot help him. Only the power of the indwelling Spirit could change things; and that will come later.

Thirdly, each section of this paragraph ends by saying (in almost identical words) that indwelling sin is responsible for the failures and defeats of the person under the law whom Paul is impersonating (16f. and 20). Both verses contain a premise and a conclusion. The premise is stated in the phrase *if I do what I do not want to do* (16a, repeated in 20), drawing attention to the radical discontinuity between will and deed. Then the first conclusion is *I agree that the law is good* (16b) and the second is that *it is no longer I myself who do it, but it is sin living in me* (17, repeated in 20). Who, then, is to blame for the good I do not do and the evil I do? This is what Paul clarifies. It is not the law, for three times he declares its holiness and goodness (12, 14, 16). Besides, in wanting so ardently to do good and avoid evil, he is thereby endorsing and approving the law. So the law is not to blame. But neither, Paul goes on, am 'I myself' responsible, the authentic 'I'. For when I do evil I do not do it voluntarily. On the contrary, I act against my better judgment, my will and my consent. It is rather the *sarx*, *sin living in me*, the false, the fallen, the counterfeit 'I'. The real I, 'I myself', is the 'I' which loves and wants the good, and hates the evil, for that is its essential orientation. Therefore the 'I' which does the opposite (doing what I hate and not doing what I want) is not the real or the genuine 'I', but rather a usurper, namely 'indwelling sin' (17, 20), or *sarx* (18). In other words, the law is neither responsible for our sinning, nor capable of saving us. It has been fatally weakened by the *sarx*.

c.   The double reality in believers under the law (21–25)

Having given a graphic description of inward conflict, as he identifies with believers under the law, Paul now summarizes the situation in terms of their double reality, even though this is not the complete story, since still the Holy Spirit is not yet included in it. He depicts this double reality four times in four different ways, as the two egos, the two laws, the two cries and the two slaveries.

First, there are two egos: *So I find this law* ('I discover this principle', REB) *at work: When I want to do good, evil is right there with me* (21). The antithesis between the 'I' who wants the good and the 'I' beside whom the evil lies is more obvious in the Greek sentence by reason of the repetition of *emoi*, meaning 'in me' or 'by me'. One might paraphrase it: 'When in me there is a desire to do good, then by me evil is close at hand.' Thus the evil and the good are both present simultaneously, for they are both part of a fallen yet regenerate personality.

Secondly there are two laws: *for in my inner being* (that is, in the real regenerate me) *I delight in God's law* (22). It is the object of my love and the source of my joy. This inner delight in the law is also called *the law of my mind* (23), because my renewed mind approves and endorses God's law (*cf.* 16). *But I see* in addition *another law*, a very different law, which is *at work in the members of my body*. This Paul calls *the law of sin* which is continuously *waging war against the law of my mind* and *making me* its *prisoner* (23). Thus the characteristic of 'the law of my mind' is that it operates 'in my inner being' and 'delights in God's law', whereas the characteristic of 'the law of sin' is that it operates 'in the members of my body', fights against the law of my mind and takes me captive. Once again, this is the condition of the person who is still under the law; it is the Holy Spirit who is missing.

Thirdly, there are two cries from the heart. One is *What a wretched man I am! Who will rescue me from this body of death?* (24). The other is *Thanks be to God – through Jesus Christ our Lord!* (25a). The former is not so much 'a heart-rending cry from the depths of despair'[76] as a cry of longing, which ends in a question mark, while the latter is a cry of confidence and thanksgiving, which ends in an exclamation mark. Yet both are the ejaculations of the same person, who is a regenerate believer, who laments his corruption, who yearns for the final deliverance at the resurrection (indeed, 'groans' in waiting for it, 8:23), who knows the impotence of the law to rescue him, and who exults in God through Christ as the only Saviour, although again the Holy Spirit is not yet

[76] Sanday and Headlam, p. 183.

213

introduced. The two cries are almost simultaneous, or at least the second is an immediate response to the first. It anticipates the declaration of Romans 8:3–4 that God has done through his Son and Spirit what the law was powerless to do.

Fourthly, there are two slaveries. *So then*, Paul concludes, *I myself* (*autos egō*, the authentic, regenerate I) *in my mind am a slave to God's law*, for I know it and love it and want it; *but in the sinful nature* (in my *sarx*, my false and fallen self, uncontrolled by the Spirit) I am a *slave to the law of sin* (25b), on account of my inability by myself to keep it. The conflict is between my renewed mind and my unrenewed *sarx*. The conflict in Galatians is different because there it is the Spirit who subdues the *sarx*.

Those who think that the 'I' of Romans 7 is an unregenerate unbeliever, who reaches the depths of wretchedness and despair in crying out for rescue, and who then immediately announces his salvation in the second cry which counters and cancels his first, find verse 25b an impossible anticlimax. It is embarrassing to the point of being intolerable, since it expresses a continuing slavery to the law of sin. The only way they can find to solve their problem is to do violence to the text (though with no manuscript support whatever) and to change the order of the verses, putting verse 25b *before* the cry of verse 24. Thus, C. H. Dodd approved James Moffatt's rearrangement, 'restoring the second part of verse 25 to what seems its original and logical position before the climax of verse 24'.[77] J. B. Phillips follows suit. So does Käsemann, who regards verse 25 as a later gloss.[78]

But verse 25b stands stubbornly there in all the manuscripts, and we have no liberty to erase it or move it. Moreover, it is seen to be an appropriate conclusion if the whole passage describes the continuing conflict within Old Testament believers. The two egos, two laws, two cries and two slaveries together constitute the double reality of people who are indeed regenerate but who are still living under the law. Indwelling sin masters them; they have not yet found the indwelling of the Spirit. Nor has Paul yet alluded to it.

When we are seeking a legitimate application of Romans 7 to ourselves today, we are likely to find verses 4–6 to be crucial. For these verses set the two orders or ages and covenants or testaments over against each other in sharp antithesis as *the old way* and *the new way*. Both are called 'service', but the old was characterized by 'letter' (a written code), while the new is characterized by 'Spirit' (his indwelling presence). In the old order we were married to the law and controlled by the flesh, and we bore fruit for death, whereas

---

[77] See Moffatt's footnote to verse 25, and Dodd's comment on pp. 114f. that Moffatt is 'surely right'.

[78] Käsemann, pp. 211f.

as members of the new order we are married to the risen Christ and liberated from the law, and we bear fruit for God. We need then to keep a watch on ourselves and others, lest we should ever slip back from the new order into the old, from a person to a system, from freedom to slavery, from the indwelling Spirit to an external code, from Christ to the law. God's purpose is not that we should be Old Testament Christians, regenerate indeed, but living in slavery to the law and in bondage to indwelling sin. It is rather that we should be New Testament Christians who, having died and risen with Christ, are living in the freedom of the indwelling Spirit.

8:1-39

11. God's Spirit in God's children

Romans 8 is without doubt one of the best-known, best-loved chapters of the Bible. If in Romans 7 Paul has been preoccupied with the place of the law, in Romans 8 his preoccupation is with the work of the Spirit. In chapter 7 the law and its synonyms were mentioned some thirty-one times, but the Holy Spirit only once (6), whereas in the first twenty-seven verses of chapter 8 he is referred to nineteen times by name. The essential contrast which Paul paints is between the weakness of the law and the power of the Spirit. For over against indwelling sin, which is the reason the law is unable to help us in our moral struggle (7:17, 20), Paul now sets the indwelling Spirit, who is both our liberator now from 'the law of sin and death' (8:2) and the guarantee of resurrection and eternal glory in the end (8:11, 17, 23). Thus the Christian life is essentially life in the Spirit, that is to say, a life which is animated, sustained, directed and enriched by the Holy Spirit. Without the Holy Spirit true Christian discipleship would be inconceivable, indeed impossible.

In handling the topic of the Holy Spirit, however, the apostle relates it to his other overarching theme in this chapter, namely the absolute security of the children of God. According to Charles Hodge, 'the whole chapter is a series of arguments, most beautifully arranged, in support of this one point'.[1] And Dr Martyn Lloyd-Jones agrees with him. 'I make bold to assert that the great theme of chapter 8 is not sanctification ... The great theme is the security of the Christian.'[2] At the same time, the two topics are intimately related. For possession of the Spirit is the hallmark of those who truly belong to Christ (9); his inner witness assures us that we are God's children and therefore his heirs (15–17); and his presence in us is the firstfruits of our inheritance, pledging the final harvest (23).

The chapter divides itself naturally into three sections. The first depicts the varied ministry of God's Spirit in liberating, indwelling,

---

[1] Hodge, p. 247.   [2] Lloyd-Jones, vol. 7, p. 264.

sanctifying, leading, witnessing to and finally resurrecting the children of God (1–17). The second treats the future glory of God's children, portrayed as a final freedom in which the whole creation will share (18–27). And thirdly Paul emphasizes the steadfastness of God's love, as he works in all things for the good of those who love him and promises that nothing will ever be allowed to separate us from his love (28–39). The apostle's perspective stretches our mind, as he ranges from eternity to eternity. He begins with 'no condemnation' (1) and ends with 'no separation' (39), in both cases for those who are 'in Christ Jesus'.

1. The ministry of God's Spirit (1–17)

The word *Therefore*, with which the chapter begins, indicates that the apostle is summing up, or expressing an interim conclusion. The deduction he draws, however, does not seem to come from chapter 7 alone, but from his whole argument thus far, and specially from what he has written in chapters 3, 4 and 5 about salvation through the death and resurrection of Christ. And the word *now* emphasizes that this salvation is already ours if we are in Christ, as opposed to being in Adam (5:12ff.).

The first blessing of salvation is expressed in the words *no condemnation*, which are equivalent to 'justification'. In fact, the opening statements of Romans 5 and Romans 8 complement each other. Chapter 5 begins with the positive declaration: 'Therefore, since we have been justified through faith, we have peace with God through our Lord Jesus Christ.' Chapter 8 begins with the negative counterpart: *Therefore, there is now no condemnation for those who are in Christ Jesus.* Paul will almost immediately go on to explain that our not being condemned is due to God's action of condemning our sin in Christ (3). Then later in the chapter he will argue that nobody can accuse us because God has justified us (33), and that nobody can condemn us because Christ died, was raised, is at God's right hand and is interceding for us (34). In other words, our justification, together with its corresponding truth of 'no condemnation', is securely grounded in what God has done for us in and through Jesus Christ.

a. The freedom of the Spirit (2–4)

The second privilege of salvation is expressed in the next statement: *because through Christ Jesus the law of the Spirit of life set me free from the law of sin and death* (2). Thus a certain 'liberation' joins 'no condemnation' as the two great blessings which are ours if we are 'in Christ Jesus' (a clause which is applied to both in the Greek

217

of verses 1 and 2). Moreover, these two blessings are linked by the conjunction *because*, indicating that our liberation is the basis of our justification. It is because we have been liberated that no condemnation can overtake us.

From what, then, have we been set free? Paul replies: *from the law of sin and death*. The context seems to demand that this is a description of God's law, of Torah. For a major emphasis of Romans 7 has been on the relation between the law on the one hand and sin and death on the other. True, Paul was at pains to stress that the law is not itself sinful, yet he added that it reveals, provokes and condemns sin (7:7–9). True again, he stressed that the law does not 'become death' to people; yet it had 'produced death' in him (7:13). So, shocking as it may sound, God's holy law could be called *the law of sin and death* because it occasioned both. In this case, to be liberated from the law of sin and death through Christ is to be no longer 'under the law', that is, to give up looking to the law for either justification or sanctification.

This liberation has been Paul's own experience. It is noteworthy that verse 2 contains the only use in Romans 8 of the first person singular (*set me free*), which has been such a prominent feature of Romans 7. By this Paul is indicating that he has himself been delivered, in Christ and through the Spirit, from the law and so from the humiliating situation with which he identified himself at the end of Romans 7.

The means of our liberation Paul calls *the law of the Spirit of life* (2) or 'the life-giving law of the Spirit' (REB). At first sight it seems strange that law should liberate us from law, especially when commentators are determined to give 'law' the same meaning in both expressions. Some take 'law' as meaning 'principle' or 'power', and translate 'the power of the Spirit of life' which frees us from 'the power of sin and death', but both expressions are then too imprecise to be meaningful. Professor Dunn argues that in both cases the law is Torah, and that Paul is reaffirming 'the two-sidedness of the law' as a law of both death and life, that is, of sin and death belonging to the old epoch, and of Spirit and life belonging to the new.[3] But it is questionable whether the Romans would have grasped this subtlety.

The alternative is to understand 'the law of the Spirit of life' as describing the gospel,[4] just as Paul calls it elsewhere 'the ministry of the Spirit'.[5] This makes the best sense, as it is certainly the gospel which has freed us from the law and its curse, and the message of life in the Spirit from the slavery of sin and death.

How the gospel liberates us from the law is elaborated in verses

---

[3] Dunn, vol. 38A, pp. 414ff.
[4] *E.g.* Hodge, pp. 250f., Moule (1894), p. 210, Lloyd-Jones, vol. 7, p. 290.
[5] 2 Cor. 3:8.

3–4. The first and fundamental truth which Paul declares is that God has taken the initiative to do *what the law* (even though it was his own law) *was powerless to do*. The law could neither justify nor sanctify. Why not? Because *it was weakened by the sinful nature* (3a), or 'because human weakness robbed it of all potency' (REB). That is, the law's impotence is not intrinsic. It is not in itself but in us, in our 'flesh' (*sarx*), our fallen selfish nature (*cf.* 7:14–20). So then, what the sin-weakened law could not do, *God did*. He made provision for both our justification and our sanctification. First, he sent his Son, whose incarnation and atonement are alluded to in verse 3, and then he gave us his Spirit through whose indwelling power we are enabled to fulfil the law's requirement, which is mentioned in verse 4 and expanded in the following paragraph. Thus God justifies us through his Son and sanctifies us through his Spirit.[6] The plan of salvation is essentially trinitarian. For God's way of justification is not law but grace (through the death of Christ), and his way of sanctification is not law but the Spirit (through his indwelling).

What *God did* Paul unfolds in five expressions. First came the *sending* of *his own Son*. The word 'sending' does not necessarily imply the Son's pre-existence, since God is also said to have 'sent' his prophets in the Old Testament and his apostles in the New, who of course were not pre-existent. Nevertheless, the statement that it was *his own Son* whom he sent may well be intended to indicate that he had enjoyed a prior life of intimacy with the Father; it certainly expresses the Father's sacrificial love in sending him (*cf.* 5:8, 10 and 8:32).

Secondly, the sending of the divine Son involved his becoming incarnate, a human being, which is expressed by the words *in the likeness of sinful man*, or better 'in the likeness of sinful flesh' (RSV). This somewhat roundabout phrase, which has puzzled commentators mainly because of its use of 'likeness', was doubtless intended to combat false views of the incarnation. That is, the Son came neither 'in the likeness of flesh', only seeming to be human, as the Docetists taught, for his humanity was real;[7] nor 'in sinful flesh', assuming a fallen nature, for his humanity was sinless,[8] but 'in the likeness of sinful flesh', because his humanity was both real and sinless simultaneously.

Thirdly, God sent his Son *to be a sin offering*. The Greek expression *peri hamartias* (literally, 'concerning sin') could be a general statement that he came 'for sin' (AV, RSV) or 'to deal with sin' (REB), without any indication how he did it. But probably the reference is

[6] *Cf.* Gal. 4:4, 6.   [7] *E.g.* 1 Jn. 4:2; 2 Jn. 7.
[8] *E.g.* 2 Cor. 5:21; Heb. 4:15; 7:26.

specifically to the sacrificial nature of his death. For *peri hamartias* was the usual LXX rendering of the Hebrew for 'sin offering' in Leviticus and Numbers, and should clearly be translated 'sin offering' in Hebrews 10:6, 8 and 13:11. And since the sin offering was prescribed specially for the atoning of 'unwilling sins', which is exactly what the sins of Romans 7 are ('I do what I do not want to do', 20), Tom Wright concludes, 'There can no longer be any room for doubt that when Paul wrote *kai peri hamartias* he meant the words to carry their regular biblical overtones, *i.e.* "and as a sin offering" '.[9] In any case, 'in the likeness of sinful flesh' is clearly an allusion to the incarnation, and 'to be a sin offering' to the atonement.

Fourthly, *God . . . condemned sin in sinful man* (3, literally, 'in the flesh'), that is, in the flesh or humanity of Jesus, real and sinless, although made sin with our sins.[10] God judged our sins in the sinless humanity of his Son, who bore them in our place. Friedrich Büchsel points out that 'when it [*sc. katakrinein*, to condemn] refers to human judgment there is a clear distinction between the condemnation and its execution'.[11] But in the case of the divine *katakrinein* 'the two can be seen as one'. Hence in Romans 8:3 'the pronouncement and execution of the sentence' are both included. The law condemns sin, in the sense of expressing disapproval of it, but when God condemned sin in his Son, his judgment fell upon it in him.[12] As Charles Cranfield puts it, 'for those who are in Christ Jesus . . . there is no divine condemnation, since the condemnation they deserve has already been fully borne for them by him'.[13]

Fifthly, Paul clarifies the ultimate reason God sent his own Son and condemned our sin in him. It was *in order that the righteous requirements of the law might be fully met in us, who do not live according to the sinful nature but according to the Spirit* (4). One might have expected Paul to write that 'God condemned sin in Jesus in order that we might escape the condemnation', that is, 'in order that we might be justified'. Indeed, this was the immediate purpose of the sin-bearing death of God's Son. Consequently, most of the early Fathers, the Reformers and subsequent Reformed commentators seem to have interpreted Paul's statement of verse 4 in the same way. Hodge, for example, insists that verse 4 'must be understood of justification, and not of sanctification. He condemned sin, in order that the demands of the law might be satisfied',[14] the law's main demand being the sentence of death for sin. Yet if God's purpose in sending his Son was limited to our justification, the

---

[9] Wright, pp. 220ff.   [10] 2 Cor. 5:21.
[11] *E.g.* Mk. 14:64: 'they all condemned him as worthy of death.' *TDNT*, vol. III, pp. 951ff.
[12] *Ibid.*   [13] Cranfield, vol. I, p. 373.   [14] Hodge, pp. 254f.

addition of the final clause (*who . . . live . . . according to the Spirit*) would be a *non sequitur*.

It is this phrase which directs our attention to law-abiding Christian behaviour as the ultimate purpose of God's action through Christ. In this case the law's *dikaiōma* or 'just requirement' (singular, not plural 'requirements' as in NIV) refers to the commandments of the moral law viewed as a whole, which God wants to be 'fulfilled' (*i.e.* 'obeyed', not 'satisfied') in his people. For Jesus had himself spoken of fulfilling the law,[15] and Paul will write later of neighbour love as the chief 'fulfilment of the law' (13:8–10).[16] Moreover, the law can be fulfilled only in those 'who walk not according to the flesh but according to the Spirit' (RSV). The flesh renders the law impotent, the Spirit empowers us to obey it. This is not perfectionism; it is simply to say that obedience is a necessary and possible aspect of Christian discipleship. Although the law cannot secure this obedience, the Spirit can.

Some modern scholars find Paul hopelessly confused, even self-contradictory, since he writes of both the abolition and the fulfilment of the law, of our being both released from it and committed to it, our discharge and our obligation being both attributable to Christ's death (7:4; 8:3–4)! The most outspoken critic of Paul's supposed inconsistency is Heikki Räisänen. He rejects all eulogies of Paul which depict him as a profound, logical, consistent theologian. Instead, 'contradictions and tensions have to be *accepted* as *constant* features of Paul's theology of the law'.[17] In particular, 'we find two conflicting lines of thought in Paul's theology of the law. Paul asserts both the abolition of the law and also its permanently normative character'.[18] Indeed, 'Paul's thought on the law is full of difficulties and inconsistencies',[19] for (Dr Räisänen presses the question) how could a divine institution be abolished or abrogated?[20] But I fail to see any inconsistency in Paul's declarations that, because the law is unable to justify or sanctify us, it has been abolished in those roles, whereas the Spirit can enable us to fulfil or keep the moral law. This was certainly the prophetic expectation. Through Ezekiel God promised, 'I will put my Spirit in you', and through Jeremiah, 'I will put my law in their minds and write it on their hearts.'[21] These promises are synonymous. When God puts his Spirit in our hearts, he writes his law there.

Verses 4 is of great importance for our understanding of Christian holiness. First, holiness is the ultimate purpose of the incarnation and the atonement. The end God had in view when sending his Son

---

[15] Mt. 5:17. [16] *Cf.* Gal. 5:14. [17] Räisänen, p. 11. [18] *Ibid.*, p. 69.
[19] *Ibid.*, p. 264. [20] *Ibid.*, p. 265. [21] Ezk. 36:26f.; Je. 31:33; *cf.* 2 Cor. 3:3.

was not our justification only, through freedom from the condemnation of the law, but also our holiness, through obedience to the commandments of the law. Secondly, holiness consists in fulfilling the just requirement of the law. This is the final answer to antinomians and adherents of the so-called 'new morality'. The moral law has not been abolished for us; it is to be fulfilled in us. Although law-obedience is not the *ground* of our justification (it is in this sense that we are 'not under law but under grace'), it is the fruit of it and the very meaning of sanctification. Holiness is Christlikeness, and Christlikeness is fulfilling the righteousness of the law. Thirdly, holiness is the work of the Holy Spirit. Romans 7 insists that we cannot keep the law because of our indwelling 'flesh'; Romans 8:4 insists that we can and must because of the indwelling Spirit.

Looking back over the whole passage which runs from 7:1 to 8:4, the continuing place of the law in the Christian life should be clear. Our freedom from the law (proclaimed for instance in 7:4, 6 and 8:2) is not freedom to disobey it. On the contrary the law-obedience of the people of God is so important to God that he sent his Son to die for us and his Spirit to live in us, in order to secure it. Holiness is the fruit of trinitarian grace, of the Father sending his Son into the world and his Spirit into our hearts.

b. The mind of the Spirit (5–8)

Paul has asserted that the only people in whom the law's righteous requirement can be fulfilled are those who live not *kata sarka* (according to flesh) but *kata pneuma* (according to spirit or better the Spirit), that is, those who follow the promptings and surrender to the control of the Spirit rather than the flesh. It is this antithesis between flesh and Spirit which Paul now develops in verses 5–8. Implicitly or explicitly, it recurs in every verse. Paul's purpose is to explain why obedience to the law is possible only to those who walk according to the Spirit.

We begin with some definitions. By *sarx* (flesh) Paul means neither the soft muscular tissue which covers our bony skeleton, nor our bodily instincts and appetites, but rather the whole of our humanness viewed as corrupt and unredeemed, 'our fallen, ego-centric human nature',[22] or more briefly 'the sin-dominated self'.[23] By *pneuma* (spirit) in this passage Paul means not the higher aspect of our humanness viewed as 'spiritual' (although in verse 16 he will refer to our human spirit), but rather the personal Holy Spirit

---

[22] Cranfield, vol. I, p. 372. *Cf.* Luther's favourite description of fallen human nature as 'deeply curved in on itself' (*e.g.* Luther, 1515, pp. 291, 313, 513).

[23] Ziesler (1987), p. 195.

himself who now not only regenerates but also indwells the people of God. This tension between 'flesh' and 'Spirit' is reminiscent of Galatians 5:16–26, where they are in irreconcilable conflict with each other. Here Paul concentrates on the 'mind', or (as we would say) 'mindset', of those who are characterized by either *sarx* or *pneuma*.

First, our mindset expresses our basic nature as Christians or non-Christians. On the one hand, there are *those who live according to the sinful nature*. They are not now those who 'walk' according to it (4, literally) but those who simply 'are' like this (5, literally). These people *have their minds set on what that nature desires*, whereas *those who live in accordance with the Spirit* (literally, 'those according to the Spirit' – there is no verb) *have their minds set on what the Spirit desires* (5). The meaning surely is not that people are like this because they think like this, although that is partly true, but that they think like this because they are like this. The expressions are descriptive. In both cases their nature determines their mindset. Moreover, since the flesh is our twisted human nature, its desires are all those things which pander to our ungodly self-centredness. Since the Spirit is the Holy Spirit himself, however, his desires are all those things which please him, who loves above all else to glorify Christ, that is, to show Christ to us and form Christ in us.

Now to 'set the mind' (*phroneō*) on the desires of *sarx* or *pneuma* is to make them the 'absorbing objects of thought, interest, affection and purpose'.[24] It is a question of what preoccupies us, of the ambitions which drive us and the concerns which engross us, of how we spend our time and our energies, of what we concentrate on and give ourselves up to. All this is determined by who we are, whether we are still 'in the flesh' or are now by new birth 'in the Spirit'.

Secondly, our mindset has eternal consequences. *The mind of sinful man* (literally, 'of the flesh') *is death, but the mind controlled by the Spirit* (literally, 'of the Spirit') *is life and peace* (6). That is, the mindset of flesh-dominated people is already one of spiritual death and leads inevitably to eternal death, for it alienates them from God and renders fellowship with him impossible in either this world or the next. The mindset of Spirit-dominated people, however, entails life and peace. On the one hand they are 'alive to God' (6:11), alert to spiritual realities, and thirsty for God like nomads in the desert,[25] like deer panting for streams.[26] On the other hand, they have peace with God (5:1), peace with their neighbour (12:15), and peace within, enjoying an inner integration

---

[24] Murray, vol. I, p. 285.   [25] Ps. 63:1.   [26] Ps. 42:1.

or harmony. We would surely pursue holiness with greater eager-ness if we were convinced that it is the way of life and peace.

Thirdly, our mindset concerns our fundamental attitude to God. The reason the mind of the flesh is death is that it *is hostile to God*, cherishing a deep-seated animosity against him. It is antagonistic to his name, kingdom and will, to his day, his people and his word, to his Son, his Spirit and his glory. In particular, Paul singles out his moral standards. In contrast to the regenerate who 'delight' in God's law (7:22), the unregenerate mind *does not submit to God's law, nor can it do so* (7), which explains why those who live according to the flesh cannot fulfil the law's righteous requirement (4). Finally, *those* who are *controlled by the sinful nature* (sarx), literally those who are 'in flesh' (*en sarki*) or unregenerate, lacking the Spirit of God, *cannot please God* (8). They *cannot* please him (8) because they *cannot* submit to his law (7), whereas, it is implied, those who are in the Spirit set themselves to please him in every-thing, even to do so 'more and more'.[27]

To sum up, here are two categories of people (the unregenerate who are 'in the flesh' and the regenerate who are 'in the Spirit'), who have two perspectives or mindsets ('the mind of the flesh' and 'the mind of the Spirit'), which lead to two patterns of conduct (living according to the flesh or the Spirit), and result in two spiritual states (death or life, enmity or peace). Thus our mind, where we set it and how we occupy it, plays a key role in both our present conduct and our final destiny.

c.   The indwelling of the Spirit (9–15)

In verse 9 Paul applies to his readers personally the truths he has so far been expounding in general terms. Having been writing in the third person plural, he now shifts to the second person and addresses his readers directly. *You, however, are controlled not by the sinful nature but by the Spirit.* 'You are controlled by' is too strong a translation of the straightforward 'you are in' the flesh or the Spirit, for Paul immediately clarifies what he means by adding *if the Spirit of God lives in you* (9a). Thus you are in the Spirit if the Spirit is in you, for the same truth can be expressed in terms either of our personal relationship to the Spirit or of his dwelling in us, the latter denoting 'a settled permanent penetrative influence'.[28] This also means, Paul continues, that *if anyone does not have the Spirit of Christ, he does not belong to Christ* (9b).

Verse 9 is of great importance in relation to our doctrine of the Holy Spirit for at least two reasons. First, it teaches that the

[27] 1 Thes. 4:1.   [28] Sanday and Headlam, p. 196.

hallmark of the authentic believer is the possession or indwelling of the Holy Spirit. Indwelling sin (7:17, 20) is the lot of all the children of Adam; the privilege of the children of God is to have the indwelling Spirit to fight and subdue indwelling sin. As Jesus had promised, 'he lives with you and will be in you'.[29] Now in fulfilment of this promise every true Christian has received the Spirit, so that our body has become 'a temple of the Holy Spirit' in which he dwells.[30] Conversely, if we do not have Christ's Spirit in us, we do not belong to Christ at all. This makes it plain that the gift of the Spirit is an initial and universal blessing, received when we first repent and believe in Jesus. Of course there may be many further and richer experiences of the Spirit, and many fresh anointings of the Spirit for special tasks, but the personal indwelling of the Spirit is every believer's privilege from the beginning. To know Christ and to have the Spirit are one. Bishop Handley Moule was wise to write that 'there is no *separable* "Gospel of the Spirit". Not for a moment are we to advance, as it were, from the Lord Jesus Christ to a higher or deeper region, ruled by the Holy Ghost.'[31]

Secondly, verse 9 teaches that several different expressions are synonyms. We have already seen that being in the Spirit is the same as having the Spirit in us. Now we note that 'the Spirit of God' is also called 'the Spirit of Christ', and that to have the Spirit of Christ in us (9b) is to have Christ in us (10a). This is not to confuse the persons of the Trinity by identifying the Father with the Son or the Son with the Spirit. It is rather to emphasize that, although they are eternally distinct in their personal modes of being, they also share the same divine essence and will. In consequence, they are inseparable. What the Father does he does through the Son, and what the Son does he does through the Spirit. Indeed, wherever each is, there are the others also.[32]

After affirming that to have the Spirit in us is the distinguishing mark of Christ's people, Paul proceeds to indicate two major consequences of his indwelling. Both verse 10 and verse 11 begin with an 'if' clause relating to this indwelling: *But if Christ is in you . . .* (10). *And if the Spirit . . . is living in you* (11). These two 'ifs' do not express any doubt about the fact of the indwelling (they could be paraphrased, 'if, as indeed is the case'), but they point to its results. What are these? The first Paul describes in terms of 'life' (10–11) and the second in terms of 'debt' or obligation (12–13).

The exact meaning of verse 10 is disputed: *your body is dead because of sin, yet your spirit is alive because of righteousness.* Two main questions are raised. The first is: what death of the body is

---

[29] Jn. 14:17.   [30] 1 Cor. 6:19.   [31] Moule (1894), p. 206.
[32] *E.g.* Jn. 14:16f.; 21, 23.

being referred to? Some suggest that *your body* (*sōma*) simply means 'you', and that you are *dead* in the sense that you have died with Christ, as explained in 6:2ff. Ernst Käsemann, for example, goes so far as to state that 'the only possible reference is to the death of the body of sin effected in baptism'.[33] But the reluctance to allow 'body' to mean our material body is strange, especially in a context which goes on to speak of its resurrection (11), and the body can hardly be already dead since the apostle goes on to write of the need to put its misdeeds to death (13). It is, therefore, much better to understand 'dead' as indicating 'mortal', that is, subject to death and destined for it. This would fit in with Paul's references in Romans to our 'mortal bodies' (*e.g.* 6:12; 8:11b) and elsewhere to our physical decaying and dying.[34] It is also true to experience. As Dr Lloyd-Jones has put it, writing as a physician as well as a pastor: 'The moment we enter into this world and begin to live, we also begin to die. Your first breath is one of the last you will ever take! . . . the principle of decay, leading to death, is in every one of us.'[35]

At the same time, in the midst of our physical mortality, our *spirit is alive*, for we have been 'quickened' or made alive in Christ (*cf.* 6:11, 13, 23). What, however, is the cause of this double condition, namely a dying body and a living spirit? The answer lies in the repeated 'because', which attributes death to sin and life to righteousness. Since Paul has already made this attribution in his Adam–Christ parallelism in chapter 5, he must surely be saying that our bodies became mortal because of Adam's sin ('to dust you will return'),[36] whereas our spirits are alive because of Christ's righteousness (5:15–18, 21), that is, because of the righteous standing he has secured for us.

The ultimate destiny of our body is not death, however, but resurrection. To this further truth Paul now proceeds in verse 11. Our bodies are not yet redeemed (23), but they will be, and we are eagerly awaiting this event. How can we be so sure about it? Because of the nature of the indwelling Spirit. He is not only 'the Spirit of life' (2), but the Spirit of resurrection. For he is *the Spirit of him who raised Jesus from the dead.* Therefore the God whose Spirit he is, namely *he who raised Christ from the dead, will also give life to your mortal bodies,* and will do it *through his Spirit, who lives in you* (11). We note this further unselfconscious allusion to the three persons of the Trinity – the resurrecting Father, the resurrected Son and the Spirit of resurrection. Further, Christ's resurrection is the pledge and the pattern of ours. The same Spirit

---

[33] Käsemann, p. 224. [34] *E.g.* 2 Cor. 4:10ff., 16.
[35] Lloyd-Jones, vol. 7, p. 69. [36] Gn. 3:19.

who raised him will also raise us. The same Spirit who gives life to our spirits (10) will also give life to our bodies (11).

This does not mean that our dead bodies will be revivified or resuscitated, and so restored to their present material existence, only to die again. No, resurrection includes transformation, the raising and changing of our body into a new and glorious vehicle of our personality, and its liberation from all frailty, disease, pain, decay and death. It is 'not that the spirit is to be freed from the body – as many, under the influence of the Greek way of thinking, have held – but rather that the Spirit will give life to the body'.[37]

'Wonderful', writes Bishop Handley Moule, 'is this deep characteristic of the Scripture: its gospel for the body. In Christ, the body is seen to be something far different from the mere clog, or prison, or chrysalis, of the soul. It is its destined implement, may we not say its mighty wings in prospect, for the life of glory.'[38] Already we express our personality through our body, especially by speech, but also by posture and gesture, by a look in our eyes or an expression on our face. We call it 'body language'. But the language which our present body speaks is imperfect; we easily miscommunicate. Our new body will not have this limitation, however. There will be a perfect correspondence between message and medium, between what we want to communicate and how we do so. The resurrection body will be the perfect vehicle of our redeemed personality.

We come now to the second consequence of the dwelling in us of God or Christ through the Spirit. The first was life; the second is a debt or obligation. *Therefore, brothers, we have an obligation* (12), or literally 'we are debtors' (AV, RSV). What is this debt? It is not now to share the gospel with the world (as in 1:14), but to live a righteous life. We have no obligation *to the sinful nature (sarx) to live according to it* (12). It has no claim on us. We owe it nothing. Our obligation is rather (this is inferred, since Paul does not complete the expected antithesis) to the Spirit, to live according to his desires and dictates.

Paul's argument seems to be this: if the indwelling Spirit has given us life, which he has (*your spirit is alive*, 10), we cannot possibly live according to the flesh, since that way lies death. How can we possess life and court death simultaneously? Such an inconsistency between who we are and how we behave is unthinkable, even ludicrous. No, we are in debt to the indwelling Spirit of life to live out our God-given life and to put to death everything which threatens it or is incompatible with it.

Verse 13 sets the option before us as a solemn life-and-death alternative,[39] which is made the more impressive by Paul's renewed

---

[37] Nygren, p. 323.   [38] Moule (1894), p. 215.   [39] Cf. Dt. 30:15ff.; Je. 21:8ff.

resort to direct address. *For if you live according to the sinful nature* (which he has just declared in verse 12 not to be a Christian obligation), *you will die; but if by the Spirit you put to death the misdeeds of the body, you will live* (13). That is, there is a kind of life which leads to death, and there is a kind of death which leads to life. Verse 13 thus becomes a very significant verse on the neglected topic of 'mortification' (the process of putting to death the body's misdeeds). It clarifies at least three truths about it.

First, what is mortification? Mortification is neither masochism (taking pleasure in self-inflicted pain), nor asceticism (resenting and rejecting the fact that we have bodies and natural bodily appetites). It is rather a clear-sighted recognition of evil as evil, leading to such a decisive and radical repudiation of it that no imagery can do it justice except 'putting to death'. In fact, the verb Paul uses normally means to 'kill someone, hand someone over to be killed, especially of the death sentence and its execution' (BAGD on *thanatoō*).[40] Elsewhere the apostle has called it a crucifixion of our fallen nature, with all its passions and desires.[41] And this teaching is Paul's elaboration of Jesus' own summons: 'If anyone would come after me, he must deny himself and take up his cross and follow me.'[42] Since the Romans compelled a condemned criminal to carry his cross to the site of crucifixion, to carry our cross is symbolic of following Jesus to the place of execution. And what we are to *put to death* there, Paul explains, is *the misdeeds of the body*, that is, every use of our body (our eyes, ears, mouth, hands or feet) which serves ourselves instead of God and other people. Some scholars, doubtless anxious to avoid the dualism which regards the body itself as evil, suggest that by *sōma* (the body) Paul really means *sarx* (the flesh, or sinful nature), and one or two manuscripts do contain this word. Thus Charles Cranfield renders the phrase 'the activities and schemings of the sinful flesh, of human self-centredness and self-assertion'.[43] But it seems better to retain *sōma*, to bear in mind that the word for *misdeeds* is actually neutral (*praxeis*, deeds or actions), and to allow the context to determine whether they are good or (as here) evil.

Secondly, how does mortification take place? We note at once that it is something that we have to do. It is not a question of dying or of being put to death, but of putting to death. In the work of mortification we are not passive, waiting for it to be done to us or for us. On the contrary, we are responsible for putting evil to death. True, Paul immediately adds that we can *put to death the misdeeds of the body* only *by the Spirit*, by his agency and power. For only he can give us the desire, determination and discipline to reject evil.

---

[40] *E.g.* Lk. 21:16. [41] Gal. 5:24. [42] Mk. 8:34. [43] Cranfield, vol. I, p. 395.

Nevertheless, it is we who must take the initiative to act. Negatively, we must totally repudiate everything we know to be wrong, and not even 'think about how to gratify the desires of the sinful nature' (13:14). This is not an unhealthy form of repression, pretending that evil does not exist in us and refusing to face it. It is the opposite. We have to 'pull it out, look at it, denounce it, hate it for what it is; then you have really dealt with it'.[44] Or, as Jesus graphically expressed it, we must gouge out our offending eye and cut off our offending hand or foot.[45] That is, if temptation comes to us through what we see, handle or visit, then we must be ruthless in not looking, not touching, not going, and so in controlling the very approaches of sin. Positively, we are to set our minds on the things the Spirit desires (5), set our hearts on things above,[46] and occupy our thoughts with what is noble, right, pure and lovely.[47] In this way 'mortification' (putting evil to death) and 'aspiration' (hungering and thirsting for what is good) are counterparts. Both verbs (verse 5, 'set their minds', and verse 13, 'put to death') are in the present tense, for they describe attitudes and activities which should be continuous, involving taking up the cross every day[48] and setting our minds on the things of the Spirit every day.

Thirdly, why should we practise mortification? It sounds an unpleasant, uncongenial, austere and even painful business. It runs counter to our natural tendency to soft and lazy self-indulgence. If we are to engage in it, we shall need strong motives. One is, as we have seen, that *we have an obligation* (12) to the indwelling Spirit of life. Another, on which Paul now insists, is that the death of mortification is the only road to life. Verse 13 contains the most marvellous promise, which is expressed in the single Greek verb *zēsesthe*, *you will live*. Paul is not now contradicting himself. Having called eternal life a free and undeserved gift (6:23), he is not now making it a reward for self-denial. Nor by 'life' does he seem to be referring to the life of the world to come. He seems to be alluding to the life of God's children, who are led by his Spirit and assured of his fatherly love, to which he comes in the next verses (14ff.). This rich, abundant, satisfying life, he is saying, can be enjoyed only by those who put their misdeeds to death. Even the pain of mortification is worth while if it opens the door to fulness of life.

This is one of several ways in which the radical principle of 'life through death' lies at the heart of the gospel. According to Romans 6 it is only by dying with Christ to sin, its penalty thereby paid, that we rise to a new life of forgiveness and freedom. According to

[44] Lloyd-Jones, vol. 7, p. 143.   [45] Mt. 5:29f.   [46] Col. 3:1f.   [47] Phil. 4:8.
[48] Lk. 9:23.

Romans 8 it is only by putting our evil deeds to death that we experience the full life of God's children. So we need to redefine both life and death. What the world calls life (a desirable self-indulgence) leads to alienation from God which in reality is death, whereas the putting to death of all perceived evil within us, which the world sees as an undesirable self-abnegation, is in reality the way to authentic life.

d.   The witness of the Spirit (14–17)

What is immediately noteworthy about this paragraph is that in each of its four verses God's people are designated his *children* or *sons* (which of course includes 'daughters'), and that in each this privileged status is related to the work of the Holy Spirit. Only in verse 16 is it specifically said that the Spirit *testifies . . . that we are God's children*. Yet the whole paragraph concerns the witness he bears us, that is, the assurance he gives us. The question is: precisely how is the Spirit's witness borne? Paul assembles four pieces of evidence. First, the Spirit leads us into holiness (verse 14 being linked to verse 13 by the conjunction *because*). Secondly, in our relationship to God he replaces fear with freedom (15a). Thirdly, in our prayers he prompts us to call God 'Father' (15b–16). Fourthly, he is the firstfruits of our heavenly inheritance (17, 23). Thus radical holiness, fearless freedom, filial prayerfulness and the hope of glory are four characteristics of the children of God who are indwelt and led by the Spirit of God. It is by these evidences that he witnesses to us that we are God's children.

First, the Spirit leads us into holiness (14). It is somewhat artificial to begin a new sub-section at verse 14, as we have done, since the topic is still the sanctifying work of the Holy Spirit. Yet verse 14 clarifies verse 13 (*because*) by changing the imagery. Those who through the Spirit put the body's misdeeds to death (13b) are now called *those who are led by the Spirit* (14a), while those who have entered into fulness of life (13c) are now called *sons of God* (14b). Both clarifications are important.

To begin with, the kind of 'leading' by the Spirit which is the characteristic experience of God's children is evidently more specific than it sounds. For it consists of, or at least includes as one of its most substantial features, the prompting and strengthening which enable them to put to death the body's misdeeds. 'The daily, hourly putting to death of the schemings and enterprises of the sinful flesh by means of the Spirit is a matter of being led, directed, impelled, controlled by the Spirit.'[49]

---

[49] Cranfield, vol. I, p. 395.

Other commentators describe God's children as 'driven' by the Spirit. For example, Godet writes that there is here 'something like a notion of holy violence; the Spirit drags the man [*sc.* the person] where the flesh would fain not go'.[50] Professor Käsemann also speaks of being 'driven by the Spirit', and interprets it of charismatic 'enthusiasts' who are 'carried away' by the Spirit.[51] Professor Dunn follows him, claiming that 'the most natural sense' is that 'of being constrained by a compelling force, of surrendering to an over-mastering compulsion'.[52] Yet the verb *agō*, although indeed it has different shades of meaning, does not, either necessarily or normally, imply the use of force.[53]

The interpretation of this verb, however, is not just a semantic question. Dr Lloyd-Jones rightly enters a theological caveat at this point, relating to the nature and operation of the Holy Spirit. 'There is no violence in Christianity . . .', he writes. 'What the Spirit does is to enlighten and persuade.'[54] Because he is a gentle, sensitive Spirit, he can easily be 'grieved'.[55] 'The Holy Spirit never browbeats us . . . The impulse can be very strong, but there is no "driving", there is no compulsion.'[56]

Next, if to be 'led by the Spirit of God' (14a) is an elaboration of to 'put to death the misdeeds of the body' by the agency of the Spirit (13b), then the statement that you *are sons of God* (14b) elaborates the promise 'you will live' (13c). The new, rich, full life, which is enjoyed by those who put their misdeeds to death, is precisely the experience of being God's children. It is evident then that the popular notion of 'the universal fatherhood of God' is not true. To be sure, all human beings are God's 'offspring' by creation,[57] but we become his reconciled 'children' only by adoption or new birth.[58] Just as it is only those who are indwelt by the Spirit who belong to Christ (9), so it is only those who are led by the Spirit who are the sons and daughters of God (14). As such we are granted a specially close, personal, loving relationship with our heavenly Father, immediate and bold access to him in prayer, membership of his worldwide family, and nomination as his heirs, to

---

[50] Godet, p. 309.   [51] Käsemann, p. 226.   [52] Dunn, vol. 38A, p. 450.

[53] The same verb is used of the Spirit 'leading' Jesus from his baptism in the Jordan to his temptation in the desert (Lk. 4:1). It is true that Mark's parallel has *ekballō* (1:12), which can mean 'drive out, expel, literally, throw out more or less forcibly'. But it can also be used of to 'send out', in this case 'without the connotation of force' (BAGD). Since in addition it expresses the action of 'removing' a splinter from the eye (Mt. 7:4f.), Dr Lloyd-Jones writes: 'Here is a man who is going to perform a very delicate eye operation; so if you insist that this word always means "force", "thrust", "drive", let me express the hope that, if ever you have a foreign object in your eye, you may not be treated by such a violent oculist, or optician!' (vol. 7, p. 172).

[54] Lloyd-Jones, vol. 7, p. 167.   [55] Eph. 4:30.   [56] Lloyd-Jones, vol. 7, p. 174.

[57] Acts 17:28.   [58] *E.g.* Jn. 1:12; Gal. 3:26; 1 Jn. 3:1, 10.

which Paul will come in verse 17. He now enlarges on some of these privileges.

Secondly, the Spirit replaces fear with freedom in our relationship to God (15). This Paul attributes to the nature of the Spirit we received (an aorist, alluding to our conversion): *For you did not receive a spirit* (or probably 'the Spirit') *that makes you a slave again to fear, but you received the Spirit of sonship* (or 'of adoption', AV, REB). F. F. Bruce reminds us that we must interpret the implications of our adoption in terms not of our contemporary culture but of the Greco-Roman culture of Paul's day. He writes: 'The term "adoption" may have a somewhat artificial sound in our ears; but in the Roman world of the first century AD an adopted son was a son deliberately chosen by his adoptive father to perpetuate his name and inherit his estate; he was no whit [*sc.* not in the smallest degree] inferior in status to a son born in the ordinary course of nature, and might well enjoy the father's affection more fully and reproduce the father's character more worthily.'[59]

Both here in verse 15 and in Galatians 4:1ff. Paul uses the imagery of slavery and freedom with which to contrast the two eras, the old age and the new, and so our pre- and post-conversion situation. The slavery of the old age led to fear, especially of God as our judge; the freedom of the new age gives us boldness to approach God as our Father. So everything has changed. True, we are still slaves of Christ (1:1), of God (6:22) and of righteousness (6:18f.), but these slaveries, far from being incompatible with freedom, are its essence. Freedom, not fear, now rules our lives.

The punctuation of the end of verse 15 and of verse 16 is disputed. Paul enunciates three truths, namely that we *received the Spirit of sonship* (15a), that *we cry*, 'Abba, *Father*' (15b), and that *the Spirit himself testifies with our spirit that we are God's children* (16). The uncertainty is how these three truths relate to one another, and in particular whether our '*Abba*, Father' cry should be attached to the clause preceding or following it. If the former is right, then we 'received ... a Spirit of adoption, enabling us to cry "Abba! Father!"' (REB). If the latter is correct, however, then the sentence reads: 'When we cry "Abba! Father!" it is the Spirit himself bearing witness with our spirit that we are children of God' (RSV). The difference is not great. In the first rendering the '*Abba*, Father' cry is the result of our receiving the Spirit of adoption; in the second it is the explanation of the Spirit's inward witness. Either way, the gift of the Spirit, the cry and the witness belong together. But on balance I prefer the second interpretation, since then Paul is seen to move on from our relationship and attitude to God in general (not

---

[59] Bruce, p. 157; *cf.* Barclay, pp. 106f.

slavery but sonship, not fear but freedom) to the particular expression of it when we pray, from the nature of the Spirit we received to the witness of the Spirit in our prayers.

Thirdly, the Spirit prompts us in our prayers to call God 'Father'. The preservation side by side of the Aramaic (*abba*) and Greek (*patēr*) words for 'father', which some commentators since Augustine have seen as a symbol of the inclusion of Jews and Gentiles in God's family, seems to go back to Jesus' agony in the garden of Gethsemane, when he is recorded as having prayed '*Abba*, Father'.[60] Joachim Jeremias' researches into the prayer literature of ancient Judaism convinced him that Jesus' use of this colloquial and familiar term of address to God was unique. '*Abba* was an everyday word, a homely family-word. No Jew would have dared to address God in this manner. Jesus did it always, in all his prayers which are handed down to us, with one single exception, the cry from the cross.'[61]

Although some scholars, both Jewish and Christian, are now suggesting that Jeremias' case was overstated and needs to be modified, his main thesis stands. Further, Jesus told his disciples to pray 'Our Father', and thus authorized them to use in their address to God the very same intimate term which he used.[62] 'He empowers them to speak to their Heavenly Father literally as the small child speaks to his father, in the same confident and childlike manner.'[63] 'Jewish usage shows how this Father–child relationship to God far surpasses any possibilities of intimacy assumed in Judaism, introducing indeed something which is wholly new.'[64]

Some maintain that the Greek verb for *we cry* (*krazō*) is such a strong one that it expresses a loud, spontaneous, emotional ejaculation.[65] Certainly it was used many times in the gospels for the shouts of demons when confronted by Jesus, and it can be translated 'cry out, scream, shriek' (BAGD). But it can equally well be rendered 'call' or 'cry', and so refer either to a liturgical acclamation in public worship or to a calling upon God in private devotion. In this case 'Paul finds the particularity of *krazein*, not in enthusiasm or ecstasy, but in childlike and joyous assurance as contrasted with the attitude of the servant'.[66]

In such prayers to the Father we experience the inward witness of the Holy Spirit. For 'when we cry, "Abba! Father!"' taking on our lips the very words which Jesus used, 'it is the Spirit himself bearing

[60] Mk. 14:36; *cf.* Gal. 4:6.
[61] J. Jeremias, *The Prayers of Jesus* (SCM, 1967), pp. 57ff.
[62] Mt. 6:9; Lk. 11:2.
[63] J. Jeremias in *Expository Times*, vol. LXXI, February 1960, p. 144.
[64] Gerhard Kittel on 'Abba' in *TDNT*, vol. I, p. 6.
[65] *E.g.* Dunn, vol. 38A, p. 462.
[66] Gottlob Schrenk on *patēr etc.* in *TDNT*, vol. V, p. 1006.

witness with our spirit that we are children of God' (15b–16, RSV). The words are ours, but the witness is his. How is his witness borne, then, and what is implied by the prefix *syn* in the verb *symmartyreō*? Normally *syn* is translated 'together with', in which case there would be two witnesses here, the Holy Spirit confirming and endorsing our own spirit's consciousness of God's fatherhood. So NEB: 'In that cry the Spirit of God joins with our spirit in testifying that we are God's children.' This would be readily understandable, since the Old Testament required two witnesses to establish a testimony.[67] On the other hand, is it really possible in experience to distinguish between the Holy Spirit and our human spirit? More important, would not these two witnesses be inappropriately matched? Surely 'we cannot stand alongside the Holy Spirit and give testimony'?[68] For 'what standing has our spirit in *this* matter? Of itself it surely has no right at all to testify to our being sons of God'.[69] In this case the prefix *syn* is simply intensive, and Paul meant that the Holy Spirit bears a strong inward witness *to* our spirit that we are God's children.

It is natural to associate this experience with what Paul has written earlier about a similar inward ministry of the Holy Spirit. According to 5:5 God through the Holy Spirit 'has poured out his love into our hearts'. According to 8:16 the Holy Spirit 'affirms to our spirit that we are God's children' (REB). Each verse gives us an example of the Holy Spirit's ministry of inward assurance, as he convinces us of the reality of God's love on the one hand and of God's fatherhood on the other. Indeed, it would be hard to separate these, since God's love has been conspicuously lavished upon us in making us his children.[70] Although we have no liberty to circumscribe God's activity in any way, it seems from Christian biographies that God gives these experiences to his people chiefly when they pray, whether in public or in private.

Fourthly, the Spirit is the firstfruits of our inheritance (17, 23). Paul cannot leave this topic of our being God's children without pointing out its implication for the future. *Now if we are children, then we are heirs as well – heirs of God and co-heirs with Christ* (17a).[71] At first sight this seems to refer to that heavenly inheritance, which 'can never perish, spoil or fade', which God is keeping in heaven for us.[72] It is possible, however, that the inheritance Paul has in mind is not something God intends to bestow on us but God himself. Indeed, 'it is difficult to suppress the richer and deeper thought that God himself is the inheritance of his children'.[73]

This notion was not unfamiliar to Israel in Old Testament days.

[67] *E.g.* Dt. 19:15. [68] Morris (1988), p. 317. [69] Cranfield, vol. I, p. 403.
[70] 1 Jn. 3:1f. [71] *Cf.* Gal. 4:7. [72] 1 Pet. 1:4.
[73] Murray, vol. I, p. 298.

The Levites, for example, knew that they had been given no inheritance among their brothers because the Lord himself was their inheritance.[74] And godly individual Israelites could confidently affirm that God was their portion. For example, 'Whom have I in heaven but you? And earth has nothing I desire besides you. My flesh and my heart may fail, but God is the strength of my heart and my portion for ever'.[75] Moreover, the day is coming when God will be 'all in all',[76] or 'everything to every one' (RSV). As for the further astonishing statement that God's heirs are also co-heirs with Christ, we recall how Jesus himself had prayed that his own might be with him, and might see his glory and share his love.[77] And although it is still future, our inheritance is certain, since the Holy Spirit is himself its firstfruit (23), guaranteeing that the harvest will follow in due course. Thus the same indwelling Spirit who assures us that we are God's children also assures us that we are his heirs.

There is a qualification, however: *if indeed we share in his sufferings in order that we may also share in his glory* (17a). Scripture lays a strong emphasis on the principle that suffering is the path to glory. It was so for the Messiah ('did not the Christ have to suffer these things and then enter his glory?').[78] It is so for the messianic community also (5:2f.). Peter teaches this as clearly as Paul: 'Rejoice that you participate in the sufferings of Christ, so that you may be overjoyed when his glory is revealed.'[79] For the essence of discipleship is union with Christ, and this means identification with him in both his sufferings and his glory.

I do not feel able to leave these verses without alluding to an interpretation of them to which Dr Martyn Lloyd-Jones has given currency. He devoted four chapters[80] to the expression 'you received the Spirit of adoption' (15) and eight more[81] to 'the witness of the Spirit' (16). Following Thomas Goodwin and other Puritans, he understood the former as 'a very special form or type of assurance',[82] more emotional than intellectual, given subsequent to conversion though not essential for salvation, and conveying a profound feeling of security in our Father's love. Similarly, he interpreted the witness of the Spirit (which he identified with the 'baptism' and the 'sealing' of the Spirit) as a distinctive and overwhelming experience which confers 'an absolute assurance'.[83] 'This is the highest form of assurance possible; there is nothing beyond it. It is the acme, the zenith of assurance and certainty of

---

[74] Dt. 18:2; 32:9.   [75] Ps. 73:25f.; *cf.* La. 3:24.   [76] 1 Cor. 15:28.
[77] Jn. 17:24ff.   [78] Lk. 24:26; *cf.* Mk. 8:31.   [79] 1 Pet. 4:13.
[80] Lloyd-Jones, vol. 7, pp. 233ff.   [81] *Ibid.*, pp. 285ff.   [82] *Ibid.*, p. 272.
[83] *Ibid.*, p. 293.

salvation.'[84] Although 'it is wrong to standardize the experience',[85] since it comes with many variations of intensity and duration, yet it is a direct and sovereign work of the Holy Spirit, unpredictable, uncontrollable and unforgettable. It brings a heightened love for God, an unspeakable joy, and an uninhibited boldness in witness. Dr Lloyd-Jones went on to defend his thesis by appealing to an impressive array of historical testimonies. Despite the diversity of their ecclesiastical backgrounds, they manifest 'a strange and curious unanimity'.[86]

I have no wish whatever to call in question the authenticity of the experiences described. Nor do I doubt that many Christian people continue to be granted similar profound encounters with God today. Nor is there any problem in affirming that the ministry of the Spirit of adoption (15) and the inner witness of the Spirit (16) are designed to bring us assurance. My anxiety is whether the biblical texts have been rightly interpreted. I have the uneasy feeling that it is the experiences which have determined the exposition. For the natural reading of Romans 8:14–17 is surely that *all* believers are 'led by the Spirit' (14), have 'received a Spirit of adoption' (15, REB), and cry '*Abba*, Father' as the Spirit himself bears witness to them that they are God's children (16) and therefore also his heirs (17). There is no indication in these four verses that a special, distinctive or overwhelming experience is in mind, which needs to be sought by all although it is given only to some. On the contrary, the whole paragraph appears to be descriptive of what is, or should be, common to all believers. Though doubtless in differing degrees of intensity, all who have the Spirit's indwelling (9) are given the Spirit's witness too (15–16).

Looking back now over the first half of Romans 8, we have seen something of the multiple ministries of the Holy Spirit. He has liberated us from the bondage of the law (2), while at the same time he empowers us to fulfil its just requirement (4). We now live each day according to the Spirit and set our minds on his desires (5). He lives in us (9), gives life to our spirits (10), and will one day give life to our bodies too (11). His indwelling obliges us to live his way (12), and his power enables us to put to death our body's misdeeds (13). He leads us as God's children (14) and bears witness to our spirit that this is what we are (15–16). He himself is also the foretaste of our inheritance in glory (17, 23). It is his indwelling which makes the fundamental difference between Romans 7 and Romans 8.

---

[84] *Ibid.*, p. 302.   [85] *Ibid.*, p. 329.   [86] *Ibid.*, p. 356.

2. The glory of God's children (18–27)

Paul now moves on from the present ministry of God's Spirit to the future glory of God's children, of which indeed the Holy Spirit is *the firstfruits* (23). What prompted this development was clearly his allusion to our sharing in the sufferings and glory of Christ (17). For 'suffering and glory' is the theme throughout this section, first the sufferings and glory of God's creation (19–22) and then the sufferings and glory of God's children (23–27). Four general, introductory points about them need to be made.

First, the sufferings and the glory belong together indissolubly. They did in the experience of Christ; they do in the experience of his people also (17). It is only after we 'have suffered a little while' that we will enter God's 'eternal glory in Christ', to which he has called us.[87] So the sufferings and the glory are married; they cannot be divorced. They are welded; they cannot be broken apart.

Secondly, the sufferings and the glory characterize the two ages or aeons. The contrast between this age and the age to come, and so between the present and the future, between the already and the not yet, is neatly summed up in the two terms *pathēmata* (sufferings) and *doxa* (glory). Moreover, the 'sufferings' include not only the opposition of the world, but all our human frailty as well, both physical and moral, which is due to our provisional, half-saved condition. The 'glory', however, is the unutterable splendour of God, eternal, immortal and incorruptible. One day it *will be revealed* (18). This end-time disclosure will be made 'to us' (RSV), because we will see it, and *in us* (NIV), because we will share in it and be changed by it.[88] It is also 'in store for us' (REB), although the precise nature of 'what we will be has not yet been made known'.[89]

Thirdly, the sufferings and the glory cannot be compared. *I consider*, writes Paul, expressing 'a firm conviction reached by rational thought on the basis of the gospel',[90] *that our present sufferings*, or literally 'the sufferings of the now time', of this continuing age, painful though they are (as Paul knows well from experience), *are not worth comparing with the glory that will be revealed in us* (18). 'Suffering' and 'glory' are inseparable, since suffering is the way to glory (see verse 17), but they are not comparable. They need to be contrasted, not compared. In an earlier letter Paul has evaluated them in terms of their 'weight'. Our present troubles, he declared, are 'light and momentary', but the glory to come is 'eternal' and 'far outweighs them all'.[91] The magnificence of God's revealed glory will greatly surpass the unpleasantness of our sufferings.

---

[87] 1 Pet. 5:10.   [88] 2 Thes. 1:10.   [89] 1 Jn. 3:2.   [90] Cranfield, vol. I, p. 408.
[91] 2 Cor. 4:17. Note that the Hebrew word for 'glory' is *kabod*, which means 'heaviness' or 'weight'.

Fourthly, the sufferings and the glory concern both God's creation and God's children. Paul now writes from a cosmic perspective. The sufferings and glory of the old creation (the material order) and of the new (the people of God) are integrally related to each other. Both creations are suffering and groaning now; both are going to be set free together. As nature shared in the curse,[92] and now shares in the pain, so it will also share in the glory. Hence *the creation waits in eager expectation for the sons of God to be revealed* (19). The word for 'eager expectation' is *apokaradokia*, which is derived from *kara*, the head. It means 'to wait with the head raised, and the eye fixed on that point of the horizon from which the expected object is to come'.[93] It depicts somebody standing 'on tiptoe' (JBP) or 'stretching the neck, craning forward'[94] in order to be able to see. And what the creation is looking for is the revelation of God's children, that is, the disclosure of their identity on the one hand and their investiture with glory on the other. This will be the signal for the renewal of the whole creation.

But what is meant by *the creation* (*hē ktisis*), an expression which occurs four times in verses 19–22, once in each verse? The REB translation 'the created universe' is something of an anachronism, since Paul had no knowledge of the galaxies. His focus will have been on the earth, as the stage on which the drama of fall and redemption is being played. By *the creation*, then, he will have intended 'the earth, with all it contains, animate and inanimate, man excepted',[95] or 'the sum-total of subhuman nature'.[96]

a. *The sufferings and glory of God's creation (20–22)*

Paul personifies 'the creation', much as we often personify 'nature'. Indeed, there is 'nothing ... unnatural, unusual or unscriptural'[97] about doing so, since such personifications are quite common in the Old Testament. For example, the heavens, earth and sea, with all their contents, the fields, trees of the forest, rivers and mountains are all summoned to rejoice and to sing to Yahweh.[98]

The apostle now makes three statements about the creation, which relate respectively to its past, future and present.

First, *the creation was subjected to frustration* (20a). This reference to the past must surely be to the judgment of God, which fell on the natural order following Adam's disobedience. The ground was cursed because of him.[99] In consequence, it would 'produce thorns and thistles', so that Adam and his descendants would

---

[92] Gn. 3:17ff. [93] Godet, p. 313. [94] Cranfield, vol. I, p. 410.
[95] Hodge, p. 271. [96] Cranfield, vol. I, p. 412.
[97] Hodge, p. 271. [98] Ps. 96:11ff.; 98:7ff.
[99] Gn. 3:17ff.; *cf.* Rev. 22:3: 'No longer will there be any curse.'

extract food from it only by 'painful toil' and sweat, until death claimed them and they returned to the dust from which they had been taken. Paul does not allude to these details. Instead, he sums up the result of God's curse by the one word *mataiotēs, frustration*. It means 'emptiness, futility, purposelessness, transitoriness' (BAGD). The basic idea is emptiness, whether of purpose or of result. It is the word chosen by the LXX translators for 'Vanity of vanities! . . . All is vanity',[100] which NIV finely renders 'Meaningless! Meaningless! . . . Utterly meaningless!' As C. J. Vaughan comments, 'the whole Book of Ecclesiastes is a commentary upon this verse'.[101] For it expresses the existential absurdity of a life lived 'under the sun', imprisoned in time and space, with no ultimate reference point to either God or eternity.

The apostle adds that the creation's subjection to frustration or 'futility' (RSV) was *not by its own choice, but by the will of the one who subjected it, in hope* (20b). These last two words are enough to prove that the person in mind, whose will subjected the creation to futility, was neither Satan nor Adam, as a few commentators have suggested. Only God, being both Judge and Saviour, entertained hope for the world he cursed.

Secondly, *the creation itself will be liberated* (21a). The word 'hope' is the pivot on which Paul turns from the past to the future of creation. Its subjection to frustration will not last for ever, God has promised. One day it will experience a new beginning, which Paul terms a 'liberation', with both a negative and a positive aspect.

Negatively, creation will be *liberated from its bondage to decay* (21b). *Phthora (decay)* seems to denote not only that the universe is running down (as we would say), but that nature is also enslaved, locked into an unending cycle, so that conception, birth and growth are relentlessly following by decline, decay, death and decomposition. In addition, there may be a passing reference to predation and pain, especially the latter which is mentioned in the next verse. So futility, bondage, decay and pain are the words the apostle uses to indicate that creation is out of joint because under judgment. It still works, for the mechanisms of nature are fine-tuned and delicately balanced. And much of it is breathtakingly beautiful, revealing the Creator's hand. But it is also in bondage to disintegration and frustration. In the end, however, it will be 'freed from the shackles of mortality' (REB), 'rescued from the tyranny of change and decay' (JBP).

Positively, creation will be *liberated . . . into the glorious freedom of the children of God* (21c), literally 'into the freedom of their glory'. These nouns correspond to those of the previous clause, for nature

---

[100] Ec. 1:2, RSV. [101] Vaughan, p. 158.

will be brought out of bondage into freedom, out of decay into glory; that is, out of corruption into incorruption. Indeed, God's creation will share in the glory of God's children, which is itself the glory of Christ (see 17–18).

This expectation that nature itself will be renewed is integral to the Old Testament prophetic vision of the messianic age, especially in the Psalms and Isaiah. Vivid images are used to express Israel's faith that the earth and the heavens will be changed like clothing;[102] that God 'will create new heavens and a new earth', including a new Jerusalem;[103] that the desert will blossom like the crocus, and so display the glory of Yahweh;[104] that wild and domestic animals will co-exist in peace, and that even the most ferocious and poisonous creatures 'will neither harm nor destroy' throughout God's new world.[105]

The New Testament writers do not take up the details of this poetic imagery. But Jesus himself spoke of the 'new birth' (*palingenesia*) of the world at his coming;[106] Peter of the 'restoration' (*apokatastasis*) of all things;[107] Paul here of the liberation, and elsewhere of the reconciliation, of all things;[108] and John of the new heaven and earth, in which God will dwell with his people, and from which all separation, sorrow, pain and death will have been eliminated.[109] It would not be wise for us to speculate, let alone dogmatize, how the biblical and the scientific accounts of reality correspond or harmonize, either in the present or in the future. The general promise of the renovation and transformation of nature is plain, including the eradication of all harmful elements and their replacement by righteousness, peace, harmony, joy and security. But we should be cautious in pressing the details. The future glory is beyond our imagination. What we do know is that God's material creation will be redeemed and glorified, because God's children will be redeemed and glorified. This is how Charles Cranfield has expressed it:

And, if the question is asked, 'What sense can there be in saying that the sub-human creation – the Jungfrau, for example, or the Matterhorn, or the planet Venus – suffers frustration by being prevented from properly fulfilling the purpose of its existence?', the answer must surely be that the whole magnificent theatre of the universe, together with all its splendid properties and all the varied chorus of sub-human life, created for God's glory, is cheated of its true fulfilment so long as man, the chief actor

---

[102] Ps. 102:25ff.   [103] Is. 65:17ff.; *cf.* 66:22.   [104] Is. 35:1ff.; *cf.* 32:15ff.
[105] Is. 11:6ff.; *cf.* 65:25.   [106] Mt. 19:28, 'the renewal of all things', NIV.
[107] Acts 3:19, 21.   [108] Eph. 1:10; Col. 1:20.
[109] Rev. 21, 22; *cf.* 2 Pet. 3:13; Heb. 12:26f.

in the great drama of God's praise, fails to contribute his rational part.[110]

Thirdly, *the whole creation has been groaning . . . right up to the present time* (22). So far the apostle has told us that the creation 'was subjected to frustration' in the past (20) and 'will be liberated' in the future (21). Now he adds that meanwhile, in the present, even while it is eagerly awaiting the final revelation (19), the creation is *groaning* in pain. Its groans are not meaningless, however, or symptoms of despair. On the contrary, they are like *the pains of childbirth*, for they provide assurance of the coming emergence of a new order. In Jewish apocalyptic literature Israel's current sufferings were frequently called 'the woes of the Messiah' or 'the birthpangs of the messianic age'. That is, they were seen as the painful prelude to, indeed the herald of, the victorious arrival of the Messiah. Jesus himself used the same expression in his own apocalyptic discourse. He spoke of false teachers, wars, famines and earthquakes as 'the beginning of birth-pains' (NIV) or 'the first birth-pangs of the new age' (REB), that is, preliminary signs of his coming.[111]

Verse 22 actually brings together the past, present and future. For not only is the creation groaning now, but it is groaning 'until now', which makes the NIV *has been groaning* legitimate. And since its groans are labour pains, they look forward to the coming new order. Although we must be careful not to impose modern scientific categories on Paul, we must hold on to his combination of present sufferings and future glory. Each verse expresses it. The creation's subjection to frustration was *in hope* (20). The bondage to decay will give place to the freedom of glory (21). The pains of labour will be followed by the joys of birth (22). There is therefore going to be both continuity and discontinuity in the regeneration of the world, as in the resurrection of the body. The universe is not going to be destroyed, but rather liberated, transformed and suffused with the glory of God.

b. The sufferings and glory of God's children (23–27)

Verses 22–23 draw an important parallel between God's creation and God's children. Verse 22 speaks of the whole creation groaning. Verse 23 begins: *Not only so, but we ourselves . . . groan inwardly . . .* Even we, who are no longer in Adam but in Christ, we who no longer live according to the flesh but *have the firstfruits of the Spirit,*

---

[110] From his essay entitled 'Some Observations on Romans 8:19–21d' in Robert Banks (ed.), *Reconciliation and Hope* (Eerdmans and Paternoster, 1974), p. 227.
[111] Mt. 24:8; Mk. 13:8; *cf.* Jn. 16:20ff.

we in whom God's new creation has already begun,[112] even we continue to groan inside ourselves *as we wait eagerly for our adoption as sons, the redemption of our bodies* (23). This is our Christian dilemma. Caught in the tension between what God has inaugurated (by giving us his Spirit) and what he will consummate (in our final adoption and redemption), we groan with discomfort and longing. The indwelling Spirit gives us joy,[113] and the coming glory gives us hope (*e.g.* 5:2), but the interim suspense gives us pain.

Paul now highlights different aspects of our half-saved condition by five affirmations.

First, *we ... have the firstfruits of the Spirit* (23a). *Aparchē*, the firstfruits, was both the beginning of the harvest and the pledge that the full harvest would follow in due time. Perhaps Paul had in mind that the Feast of Weeks, which celebrated the reaping of the firstfruits, was the very festival (called in Greek 'Pentecost') on which the Spirit had been given. Replacing this agricultural metaphor with a commercial one, Paul also described the gift of the Spirit as God's *arrabōn*, the 'first instalment, deposit, down payment, pledge' (BAGD), which guaranteed the future completion of the purchase.[114] Although we have not yet received our final adoption or redemption, we have already received the Spirit as both foretaste and promise of these blessings.

Secondly, *we ... groan inwardly* (23b). The juxtaposition of the Spirit's indwelling and our groaning should not surprise us. For the very presence of the Spirit (being only the firstfruits) is a constant reminder of the incompleteness of our salvation, as we share with the creation in the frustration, the bondage to decay and the pain. So one reason for our groaning is our physical frailty and mortality. Paul expresses this elsewhere: 'Meanwhile we groan, longing to be clothed with our heavenly dwelling [meaning probably our resurrection body] ... For while we are in this tent [our temporary, flimsy, material body], we groan and are burdened ....'[115] But it is not only our fragile body (*sōma*) which makes us groan; it is also our fallen nature (*sarx*), which hinders us from behaving as we should, and would altogether prevent us from it, were it not for the indwelling Spirit (7:17, 20). We long, therefore, for our *sarx* to be destroyed and for our *sōma* to be transformed. Our groans express both present pain and future longing. Some Christians, however, grin too much (they seem to have no place in their theology for pain) and groan too little.

Thirdly, *we wait eagerly for our adoption as sons, the redemption of our bodies* (23c). Just as the groaning creation waits eagerly for God's sons to be revealed (19), so we groaning Christians wait

---

[112] *Cf.* 2 Cor. 5:17.   [113] *E.g.* Gal. 5:22; 1 Thes. 1:6.
[114] See 2 Cor. 1:22; 5:5; Eph. 1:4.   [115] 2 Cor. 5:2, 4.

eagerly for our adoption as sons, even our bodily redemption. We have, of course, already been adopted by God (15), and the Spirit assures us that we are his children (16). Yet there is an even deeper and richer child–Father relationship to come when we are fully 'revealed' as his children (19) and 'conformed to the likeness of his Son' (29). Again, we have already been redeemed,[116] but not yet our bodies. Already our spirits are alive (10), but one day the Spirit will also give life to our bodies (11). More than that, our bodies will be changed by Christ to be 'like his glorious body'.[117] 'Bondage to decay' will be replaced by the 'freedom of glory' (21).

Fourthly, *in this hope we were saved* (24a). *We were saved* (*esōthēmen*) is an aorist tense. It bears witness to our decisive past liberation from the guilt and bondage of our sins, and from the just judgment of God upon them.[118] Yet we remain only half-saved. For we have not yet been saved from the outpouring of God's wrath in the day of judgment (5:9), nor have the final vestiges of sin in our human personality been eradicated. Not yet has our *sarx* been obliterated; not yet has our *sōma* been redeemed. So we were saved *in hope* of our total liberation (24a), as the creation was subjected to frustration *in . . . hope* of being set free from it (20). This double hope looks to the future and to things which, being future, are so far unseen. For *hope that is seen*, having been realized in our experience, *is no hope at all. Who hopes for what he already has?* (24b). Instead, *we hope for what we do not yet have* (25a).[119]

Fifthly, *we wait for it patiently* (25b), that is, for the fulfilment of our hope. For we are confident in God's promises that the firstfruits will be followed by the harvest, bondage by freedom, decay by incorruption, and labour pains by the birth of the new world. This whole section is a notable example of what it means to be living 'in between times', between present difficulty and future destiny, between the already and the not yet, between sufferings and glory. 'We were saved in hope' brings them together. And in this tension the correct Christian posture is that of waiting, waiting 'eagerly' (23, *cf.* 19) with keen expectation, and waiting 'patiently' (25), steadfast in the endurance of our trials (*hypomonē*). The same verb occurs in both verses (*apekdechomai*, 23 and 25, as also in 19), and includes in itself the note of 'eagerness', whereas 'patience' or 'perseverance' is added to it in verse 25. The combination is significant. We are to wait neither so eagerly that we lose our patience, nor so patiently that we lose our expectation, but eagerly and patiently together.

---

[116] *Cf.* Eph. 1:7; Col. 1:14; *cf.* Rom. 3:24; 1 Cor. 1:30.
[117] Phil. 3:21; *cf.* 1 Cor. 15:35ff.   [118] *Cf.* Eph. 2:8.   [119] *Cf.* Heb. 11:1.

Yet it is hard to keep this balance. Some Christians over-emphasize the call to patience. They lack enthusiasm and lapse into lethargy, apathy and pessimism. They have forgotten God's promises, and are guilty of unbelief. Others grow impatient of waiting. They are so carried away with enthusiasm that they almost try to force God's hand. They are determined to experience now even what is not available yet. Understandably anxious to emerge out of the painful present of suffering and groaning, they talk as if the resurrection had already taken place, and as if the body should no longer be subject to weakness, disease, pain and decay. Yet such impatience is a form of presumption. It is to rebel against the God of history, who has indeed acted conclusively for our salvation, and who will most assuredly complete (when Christ comes) what he has begun, but who refuses to be hustled into changing his planned timetable just because we do not enjoy having to go on waiting and groaning. God give us a patient eagerness and an eager patience as we wait for his promises to be fulfilled!

In this life of expectancy Paul now brings us another encouragement. It again concerns the ministry of the Holy Spirit. This ministry he has so far portrayed in relation first to the law which he enables us to fulfil (2–8), secondly to our fallen nature which he subdues (9–13), thirdly to our adoption into God's family, of which he assures us (14–17), and fourthly to our final inheritance of which he is the guarantee and foretaste (18–23). Now, fifthly, he writes of the Holy Spirit in relation to our prayers (26–27). Indeed, true Christian prayer is impossible without the Holy Spirit. It is he who causes us to cry 'Abba, *Father*' (15) when we pray. Prayer is in itself an essentially trinitarian exercise. It is access to the Father through the Son and by the Spirit.[120] The inspiration of the Spirit is just as necessary for our prayers as the mediation of the Son. We can approach the Father only through the Son and only by the Spirit.

In the same way, Paul begins (26), probably meaning that as our Christian hope sustains us, so does the Holy Spirit. In general, *the Spirit helps us in our weakness* (26a), that is, in the ambiguity and frailty of our 'already–not yet' existence. In particular, he helps our weakness in prayer. In this sphere our infirmity is our ignorance: *We do not know what we ought to pray for* (26b). But he knows what we do not know. In consequence, *the Spirit himself intercedes for us* (26c). Thus 'the children of God have two divine intercessors', writes John Murray. 'Christ is their intercessor in the court of heaven ...', while 'the Holy Spirit is their intercessor in the theatre of their own hearts.'[121]

Moreover, the Holy Spirit's intercession is said to be *with groans*

---

[120] Eph. 2:18.   [121] Murray, vol. I, p. 311.

that words cannot express (26d), or 'sighs too deep for words' (RSV). Strictly speaking, these translations are inaccurate. For the adjective *alalētos* simply means 'wordless' (BAGD). The point Paul is making is not that the groans cannot be put into words, but that in fact they are not. They are unexpressed, rather than inexpressible. In the context, these wordless groans must surely be related to the groans both of God's creation (22) and of God's children (23), namely 'agonized longings' (JBP) for final redemption and the consummation of all things. Why do we not know what to pray for? Perhaps because we are unsure whether to pray for deliverance from our sufferings or for strength to endure them.[122] Also, since we do not know what we will be,[123] or when or how, we are in no position to make precise requests. So the Spirit intercedes for us, and does so with speechless groans.

It is truly amazing that, having written of the groaning creation and of the groaning church, Paul should now write of the groaning Spirit. Indeed, some commentators have resisted this, declaring that the Spirit never groans, and that Paul means only that he causes us to groan. Yet Paul's language is clear. The Spirit intercedes for us in unspoken groanings. That is, his intercession is accompanied by them and expressed in them. True, God's creation and God's children groan because of their present state of imperfection, and there is nothing imperfect about the Holy Spirit. It must be, therefore, that the Holy Spirit identifies with our groans, with the pain of the world and the church, and shares in the longing for the final freedom of both. We and he groan together.

These groans can hardly be *glossolalia*,[124] since those 'tongues' or languages were expressed in words which some could understand and interpret.[125] Here Paul is referring rather to inarticulate groans. Although wordless, however, they are not meaningless. For God the Father, *who searches our hearts* – a uniquely divine activity[126] – *knows the mind of the Spirit, because the Spirit intercedes for the saints* (that is, the people of God) *in accordance with God's will* (27).[127]

So three persons are involved in our praying. First, we ourselves in our weakness do not know what to pray for. Secondly, the indwelling Spirit helps us by interceding for us and through us, with speechless groans but according to God's will. Thirdly, God the Father, who both searches our hearts and knows the Spirit's mind, hears and answers accordingly. Of these actors, however, it is the

[122] *Cf.* Phil. 1:19ff.; *cf.* Jn. 12:27.   [123] 1 Jn. 3:2.
[124] *Pace* Käsemann, pp. 240–242.
[125] Acts 2:4ff.; 1 Cor. 14:13ff., 26ff.
[126] *Cf.* 1 Sa. 16:7; Ps. 7:9; 139:1ff.; Je. 17:10; Acts 15:8; 1 Thes. 2:4.
[127] *Cf.* 1 Jn. 5:14.

Spirit who is emphasized. Paul makes three statements about him. First, 'the Spirit helps us' (because of our weakly, half-saved situation); secondly, 'the Spirit intercedes for us' (because of our ignorance of what to pray for); and thirdly, 'the Spirit intercedes according to God's will' (and therefore God listens and responds).

3.   The steadfastness of God's love (28–39)

In the last twelve verses of Romans 8 the apostle soars to sublime heights unequalled elsewhere in the New Testament. Having described the chief privileges of justified believers – peace with God (5:1–11), union with Christ (5:12 – 6:23), freedom from the law (7:1–25) and life in the Spirit (8:1–27) – his great Spirit-directed mind now sweeps over the whole plan and purpose of God from a past eternity to an eternity still to come, from the divine foreknowledge and predestination to the divine love from which absolutely nothing will ever be able to separate us.

To be sure, at present we experience sufferings and groans, but we are sustained in the midst of them by the hope of glory. So far it is only a 'hope', because it is still future, unseen and unrealized, but it is not on that account uncertain. On the contrary, our Christian hope is solidly grounded on the unwavering love of God. So the burden of Paul's climax is the eternal security of God's people, on account of the eternal unchangeability of God's purpose, which is itself due to the eternal steadfastness of God's love.

These tremendous truths the apostle declares three times over, although from three different perspectives. He begins with five unshakeable convictions (28) about God working all things together for the good of his people. He continues with five undeniable affirmations (29–30) regarding the successive stages of God's saving purpose from eternity to eternity. And he concludes with five unanswerable questions (31–39), in which he challenges anybody to contradict the convictions and the affirmations which he has just expressed.

a.   Five unshakeable convictions (28)

Romans 8:28 is surely one of the best-known texts in the Bible. On it believers of every age and place have stayed their minds. It has been likened to a pillow on which to rest our weary heads.

We note that verse 28 begins with the statement *we know*. Verse 22 began likewise. So here are two assertions of Christian knowledge, one about the groaning creation and the other about God's providential care. Yet there are many other things which we do not know. For example, 'we do not know what we ought to pray for'

(26). In fact, we are caught in a continuous tension between what we know and what we do not know. It is just as foolish to claim to know what we do not know as it is to confess not to know what we do know. In those areas in which God has not plainly revealed his mind, the right attitude for us to adopt is that of Christian agnosticism.[128] But in verse 28 Paul lists five truths about God's providence which *we know*.

First, we know that *God works*, or is at work, in our lives. The familiar AV rendering that 'all things work together for good' is surely to be rejected, since all things do not automatically work themselves together into a pattern of good. The AV statement would be acceptable only if 'it is the sovereign guidance of God that is presumed as the undergirding and directing force behind all the events of life'.[129] An early copyist evidently felt the need to make this explicit by adding 'God' as the subject of the verb. But the manuscript support for this reading, although 'both ancient and noteworthy',[130] is insufficient to secure its acceptance. The addition is also unnecessary, for the order of words permits the translation, 'we know that for those who love God he is working . . .'. He is ceaselessly, energetically and purposefully active on their behalf.

Secondly, God is at work *for the good of* his people. Being himself wholly good, his works are all expressions of his goodness and are calculated to advance his people's good. Moreover, the 'good' which is the goal of all his providential dealings with us is our ultimate well-being, namely our final salvation. Verses 29–30 make this plain.

Thirdly, God works for our good *in all things*. The NIV translation understands *panta* ('all things') not as the object of the verb ('God works everything for good') but as an accusative of respect ('in everything God works for good'). Either way, 'all things' must include the sufferings of verse 17 and the groanings of verse 23. 'Thus all that is negative in this life is seen to have a positive purpose in the execution of God's eternal plan.'[131] Nothing is beyond the overruling, overriding scope of his providence.

Fourthly, God works in all things for the good of *those who love him*. This is a necessary limitation. Paul is not expressing a general, superficial optimism that everything tends to everybody's good in the end. No, if the 'good' which is God's objective is our completed salvation, then its beneficiaries are his people who are described as those who love him. This is an unusual phrase for Paul, because his references in Romans to love are rather to God's love for us (*e.g.* 5:5, 8; 8:35, 37, 39). Nevertheless, he does elsewhere allude to our

---

[128] See Dt. 29:29.   [129] Moo, p. 565.   [130] Metzger (1975), p. 518.
[131] Nygren, p. 338.

love for God,[132] and this is a common biblical concept, since the first and great commandment is that we love God with all our being.[133]

Fifthly, those who love God are also described as those *who have been called according to his purpose*. For 'their love for him is a sign and token of his prior love for them',[134] which has found expression in his eternal purpose and his historical call. So God has a saving purpose, and is working in accordance with it. Life is not the random mess which it may sometimes appear.

These are the five truths about God which, Paul writes, *we know*. We do not always understand what God is doing, let alone welcome it. Nor are we told that he is at work for our comfort. But we know that in all things he is working towards our supreme good. And one of the reasons we know this is that we are given many examples of it in Scripture. For instance, this was Joseph's conviction about his brothers' cruelty in selling him into Egypt: 'You intended to harm me, but God intended it for good ... the saving of many lives.'[135] Similarly, Jeremiah wrote in God's name a letter to the Jews in Babylonian exile after the catastrophic destruction of Jerusalem: '"I know the plans I have for you," declares the LORD, "plans to prosper you and not to harm you, plans to give you hope and a future."'[136] The same concurrence of human evil and divine plan had its most conspicuous display in the cross, which Peter attributed both to the wickedness of men and to 'God's set purpose and foreknowledge'.[137]

b. Five undeniable affirmations (29–30)

In these two verses Paul elaborates what he meant in verse 28 by God's 'purpose', according to which he has called us and is working everything together for our good. He traces God's good and saving purpose through five stages from its beginning in his mind to its consummation in the coming glory. These stages he names foreknowledge, predestination, calling, justification and glorification.

First comes a reference to *those God foreknew*. Since the common meaning of 'to foreknow' is to know something beforehand, in advance of its happening, some commentators both ancient and modern have concluded that God foresees who will believe, and that this foreknowledge is the basis of his predestination. But this cannot be right, for at least two reasons. First, in this sense God

---

[132] *E.g.* 1 Cor. 2:9; 8:3; *cf.* Eph. 6:24.   [133] Dt. 6:5; Mk. 12:30.
[134] Cranfield, vol. I, p. 431; *cf.* 1 Jn. 4:19.
[135] Gn. 50:20.   [136] Je. 29:11.   [137] Acts 2:23; *cf.* 4:27f.

foreknows everybody and everything, whereas Paul is referring to a particular group. Secondly, if God predestines people because they are going to believe, then the ground of their salvation is in themselves and their merit, instead of in him and his mercy, whereas Paul's whole emphasis is on God's free initiative of grace.

Other commentators have therefore reminded us that the Hebrew verb 'to know' expresses much more than mere intellectual cognition; it denotes a personal relationship of care and affection. Thus, when God 'knows' people, he watches over them,[138] and when he 'knew' the children of Israel in the desert, what is meant is that he cared for them.[139] Indeed, Israel was the only people out of all the families of the earth whom Yahweh had 'known', that is, loved, chosen and formed a covenant with.[140] The meaning of 'foreknowledge' in the New Testament is similar. 'God did not reject his people [Israel], whom he foreknew', that is, whom he loved and chose (11:2).[141] In the light of this biblical usage John Murray writes: ' "Know" . . . is used in a sense practically synonymous with "love" . . . "Whom he foreknew" . . . is therefore virtually equivalent to "whom he foreloved".'[142] Foreknowledge is 'sovereign, distinguishing love'.[143] This fits in with Moses' great statement: 'The Lord did not set his affection on you and choose you because you were more numerous than other peoples . . . But it was because the Lord loved you . . . .'[144] The only source of divine election and predestination is divine love.

Secondly, *those God foreknew*, or foreloved, *he also predestined to be conformed to the likeness of his Son, that he might be the firstborn among many brothers* (29). The verb *predestined* translates *proorizō*, which means to 'decide upon beforehand' (BAGD), as in Acts 4:28 ('They did what your power and will had decided beforehand should happen'). Clearly, then, a decision is involved in the process of becoming a Christian, but it is God's decision before it can be ours. This is not to deny that we 'decided for Christ', and freely, but to affirm that we did so only because he had first 'decided for us'. This emphasis on God's gracious, sovereign decision or choice is reinforced by the vocabulary with which it is associated. On the one hand, it is attributed to God's 'pleasure', 'will', 'plan' and 'purpose',[145] and on the other it is traced back to 'before the creation of the world'[146] or 'before time began'.[147] C. J. Vaughan sums the issue up in these words:

---

[138] Ps. 1:6; 144:3.   [139] Ho. 13:5.   [140] Am. 3:2.   [141] *Cf.* 1 Pet. 1:2.
[142] Murray, vol. I, p. 317.   [143] *Ibid.*, p. 318.
[144] Dt. 7:7f.; *cf.* Eph. 1:4f.   [145] Eph. 1:5, 9, 11; 3:11.
[146] *E.g.* Eph. 1:4.
[147] 1 Cor. 2:7; 2 Tim. 1:9; *cf.* 1 Pet. 1:20; Rev. 13:8.

Everyone who is eventually saved can only ascribe his salvation, from the first step to the last, to God's favour and act. Human merit must be excluded: and this can only be by tracing back the work far beyond the obedience which evidences, or even the faith which appropriates, salvation; even to an act of spontaneous favour on the part of that God who foresees and foreordains from eternity all his works.[148]

Neither Scripture nor experience allows us to weaken this teaching. As for Scripture, not only throughout the Old Testament is Israel acknowledged as 'the one nation on earth that God went out to redeem as a people for himself', to be his special 'treasured possession',[149] but throughout the New Testament it is recognized that human beings are by nature blind, deaf and dead, so that their conversion is impossible unless God gives them sight, hearing and life.

Our own experience confirms this. Dr J. I. Packer, in his fine essay *Evangelism and the Sovereignty of God*,[150] points out that in fact all Christian people believe in God's sovereignty in salvation, even if they deny it. 'Two facts show this,' he writes. 'In the first place, you give God thanks for your conversion. Now why do you do that? Because you know in your heart that God was entirely responsible for it. You did not save yourself; he saved you . . . There is a second way in which you acknowledge that God is sovereign in salvation. You pray for the conversion of others . . . You ask God to work in them everything necessary for their salvation.' So our thanksgivings and our intercessions prove that we believe in divine sovereignty. 'On our feet we may have arguments about it, but on our knees we are all agreed.'[151]

Yet the mysteries remain. And as finite and fallen creatures we have no right to demand explanations from our infinite and perfect Creator. Nevertheless, he has thrown light on our problem in such a way as to contradict the chief objections which are raised and to show that the consequences of predestination are the opposite of what is popularly supposed. I give five examples.

1. Predestination is said to foster arrogance, since (it is alleged) God's elect boast of their favoured status. But on the contrary, predestination excludes boasting. For it fills God's people with astonishment that he should ever have had mercy on undeserving sinners like them. Humbled before the cross, they desire to live the rest of their lives only 'to the praise of his glorious grace'[152] and to spend eternity worshipping the Lamb who was slain.[153]

---

[148] Vaughan, p. 163.
[149] 2 Sa. 7:22ff.; *cf.* Ex. 19:3ff.; Dt. 7:6; 10:15; 14:2; Ps. 135:4.
[150] Inter-Varsity Press, 1961.   [151] *Ibid.*, pp. 12ff.   [152] Eph. 1:6, 12, 14.
[153] Rev. 5:11ff.

2. Predestination is said to foster uncertainty, and to create in people a neurotic anxiety as to whether they are predestined and saved or not. But this is not so. If they are unbelievers, they are entirely unconcerned about their salvation, until and unless the Holy Spirit brings them under conviction of sin as a prelude to their conversion. If they are believers, however, even when passing through a period of doubt, they know that in the end their security lies only in the eternal, predestinating will of God. Nothing else can bring such assurance and comfort. As Luther wrote in his comment on verse 28, predestination 'is a wonderfully sweet thing for those who have the Spirit'.[154]

3. Predestination is said to foster apathy. For if salvation is entirely God's work and not ours, people argue, then all human responsibility before God has been undermined. But again this is not so. On the contrary, it is abundantly clear that Scripture's emphasis on God's sovereignty never diminishes our responsibility. Instead, the two lie side by side in an antinomy, which is an apparent contradiction between two truths. Unlike a paradox, an antinomy is 'not deliberately manufactured; it is forced upon us by the facts themselves . . . We do not invent it, and we cannot explain it. Nor is there any way to get rid of it, save by falsifying the very facts that led us to it.'[155] A good example is found in the teaching of Jesus, who declared both that 'no-one can come to me unless the Father . . . draws him'[156] and that 'you refuse to come to me to have life'.[157] Why do people not come to Jesus? Is it that they cannot? Or is it that they will not? The only answer which is compatible with his own teaching is, 'Both, even though we cannot reconcile them.'

4. Predestination is said to foster complacency, and to breed antinomians. For, if God has predestined us to eternal salvation, why should we not live as we please, without moral restraint, and in defiance of divine law? Paul has already answered this objection in chapter 6. Those whom God has chosen and called he has united to Christ in his death and resurrection. Having died to sin, they now live a new life to God. And elsewhere Paul writes that 'he chose us in him before the creation of the world to be holy and blameless in his sight'.[158] Indeed, he has predestined us *to be conformed to the likeness of his Son* (29).

5. Predestination is said to foster narrow-mindedness, as the elect people of God become absorbed only in themselves. The opposite is the case. The reason God called one man Abraham and his one family was not for their blessing only, but that through them all the families of the earth might be blessed.[159] Similarly, the reason God

---

[154] Luther (1515), p. 371. [155] Packer, *op. cit.*, p. 21. [156] Jn. 6:44.
[157] Jn. 5:40. [158] Eph. 1:4; *cf.* 2 Tim. 1:9. [159] Gn. 12:1ff.

chose his Servant, that shadowy figure in Isaiah whom we see partly fulfilled in Israel, but specially in Christ and his people, was not only to glorify Israel but to bring light and justice to the nations.[160] Indeed these promises were a great spur to Paul (as they should be to us) when he courageously broadened his evangelistic vision to include the Gentiles.[161] Thus, God has made us his own people, not that we should be his favourites, but that we should be his witnesses, 'to proclaim the glorious deeds of him who has called you out of darkness into his marvellous light'.[162]

So the doctrine of divine predestination promotes humility, not arrogance; assurance, not apprehension; responsibility, not apathy; holiness, not complacency; and mission, not privilege. This is not to claim that there are no problems, but to indicate that they are more intellectual than pastoral.

Certainly the point Paul singles out for emphasis in verse 29 is pastoral. It concerns the two practical purposes of God's predestination. The first is that we should *be conformed to the likeness of his Son*. In the simplest possible terms, God's eternal purpose for his people is that we should become like Jesus. The transformation process begins here and now in our character and conduct, through the work of the Holy Spirit,[163] but will be brought to completion only when Christ comes and we see him,[164] and our bodies become like the body of his glory.[165] The second purpose of God's predestination is that, as a result of our conformity to the image of Christ, *he might be the firstborn among many brothers*, enjoying both the community of the family and the pre-eminence of the firstborn.[166]

We now come to Paul's third affirmation: *those he predestined, he also called* (30a). The call of God is the historical application of his eternal predestination. His call comes to people through the gospel,[167] and it is when the gospel is preached to them with power, and they respond to it with the obedience of faith, that we know God has chosen them.[168] So evangelism (the preaching of the gospel), far from being rendered superfluous by God's predestination, is indispensable, because it is the very means God has ordained by which his call comes to his people and awakens their faith. Clearly, then, what Paul means by God's call here is not the general gospel invitation but the divine summons which raises the spiritually dead to life. It is often termed God's 'effective' or 'effectual' call. Those whom God thus calls (30) are the same as those 'who have been called according to his purpose' (28).

---

[160] Is. 42:1ff.; 49:5ff.   [161] *E.g.* Acts 13:47; 26:23.   [162] 1 Pet. 2:9f., REB.
[163] 2 Cor. 3:18.   [164] 1 Jn. 3:2f.   [165] 1 Cor. 15:49; Phil. 3:21.
[166] *Cf.* Col. 1:18.   [167] 2 Thes. 2:13f.   [168] 1 Thes. 1:4f.

Fourthly, *those he called, he also justified* (30b). God's effective call enables those who hear it to believe, and those who believe are justified by faith. Since justification by faith has been an overarching topic of Paul's earlier chapters, it is not necessary to repeat what has already been said, except perhaps to emphasize that justification is more than forgiveness or acquittal or even acceptance; it is a declaration that we sinners are now righteous in God's sight, because of his conferment upon us of a righteous status, which is indeed the righteousness of Christ himself. It is 'in Christ', by virtue of our union with him, that we have been justified.[169] He became sin with our sin, so that we might become righteous with his righteousness.[170]

Fifthly, *those he justified, he also glorified* (30c). Paul has already several times used the noun 'glory'. It is essentially the glory of God, the manifestation of his splendour, of which all sinners fall short (3:23), but which we rejoice in hope of recovering (5:2). Paul also promises both that if we share Christ's sufferings we will share his glory (8:17) and that the creation itself will one day be brought into the freedom of the glory of God's children (8:21). Now he uses the verb: *those he justified, he also glorified*. Our destiny is to be given new bodies in a new world, both of which will be transfigured with the glory of God.

Many students have noticed that the process of sanctification has been omitted in verse 30 between justification and glorification. Yet it is implicitly there, both in the allusion to our being conformed to the image of Christ and as the necessary preliminary to our glorification. For 'sanctification is glory begun; glory is sanctification consummated'.[171] Moreover, so certain is this final stage that, although it is still future, Paul puts it into the same aorist tense, as if it were past, as he has used for the other four stages which *are* past. It is a so-called 'prophetic past' tense. James Denney writes that 'the tense in the last word is amazing. It is the most daring anticipation of faith that even the New Testament contains.'[172]

Here then is the apostle's series of five undeniable affirmations. God is pictured as moving irresistibly from stage to stage; from an eternal foreknowledge and predestination, through a historical call and justification, to a final glorification of his people in a future eternity. It resembles a chain of five links, each of which is unbreakable.

c. Five unanswerable questions (31–39)

Paul introduces the last nine verses of this chapter with a concluding formula, which he has already used three times (6:1, 15; 7:7): *What,*

---

[169] Gal. 2:17.   [170] 2 Cor. 5:21.   [171] Bruce, p. 168.   [172] Denney, p. 652.

then, shall we say in response to this? (31a). That is, in the light of his five convictions (28) and five affirmations (29–30), 'what is there left to say?' (JBP), or 'what can we add?' (JB). The apostle's answer to his own question is to ask five more questions, to which there is no answer. He hurls them into space, as it were, in a spirit of bold defiance. He challenges anybody and everybody, in heaven, earth or hell, to answer them and to deny the truth which they contain. But there is no answer. For no-one and nothing can harm the people whom God has foreknown, predestined, called, justified and glorified.

If we are to understand the significance of these questions, it is essential to grasp why each remains unanswered. It is because of a truth which in each case is either contained in the question, or is attached to it by an 'if' clause. It is this truth, whether explicit or implicit, which renders the question unanswerable. The clearest example is the first.

Question 1: If God is for us, who can be against us? (31b).

If Paul had simply asked, 'Who is against us?' there would immediately have been a barrage of replies. For we have formidable foes arrayed against us. What about the catalogue of hardships which he lists in verse 35; are they not against us? The unbelieving, persecuting world is opposed to us.[173] Indwelling sin is a powerful adversary. Death is still an enemy, defeated but not yet destroyed. So is he 'who holds the power of death, that is, the devil',[174] together with all the principalities and powers of darkness which are mentioned in verse 38.[175] Indeed, the world, the flesh and the devil are together marshalled against us, and are much too strong for us. 'Sometimes under calamity the whole universe seems to be against us.'[176]

But Paul does not ask this naïve question. The essence of his question is contained in the 'if' clause: 'If [rather, 'since'] God is for us, who can be against us?' Paul is not saying that the claim 'God is for us' can be made by everybody. In fact, perhaps the most terrible words which human ears could ever hear are those which God uttered many times in the Old Testament: '"I am against you," declares the LORD.' They occur most frequently in the prophetic oracles against the nations, for example, against Assyria, Babylon, Egypt, Tyre and Sidon, and Edom.[177] More terrible still, they were sometimes spoken against Israel herself in her disobedience and

---

[173] *Cf.* 1 Cor. 16:9: 'there are many who oppose me'.

[174] 1 Cor. 15:26; Heb. 2:14.   [175] *Cf.* Eph. 6:12.

[176] Dodd, p. 146.

[177] Assyria and its capital Nineveh (Na. 2:13; 3:5); Babylon (Je. 50:31; 51:25); Egypt (Ezk. 29:3, 10; 30:22); Tyre and Sidon (Ezk. 26:3; 28:22) and Edom (Ezk. 35:1ff.).

idolatry,[178] and specially against her false shepherds and false prophets.[179]

But this is not the case in Romans 8:31. On the contrary, the situation Paul envisages is one in which 'God is for us', since he has foreknown, predestined, called, justified and glorified us. This being so, who can be against us? To that question there is no answer. All the powers of hell may set themselves together against us. But they can never prevail, since God is on our side.

Question 2: He who did not spare his own Son, but gave him up for us all – how will he not also, along with him, graciously give us all things? (32).

Again, suppose the apostle had asked the simple question: 'Will God not graciously give us all things?' In response, we might well have demurred and given an equivocal answer. For we need many things, some of which are difficult and demanding. How then can we possibly be sure that God will supply all our needs?

But the way Paul phrases his question banishes these doubts. For he points us to the cross. The God concerning whom we are asking our question whether or not he will give us all things is the God who has already given us his Son. On the one hand, and negatively, he *did not spare his own Son*, a statement which surely echoes God's word to Abraham: 'You . . . have not withheld [LXX 'spared', as in Rom. 8:32] your son, your only son.'[180] On the other hand, and positively, God *gave him up for us all*. The same verb is used in the gospels of Judas, the priests and Pilate who 'handed Jesus over' to death. Yet Octavius Winslow was correct to write: 'Who delivered up Jesus to die? Not Judas, for money; not Pilate, for fear; not the Jews, for envy; – but the Father, for love!'[181]

Here in 8:32, as earlier in 5:8–10, Paul argues from the greater to the lesser, namely that since God has already given us the supreme and costliest gift of his own Son, 'how can he fail to lavish every other gift upon us?' (REB). In giving his Son he gave everything. The cross is the guarantee of the continuing, unfailing generosity of God.

Question 3: Who will bring any charge against those whom God has chosen? It is God who justifies (33).

This question and the next (asking who will accuse us and who will condemn us) bring us in imagination into a court of law. Paul's argument is that no prosecution can succeed, since God our judge has already justified us; and that we can never be condemned, since Jesus Christ our advocate has died for our sins, was raised from the

[178] *E.g.* Lv. 26:17; Ezk. 5:8; 14:8; 15:7; 21:3.
[179] *E.g.* Ezk. 13:8f., 20; 14:9; 34:10.   [180] Gn. 22:16.
[181] Quoted from John Murray, *No Condemnation in Christ Jesus* (1857), p. 324.

dead, is seated at God's right hand, and is interceding for us.

So who will accuse us? Once again, if this question stood on its own, many voices would be raised in accusation. Our conscience accuses us. The devil never ceases to press charges against us, for his title *diabolos* means 'slanderer' or 'calumniator', and he is called 'the accuser of the brothers'.[182] In addition, we doubtless have human enemies who delight to point an accusing finger at us. But none of their allegations can be sustained. Why not? Because God has chosen us (we are 'God's elect', rsv) and because God has justified us. Therefore all accusations fall to the ground. They glance off us like arrows off a shield. The apostle is surely echoing the words of the Servant in Isaiah 50:8–9:

> He who vindicates me is near.
> Who then will bring charges against me?
> Let us face each other!
> Who is my accuser?
> Let him confront me!
> It is the Sovereign Lord who helps me.
> Who is he who will condemn me?

Question 4: Who is he that condemns? Christ Jesus, who died – more than that, who was raised to life – is at the right hand of God and is also interceding for us (34).

In answer to the opening question as to who will condemn us, there are without doubt many who are wanting to. Sometimes our own 'heart' condemns us.[183] It certainly tries to. And so do our critics, our detractors, our enemies, yes, and all the demons of hell.

But their condemnations will all fail. Why? Because of Christ Jesus. Commentators differ as to whether the next clauses are questions (rsv, 'Is it Christ Jesus who died . . .?') or assertions ('It is Christ Jesus who died . . .'), or denials (reb, 'Not Christ, who died . . .!'). But in every case the sense is the same, namely that Christ rescues us from condemnation, in particular by his death, resurrection, exaltation and intercession.

First, *Christ Jesus . . . died* – died for the very sins for which otherwise we would deservedly be condemned. But instead God 'condemned sin' (our sin) in the humanity of Jesus (8:3), and so Christ has redeemed us from the curse or condemnation of the law 'by becoming a curse for us'.[184] There is *more than that*, however, in the saving work of Christ. For secondly, after death he *was raised to life*. It is not just that he rose, although this is affirmed in the New Testament, but that he was raised by the Father, who thus demonstrated his acceptance of the sacrifice of his Son as the only

---

[182] Rev. 12:10; *cf.* Zc. 3:1.   [183] 1 Jn. 3:20f.   [184] Gal. 3:13.

satisfactory basis for our justification (4:25).[185] And now, thirdly, the crucified and resurrected Christ *is at the right hand of God*, resting from his finished work,[186] occupying the place of supreme honour,[187] exercising his authority to save,[188] and waiting for his final triumph.[189] Fourthly, he *is also interceding for us*, for he is our heavenly advocate[190] and high priest.[191] His very presence at the Father's right hand is evidence of his completed work of atonement, and his intercession means that he 'continues . . . to secure for his people the benefits of his death'.[192] With this Christ as our Saviour (who died, was raised, has been exalted and is interceding), we know that 'there is now no condemnation' for those who are united to him (8:1). We can therefore confidently challenge the universe, with all its inhabitants human and demonic: *Who is he that condemns?* There will never be any answer.

Question 5: Who shall separate us from the love of Christ? (35a).

'We are climbing a grand staircase here,'[193] and this fifth question is the top step. As we stand on it, Paul himself now does what we have been trying to do with his other questions. He first asks who will separate us from Christ's love and then looks round for an answer. He brings forward a sample list of adversities and adversaries that might be thought of as coming between us and Christ's love. He mentions seven possibilities (35b). He begins with *trouble* (*thlipsis*), *hardship* (*stenochōria*) and *persecution* (*diōgmos*), which together seem to denote the pressures and distresses caused by an ungodly and hostile world. He goes on to *famine or nakedness*, the lack of adequate food and clothing. Since in the Sermon on the Mount Jesus promised these to the heavenly Father's children,[194] would not their absence suggest that after all he does not care?

Paul concludes his list with *danger or sword*, meaning perhaps the risk of death on the one hand and the experience of it on the other, whether 'the sword' be 'the final sword thrust of bandit or enemy soldier or executioner'.[195] A willingness for martydom is certainly the final test of Christian faith and faithfulness. In order to enforce this, the apostle quotes from a psalm, which depicts the persecution of Israel by the nations. They were not suffering because they had forgotten Yahweh or turned to a foreign god. Instead, they were suffering for Yahweh's sake, because of their very loyalty to him:

> [36]*'For your sake we face death all day long;*
> *we are considered as sheep to be slaughtered.'*[196]

---

[185] *Cf.* 1 Cor. 15:14ff.   [186] *E.g.* Heb. 1:3; 10:11ff.   [187] Phil. 2:9ff.
[188] Acts 2:33; 5:31.   [189] Ps. 110:1.   [190] *E.g.* 1 Jn. 2:1f.
[191] *E.g.* Heb. 7:23ff.   [192] Hodge, p. 290.   [193] Lloyd-Jones, vol. 8, p. 425.
[194] Mt. 6:25f.   [195] Dunn, vol. 38A, p. 512.   [196] *Cf.* Ps. 44:22, LXX.

So what about these seven afflictions – and others too, since the list could be considerably lengthened? They are real sufferings all right – unpleasant, demeaning, painful, hard to bear and challenging to faith. And Paul knew what he was talking about, because he had himself experienced them all, and worse.[197] Perhaps the Roman Christians were also having to endure similar trials. Indeed some of them did a few years later, when they were burned as living torches for the sadistic entertainment of the Emperor Nero. Those of us who have never had to suffer physically for Christ should perhaps read verses 35–39 alongside verses 35–39 of Hebrews 11, which list unnamed people of faith who were tortured, jeered at, flogged, chained, stoned, and even sawn in half. Faced with such heroism, there is no place for glibness or complacency.

Nevertheless, can pain, misery and loss separate Christ's people from his love? *No!* On the contrary, far from alienating us from him, *in all these things* (even while we are enduring them) Paul dares to claim that *we are more than conquerors (hypernikōmen)*. For we not only bear them with fortitude but triumph over them, and so 'are winning a most glorious victory' (BAGD) *through him who loved us* (37). This second reference to Christ's love is significant, and the aorist tense shows that it alludes to the cross. Paul seems to be saying that, since Christ proved his love for us by *his* sufferings, so *our* sufferings cannot possibly separate us from it. In the context, which began with a reference to our sharing Christ's sufferings (17), they 'should be seen as evidence of union with the crucified one, not a cause for doubting his love'.[198]

Paul now reaches his climax. He began with *we know* (28); he ends more personally with *I am convinced*. He deliberately uses the perfect tense (*pepeismai*), meaning, 'I have become and I remain convinced', for the conviction he expresses is rational, settled and unalterable. He has asked questions whether anything will separate us from Christ's love (35–36); he now declares that nothing can and so nothing will (37–39). He chooses ten items which some might think powerful enough to create a barrier between us and Christ, and he mentions them in four pairs, while leaving the remaining two on their own. *Neither death nor life* presumably alludes to the crisis of death and the calamities of life. *Neither angels nor demons* is more debatable. *Demons* translates *archai*, which elsewhere are certainly evil principalities.[199] One would therefore expect the contrasting *angels* to be good. But how can unfallen angels threaten God's people? Perhaps, then, this couplet is more indefinite and is simply meant to include all cosmic, superhuman agencies, whether

---

[197] *E.g.* 2 Cor. 11:23ff.   [198] Dunn, vol. 38A, p. 504.
[199] *E.g.* Eph. 6:12; Col. 2:15.

good or bad. Since Christ has triumphed over them all,[200] and they are now 'in submission to him',[201] it is certain that they cannot harm us.

The next two pairs refer in modern language to 'time' (*neither the present nor the future*) and 'space' (*neither height nor depth*), while in between them, on their own, come unspecified *powers*, perhaps 'the forces of the universe' (REB). Some of these words, however, were technical terms for 'the astrological powers by which (as many in the Hellenistic world believed) the destiny of mankind was controlled'.[202] Alternatively, Paul's language may have been more rhetorical than technical, as he affirms like Psalm 139:8 that 'neither the highest height nor the deepest depth',[203] neither heaven nor earth nor hell, can separate us from Christ's love. He concludes with *or anything else in all creation*, in order to make sure that his inventory is comprehensive, and that nothing has been left out. Everything in creation is under the control of God the Creator and of Jesus Christ the Lord. That is why nothing *will be able to separate us from the love of God that is in Christ Jesus our Lord* (39b).

Paul's five questions are not arbitrary. They are all about the kind of God we believe in. Together they affirm that absolutely nothing can frustrate God's purpose (since he is for us), or quench his generosity (since he has not spared his Son), or accuse or condemn his elect (since he has justified them through Christ), or sunder us from his love (since he has revealed it in Christ).

Here then are five convictions about God's providence (28), five affirmations about his purpose (29, 30) and five questions about his love (31–39), which together bring us fifteen assurances about him. We urgently need them today, since nothing seems stable in our world any longer. Insecurity is written across all human experience. Christian people are not guaranteed immunity to temptation, tribulation or tragedy, but we are promised victory over them. God's pledge is not that suffering will never afflict us, but that it will never separate us from his love.

This is the love of God which was supremely displayed in the cross (5:8; 8:32, 37), which has been poured into our hearts by the Holy Spirit (5:5), which has drawn out from us our responsive love (8:28), and which in its essential steadfastness will never let us go, since it is committed to bringing us safe home to glory in the end (8:35, 39). Our confidence is not in our love for him, which is frail, fickle and faltering, but in his love for us, which is steadfast, faithful and persevering. The doctrine of 'the perseverance of the

[200] *E.g.* Eph. 1:21f.   [201] 1 Pet. 3:22.   [202] Barrett, p. 174.
[203] Cranfield, vol. I, p. 443.

saints'[204] needs to be re-named. It is the doctrine of the perseverance of God with the saints.

> Let me no more my comfort draw
> From my frail hold of thee;
> In this alone rejoice with awe –
> Thy mighty grasp of me.

[204] One of the most thorough statements and defences of this doctrine is given by D. M. Lloyd-Jones in his exposition of Rom. 8:17–39 entitled *The Final Perseverance of the Saints* (Banner of Truth, 1975). Chapters 16–36 (pp. 195–457) are specifically devoted to this great theme.

C.   The plan of God
for Jews and Gentiles
Romans 9 – 11

'Romans 9 – 11 is as full of problems as a hedgehog is full of prickles,' Dr Tom Wright has written. 'Many have given it up as a bad job, leaving Romans as a book with eight chapters of "gospel" at the beginning, four of "application" at the end, and three of puzzle in the middle.'[1] Some regard Romans 9 – 11 as no more than a 'parenthesis', 'excursus' or 'appendix'. Even Martyn Lloyd-Jones calls these chapters 'a kind of postscript' dealing with a specific topic,[2] although he fully recognizes their great importance. Others go to the opposite extreme and consider Romans 9 – 11 the heart of the letter, to which the remaining chapters are only introduction and conclusion. These chapters are 'the climax of Romans', writes Bishop Stendahl,[3] its 'real centre of gravity'.[4] In between these more extreme positions, most commentators recognize that, far from being a digression, Romans 9 – 11 are integral to the apostle's developing argument, and are 'an essential part of the letter'.[5]

It is also almost universally acknowledged that these three chapters are concerned with relations between Jews and Gentiles, and particularly with the unique position of the Jews in God's purpose. Paul has already alluded to these topics in a number of previous passages.[6] Now he elaborates them. But within these general parameters, on what does he concentrate? It is here that there is widespread disagreement. His focus is said by different scholars to be on God's sovereign election in relation to Jews and Gentiles (Robert Haldane), on the inclusion of the Gentiles and the exclusion of the Jews (Charles Hodge), on the place of the Jews in the fulfilment of prophecy (a contemporary evangelical preoccupation), on Jewish–Gentile solidarity in the family of God (Krister Stendahl), on whether justification by faith is compatible with the promises of

---

[1] Wright, p. 231.   [2] Lloyd-Jones, vol. 8, pp. 367f.   [3] Stendahl, p. 4.
[4] *Ibid.*, p. 28.   [5] Nygren, p. 357.
[6] *E.g.* 1:16; 2:9f.; 17ff.; 3:1ff., 29ff.; 4:1ff.; 5:20; 6:14f.; 7:1ff.; 8:2ff.

God to Israel (Anders Nygren, John Ziesler), on the Christian mission to Gentiles which also includes Jews (Tom Wright), and on the vindication of God in relating his purpose and promises to present Jewish unbelief (John Murray, James Denney, D. M. Lloyd-Jones). Even those scholars who seek to identify a single major theme readily acknowledge that these chapters also contain subsidiary themes.

The dominant theme is Jewish unbelief, together with the problems which it raised. How could the privileged people of God have failed to recognize their Messiah? Since the gospel had been 'promised beforehand ... in the Holy Scriptures' (1:2; cf. 3:21), why did they not embrace it? If the good news was truly God's saving power 'first for the Jews' (1:16), why were they not the first to accept it? How could their unresponsiveness be reconciled with God's covenant and promises? How did the conversion of the Gentiles, and Paul's unique mission as apostle to the Gentiles, fit in with God's plan? And what was God's future purpose for both Jews and Gentiles? Each chapter handles a different aspect of God's relation to Israel, past, present and future:

1. Israel's fall (9:1–33): God's purpose of election
2. Israel's fault (10:1–21): God's dismay over her disobedience
3. Israel's future (11:1–32): God's long-term design
4. Doxology (11:33–36): God's wisdom and generosity

9:1–33
12. Israel's fall:
God's purpose of election

Each of these three chapters (9, 10 and 11) begins with a personal statement by Paul, in which he identifies himself with the people of Israel and expresses his profound concern for them. To him Israel's unbelief is far more than an intellectual problem. He writes of the sorrow and anguish he feels over them (9:1ff.), of his prayerful longing for their salvation (10:1), and of his conviction that God has not rejected them (11:1f.).

It may be helpful to sum up the argument of chapter 9. Paul begins by confessing that Jewish unbelief causes him not only anguish of heart (1–3), but also perplexity of mind as he asks himself how the people of Israel with their eight unique privileges could have rejected their own Messiah (4–5). How can their apostasy be explained? Paul's questions and answers proceed consecutively.

First, is it that *God's word* has *failed* (6a)? No, God has kept his promise, which was addressed, however, not to all Israel but to true, spiritual Israel (6b) whom he had called according to his own 'purpose in election' (11–12).

Secondly, *is God* not *unjust* to exercise his sovereign choices (14)? No. To Moses he stressed his mercy (15), and to Pharaoh his power in judgment (17). But it is not unjust either to show mercy to the undeserving or to harden those who harden themselves (18). Both mercy and judgment are fully compatible with justice.

Thirdly, *why* then *does God still blame us?* (19). Paul's threefold response to this question uncovers the misunderstandings of God which it implies. (a) God has the right of a potter to shape his clay, and we have no right to challenge him (20–21). (b) God must reveal himself as he is, making known his wrath and his glory (22–23). (c) God has foretold in Scripture both the inclusion of the Gentiles and the exclusion of Israel except for a remnant (24–29).

Fourthly, *what then shall we say* in conclusion (30)? The explanation of the church's composition (a Gentile majority and a Jewish remnant) is that the Gentiles believed in Jesus whereas the majority of Israel stumbled over him, the stone God had laid (30–33). Thus the acceptance of the Gentiles is attributed to the sovereign mercy of God, and the rejection of Israel to their own rebellion.

Paul begins with a strong threefold affirmation, intended to put his sincerity beyond question and to persuade his readers to believe him. First, *I speak the truth in Christ*. He is conscious of his relationship to Christ and of Christ's presence with him as he writes. Secondly, as a negative counterpart, *I am not lying*, or even exaggerating. Thirdly, *my conscience confirms it in the Holy Spirit* (1). He knows that the human conscience is fallible and culturally conditioned, but he claims that his is illumined by the Spirit of truth himself.

What, then, is this truth which he asserts with such force? It concerns his continuing love for his people Israel, who have rejected Christ. They cause him *great sorrow and unceasing anguish of heart* (2). He goes on to call them his *brothers* and those of his *own race*. For membership of the Christian brotherhood and of God's 'holy nation' does not cancel our natural ties of family and nationality. *I could wish*, he continues, *that* for their sake *I myself were cursed (anathema) and cut off from Christ* (3). Paul is not literally expressing this wish, since he has just stated his conviction that nothing could ever separate him from God's love in Christ (8:35, 38f.) His use of the imperfect tense conveys the sense that he could entertain such a wish, if it could possibly be granted. Like Moses, who in his plea for Israel's forgiveness dared to pray that otherwise God would blot him out of the book of life,[1] Paul says he would be willing even to be damned if only thereby Israel might be saved. Denney calls it 'a spark from the fire of Christ's substitutionary love', for he is prepared to die in their place.[2] And Luther comments: 'It seems incredible that a man would desire to be damned, in order that the damned might be saved.'[3]

The apostle's anguish over unbelieving Israel is the more poignant because of her unique privileges, some of which he has mentioned earlier (2:17ff. and 3:1ff.), but of which he now gives a fuller inventory. *Theirs is the adoption as sons*, since God had said, 'Israel is my firstborn son'[4] and 'I am Israel's father';[5] *theirs the divine glory*, namely the visible splendour of God, which filled first the tabernacle[6] and then the temple,[7] and which came to be permanently localized in the inner sanctuary, so that Yahweh could be described as 'enthroned between the cherubim that are on the ark'.[8]

---

[1] Ex. 32:32.   [2] Denney, p. 657.   [3] Luther (1515), p. 380.
[4] Ex. 4:22; *cf.* Ho. 11:1.   [5] Je. 31:9.   [6] Ex. 29:42ff.; 40:34ff.   [7] 1 Ki. 8:10f.
[8] 2 Sa. 6:2; *cf.* Lv. 16:2; Heb. 9:5.

Theirs too are *the covenants*, especially of course God's founda-
tional covenant with Abraham, but also its multiple renewals and
elaborations to Isaac and Jacob, Moses[9] and David;[10] *the receiving
of the law*, the unique revelation of God's will spoken by his voice
and written with his finger;[11] *the temple worship* (though 'temple'
does not occur in the Greek sentence), comprising all the prescribed
regulations for the priesthood and sacrifices; *and the promises* (4),
particularly those relating to the coming of the Messiah as God's
prophet, priest and king. In addition, *theirs are the patriarchs*, not
only Abraham, Isaac and Jacob, but also the progenitors of the
twelve tribes and other great figures such as Moses, Joshua, Samuel
and David; and above all, *from them is traced the human ancestry of
Christ* (5a), literally 'the Christ according to the flesh', whose
genealogy Matthew traces back to Abraham, and Luke to Adam.
Calvin justly comments: 'If he honoured the whole human race
when he connected himself with it by sharing our nature, much
more did he honour the Jews, with whom he desired to have a close
bond of affinity.'[12]

Paul does not stop there, however. The final words of verse 5 are:
who is God over all, for ever praised! Amen. The question is
whether these words refer to Christ or to God the Father. And the
difficulty in deciding for certain is due to the absence of punctuation
in the original manuscript. We have to supply it. Three main positions are held.

First, the traditional view from the early Greek Fathers onwards
has been to apply all three expressions ('over all', 'God' and 'for
ever praised') to Christ, as – with slight differences – in AV, JB, JBP
and NIV, and in the margin of RSV and REB. The second view applies
the expressions to God the Father. By placing a full stop after
'Christ', what follows becomes an independent sentence: 'God who
is over all be blessed for ever' (RSV; *cf.* REB). The third way is a
compromise. It applies the words 'over all' to Christ, but the
remaining words to God the Father (REB mg.).

The real problem is not whether Paul would have described
Christ as 'over all', since he regularly affirmed his universal
sovereignty,[13] but whether he would have called him 'God' and
ascribed to him everlasting praise. It is argued that Paul usually
designated Jesus 'Son of God' (*e.g.* 1:3f., 9; 5:10; 8:29) or God's
'own Son' (*e.g.* 8:3, 32), not 'God', and also that biblical doxologies
are normally addressed to God,[14] not to Jesus.

On the other hand, Paul gives Jesus the divine title 'Lord',[15] calls
him 'the Lord of both the dead and the living' (14:9), affirms his

---

[9] Ex. 24:8.   [10] 2 Sa. 23:5.   [11] Dt. 4:7f.   [12] Calvin, p. 195.
[13] *E.g.* Rom. 14:9; Eph. 1:20ff.; Phil. 2:9ff.; Col. 1:18f.
[14] *E.g.* 2 Cor. 1:3; Eph. 1:3; *cf.* 1 Pet. 1:3.   [15] *E.g.* Rom. 10:9, 13; Phil. 2:9ff.

pre-existence,[16] describes him as both 'in the form of God' and having 'equality with God',[17] and declares that 'all the fulness of the deity lives in bodily form' in him.[18] These expressions accord him divine honours and powers, which are tantamount to calling him 'God'. Further, Hebrews 13:21 appears to contain a doxology to Christ.

Charles Cranfield regards it as 'virtually certain' that Paul intended to describe Christ as 'God over all, for ever praised'. He adds: 'There is ... no good ground for denying that Paul here affirms that Christ, who, in so far as his human existence is concerned, is of Jewish race, is also Lord over all things and by nature God blessed for ever.'[19]

One would think that Israel, favoured with these eight blessings, prepared and educated for centuries for the arrival of her Messiah, would recognize and welcome him when he came. How then can one reconcile Israel's privileges with her prejudices? How can one explain her 'hardening' (11:25)? Paul now addresses himself to this mystery. He asks himself, or his imaginary interlocutor, four questions.

Question 1: Has God's promise failed? (6–13).

At first sight it would appear that God's promise to Israel had failed, or literally 'fallen'. For he had promised to bless them, but they had forfeited his blessing through unbelief. Israel's failure was her own failure, however; it was not due to the failure of God's word (6a). *For not all who are descended from Israel are Israel* (6b). That is, there have always been two Israels, those physically descended from Israel (Jacob) on the one hand, and his spiritual progeny on the other; and God's promise was addressed to the latter, who had received it. The apostle has already made this distinction earlier in his letter between those who were Jews outwardly, whose circumcision was in the body, and those who were Jews inwardly, who had received a circumcision of the heart by the Spirit (2:28f.).

He now refers to two well-known Old Testament situations in order to illustrate and prove his point. The first concerns Abraham's family. Just as not all who are descended from Israel are Israel, so not all who are descended from Abraham are *Abraham's children*, his true offspring (*cf.* Rom. 4). *On the contrary*, as Scripture says, '*It is through Isaac that your offspring will be reckoned*' (7),[20] and not through Abraham's other son Ishmael, who is not even mentioned. *In other words*, who are *God's children*, who can also be designated *Abraham's offspring*? It is not *the natural children*, literally 'the children of the flesh', but *the children of the promise*, who were

---

[16] Gal. 4:4; 2 Cor. 8:9. [17] Phil. 2:6 mg. [18] Col. 2:9.
[19] Cranfield, vol. II, p. 840. *Cf.* also Metzger (1973), pp. 95ff.
[20] Gn. 21:12; *cf.* Gal. 4:23ff.

born as a result of God's promise (8). And this was the wording of the promise: *'At the appointed time I will return, and Sarah will have a son'* (9).[21]

From Abraham and his two sons Isaac and Ishmael, Paul turns for his second illustration to Isaac and his two sons Jacob and Esau. He shows that just as God chose Isaac, not Ishmael, to be the recipient of his promise, so he chose Jacob, not Esau. In this case, however, it was even clearer that God's decision had nothing whatever to do with any eligibility in the boys themselves, for there was nothing to distinguish them from one another. Isaac and Ishmael had had different mothers, but Jacob and Esau had the same mother (Rebekah). *Not only that, but Rebekah's children had one and the same father*, namely *Isaac* (10), and moreover they were twins. *Yet, before the twins were born or had done anything good or bad*, God had made his decision and revealed it to their mother. This was deliberate, *in order that God's purpose in election*, his eternal purpose which operates according to the principle of election, *might stand* (11).

Perhaps there is a conscious contrast between the question whether God's promise had 'fallen' (6, literally) and the statement that his purpose must *stand* (11). What 'God's purpose in [literally, according to] election' means is clear beyond doubt. It is that God's choice of Isaac (not Ishmael), and of Jacob (not Esau), does not originate in them or in any *works* they may have done, but in the mind and will of *him who calls* (12a). To clinch this, Paul quotes two Scriptures referring to Jacob and Esau. The first declares that *'The older will serve the younger'* (12b),[22] putting Jacob above Esau.

The second Scripture says: *'Jacob I loved, but Esau I hated'* (13).[23] This bald statement sounds shocking in Christian ears and cannot possibly be taken literally. Although there is such an emotion as 'holy hatred', it is directed only to evildoers and would be inappropriate here. So several suggestions for softening the statement have been proposed. Some suggest that the reference is less to the individuals Jacob and Esau than to the peoples they fathered, the Israelites and the Edomites, and to their historical destinies. Others interpret the sentence as meaning, 'I chose Jacob and rejected Esau.'[24] But the third option seems best, which is to understand the antithesis as a Hebrew idiom for preference. Jesus himself gives us this interpretative clue, since according to Luke he told us that we cannot be his disciples unless we hate our family,[25] whereas according to Matthew we are forbidden rather to love them more than him.[26] Although this makes the wording more acceptable, the reality behind it

---

[21] Gn. 18:10, 14.   [22] Gn. 25:23.   [23] Mal. 1:2f.   [24] Calvin, p. 202.
[25] Lk. 14:26.   [26] Mt. 10:37.

267

stands, namely that God put Jacob above Esau – as individuals too, not just in the sense that the Israelites were God's people, not the Edomites.

We have also to remember that Esau forfeited his birthright because of his own worldliness[27] and lost his rightful blessing because of his brother's deceit,[28] so that human responsibility was interwoven with divine sovereignty in their story. We should also recall that the rejected brothers, Ishmael and Esau, were both circumcised, and therefore in some sense they too were members of God's covenant, and were both promised lesser blessings. Nevertheless, both stories illustrate the same key truth of 'God's purpose according to election'. So God's promise did not fail; but it was fulfilled only in the Israel within Israel.

Many mysteries surround the doctrine of election, and theologians are unwise to systematize it in such a way that no puzzles, enigmas or loose ends are left. At the same time, in addition to the arguments developed in the exposition of Romans 8:28–30, we need to remember two truths. First, election is not just a Pauline or apostolic doctrine; it was also taught by Jesus himself. 'I know those I have chosen,' he said.[29] Secondly, election is an indispensable foundation of Christian worship, in time and eternity. It is the essence of worship to say: 'Not to us, O LORD, not to us, but to your name be the glory.'[30] If we were responsible for our own salvation, either in whole or even in part, we would be justified in singing our own praises and blowing our own trumpet in heaven. But such a thing is inconceivable. God's redeemed people will spend eternity worshipping him, humbling themselves before him in grateful adoration, ascribing their salvation to him and to the Lamb, and acknowledging that he alone is worthy to receive all praise, honour and glory.[31] Why? Because our salvation is due entirely to his grace, will, initiative, wisdom and power.

Question 2: Is God unjust? (14–18).

Granted that God's promise has not failed, but has been fulfilled in Abraham, Isaac and Jacob, and in their spiritual lineage, is not 'God's purpose according to election' intrinsically unjust? To choose some for salvation and pass by others looks like a breach of elementary justice. Is it? *What then shall we say? Is God unjust?* Paul's immediate retort is *Not at all!* (14). He then goes on to explain. *For he says to Moses, 'I will have mercy on whom I have mercy, and I will have compassion on whom I have compassion'* (15). Thus Paul's way of defending God's justice is to proclaim his mercy. It sounds like a complete *non sequitur*. But it is not. It

---

[27] Gn. 25:29ff. [28] Gn. 27:1ff. [29] Jn. 13:18; *cf.* 15:16; 17:6. [30] Ps. 115:1.
[31] Rev. 5:12f.; 7:10ff.

simply indicates that the question itself is misconceived, because the basis on which God deals savingly with sinners is not justice but mercy. For salvation *does not . . . depend on man's desire or effort*, that is, on anything we want or strive for, *but on God's mercy* (16).

Having quoted God's word to Moses (15),[32] Paul now quotes his word to Pharaoh (17),[33] although it is noteworthy that he writes of what *the Scripture says to Pharaoh*, since to him what God says and what Scripture says are synonyms: '*I raised you up for this very purpose*, that is, 'brought you on the stage of history',[34] *that I might display my power in you and that my name might be proclaimed in all the earth*' (17). Indeed, the refrain in the narrative of Pharaoh and the plagues is 'so that you may know there is no-one like the LORD our God'.[35]

Paul sees these divine words to Moses (15) and Pharaoh (17), both recorded in Exodus, as complementary, and sums them up in verse 18: *Therefore God has mercy on whom he wants to have mercy* (the message to Moses), *and he hardens whom he wants to harden* (the message to Pharaoh). Dr Leon Morris rightly comments: 'Neither here nor anywhere else is God said to harden anyone who had not first hardened himself.'[36] That Pharaoh hardened his heart against God and refused to humble himself is made plain in the story.[37] So God's hardening of him was a judicial act, abandoning him to his own stubbornness,[38] much as God's wrath against the ungodly is expressed by 'giving them over' to their own depravity (1:24, 26, 28). The same combination of human obstinacy and divine judgment in the hardening of the heart is seen in God's word to Isaiah ('Make the heart of this people calloused'), which Jesus applied to his own teaching ministry, and Paul applied to his.[39]

So God is not unjust. The fact is, as Paul demonstrated in the early chapters of his letter, that all human beings are sinful and guilty in God's sight (3:9, 19), so that nobody deserves to be saved. If therefore God hardens some, he is not being unjust, for that is what their sin deserves. If, on the other hand, he has compassion on some, he is not being unjust, for he is dealing with them in mercy. The wonder is not that some are saved and others not, but that anybody is saved at all. For we deserve nothing at God's hand but judgment. If we receive what we deserve (which is judgment), or if we receive what we do not deserve (which is mercy), in neither case

[32] Ex. 33:19. [33] Ex. 9:16. [34] Denney, p. 662.

[35] *E.g.* Ex. 8:10; *cf.* Ezk. 6:7, 14, *etc.*

[36] Morris (1988), p. 361.

[37] *E.g.* Ex. 4:42ff.; 7:13, 14, 22; 8:15, 19, 32; 9:7, 17, 27, 34f.; 10:3, 16; 11:9; 13:15; 14:5.

[38] *E.g.* Ex. 4:21; 7:3; 9:12; 10:1, 20, 27; 11:10; 14:4, 8, 17.

[39] Is. 6:9f.; Mt. 13:13ff.; Mk. 4:11f.; Jn. 12:39f.; Acts 28:25ff.

is God unjust. If therefore anybody is lost, the blame is theirs, but if anybody is saved, the credit is God's. This antinomy contains a mystery which our present knowledge cannot solve; but it is consistent with Scripture, history and experience.

Question 3: Why does God still blame us? (19–29).

If salvation is due entirely to God's will (which it is, as stated twice in verse 15 and twice more in verse 18), and if we do not resist his will (which we do not, and indeed could not), *one of you will say to me: 'Then why does God still blame us? For who resists his will?'* (19). In other words, is it fair of God to hold us accountable to him, when he makes the decisions? To this question Paul makes three responses, all of which concern who God is. Most of our problems arise and seem insoluble because our image of God is distorted.

First, *God has the right of a potter over his clay* (20–21). Paul's first response to his critic's two questions is to pose three counter-questions which all concern our identity. They ask whether we know who we are (*Who are you, O man . . .?* 20a), what kind of relationship we think exists between us and God, and what attitude to him we consider appropriate to this relationship. Moreover, all three counter-questions emphasize the gulf which yawns between a human being and God (20a), between a crafted object and the craftsman (between *what is formed* and *him who formed it*, 20b), and between a *lump of clay* and *the potter* who is shaping it (21). Since this is the relationship between us, do we really think it fitting for a human being to *talk back to God* (20a), for art to ask the artist why he has made it as he has (20b), or for a pot to challenge the potter's right to shape the same lump of clay into pottery for different uses (21)?

We need to recall the Old Testament background to Paul's questions. The village potter at his wheel was a familiar figure in Palestine, and his craft was used to illustrate several different truths. For example, Jeremiah watches the potter's skill and determination in re-shaping a vessel which has been spoiled.[40] This is not in Paul's mind here, however. He is alluding rather to two texts in Isaiah. The first contains God's striking complaint to Israel, 'You turn things upside down.' That is, refusing to allow God to be God, they even attempt to reverse roles, as if the potter had become the pot and the pot the potter.[41] In the second text God pronounces a 'woe' to 'him who quarrels with his Maker', to him who is himself only a potsherd, yet challenges the potter to explain what he is making.[42]

What then is Paul condemning? Some commentators betray their embarrassment at this point, and others are brash enough to reject Paul's teaching. 'It is the weakest point in the whole epistle,'

---

[40] Je. 18:1ff.   [41] Is. 29:16.   [42] Is. 45:9.

declares C. H. Dodd.[43] But we need to draw a distinction. Paul is not censuring someone who asks sincerely perplexed questions, but rather someone who 'quarrels' with God, who talks back (20) or answers back (RSV). Such a person manifests a reprehensible spirit of rebellion against God, a refusal to let God be God and acknowledge his or her true status as creature and sinner. Instead of such presumption we need, like Moses, to keep our distance, take off our shoes in recognition of the holy ground on which we stand, and even hide our face from him.[44] Similarly, we need, like Job, to put our hand over our mouth, confess that we tend to speak things we do not understand, despise ourselves, and repent in dust and ashes.[45] Job had been right to reject the traditional claptrap of his so-called 'comforters', and in his dialogue with them he had been in the right and they in the wrong.[46] Where Job had gone wrong was in daring to 'contend' with the Almighty, to 'accuse' him and attempt to 'correct' him.[47]

But still the whole story has not yet been told. For human beings are not merely lumps of inert clay, and this passage well illustrates the danger of arguing from an analogy. To liken humans to pottery is to emphasize the disparity between us and God. But there is another strand in biblical teaching which affirms not our unlikeness but our likeness to God, because we have been created in his image, and because we still bear it (though distorted) even since the fall.[48] As God's image-bearers, we are rational, responsible, moral and spiritual beings, able to converse with God, and encouraged to explore his revelation, to ask questions and to think his thoughts after him. In consequence, there are occasions in which biblical characters who have fallen on their faces before God are told to stand up on their feet again, especially to receive God's commission.[49] In other words, there is a right kind of prostration before God, which is a humble acknowledgment of his infinite greatness, and a wrong kind which is a grovelling denial of our human dignity and responsibility before him.

Returning to Romans, Paul is not wishing to stifle genuine questions. After all, he has been asking and answering questions throughout the chapter and indeed the whole letter. No, 'it is the God-defying rebel and not the bewildered seeker after the truth whose mouth he [sc. Paul] so peremptorily shuts'.[50]

Paul's emphasis in this paragraph is that as the potter has the right to shape his clay into vessels for different purposes, so God has the right to deal with fallen humanity according to both his wrath and his mercy, as he has argued in verses 10–18. 'In the sovereignty here

[43] Dodd, p. 159.   [44] Ex. 3:5f.   [45] Jb. 40:4; 42:3, 6.   [46] Jb. 42:7f.
[47] Jb. 40:2; cf. 1:22; 2:10.   [48] E.g. Gn. 9:6.
[49] E.g. Ezk. 1:28; 2:1f.; Dn. 10:7ff.   [50] Bruce, p. 179.

asserted,' writes Hodge, 'it is God as moral governor, and not God as creator, who is brought to view.' It is nowhere suggested that God has the right to 'create sinful beings in order to punish them', but rather that he has the right to 'deal with sinful beings according to his good pleasure', either to pardon or to punish them.[51]

Secondly, *God reveals himself as he is* (22–23). The apostle continues to demonstrate that God's freedom to show mercy to some and to harden others is fully compatible with his justice. The burden of his theodicy is that we must allow God to be God, not only in renouncing every presumptuous desire to challenge him (20–21), but also in assuming that his actions are without exception in harmony with his nature. For God is always self-consistent and never self-contradictory. He determines to be himself and to be seen to be himself.

Verses 22 and 23, which are parallel to each other, plainly express this theme. The word that is common to both is the verb 'to make known'. Verse 22 speaks of the revelation of God's *wrath* and *power . . .* to *the objects of his wrath*, and verse 23 of the revelation of *the riches of his glory . . . to the objects of his mercy*. The NIV also makes both verses begin with the same rhetorical question (*What if God . . .? What if he . . .?*), which in both cases is left unanswered. Their meaning is readily intelligible, however. Paul is implying that if God acts in perfect accordance with his wrath and mercy, there can be no possible objection.

Although the structure of the two verses is the same, there are also significant differences to be noted. First, God is said to bear *with great patience the objects of his wrath*, instead of visiting it upon evildoers immediately. The implication seems to be that his forebearance in delaying the hour of judgment will not only keep the door of opportunity open longer, but also make the ultimate outpouring of his wrath the more dreadful. This was so in the case of Pharaoh, and it is still the situation today as we wait for the Lord's return.[52] Secondly, although Paul describes the objects of God's mercy as those *whom he prepared in advance for glory* (23), he describes the objects of God's wrath simply as *prepared for destruction*, ready and ripe for it, without indicating the agency responsible for this preparation. Certainly God has never 'prepared' anybody for destruction; is it not that by their own evildoing they prepare themselves for it?

There is a third difference between verses 22 and 23. Although they are complementary, NIV seems to be right in making verse 23 dependent on verse 22: *What if God, choosing to show his wrath . . . bore with great patience the objects of his wrath . . .? What if he did*

---

[51] Hodge, p. 319.   [52] 2 Pet. 3:3ff.; *cf.* Rom. 2:4.

this in order *to make the riches of his glory known . . .?* The double question implies that this is indeed what God did. That is, the revelation of his wrath to the objects of his wrath was with a view to the revelation of his glory to the objects of his mercy. The pre-eminent disclosure will be of the riches of God's glory; and the glory of his grace will shine the more brightly against the sombre background of his wrath. 'Glory' is of course shorthand for the final destiny of the redeemed, in which the splendour of God will be shown to and in them, as first they are transformed and then the universe (*cf.* 8:18f.).

So God's two actions, summed up in verse 18 as 'showing mercy' and 'hardening', have now been traced back to his character. It is because he is who he is that he does what he does. And although this does not solve the ultimate mystery why he prepares some people in advance for glory and allows others to prepare themselves for destruction, yet both are revelations of God, of his patience and wrath in judgment and above all of his glory and mercy in salvation.

Paul is responding to the question 'Why does God still blame us?' (19). He now gives a third explanation. It is that *God foretold these things in Scripture* (24–29). Among the objects of God's mercy, whom he has prepared in advance for glory (23), Paul now includes *even us*, himself and his readers, *whom he also called, not only from the Jews but also from the Gentiles* (24). For God's way of dealing with Jews and Gentiles was another illustration of his 'purpose in election' (11) and had been clearly foretold in Old Testament Scripture. In verses 25–26 Paul quotes two texts from Hosea, to explain God's amazing inclusion of the Gentiles, and then in verses 27–29 two texts from Isaiah, to explain his equally amazing reduction of Jewish inclusion to a remnant.

The background to the Hosea texts was Hosea's marriage to his 'adulterous wife', Gomer, together with their three children whose names symbolized God's judgment on the unfaithful northern kingdom of Israel. He told them to call their second child, a daughter, 'Lo-Ruhamah' ('not loved') because, he said, 'I will no longer show love to the house of Israel.'[53] He then told them to call their third child, a boy, 'Lo-Ammi' ('not my people') because, he added, 'you are not my people, and I am not your God'.[54] Yet God went on to promise that he would reverse the situation of rejection implicit in the children's names. These are the texts Paul quotes.

> [25]*'I will call them "my people" who are not my people;*
> *and I will call her "my loved one" who is not my loved*
> *one'*,[55]

---

[53] Ho. 1:6.   [54] Ho. 1:9.   [55] Ho. 2:23.

and,

> [26]*'It will happen that in the very place where it was said to them,*
> *"You are not my people,"*
> *they will be called "sons of the living God".* '[56]

In order to understand Paul's handling of these texts, we need to remember that, according to the New Testament, Old Testament prophecies often have a threefold fulfilment. The first is immediate and literal (in the history of Israel), the second intermediate and spiritual (in Christ and his church), and the third ultimate and eternal (in God's consummated kingdom). A good example is the prophecies of the rebuilding of the temple. Here, however, the prophecy takes the form of God's promise in mercy to overturn an apparently hopeless situation, to love again those he had declared unloved, and to welcome again as his people those he had said were not. The immediate and literal application was to Israel in the eighth century BC, repudiated and judged by Yahweh for apostasy, but promised a reconciliation and reinstatement.

Paul the apostle, however, is shown that God's promise has a further and gospel fulfilment in the inclusion of the Gentiles. They had been 'separate from Christ, excluded from citizenship in Israel and foreigners to the covenants of promise, without hope and without God in the world. But now in Christ Jesus', Paul continues, 'you who once were far away have been brought near through the blood of Christ . . . Consequently, you are no longer foreigners and aliens, but fellow-citizens with God's people and members of God's household.'[57] The apostle Peter also applies Hosea's prophecy to the Gentiles.[58] Their inclusion is a marvellous reversal of fortunes by God's mercy. The outsiders have been welcomed inside, the aliens have become citizens, and the strangers are now beloved members of the family.

Next Paul turns from Hosea to Isaiah, and so from the inclusion of the Gentiles to the exclusion of the Jews, apart from a remnant. The historical background to the two Isaiah texts is again one of national apostasy in the eighth century BC, although it now relates to the southern kingdom of Judah. The 'sinful nation' has forsaken Yahweh and has been judged through an Assyrian invasion, so that the whole country lies desolate and only a few survivors are left.[59] God goes on to promise, however, that Assyria will be punished for its arrogance, and that a believing remnant will return to the Lord.[60] Indeed, the name of Isaiah's son symbolized this promise, as Shear-Jashub means 'a remnant will return'.[61]

---

[56] Ho. 1:10.   [57] Eph. 2:12f., 19.   [58] 1 Pet. 2:10.   [59] Is. 1:4ff.
[60] Is. 10:12ff.   [61] Is. 7:3.

²⁷*Isaiah cries out concerning Israel:*

'*Though the number of the Israelites be like the sand by the sea,*
  only the remnant will be saved.
²⁸*For the Lord will carry out*
  his sentence on earth with speed and finality.'⁶²

²⁹*It is just as Isaiah said previously:*

'*Unless the Lord Almighty*
  had left us descendants,
we would have become like Sodom,
  we would have been like Gomorrah.'⁶³

The significance of both texts lies in the contrast they contain between the majority and the minority. In verse 27 (quoting Is. 10:22) it is said that *the number of the Israelites* will be *like the sand by the sea*. This was God's promise to Abraham after his surrender of Isaac, although he added the second metaphor, 'as the stars in the sky'.⁶⁴ But in comparison with the countless number of Israelites, like stars and grains of sand, only a remnant would be saved, the Israel within Israel (6). Similarly, in verse 29, out of the total destruction of Sodom and Gomorrah only a handful was spared, in fact only Lot and his two daughters.

By bringing the Hosea and Isaiah texts together, Paul provides Old Testament warrant for his vision. On the one hand, God has called us, he writes, not only from the Jews but also from the Gentiles (24). So there is a fundamental Jewish–Gentile solidarity in God's new society. On the other hand, Paul is conscious of the serious imbalance between the size of the Gentile participation and the size of the Jewish participation in the redeemed community. As Hosea prophesied, multitudes of Gentiles, formerly disenfranchised, have now been welcomed as the people of God. As Isaiah prophesied, however, the Jewish membership was only a remnant of the nation, so small in fact as to constitute not the inclusion of Israel but its exclusion, not its acceptance but its 'rejection' (11:15). Jesus himself had foretold this situation, when he said: 'I say to you that many will come from the east and the west, and will take their places at the feast with Abraham, Isaac and Jacob in the kingdom of heaven. But the subjects of the kingdom will be thrown outside . . . .'⁶⁵

Question 4: What then shall we say in conclusion? (30–33).

Paul's fourth and final question, repeated from verse 14, is addressed to himself. In the light of the argument he has been developing, what conclusion would it be legitimate to draw? In particular, faced with the unbelief of the majority of Israel and the

---

⁶² Is. 10:22f.   ⁶³ Is. 1:9.   ⁶⁴ Gn. 22:17; *cf*. 15:5.   ⁶⁵ Mt. 8:11f.

minority status of believing Israel, how have these things come about? In response, Paul begins with a description, continues with an explanation, and ends with a biblical confirmation.

The situation he describes is completely topsy-turvy. On the one hand, *the Gentiles* (better 'Gentiles' without the definite article), *who did not pursue righteousness, have obtained it, a righteousness that is by faith* (30). To describe pagans as 'not pursuing righteousness' is a major understatement. Most of them at least are godless and self-centred, going their own way, lovers of themselves, of money and pleasure, rather than lovers of God and of goodness.[66] Nevertheless, they obtained what they did not pursue. Indeed, when they heard the gospel of justification by faith, the Holy Spirit worked in them so powerfully that they 'laid hold' of it almost with violence (*katalambanō*) by faith. *But Israel*, on the other hand, *who pursued a law of righteousness, has not attained it* (31). Israel's pursuit of righteousness was almost proverbial. They were imbued with a religious and moral zeal which some would call fanaticism. Why, then, did they not 'attain' it? Paul uses a different verb (*phthanō*), meaning to 'reach' or 'arrive at'. And the reason they did not arrive is that they were pursuing an impossible goal. Paul anticipates what he will say in the next verse by setting over against the Gentiles' *righteousness* that is by faith what he calls *a law of righteousness*, which must be a reference to Torah viewed as a law to be obeyed. Here, then, is Paul's description of the upside-down religious situation of his day. The Jews who pursued righteousness never reached it; the Gentiles who did not pursue it laid hold of it.

But why was this so? And with regard to the Jews who did not arrive, *why not?* Significantly, Paul's answer on this occasion makes no reference to God's 'purpose in election' (11), but instead attributes Israel's failure to arrive to her own folly: *because they pursued it not by faith* (which is how the Gentiles laid hold of it, 30) *but as if it were by works*, that is, as if the accumulation of works-righteousness were God's way of salvation. So *they stumbled over the 'stumbling-stone'* (*proskomma*, 32). What Paul means by this is not in doubt, since he uses the same imagery (although a different vocabulary) elsewhere. In particular, he calls the proclamation of Christ crucified 'a stumbling-block (*skandalon*) to Jews',[67] and refers also to 'the offence (*skandalon*) of the cross'.[68] And why do people stumble over the cross? Because it undermines our self-righteousness. For 'if righteousness could be gained through the law, Christ died for nothing'.[69] That is, if we could gain a righteous standing before God by our own obedience to his law, the cross would be superfluous. If we could save ourselves, why should

---

[66] 2 Tim. 3:1ff.   [67] 1 Cor. 1:23.   [68] Gal. 5:11.   [69] Gal. 2:21.

Christ have bothered to die? His death would have been redundant. The fact that Christ died for our sins is proof positive that we cannot save ourselves. But to make this humiliating confession is an intolerable offence to our pride. So instead of humbling ourselves, we 'stumble over the stumbling-stone'.

It only remains for the apostle to provide biblical support for what he has written (33). Like Peter in his first letter,[70] he brings together two rock-sayings from Isaiah. But Paul goes further than Peter and conflates them. The first and final phrases he quotes are from Isaiah 28:16: *See, I lay in Zion a stone*, and *the one who trusts in him will never be put to shame.* In between these, however, the other two phrases come from Isaiah 8:14: *a stone that causes men to stumble and a rock that makes them fall.* The primary affirmation is that God himself has laid down a solid rock or stone. It is, of course, Jesus Christ. He boldly applied to himself the prophecy of Psalm 118: 'the stone the builders rejected has become the capstone'.[71] In addition, 'no-one can lay any foundation other than the one already laid, which is Jesus Christ'.[72] So everybody has to decide how to relate to this rock which God has laid down. There are only two possibilities. One is to put our trust in him, to take him as the foundation of our lives and build on him. The other is to bark our shins against him, and so to stumble and fall.

Paul began this chapter with the paradox of Israel's privilege and prejudice (1–5). How can her unbelief be explained?

It is not because God is unfaithful to his promises, for he has kept his word in relation to the Israel within Israel (6–13).

It is not because God is unjust in his 'purpose according to election', for neither his having mercy on some nor his hardening of others is incompatible with his justice (14–18).

It is not because God is unfair to blame Israel or hold human beings accountable, for we should not answer him back, and in any case he has acted according to his own character and according to Old Testament prophecy (19–29).

It is rather because Israel is proud, pursuing righteousness in the wrong way, by works instead of faith, and so has stumbled over the stumbling-block of the cross (30–33).

Thus this chapter about Israel's unbelief begins with God's purpose of election (6–29) and concludes by attributing Israel's fall to her own pride (30–33). In the next chapter Paul calls her 'a disobedient and obstinate people' (10:21).

[70] 1 Pet. 2:6, 8.   [71] Ps. 118:22; Mk. 12:10; *cf.* Acts 4:11; 1 Pet. 2:7.
[72] 1 Cor. 3:11.

Liberal commentators are not lacking who insist that, by ascribing Jewish unbelief now to God's purpose of election and now to Israel's own blindness and arrogance, the apostle was contradicting himself. But that is a shallow conclusion, and inadmissible to anybody who accepts Paul's apostolic authority. No, 'antinomy' is the right word to use, not 'contradiction'. Dr Lloyd-Jones sums up Paul's position in these words: 'In verses 6 to 29 he explains why anybody is saved; it is the sovereign election of God. In these verses (30–33) he is showing us why anybody is lost, and the explanation of that is their own responsibility.'[73]

Few preachers can have maintained this balance better than Charles Simeon of Cambridge in the first half of the nineteenth century. He lived and ministered at a time when the Arminian–Calvinist controversy was bitter, and he warned his congregation of the danger of forsaking Scripture in favour of a theological system. 'When I come to a text which speaks of election', he said to J. J. Guerney in 1831, 'I delight myself in the doctrine of election. When the apostles exhort me to repentance and obedience, and indicate my freedom of choice and action, I give myself up to that side of the question.'[74] In defence of his commitment to both extremes, Simeon would sometimes borrow an illustration from the Industrial Revolution: 'As wheels in a complicated machine may move in opposite directions and yet subserve a common end, so may truths apparently opposite be perfectly reconcilable with each other, and equally subserve the purposes of God in the accomplishment of man's salvation.'[75]

---

[73] Lloyd-Jones, vol. 9, p. 285.

[74] *Memoirs of the Life of the Rev. Charles Simeon*, ed. William Carus (Hatchard, 1848), pp. 674f.

[75] Preface to the *Horae Homileticae* in 21 volumes (1832), p. 5.

10:1–21
13. Israel's fault:
God's dismay over her disobedience

Chapters 9 – 11 of Romans all address the problem of Jewish unbelief. In chapter 9 the emphasis was on God's purpose according to election; the emphasis of chapter 10, however, is on the human factors, on the need for an understanding of the gospel (5–13), for the proclamation of the gospel (14–15), and for the response of faith (16–21). With chapter 10 Paul turns from the past to the present, from his explanation of the Israelites' unbelief to his hope that they will yet hear and believe the gospel. This vision for the future he will elaborate further in chapter 11.

1. Israel's ignorance of the righteousness of God (1–4)

Paul begins this chapter, as he began the last, with a very personal reference to his love and longing for 'them'. In the Greek sentence they are not specified, but NIV is certainly right to insert *the Israelites*. There are several similarities between the openings of the two chapters. In both Paul mentions his heart: his heart's sorrow and anguish because the unbelieving people of Israel are lost (9:2f.), and his *heart's desire and prayer to God . . . that they may be saved* (1). J. B. Phillips catches the earnestness of the apostle's cry: 'My brothers, from the bottom of my heart I long and pray to God that Israel may be saved!' At the beginning of chapter 9 he expresses the hypothetical wish that he himself might be cursed if thereby they could be spared (9:3); at the beginning of chapter 10 he expresses an ardent, prayerful wish for their salvation. Moreover, as his pain is increased by their combination of privilege and prejudice (9:4f.), so his longing is increased by their combination of zeal and ignorance (2).

Paul has no doubt of their religious sincerity. He *can testify about them* from his own experience *that they are zealous for God*. And he knows what he is talking about, because he himself in his

pre-conversion life was 'extremely zealous' in his religion,[1] as seen
in his persecution of the church.[2] Indeed he was 'just as zealous for
God' as any of his contemporaries,[3] and could even describe his zeal
at that time as an 'obsession'.[4] So he is obliged to say of the Israelites
that *their zeal is not based on knowledge* (2). Yet Scripture says that
'it is not good to have zeal without knowledge'.[5] Sincerity is not
enough, for we may be sincerely mistaken. The proper word for
zeal without knowledge, commitment without reflection, or enthusiasm without understanding, is fanaticism. And fanaticism is a horrid
and dangerous state to be in.

Having asserted their general condition of ignorance, Paul now
particularizes in two negatives: *they did not know the righteousness
that comes from God* and *they did not submit to God's righteousness.* Instead, they *sought to establish their own* (3). Recent commentators who have accepted Professor E. P. Sanders' thesis of
'covenantal nomism'[6] offer an interpretation of this verse which is
very different from the traditional understanding. Professor Dunn,
for example, argues that the Jews were right to see 'righteousness' as
obedience to the law and so loyalty to the covenant (the meaning of
'covenantal nomism'), but wrong to construe it in terms of circumcision, sabbath observance, dietary regulations and ritual purity.
This understanding of the law was not only 'too superficial' but also
'too nationalistic',[7] because it disenfranchised the Gentiles whom
God wanted to include. 'Their own righteousness', therefore, meant
a righteousness which was peculiarly and exclusively their own, and
was being contrasted not with God's but with other people's.[8] And
their attempt to 'establish' this righteousness of their own was an act
not of creation (producing something out of nothing) but of confirmation (preserving what was already in existence, namely their
covenant membership and righteousness). What Paul objected to
was 'Israel's attempt to maintain a claim of national monopoly to
that covenant righteousness'.[9] What then does it mean that *Christ is
the end of the law* ... (4)? What Christ terminated was not the law
as the way of attaining a righteous standing before God, but 'the law
seen as a way ... of documenting God's special regard for Israel, of
marking Israel out from the other nations ...'.[10]

What disturbs me about this attempted reconstruction, I confess,
is not so much what is being affirmed (for the Jews were ethnically

---

[1] Gal. 1:14.   [2] Gal. 1:13; Phil. 3:6.   [3] Acts 22:3.   [4] Acts 26:9ff.
[5] Pr. 19:2.   [6] See Preliminary Essay, pp. 25ff.   [7] Dunn, vol. 38B, p. 593.
[8] *Ibid.*, pp. 587, 595. Compare E. P. Sanders (1883): '"their own righteousness"
... means "that righteousness which the Jews alone are privileged to obtain" rather
than "self-righteousness which consists in individuals presenting their merits as a
claim upon God"', p. 38.
[9] Dunn, vol. 38B, p. 588.   [10] *Ibid.*, p. 598.

exclusive), but what is being denied. For example, the statement that 'their own righteousness' is not being contrasted with God's is plainly not so in 10:3, and more plainly still in Philippians 3:9. I think the Jews (like all human beings) were more self-righteous than Professors Sanders and Dunn allow. As Calvin justly commented, 'the first step to obtaining the righteousness of God is to renounce our own righteousness'.[11]

To other commentators the assertion that the Jews *did not know the righteousness that comes from God* means that they had not yet learned the way of salvation, how the righteous God puts the unrighteous right with himself by bestowing upon them a righteous status. This is 'the righteousness of God' which is revealed in the gospel, and is received by faith altogether apart from the law, as Paul has written earlier (1:17; 3:21). The tragic consequence of the Jews' ignorance was that, recognizing their need of righteousness if they were ever to stand in God's righteous presence, they *sought to establish their own*, and *they did not submit to God's righteousness* (3).

This ignorance of the true way, and this tragic adoption of the false way, are by no means limited to Jewish people. They are widespread among religious people of all faiths, including professing Christians. All human beings, who know that God is righteous and they are not (since 'there is no-one righteous, not even one', 3:10), naturally look around for a righteousness which might fit them to stand in God's presence. There are only two possible options before us. The first is to attempt to build or establish our own righteousness, by our good works and religious observances. But this is doomed to failure, since in God's sight even 'all our righteous acts are like filthy rags'.[12] The other way is to submit to God's righteousness by receiving it from him as a free gift through faith in Jesus Christ.[13] In verses 5–6 Paul calls the first *the righteousness that is by the law* and the second *the righteousness that is by faith*.

The fundamental error of those who are seeking to establish their own righteousness is that they have not understood Paul's next affirmation: *Christ is the end (telos) of the law so that there may be righteousness for everyone who believes* (4). *Telos* could mean 'end' in the sense of 'goal' or 'completion', indicating that the law pointed to Christ and that he has fulfilled it. Or it could mean 'end' in the sense of 'termination' or 'conclusion', indicating that Christ has abrogated the law. Paul must surely mean the latter. But the abrogation of the law gives no legitimacy either to antinomians, who claim that they can sin as they please because they are 'not under

[11] Calvin, p. 221.   [12] Is. 64:6.   [13] Phil. 3:9.

law but under grace' (6:1, 15), or to those who maintain that the very category of 'law' has been abolished by Christ and that the only absolute left is the command to love. When Paul wrote that we have 'died' to the law, and been 'released' from it (7:4, 6), so that we are no longer 'under' it (6:15), he was referring to the law as the way of getting right with God. Hence the second part of verse 4. The reason Christ has terminated the law is *so that there may be righteousness for everyone who believes*. In respect of salvation, Christ and the law are incompatible alternatives. If righteousness is by the law it is not by Christ, and if it is by Christ through faith it is not by the law. Christ and the law are both objective realities, both revelations and gifts of God. But now that Christ has accomplished our salvation by his death and resurrection, he has terminated the law in that role. 'Once we grasp the decisive nature of Christ's saving work', writes Dr Leon Morris, 'we see the irrelevance of all legalism.'[14]

2. Alternative ways of righteousness (5–13)

Paul has already stated three antitheses – between faith and works (9:32), between God's righteousness to which we should submit and our own righteousness which we mistakenly seek to establish (3), and between Christ and the law (4). Now he draws out the implications of the latter by contrasting *the righteousness that is by the law* (5) with *the righteousness that is by faith* (6). He does so by appealing to Scripture, quoting a text on each side. He thus sets Moses against Moses, that is, Moses in Leviticus against Moses in Deuteronomy.

On the one hand, *Moses describes in this way the righteousness that is by the law: 'The man who does these things will live by them'* (5).[15] The natural interpretation of these words is that the way to life (*i.e.* salvation) is by obedience to the law. This is how Paul himself understood the sentence when he quoted it in Galatians 3:12. But 'clearly', he added in that context, 'no-one is justified before God by the law', because no-one has succeeded in obeying it. The weakness of the law is our own weakness (8:3). Because we disobey it, instead of bringing us life it brings us under its curse, and that would be our position still if Christ had not redeemed us from the law's curse by becoming a curse for us.[16] It is in this sense that 'Christ is the end of the law'. Righteousness is not to be found that way.

So, on the other hand, *the righteousness that is by faith*, which Paul now personifies, proclaims a different message. It sets before

---

[14] Morris (1988), p. 380.   [15] Lv. 18:5.   [16] Gal. 3:10ff.

us for salvation not the law but Christ, and assures us that unlike the law, Christ is not unattainable, but readily accessible. The passage Paul quotes (from Dt. 30) begins with a stern prohibition, which the righteousness by faith endorses: *'Do not say in your heart, "Who will ascend into heaven?" (that is, to bring Christ down)* (6) *or "Who will descend into the deep?" (that is, to bring Christ up from the dead)'* (7). To ask such questions would be as absurd as they are unnecessary. There is no need whatever for us to scale the heights or plumb the depths in search of Christ, for he has already come, died and risen, and so is accessible to us.

What, then, is the positive message of the righteousness of faith? *What does it say? 'The word is near you; it is in your mouth and in your heart',* that is, Paul explains, *the word of faith* (the message requiring a response of faith, *i.e.* the gospel) which *we* (apostles) *are proclaiming* (8). Taking his cue from the reference to the people's 'mouth' and 'heart' in Deuteronomy 30:14, just quoted, Paul now summarizes the gospel in these terms: *That if you confess with your mouth, 'Jesus is Lord'* (the earliest and simplest of all Christian creeds), *and believe in your heart that God raised him from the dead, you will be saved* (9). Thus heart and mouth, inward belief and outward confession, belong essentially together. 'Confession without faith would be vain ... But likewise faith without confession would be shown to be spurious.'[17] *For it is with your heart that you believe and are justified, and it is with your mouth that you confess and are saved* (10). The parallelism is reminiscent of Hebrew poetry in the Old Testament, and the two clauses in verses 9–10 are to be held together rather than separately. Thus, there is no substantive difference here between being 'justified' and being 'saved'. Similarly, the content of the belief and that of the confession need to be merged. Implicit in the good news are the truths that Jesus Christ died, was raised, was exalted, and now reigns as Lord and bestows salvation on those who believe. This is not salvation by slogan but by faith, that is, by an intelligent faith which lays hold of Christ as the crucified and resurrected Lord and Saviour. This is the positive message of 'the righteousness that is by faith'.

But is Paul's use of Deuteronomy 30:11–14 legitimate? Or is he guilty of an unprincipled allegorization, and of reading into Scripture what is not there? We begin by noting that his only actual quotation (as opposed to allusion) is Deuteronomy 30:14, which is reproduced almost exactly in verse 8: *'the word is near you; it is in your mouth and in your heart'.* There Paul stops, for the Deuteronomy text goes on to say that the reason the word was near them was 'so that you may obey it', whereas Paul calls it 'the word

[17] Murray, vol. II, p. 56.

of faith'. How then can Paul take a verse about the law which is to be obeyed and apply it to the gospel which is to be believed? It sounds a fundamental contradiction, especially while he is commending 'righteousness by faith'. But it is not.

How does Paul use the Deuteronomy passage? He is not claiming either that Moses explicitly foretold the death and resurrection of Jesus, or that he preached the gospel under the guise of the law. No. The similarity he sees and stresses between Moses' teaching and the apostles' gospel lies in their easy accessibility. He knows that Moses began this part of his speech (although he does not quote it) by telling the Israelites that his teaching was neither 'too difficult' for them nor 'beyond their reach'. Moses went on, using dramatic imagery, that it was neither up in heaven nor beyond the sea – remote, unrevealed and unknown – so that they would have to find someone to ascend into heaven or cross the sea in order to bring it to them. On the contrary, his teaching was very near them. They knew it already. Far from being above or beyond them, it was actually inside them, in their hearts and in their mouths.

What Moses had said about his teaching, Paul now affirms about the gospel. It is neither remote nor unavailable. There is no need to ask who will ascend to heaven to bring Christ down or descend to Hades to bring Christ up. Storming the ramparts of heaven and potholing in Hades, in search of Christ, are equally unnecessary. For Christ has come and died, and been raised, and is therefore immediately accessible to faith. We do not need to do anything. Everything that is necessary has already been done. Moreover, because Christ himself is near, the gospel of Christ is also near. It is in the heart and mouth of every believer. The whole emphasis is on the close, ready, easy accessibility of Christ and his gospel.

Verses 11–13 build on this. They stress that Christ is not only *easily* accessible, but *equally* accessible to all, to *anyone* (11) and to *everyone* (13), since *there is no difference* (12), no favouritism. All three verses refer to Christ and affirm his availability to faith, although each describes in different terms both the nature of faith and how Christ responds to believers. In verse 11 we 'trust in him' and will *never be put to shame.* In verse 12 we *call on him,* and he *richly blesses* us. In verse 13 we call *on the name of the Lord* and are *saved.* Let us now consider the three verses separately.

First, verse 11: *As the Scripture says, 'Anyone who trusts in him will never be put to shame.'* This is a second quotation of Isaiah 28:16, the first having been in 9:33. The designation of saving faith as 'trust' shows that the 'belief' and the 'confession' of the two previous verses (9–10) are not to be understood as a mere subscription to credal formulae.

Secondly, verse 12: *For there is no difference between Jew and*

284

Gentile – the same Lord is Lord of all and richly blesses all who call on him. It is a marvellous affirmation that through Christ there is no distinction between Jew and Gentile. Of course there is a fundamental distinction between those who seek righteousness by the law and those who seek it by faith. But between those who have been justified by faith and are now in Christ, all distinctions, not only of race, but also of sex and culture, are not so much abolished (since Jews are still Jews, Gentiles Gentiles, men men and women women) as rendered irrelevant.[18] Just as there is no distinction between us because in Adam we are all sinners (3:22f.), so now there is no distinction between us because in Christ, who is *Lord of all*, all who call on him are richly blessed. Far from impoverishing us, we all receive his 'unsearchable riches'.[19]

In the third verse (13) both our calling on him and his blessing of us are elaborated. To *call on him* is, more precisely, to call *on the name of the Lord*, that is, to appeal to him to save us in accordance with who he is and what he has done. *Everyone* who thus calls on him, we are assured, *will be saved* (13). In the first place this is a quotation from Joel 2:32. But Peter cited it on the day of Pentecost, transferring the text from Yahweh to Jesus,[20] which is also what Paul does here. Indeed, this appeal to Jesus for salvation became so characteristic of Christian people that Paul could describe the worldwide community as 'those everywhere who call on the name of our Lord Jesus Christ'.[21]

What then, according to this section, is necessary to salvation? First the fact of the historic Jesus Christ, incarnate, crucified, risen, reigning as Lord, and accessible. Secondly, the apostolic gospel, *the word of faith* (8), which makes him known. Thirdly, simple trust on the part of the hearers, calling on the name of the Lord, combining faith in the heart and confession with the mouth. But still something is missing. There is, fourthly, the evangelist who proclaims Christ and urges people to put their trust in him. It is of Christian evangelists that Paul writes in the next paragraph.

3. The necessity of evangelism (14–15)

In order to demonstrate the indispensable necessity of evangelism, Paul asks four consecutive questions.

First, if, in order to be saved, sinners must call on the name of the Lord (13), *How, then, can they call on the one they have not believed in?* (14a). For calling on his name presupposes that they know and believe his name (*i.e.* that he died, was raised and is Lord). This is the only occasion in his letters on which Paul uses the

---

[18] See Gal. 3:28.　　[19] Eph. 3:8.　　[20] Acts 2:21.　　[21] 1 Cor. 1:2.

term 'believe in (*eis*)', which is the regular expression in John's writings for saving faith. Here, however, since saving faith is presented as 'calling on' Christ's name, the kind of 'belief' Paul has in mind must be the prior stage of believing the facts about Jesus which are included in his 'name'.

Secondly, *how can they believe in the one of whom they have not heard?* (14b). Just as believing is logically prior to calling, so hearing is logically prior to believing. What kind of hearing, however? 'In accordance with normal grammatical usage', the phrase *the one of whom* (*hou*) should be translated 'the one whom' and so means 'the speaker rather than the message'.[22] In other words, they will not believe Christ until they have heard him speaking through his messengers or ambassadors.[23]

Thirdly, *how can they hear without someone preaching* (*kēryssō*, to 'herald') *to them?* (14c). In ancient times, before the development of the mass media of communication, the role of the herald was vital. The major means of transmitting news was his public proclamations in the city square or the marketplace. There could be no hearers without heralds.

Fourthly, *how can they preach unless they are sent?* (15a). It is not clear from the text what kind of 'sending' Paul has in mind. Because he uses the verb *apostellō*, commentators have tended to assume that he has himself in mind as an apostle (see 1:1, 5; 11:13),[24] together with his fellow apostles, for they had been directly commissioned by Christ.[25] There were also 'apostles of the churches', however, sent out as missionaries.[26] The latter is a broader concept, for, although the apostles of Christ were appointed by him and required no endorsement by the church, the churches sent out only those whom Christ had chosen to send.[27] The need for heralds is now confirmed from Scripture: *As it is written, 'How beautiful are the feet of those who bring good news!'* (15b).[28] If those who proclaimed the good news of release from Babylonian exile were thus celebrated, how much more welcome the heralds of the gospel of Christ should be!

The essence of Paul's argument is seen if we put his six verbs in the opposite order: Christ sends heralds; heralds preach; people hear; hearers believe; believers call; and those who call are saved. And the relentless logic of Paul's case for evangelism is felt most forcibly when the stages are stated negatively and each is seen to be essential to the next. Thus, unless some people are commissioned for the task, there will be no gospel preachers; unless the gospel is

---

[22] Dunn, vol. 38B, p. 620.   [23] *Cf.* 2 Cor. 5:20; 13:3.   [24] *Cf.* Gal. 1:15f.
[25] *E.g.* Lk. 6:12f.; Gal. 1:1.   [26] 2 Cor. 8:23.   [27] *E.g.* Acts 13:1ff.
[28] *Cf.* Is. 52:7.

preached, sinners will not hear Christ's message and voice; unless they hear him, they will not believe the truths of his death and resurrection; unless they believe these truths, they will not call on him; and unless they call on his name, they will not be saved. Since Paul began this chapter by expressing his longing that the Israelites will be saved (1), he must surely have had them specially in mind when developing his evangelistic strategy in these verses. His next paragraph confirms this.

4. The reason for Israel's unbelief (16–21)

If evangelism is made up of a series of successive stages, beginning with heralds being sent and ending with sinners being saved, how is the unbelief of Israel to be explained? For *not all the Israelites accepted the good news* (16a) – a surprising understatement in view of what he has written earlier about 'only the remnant' (9:27). It is partly for this reason that some understand these verses as relating to Paul's mission to the Gentiles. But NIV is surely right (as in verse 1) to supply the word 'Israelites', which is missing from the Greek sentence. The whole section is about the Jewish response – or rather non-response – to the gospel. Their unbelief, Paul now shows, was foretold by Isaiah in his rhetorical question: *'Lord, who has believed our message?'* (16b).[29] Yet they should have believed. Verse 17 reverts to the argument of verse 14, although it reduces the five stages to only three; *faith comes from hearing* (NEB 'is awakened by') *the message, and the message is heard through the word of Christ*, that is, 'the word of which Christ is both content and author'.[30] Thus preaching leads to hearing, and hearing to believing. Why then have the Israelites not believed? In answer to this perplexing question Paul ventilates and rejects two possible explanations (18–19), and then supplies his own explanation (20–21).

First, *did they not hear?* This is the right first question to ask, since believing depends on hearing. But Paul no sooner asks the question than he summarily dismisses it: *Of course they did* (18a). As evidence of this assertion he quotes Psalm 19:4:

> 18b*'Their voice has gone out into all the earth,*
> *their words to the ends of the world.'*

Paul's choice of biblical quotation is surprising, since what Psalm 19 celebrates is not the worldwide spread of the gospel, but the universal witness of the heavens to their Creator. Paul of course knew this perfectly well. It is entirely gratuitous to conclude that he misremembered, misunderstood or misrepresented

---

[29] *Cf.* Is. 53:1.   [30] Dunn, vol. 38B, p. 623.

his text. It seems perfectly reasonable instead to suggest that he was transferring eloquent biblical language about global witness from the creation to the church, taking the former as symbolic of the latter. If God wants the general revelation of his glory to be universal, how much more must he want the special revelation of his grace to be universal too!

But is it true that the gospel has *gone out into all the earth* and *to the ends of the world*? As an understandable hyperbole I think it is, just as Paul was to say later to the Colossians that the gospel 'has been proclaimed to every creature under heaven', so that in consequence 'all over the world this gospel is bearing fruit and growing'.[31] Since Paul is here alluding to the spread of the good news in Jewry, however, it may be better to understand Paul's claim as what F. F. Bruce has called 'representative universalism', meaning that 'wherever there were Jews', and in particular wherever a Jewish community existed, 'there the gospel had been preached'.[32] So the Jews *have* heard; they cannot blame their not believing on their not hearing.

Secondly, then, *Did Israel not understand?* (19a). For we take Paul's point that it is quite possible to hear without understanding, as Jesus warned us in his parable of the sower.[33] But no, Paul also rejects this explanation of Jewish unbelief, and backs up his position by quoting from Moses *first*. Perhaps he means that he will then quote Isaiah second (20), so that the law and the prophets constitute two witnesses. The Mosaic verse he appeals to is this:

> [19b]'*I will make you envious by those who are not a nation;*
> *I will make you angry by a nation that has no*
> *understanding'.*[34]

This text indicates that there are people with 'no understanding'. But they are not the Jews; they are the Gentiles, whom Moses also describes as 'not a nation', reminding us of God's word to Hosea which Paul has earlier applied to the Gentiles, namely that they were 'not my people' (9:25f.).[35] God reveals his intention to make Israel both 'envious' of and 'angry' at the 'no-nation', 'no-understanding' Gentiles because of the blessings he would give them.

If, then, Israel's rejection of the gospel cannot be attributed either to her not hearing it or to her not understanding it, she must be without excuse. This is the third possible explanation of her unbelief, which Paul now accepts. Israel is simply stubborn. True, the Israelites were ignorant of God's righteousness (3), but this is

---

[31] Col. 1:23, 6.   [32] Bruce, p. 194.   [33] Mt. 13:19.   [34] *Cf.* Dt. 32:21.
[35] Ho. 1:9f.; 2:23.

now seen to be wilful ignorance. They had 'stumbled over the "stumbling-stone"', namely Christ (9:32).

In order to enforce this, Paul now quotes what *Isaiah boldly says.* The prophet's 'bold' words are those recorded in Isaiah 65:1f.; they prove to come from the lips of Yahweh himself. In these two verses he draws a sharp contrast between the Gentiles and the Jews, his actions towards them and their attitudes towards him. Take the Gentiles first:

> [20]'*I was found by those who did not seek me;*
> *I revealed myself to those who did not ask for me'.*[36]

Paul could have added the third clause of Isaiah 65:1:

> '*To a nation that did not call on my name,*
> *I said, "Here am I, here am I."* '

Taken together, the three clauses complete the picture. God deliberately reverses the roles between himself and the Gentiles. It would normally be for them to ask, seek and knock (as Jesus was later to put it), and to adopt towards him the respectful attitude of a servant at his master's disposal, saying, 'Here I am.' Instead, although they did not ask or seek or offer themselves to his service, he allowed himself to be found by them, he revealed himself to them, and he even offered himself to them, saying humbly to them, 'Here am I.' This is dramatic imagery for grace, God taking the initiative to make himself known.

> [21]*But concerning Israel he says,*
> '*All day long I have held out my hands*
> *to a disobedient and obstinate people.'*[37]

God's initiative to Israel is even more pronounced. He does not simply allow himself to be found; he actively holds out his hands to them. Like a parent inviting a child to come home, offering a hug and a kiss, and promising a welcome, so God has opened and stretched out his arms to his people, and has kept them continuously outstretched, *all day long*, pleading with them to return. But he has received no response. They do not even give him the neutral response of the Gentiles, who decline either to ask or to seek. No, their response is negative, resistant, recalcitrant, dismissive. They are determined to remain *a disobedient and obstinate people.* We feel God's dismay, his grief.

So Paul concludes his second exploration into the unbelief of Israel. In chapter 9 he attributed it to God's purpose of election, on account of which many were passed by, and only a remnant was

---

[36] Is. 65:1.   [37] Is. 65:2.

left, an Israel within Israel. In chapter 10, however, he attributes it to Israel's own disobedience. Their fall was their fault. The antinomy between divine sovereignty and human responsibility remains.

One of the notable features of Romans 10 is that it is saturated with Old Testament allusion and quotation. Paul cites Scripture here in order to confirm or illustrate eight truths: first, the ready accessibility of Christ to faith (6–8 = Dt. 30:12ff.); second, the promise of salvation to all who believe (11 = Is. 28:16; 13 = Joel 2:32); third, the glorious necessity of evangelism (15 = Is. 52:7); fourth, the unresponsiveness of Israel (16 = Is. 53:1); fifth, the universality of the gospel (18 = Ps. 19:4); sixth, the Gentiles' provocation of Israel (19 = Dt. 32:21); seventh, the divine initiative of grace (20 = Is. 65:1); and eighth, the patient grief of God the evangelist (21 = Is. 65:2). Thus Paul's emphasis is not only on the authority of Scripture, but also on the fundamental continuity which unites the Old and the New Testament revelations.

11:1–32
14. Israel's future: God's long-term design

Paul began these three chapters with the tragic paradox of Israel's condition, uniquely privileged by God and yet entrenched in unbelief (9:1ff.). This was not to be attributed to either unfaithfulness or injustice on the part of God (9:6ff.), but rather both to his own 'purpose in election' (9:11) and also to Israel's stumbling over Christ (9:32), and her obstinate rejection of God's persistent advances (10:21).

Paul now addresses himself to the implications of Israel's disobedience. He asks two questions, to both of which he immediately responds with the same indignant riposte.

Question 1: I ask then: Did God reject his people? By no means! (1a).

One might have expected that, since they have rejected God, God has rejected them. But this is not so. They are not the abandoned nation they may seem. Their rejection is only partial; a believing remnant remains, as Paul shows in verses 1–10.

Question 2: Again I ask: Did they stumble so as to fall beyond recovery? Not at all! (11a).

Far from Israel's fall being the end, it is going to be only temporary. Already, in fact, her transgression has resulted in unexpected blessings, and God's historical providence is going to occasion many more, as Paul will explain in verses 12–32.

So then 'the rejection of the Jews was neither total nor final'.[1] That is the theme of this chapter. There is still an Israelite remnant in the present, and there is going to be an Israelite recovery in the future, which will itself lead to blessing for the whole world.

---

[1] Hodge, p. 353. In fact, Paul emphasizes 'its temporal and providential character' (Fitzmyer, p. 608).

1. The present situation (1–10)

In verse 1 the apostle asks his straight question: *Did God reject his people?* In verse 2 he replies emphatically, *God did not reject his people.* Perhaps he is consciously echoing the confident assertion of the psalmist: 'The LORD will not reject his people; he will never forsake his inheritance.'[2] He does not rely on dogmatic statement alone, however; he brings forward four pieces of evidence to back it up.

The first is *personal*: *I am an Israelite myself, a descendant of Abraham, from the tribe of Benjamin* (1b). He may be writing as a patriotic Jew: how could he entertain the preposterous idea that God had repudiated his own people? But a more natural interpretation is that he himself as a Jew was proof that God had not rejected his people, not even him, the blasphemer and persecutor 'who with all his strength had contended against God'.[3]

The second piece of evidence is *theological*. The apostle has anticipated it in the words in which he has posed the question, whether God has rejected *his people*, that is, his special chosen people, the people of his covenant, which he has declared unbreakable.[4] Now in answering his question he underlines this by describing them as *his people, whom he foreknew* (2a). In the exposition of Romans 8:29 it was suggested that to 'foreknow' means to 'forelove' and to 'choose'. Although here it is the nation, not an elect remnant, whom God is said to have foreknown, still foreknowledge and rejection are mutually incompatible.

Thirdly, Paul brings forward some *biblical* evidence, namely the situation in the time of Elijah. After the prophet's victory over the prophets of Baal at Mount Carmel, he fled from Queen Jezebel into the desert, and later took refuge in a cave on Mount Horeb. There *he appealed to God against Israel* (2b), saying: *'Lord, they have killed your prophets and torn down your altars; I am the only one left, and they are trying to kill me'* (3).[5] God's reply to Elijah was that he had got his arithmetic wrong. He was by no means the sole surviving loyalist. On the contrary, God said: *'I have reserved for myself seven thousand who have not bowed the knee to Baal'* (4).[6] So Israel's national apostasy was not complete. Although the doctrine of the remnant was not developed until Isaiah's time, the faithful remnant itself already existed during the prophetic ministry of Elijah at least a century earlier.

Paul's fourth evidence that God had not totally rejected his people was *contemporary*. Just as in Elijah's day there was a

---

[2] Ps. 94:14. See also 1 Sa. 12:22.   [3] Luther (1515), p. 421.   [4] Je. 33:19ff.
[5] 1 Ki. 19:10.   [6] 1 Ki. 19:18.

remnant of 7,000, *so too, at the present time*, namely in Paul's day, *there is a remnant ...* (5). It was probably sizeable. James was soon to tell Paul in Jerusalem that there were 'many thousands' of believing Jews.[7] Moreover, the chief characteristic of this remnant was that it had been *chosen by grace* (5b). Literally, it had come into existence 'according to the election of grace', just as God's purpose is 'according to election' (*kat' eklogēn* here as in 9:11). 'Grace' emphasizes that God has called the remnant into being, just as he had 'reserved' for himself the loyal minority in Elijah's day (4). For grace is God's gracious kindness to the undeserving, so that if his election is *by grace, then it is no longer by works; if it were, grace would no longer be grace* (6). It is refreshing, in our era of relativistic fog, to see Paul's resolve to maintain the purity of verbal meanings. His objective is to insist that grace excludes works, that is, God's initiative excludes ours. 'If you confuse such opposites as faith and works, then words will simply lose their meaning.'[8]

What then? That is, how does Paul apply this remnant theology to the facts of his own day and experience? It obliges him to stop generalizing about 'Israel' and to make a division. For *what Israel sought so earnestly* (presumably the righteousness of 9:31) *it did not obtain*, at least not as a whole; *but the elect did*, namely those who were *chosen by grace* (5) and so justified by faith. *The others*, the unbelieving Israelite majority, *were hardened* (7). There can be little doubt that Paul meant they were hardened by God (since the next verse says that *God gave them a spirit of stupor*). Nevertheless, as with the hardening of Pharaoh and those he represented (9:18; *cf.* 11:25), a judicial process is in mind (*a retribution*, in fact, verse 9) by which God gives people up to their own stubbornness. What this 'hardening' means in practice Paul goes on to indicate from two Old Testament quotations, both of which refer to eyes which cannot see.

The first quotation (8) is a conflation of Deuteronomy 29:2ff. and Isaiah 29:10. In the former text Moses tells the Israelites that, although they have witnessed his wonders, yet he has not given them 'a mind that understands or eyes that see or ears that hear' (Dt. 29:4). From the Isaiah text Paul quotes only the first sentence, to the effect that God has given them *a spirit of stupor*, a complete loss of spiritual sensitivity which (as the context makes clear) was self-induced before it became a divine judgment. Moreover, this condition, Paul adds, continues to afflict Israel to this very day:

> [8]*'God gave them a spirit of stupor,*
> *eyes so that they could not see.*

[7] Acts 21:20.   [8] Barrett, p. 209.

> *and ears so that they could not hear,*
> *to this very day.'*

The second quotation (9) comes from Psalm 69, which portrays a righteous person's experience of persecution. Jesus applied it to himself ('They hated me without reason'),[9] and early Christians therefore quickly identified it as messianic. This victim of unprovoked hostility prays both that God will vindicate him and that God's just judgment will fall on his enemies. Because of the messianic nature of the psalm Paul is able to reverse its application. Instead of Israel being the persecuted, she has become (in her rejection of Christ) the persecutor. This is what the psalmist prays:

> [9] *'May their table become a snare and a trap,*
> *a stumbling-block and a retribution for them.*
> [10] *May their eyes be darkened so they cannot see,*
> *and their backs be bent for ever.'*

The imagery is not easy to interpret. But *their table* seems to be a symbol of the security, well-being and community which are enjoyed at home, and which somehow can be turned into the opposite, becoming *a snare and a trap, a stumbling-block and a retribution for them.* The reference to *their backs* being *bent for ever* is also obscure, although the bent back is normally a picture of carrying a heavy load, whether in this case of grief, fear or oppression.

2. The future prospect (11–32)

Paul's answer to his first question whether God has rejected his people is that, although not rejected, they have been hardened. Or, more accurately, while a believing remnant remains, the others (who are the majority) are hardened. That is the present situation. Is it permanent, even hopeless? What about the future? Paul is now ready to ask his second question. *Again I ask: Did they stumble so as to fall beyond recovery? Not at all!* (11a). And as the apostle elaborates his strong negative, it becomes clear that Israel's fall, which in the first paragraph he has proved to be not total, is not final either. On the contrary, far from their being on a downward spiral, the spiral is upwards. They have not stumbled *so as to fall beyond recovery*, but rather to rise, and in that rise both to experience, and to cause Gentiles to experience, greater blessings than would have been the case if they had not fallen in the first place. Such is God's merciful providence.

[9] Jn. 15:25 = Ps. 69:4.

a. A chain of blessing (11–16)

It is essential to grasp Paul's sequence of thought in this paragraph, since it recurs with modifications throughout the chapter. It is like a chain with three links.

First, already through Israel's fall salvation has come to the Gentiles.

Secondly, this Gentile salvation will make Israel envious and so lead to her restoration or 'fulness'.

Thirdly, Israel's fulness will bring yet much greater riches to the world.

Thus the blessing ricochets from Israel to the Gentiles, from the Gentiles back to Israel, and from Israel to the Gentiles again. Of these stages the first has already taken place; it constitutes the ground on which the second and third may confidently be expected to follow. Moreover, in this paragraph Paul traces the same development twice, first in general terms (11–12) and then with particular reference to his personal ministry as apostle to the Gentiles (13–16).

In his general statement Paul describes the first stage thus: *because of their (sc.* Israel's) *transgression, salvation has come to the Gentiles* (11a). Thus the apostle 'is giving a theological interpretation to historical events'.[10] On no fewer than four separate and significant occasions Luke records in the Acts how the Jews' rejection of the gospel led to its offer to and acceptance by Gentiles. During the first missionary journey, in Pisidian Antioch, Paul and Barnabas said to the Jews: 'We had to speak the word of God to you first. Since you reject it and do not consider yourselves worthy of eternal life, we now turn to the Gentiles.'[11]

During the second and third missionary journeys, in Corinth and Ephesus respectively, Paul again ('as usual') began his ministry in the synagogue. But when the Jews opposed him and rejected the gospel, he took a decisive step, left them, and opened up a Gentile mission in a nearby secular building.[12] The fourth example would take place later, when he arrived in Rome.[13]

In each of these epoch-making decisions the same double event had taken place. The Jews had rejected the gospel and the Gentiles had accepted it. The second naturally followed the first, as Jesus himself had predicted.[14] But now Paul turns history into theology, by implying that the first event took place with a view to the second. God thus overruled the sin of Israel for the salvation of the Gentiles.

---

[10] Ziesler (1989), p. 273.   [11] Acts 13:46.   [12] Acts 14:1; 18:6; 19:8f.
[13] Acts 28:28.   [14] Mt. 8:11f.; 21:43.

That stage (*sc.* Gentiles being saved) had already taken place. But Paul goes on to the next stage, namely that *salvation has come to the Gentiles* in order (*eis*) *to make Israel envious* (11b; *cf.* 10:19). In the Acts, Luke several times mentions Jewish envy of the apostles.[15] He seems to mean that the Jews were jealous of their success, of their influence on the people, and of the large crowds they attracted. But Paul envisages a more productive kind of envy than this. He knows that when Israel sees the blessings of salvation being enjoyed by believing Gentiles (their reconciliation to God and to each other, their forgiveness, their love, joy and peace through the Spirit), they will covet these blessings for themselves and, it is implied, will repent and believe in Jesus in order to secure them. Thus provoked to envy, they will be led to conversion.

But this restoration of Israel will lead to a third stage, as the salvation now enjoyed by Israel will spill over in further blessing to the world. In expressing it, moreover, Paul is not content with a simple arithmetical progression from transgression to salvation to envy (or from the salvation of the Gentiles to the salvation of the Jews, verses 11, 14); instead he sets down a geometric, *a fortiori* progression: *if their transgression means riches for the world, and their loss means riches for the Gentiles, how much greater riches will their fulness bring!* (12). This is a compact sentence which telescopes two progressions. The first concerns Israel, and the second the Gentile world. As for Israel, the *a fortiori* argument is that if her 'fall' (*transgression*) and 'defeat' or 'overthrow' (*loss*) brought blessing to the Gentiles, how much more blessing will her *fulness* (*plērōma*) bring, which seems to mean not only her conversion and restoration but also her increase in numbers until the remnant (*leimma*) has grown into a substantial majority. As for the Gentiles, the blessing they have received through Israel's fall is called *salvation* or *riches*; but the blessing which they will receive through Israel's fulness is called *much greater riches*. What this will be we are not told; Paul leaves us, at least at the moment, to guess.

After this general statement of 'the chain of blessing', Paul now particularizes by relating it to his own ministry. He develops the same logic a second time. *I am talking to you Gentiles*, he writes, referring to the Gentile Christians in the church in Rome, who seem to have made up the majority. *I am the apostle to the Gentiles*, he continues, as he has already affirmed (1:1, 5) and will affirm again before he finishes his letter (15:16).[16] And *inasmuch as* this is so, he goes on, *I make much of* (*doxazō*, 'glorify') *my ministry* (13). He does this 'by giving himself to it wholly and

[15] Acts 5:17; 13:45; 17:5.
[16] For other references to his unique apostolic ministry to Gentiles see Acts 9:15f.; 22:21; 26:16ff.; Gal. 1:1, 16; 2:7ff.; 1 Tim. 2:7.

unreservedly'.[17] He 'fulfils it with all his might and devotion'.[18]

Paul now explains why he 'glorifies' his ministry, devoting himself to it with such energy and perseverance. It is because of what he hopes to achieve by it: *in the hope that I may somehow arouse my own people to envy and* so, by persuading them to believe in Christ, *save some of them* (14). This is a remarkable statement of his ministerial goals on several counts. First, to characterize his ministry to his own people in terms of arousing their 'envy', and to encourage them to come to Christ as a result of such 'envy', sounds like stimulating unworthy motives in both him and them. But this is not so. Not all envy is tainted with selfishness, because it is not always either a grudging discontent or a sinful covetousness. At base, envy is 'the desire to have for oneself something possessed by another', and whether envy is good or evil depends on the nature of the something desired and on whether one has any right to its possession. If that something is in itself evil, or if it belongs to somebody else and we have no right to it, then the envy is sinful. But if the something desired is in itself good, a blessing from God, which he means all his people to enjoy, then to 'covet' it and to 'envy' those who have it is not at all unworthy. This kind of desire is right in itself, and to arouse it can be a realistic motive in ministry.

A second reason Paul's statement is surprising is that his hope to *save some* sounds too low an expectation. We need to remember, however, that his vision focuses on the coming 'fulness' of Israel; his hope that he will himself 'save some' relates only to his own modest personal contribution to this end.

Thirdly, and most remarkably, Paul regards arousing his own (Jewish) people to envy as an aspect of his ministry to Gentiles. How could this be? It is an example of the continuing interaction between Jews and Gentiles which he perceives, and which is woven into his mission strategy. Perhaps he feels embarrassed, as he writes to the largely Gentile Roman church, that he the apostle to the Gentiles should have so much to say about the Jews. So he demonstrates that the two cannot be separated. Already it has been as a result of the Jewish rejection of the gospel that his distinctive ministry to the Gentiles has begun; now he shows that his ministry of arousing the Jews to envy will have a directly beneficial effect on the Gentile world.

This Paul now elaborates. What are the *much greater riches* which the fulness of Israel will bring to the Gentiles (12)? He responds: *For if their rejection is the reconciliation of the world, what will their acceptance be but life from the dead?* (15). We note how, in this restatement of what he has already written, his vocabulary has

---

[17] Dunn, vol. 38B, p. 656.   [18] Cranfield, vol. II, p. 560.

advanced. Israel's 'fall', 'transgression' and 'defeat' have now become her 'rejection' by God, even though God has not rejected his people altogether or for ever (1–2). The 'salvation' and 'riches' which the Gentiles have already received are now said to be 'the reconciliation of the world', surely because Christ 'has destroyed the barrier, the dividing wall of hostility' both between them and God and between them and the Jews.[19] The 'fulness' of restored Israel is now called their 'acceptance', reversing their temporary and partial 'rejection'. And the 'much greater riches' which Israel's fulness will bring to the Gentiles are defined as 'life from the dead'. This last expression has brought much puzzlement to commentators. There are three main interpretations.

The first is *literal*, namely that Paul is referring to the general resurrection on the last day, 'the final consummation, the resurrection of the dead, and that eternal life that follows'.[20] Thus the conversion of Israel 'will be the signal for the resurrection, the last stage of the eschatological process initiated by the death and resurrection of Jesus'.[21] Certainly in Jewish apocalyptic the restoration of Israel was usually associated with the resurrection of the dead, and certainly Paul has used 'life' in referring to the body (8:11). Nevertheless, 'life from the dead' would be a most unusual expression for resurrection, especially when *anastasis* was a perfectly good word which was ready to hand. Also, did Paul really believe that his own ministry to Jews and Gentiles would trigger the parousia and the resurrection? The evidence for this is lacking.

A second interpretation is *spiritual*, namely that Paul is referring to our being 'raised' with Christ, which is one of his favourite themes.[22] And earlier he has described us as 'those who have been brought from death to life' (6:13). But this is the status and experience of all Christian people. It belongs to the 'salvation' and 'riches' which Gentile Christians have already received. *Much greater riches* demands to be understood as something new, even spectacular. To refer it to the new life in Christ which we already enjoy would be an anticlimax.

Thirdly, there is the *figurative* interpretation. Paul foresees that 'unimaginable blessing'[23] is going to enrich the Gentiles, a worldwide blessing which will so far surpass anything before experienced that it can only be likened to new life out of death. Perhaps Paul is taking a backward glance to Ezekiel's vision, in which the restoration of Israel is depicted as the coming together of dead, dry bones which are then given both flesh and life.[24] Does Paul now apply this

---

[19] Eph. 2:11ff.   [20] Sanday and Headlam, p. 319.
[21] Barrett, p. 215. So too Cranfield, vol. II, p. 563, Dunn, pp. 658, 670, and Käsemann, p. 307.
[22] *E.g.* Eph. 2:1ff.; Col. 3:1ff.   [23] Denney, p. 679.   [24] Ezk. 37:3ff.

vision to the Gentile world? Does he prophesy 'a vast and intense revival of true religion from a state which, by comparison, was religious death',[25] 'an unprecedented quickening for the world in the expansion and success of the gospel'?[26] If God could use the tragedy of Israel's rejection to bring salvation to the Gentiles, with what further blessing could he not enrich the world through Israel's acceptance and fulness?

The apostle now uses two little metaphors, which function like proverbs, one taken from the ceremonial life of Israel, and the other from the agricultural. Both are clearly intended in some way to justify Paul's confidence in the spread or escalation of blessings which he has been describing, and, like verse 15, both parts of verse 16 are 'if' clauses. *If the part of the dough offered as firstfruits is holy, then the whole batch is holy* (16a).[27] Perhaps this should be interpreted as follows. As when a representative piece is consecrated to God, the whole belongs to him, so when the first converts believe, the conversion of the rest can be expected to follow. Next, *if the root is holy, so are the branches* (16b), perhaps meaning that as the Jewish patriarchs belong to God by covenant, so do their descendants who are included in the covenant. It seems to be this 'root' and 'branches' picture which leads Paul now to develop his allegory of the olive tree.

b. The allegory of the olive tree (17–24)

The olive, cultivated in groves or orchards throughout Palestine, was an accepted emblem of Israel,[28] as was also the vine.[29] Paul now develops the metaphor in such a way as to accommodate and illustrate his teaching about Jews and Gentiles. The cultivated olive is the people of God, whose root is the patriarchs and whose stem represents the continuity of the centuries. Now *some of the branches have been broken off*, standing for the unbelieving Jews who have been temporarily discarded, *and you* (Gentile believers), *though a wild olive shoot, have been grafted in among the others* (the Jewish remnant), so that you *now share* with them *in the nourishing sap from the olive root* (17).

Some commentators make heavy weather of Paul's allegory. They point out that, according to the normal procedure, 'grafts must necessarily be of branches from a cultivated olive inserted into a wild stock, the reverse process being one which would be valueless and is never performed'.[30] C. H. Dodd goes further and makes merry at Paul's expense. 'Paul had the limitations of the town-bred

---

[25] Moule (1884), p. 193.   [26] Murray, vol. II, p. 84.   [27] Cf. Nu. 15:17ff.
[28] Je. 11:16; Ho. 14:6.   [29] E.g. Ps. 80:8ff.
[30] Sanday and Headlam, p. 328.

man . . . and he had not the curiosity to inquire what went on in the olive-yards which fringed every road he walked.'[31] Poor ignorant city boy! So some scholars draw attention to Paul's reference in verse 24 to what is 'contrary to nature' and suggest that Paul knew what he was saying and was deliberately wishing to teach theological rather than horticultural lessons.

In 1905, however, Sir William Ramsay wrote an interesting article, which is still quoted, in which he drew on both ancient and modern authorities. The process Paul described, he wrote, was still in use in Palestine 'in exceptional circumstances . . .', for 'it is customary to reinvigorate an olive tree which is ceasing to bear fruit by grafting it with a shoot of the wild-olive, so that the sap of the tree ennobles this wild shoot and the tree now again begins to bear fruit'.[32] Paul's reference, therefore, is not to 'the ordinary process of grafting the young olive-tree' but to 'the method of invigorating a decadent olive-tree'.[33] In this case what is 'contrary to nature' is not the 'grafting' but the 'belonging', namely that the shoot has been cut from the wild olive to which it naturally belonged and has been grafted into the cultivated olive to which it does not naturally belong.[34]

Paul develops his allegory in such a way as to play on the themes of 'broken off' and 'grafted in', and to teach two complementary lessons. The first is a warning to the Gentile believers not to presume (17–22), and the second a promise to the Israelite unbelievers that they could be restored (23–24).

The warning to the believing Gentiles is clear. The olive has experienced both a pruning and a grafting. Some branches have been cut out of the cultivated tree. That is, some Jews have been rejected. And in their place a wild shoot has been grafted in. That is, some Gentiles have believed and been welcomed into God's covenant people. *Do not boast over those branches.* This is the warning, which Paul corroborates with a number of arguments. First, he says, you must remember your dependence on the root, for branches have no life in themselves. *Consider this: You do not support the root, but the root supports you* (18). Secondly, you must reflect that your stability is due to your faith alone. You may protest that *'Branches were broken off so that I could be grafted in'* (19). This is formally true. *Granted. But they were broken off because of unbelief, and you stand by faith (20).* So your position is decidedly vulnerable.

Thirdly, *do not be arrogant, but be afraid* (20). For you must not

<hr />

[31] Dodd, p. 180.

[32] Page 19. The article appeared in W. Robertson Nicoll (ed.), *The Expositor*, 6th series, vol. XI (Hodder and Stoughton, 1905), pp. 16ff. and 152ff., and was later included in Ramsay's *Pauline and Other Studies* (1906), pp. 217ff.

[33] *Ibid.*, pp. 24, 34.   [34] Ziesler (1989), p. 281.

forget what happened to unbelieving Israel, which belonged naturally to the olive tree. *For if God did not spare the natural branches,
he will not spare you either* (21), for you do not naturally belong.
Fourthly, you must constantly meditate on the character of God.
Consider therefore the kindness and sternness of God, sternness in
judgment upon *those who fell,* the apostate Jews, *but kindness to
you,* believing Gentiles, who have been incorporated by his sheer
grace alone, *provided that you continue in his kindness. Otherwise
you will be cut off* (22). Not that those who truly belong to him will
ever be rejected, but that continuance or perseverance is the hallmark of God's authentic children.[35]

This exhortation to Gentile believers not to boast, together with
the arguments with which it was buttressed, was undoubtedly much
needed in Rome. For, although the Jews were tolerated and protected by law from Gentile molestation, they suffered a great deal of
popular Gentile ill will and sometimes from outbreaks of violence.
Resisting assimilation to Gentile culture, and refusing to abandon or
modify their own practices, 'their exclusiveness bred the
unpopularity out of which anti-Semitism was born. The Jew was a
figure of amusement, contempt or hatred to the Gentiles among
whom he lived.'[36] Paul was determined that Gentile believers in
Rome would have no share in such anti-Semitic prejudice.

After this warning to Gentile believers against pride and presumption, Paul is ready with his promise to Jewish unbelievers. His
argument is that if those grafted in could be cut off, then those cut
off could be grafted in again. The key word is *persist* (*epimenō*), the
same verb as is rendered 'continue' in the previous verse: *And if
they do not persist in unbelief, they will be grafted in, for God is able
to graft them in again* (23). Moreover, the assurance of this is drawn
from the contrast between the natural and the unnatural branches:
After all, if you (sc. Gentile believers) *were cut out of an olive tree
that is wild by nature, and contrary to nature were grafted into a
cultivated olive tree, how much more readily will these* (sc. Jewish
believers), *the natural branches, be grafted into their own olive tree!*
(24). In other words, 'the restoration of Israel is an easier process
than the call of the Gentiles'.[37]

Much of the 'chain of blessing', then, is included in the allegory of
the olive tree, especially the rejection of the Jews (cultivated
branches broken off), the incorporation of the Gentiles (the wild
shoot grafted in) and the expected restoration of the Jews (natural
branches grafted back in again). What the allegory does not permit

[35] *E.g.* Heb. 3:14; 1 Jn. 2:19.
[36] E. M. Smallwood, *The Jews under Roman Rule from Pompey to Diocletian*
(Leiden, 1976), pp. 123f.
[37] Sanday and Headlam, p. 330.

is the further truth that through Israel's restoration the Gentiles will be yet more richly blessed. The warning and the promise are paramount, however. First the warning: since the natural branches were broken off, the wild ones could be too (21). The Gentiles could be rejected like the Jews. There is no room for complacency. Secondly the promise: since the wild branches were grafted in, the natural ones could be too (24). The Jews could be accepted like the Gentiles. There is no room for despair.

c. The divine mystery (25–32)

Having completed his allegory of the olive tree, Paul again addresses his readers directly, his 'brothers', probably including both Gentile and Jewish church members, since he is now going to refer to the future of both. *I do not want you to be ignorant of this mystery, brothers, so that you may not be conceited* (25a). He has already warned them against boasting (18) and arrogance (20), and now against conceit. 'Not ignorant so that not conceited' is the essence of what he writes, for he knows that ignorance is the cause of conceit. It is when we have false or fantasy images of ourselves that we grow proud. Conversely, knowledge is conducive to humility, for humility is honesty, not hypocrisy. The complete antidote to pride is truth. If only the Jewish and Gentile members of the church in Rome can grasp their position *vis-à-vis* one another in the purpose of God, they will have nothing to boast about.

What Paul specially wants them to know is *this mystery*. By a 'mystery' he means not a secret which is known only by the initiated, but a secret which has now been openly revealed and has therefore become public truth. Essentially this is Christ himself, 'in whom are hidden all the treasures of wisdom and knowledge'.[38] But in particular it is the good news that in Christ Gentiles are now equal beneficiaries with the Jews of the promises of God and equal members of his family (16:25f.).[39] In this passage in Romans, however, the mystery seems to be what he is about to tell them. It consists of three consecutive truths. The first is that *Israel has experienced a hardening in part* (25b). This fact is not new, since Paul has already stated it in verse 7. As we have already seen, it is God who 'hardens' (9:18), although this is a judicial process by which he hands people over to their own stubbornness. The 'hardening' takes the form of spiritual insensitivity. In the case of Israel it is the same as the 'veil' which Paul elsewhere says lies over their hearts and minds.[40]

---

[38] Col. 2:2f.; 4:3.   [39] Eph. 1:9; 3:3ff.; Col. 1:26f.; 3:11.
[40] 2 Cor. 3:14ff.; 4:3f.

But now the apostle stresses that it is only partial (*in part*), since not all Israelites have experienced it (*i.e.* not the believing remnant), and only temporary (*until...*), since it will last only until the second stage of God's unfolding plan. This Paul now states: *until the full number of the Gentiles has come in* (25c). While Israel remains hardened, and continues to reject Christ, the gospel will be preached throughout the world,[41] and more and more Gentiles will hear and respond to it. And this process will continue until *the full number* or full complement (*plērōma*, the same word having been used of Israel in verse 12) *of the Gentiles* has been made up.

This will bring about the third stage: *And so all Israel will be saved* (26a). The three main words in this statement, namely 'all', 'Israel' and 'saved', need some investigation.

First, what is the identity of *Israel* which is to be saved? Calvin believed it was a reference to the church. 'I extend the word *Israel*', he wrote, 'to include all the people of God', so that, when the Gentiles have come in and the Jews have returned, 'the salvation of the whole Israel of God, which must be drawn from both, will thus be completed....'[42] It is of course true that Paul referred to the church as 'the Israel of God' in Galatians 6:16, but throughout Romans 'Israel' means ethnic or national Israel, in contrast to the Gentile nations. This is plainly so in verse 25 of this context; so the word could hardly take on a different meaning in the very next verse (26). The natural interpretation of the 'mystery' is that Israel as a people is hardened until the fulness of the Gentiles has come in, and then at that point (it is implied) Israel's hardening will be over and 'all Israel will be saved'. I do not think John Murray was putting it too strongly when he wrote: 'It is exegetically impossible to give to "Israel" in this verse any other denotation than that which belongs to the term throughout this chapter.'[43]

Secondly, there is the word *all*. Whom does Paul intend to include in 'all Israel'? At present Israel is hardened except for a believing remnant, and will remain so until the Gentiles have come in. Then 'all Israel' must mean the great mass of the Jewish people, comprising both the previously hardened majority and the believing minority. It need not mean literally every single Israelite. This is in keeping with contemporary usage. ' "All Israel" is a recurring expression in Jewish literature,' writes F. F. Bruce, 'where it need not mean "every Jew without a single exception", but "Israel as a whole".'[44]

The third word is *saved*. What kind of salvation is in view? The scriptural foundation, which Paul now supplies, will help us to

[41] *Cf.* Mk. 13:10; *cf.* Rev. 7:9ff.   [42] Calvin, p. 255.   [43] Murray, vol. II, p. 96.
[44] Bruce, p. 209.

answer this question. It is a potpourri of three texts about the salvation of God's people.

> [26b]*'The deliverer will come from Zion;*
> *he will turn godlessness away from Jacob.*
> [27]*And this is my covenant with them*
> *when I take away their sins'.*

These verses together make three affirmations. First, *the deliverer will come from Zion.*[45] This was, in Isaiah's original, a reference to Christ's first coming. Secondly, what he would do when he came was described in moral terms: he would *'turn godlessness away from Jacob'.* This seems to be an allusion to Isaiah 27:9, where Jacob's guilt would be atoned for and removed. Thirdly, the deliverer would establish God's covenant, which promised the forgiveness of sins.[46] Putting these truths together, the deliverer would come to bring his people to repentance and so to forgiveness, according to God's covenant promise. It is clear from this that the 'salvation' of Israel for which Paul has prayed (10:1), to which he will lead his own people by arousing their envy (11:14), which has also come to the Gentiles (11:11; *cf.* 1:16), and which one day 'all Israel' will experience (11:26), is salvation from sin through faith in Christ. It is not a national salvation, for nothing is said about either a political entity or a return to the land. Nor is there any hint of a special way of salvation for the Jews which dispenses with faith in Christ.

It is understandable that since the holocaust Jews have demanded an end to Christian missionary activity among them, and that many Christians have felt embarrassed about continuing it. It is even mooted that Jewish evangelism is an unacceptable form of anti-Semitism. So some Christians have attempted to develop a theological basis for leaving Jews alone in their Judaism. Reminding us that God's covenant with Abraham was an 'everlasting covenant', they maintain that it is still in force, and that therefore God saves Jewish people through their own covenant, without any necessity for them to believe in Jesus. This proposal is usually called a 'two-covenant theology'. Bishop Krister Stendahl was one of the first scholars to argue for it,[47] namely that there are two different salvation 'tracks' the Christian track for the believing remnant and believing Gentiles, and the track for historical Israel which relies on God's covenant with them. Professor Dunn is surely right to reject this as 'a false and quite unnecessary antithesis'.[48]

---

[45] Is. 59:20.   [46] Je. 31:33f.   [47] Stendahl, p. 4.

[48] Dunn, vol. 38B, p. 683. *Cf.* Sanders (1983), pp. 194ff. and p. 205, n. 88, and Ziesler (1989), p. 285. For a comprehensive and sensitive statement on the propriety of Jewish evangelism, see *The Willowbank Declaration on the Christian Gospel and the Jewish People* (World Evangelical Fellowship, 1989).

Romans 11 stands in clear opposition to this trend because of its insistence on the fact that there is only one olive tree, to which Jewish and Gentile believers both belong. Jewish people 'will be grafted in' again 'if they do not persist in unbelief' (23). So faith in Jesus is essential for them. Whether or not Dr Tom Wright is correct in rejecting the notion of 'a large-scale, last-minute salvation of ethnic Jews',[49] his emphasis on present evangelism ('now', three times in verses 30 and 31) is healthy: 'Paul is envisaging a steady flow of Jews into the church, by grace through faith.'[50] The two-covenant theology also has the disastrous effect of perpetuating the distinction between Jews and Gentiles which Jesus Christ has abolished. 'The irony of this', writes Tom Wright, 'is that the late twentieth century, in order to avoid anti-Semitism, has advocated a position (the non-evangelization of the Jews) *which Paul regards precisely as anti-Semitic.*'[51] 'It would be quite intolerable to imagine a church at any period which was simply a Gentile phenomenon' or 'consisted only of Jews'.[52]

Looking back over verses 11–27, we note that Paul rehearses four times, with modifications, the same Jews–Gentiles–Jews–Gentiles sequence. First, in his 'chain of blessing' (11–12) he moves from Israel's transgression to salvation for the Gentiles, to Israel's envy and fulness, to 'much greater riches'. Secondly, in reference to his own ministry (13–16) he writes of Israel's rejection, the reconciliation of the world, Israel's acceptance and 'life from the dead'. Thirdly, in the allegory of the olive tree (17–24), the breaking off of the natural branches is followed by the grafting in of the wild shoot, with the prospect that the natural branches will be grafted back in again and that the wild branches must continue in God's kindness. Fourthly, in Paul's statement of the divine mystery (25–26), he moves from Israel's partial, temporary hardening to the fulness of the Gentiles to the salvation of all Israel, though the grand finale of blessing to the world is not mentioned.

The conclusion to Romans 11 (28–32), apart from the doxology (33–36), contains two distinct statements. Both are very finely chiselled and sculptured. Both focus on still unbelieving Israel ('they'), although in relation to believing Gentiles ('you'). Both not only describe present reality (which includes continuing Jewish unbelief), but also indicate the grounds for confidence that God has neither rejected his people (1–2) nor allowed them to fall beyond recovery (11). What are these grounds? They are God's election (28–29) and God's mercy (30–32).

First, God's election is irrevocable. *As far as the gospel is concerned, they are enemies on your account; but as far as election is*

---

[49] Wright, p. 233.   [50] *Ibid.*, p. 249.   [51] *Ibid.*, p. 253.   [52] *Ibid.*, p. 249.

concerned, they are loved on account of the patriarchs (28), *for God's gifts and his call are irrevocable* (29).

Here are two contrasting ways of evaluating the Jewish people. The essence of the antithesis is in the words 'they are enemies' and 'they are loved'. Because 'loved' is passive, 'enemies' must be passive too. That is, it denotes God's hostility to them, in the sense that they are under his judgment. Indeed, verse 28 insists that they are objects of God's love and wrath simultaneously. The same verse includes two further explanatory contrasts, which develop the antithesis between 'they' (unbelieving Jews) and 'you' (believing Gentiles). In relation to the gospel they are enemies because of you; in relation to election they are loved because of the patriarchs. This needs elaboration. On the one hand, the Jews are not only rejecting the gospel but actively opposing it and doing their best to prevent you Gentiles from hearing it. So then, in relation to the gospel, and for your sake (because God wants you to hear and believe), he is hostile to them. On the other hand, the Jews are the chosen, special people of God, the descendants of the noble patriarchs with whom the covenant was made, and to whom the promises were given. So then, in relation to election, and for the sake of the patriarchs (because God is faithful to his covenant and promises), he loves them and is determined to bring them to salvation. For the fact is that God never goes back on his gifts or call (29). Both are *irrevocable*. His gifts are the privileges he bestowed on Israel, which are listed in 9:4–5. As for his call, 'God is not a man, that he should lie, nor a son of man, that he should change his mind. Does he speak and then not act? Does he promise and not fulfil?'[53] It is because of God's steadfast faithfulness that we can have confidence in Israel's restoration.

The second ground for confidence that God has a future for his people is his mercy. For God's mercy is shown to the disobedient. *Just as you who were at one time disobedient to God have now received mercy as a result of their disobedience* (30), *so they too have now become disobedient in order that they too may now receive mercy as a result of God's mercy to you* (31).

These carefully constructed verses contain a parallel rather than a contrast. Human disobedience and divine mercy are depicted in the experience of both Gentiles and Jews; the obvious difference is that, whereas God has already been merciful to disobedient but repentant Gentiles, his mercy to disobedient Israel belongs largely to the future. But there is another difference, namely in the reasons given for God's mercy, which are expressed in the Greek sentence by simple datives. Thus, you received mercy 'by their disobedience' (30), whereas they will receive mercy 'by your mercy' (31). More

[53] Nu. 23:19.

fully, it is because of disobedient Israel that disobedient Gentiles have received mercy, and it is because of this mercy to disobedient Gentiles that disobedient Jews will receive mercy too. We detect yet again the 'chain of blessing', as Israel's disobedience has led to mercy for the Gentiles, which in turn will lead to mercy for Israel.

Verse 32 sums up the argument in such a way as to disclose God's overruling purpose and plan. *For God has bound all men over to disobedience so that he may have mercy on them all.* Disobedience is likened to a dungeon in which God has incarcerated all human beings, so that 'they have no possibility of escape except as God's mercy releases them'.[54] This has been the argument of this letter, as in its first three chapters Paul demonstrated that all human beings are sinful, guilty and without excuse, and then from 3:21 onwards unfolded the way of salvation by grace through faith in Christ. He writes something similar in Galatians. 'The Scripture declares that the whole world is a prisoner of sin ... We were held prisoners by the law, locked up until faith should be revealed. So the law was put in charge (RSV, 'was our custodian') to lead us to Christ....'[55] Thus human disobedience is the prison from which divine mercy liberates us.

But who are the 'all men' who are bound over to disobedience, and the 'all' on whom God will have mercy (32)? On this verse some have built their universalistic dreams. And, isolated from its context in Romans, it could be understood to promise universal salvation in the end. But Romans will not allow this interpretation, since in it Paul declares that there is to be a 'day of God's wrath' (2:5), on which some will receive 'wrath and anger', 'trouble and distress' (2:8f.). What, then, is the alternative? It is to note that in both halves of verse 32, regarding those whom God has imprisoned in disobedience and those on whom he will have mercy, Paul does not actually write of 'all men' or of 'all', but of 'the all' (*tous pantas*). And this expression in its context refers to the two groups who are contrasted throughout the chapter, and especially in verses 28 and 31, namely the 'they' and the 'you', the Jews and the Gentiles.

Paul has been at pains to argue that there is no distinction between Jews and Gentiles either in sin (3:9, 22) or in salvation (10:12). Now he writes that, as they have been together in the prison of their disobedience, so they will be together in the freedom of God's mercy. Moreover, he has predicted the future 'fulness' both of Israel (12) and of the Gentiles (25). It is when these two 'fulnesses' have been fused that the new humanity will have been realized, consisting of huge numbers of the redeemed, the great

[54] Cranfield, vol. II, p. 587.   [55] Gal. 3:22ff.

multinational multitude which no-one can count,[56] 'the many' who were formerly in Adam but are now in Christ, experiencing his overflowing grace and reigning with him in life (5:12ff.). The end of God's ways will be 'mercy, mercy uncompromised',[57] mercy on the fulness of both Jews and Gentiles, mercy on 'them all', that is, 'on all without distinction, rather than on all without exception'.[58]

---

[56] Rev. 7:9.   [57] Cranfield, vol. II, p. 587.   [58] Bruce, p. 211.

11:33–36
15. Doxology

For eleven chapters Paul has been giving his comprehensive account
of the gospel. Step by step he has shown how God has revealed his
way of putting sinners right with himself, how Christ died for our
sins and was raised for our justification, how we are united with
Christ in his death and resurrection, how the Christian life is lived
not under the law but in the Spirit, and how God plans to incorporate the fulness of Israel and of the Gentiles into his new
community. Paul's horizons are vast. He takes in time and eternity,
history and eschatology, justification, sanctification and glorification. Now he stops, out of breath. Analysis and argument must give
way to adoration. 'Like a traveller who has reached the summit of
an Alpine ascent,' wrote F. L. Godet of Neuchâtel, Switzerland,
'the apostle turns and contemplates. Depths are at his feet; but
waves of light illumine them, and there spreads all around an
immense horizon which his eye commands.'[1] Before Paul goes on
to outline the practical implications of the gospel, he falls down
before God and worships (33–36).

Paul's praise is informed by Scripture, and is full of Old Testament phraseology. Yet it is his own expression of humble wonder
and dependence.

He begins with *an astonished exclamation*: *Oh, the depth of the
riches of the wisdom and knowledge of God! How unsearchable his
judgments, and his paths beyond tracing out!* (33). There are two
possible ways of interpreting the opening sentence. The first is to
understand Paul to be referring to one truth, namely God's wisdom
and knowledge, whose profound riches he celebrates (NIV, 'the depth
of the riches *of* the wisdom and knowledge of God'). The second is
to understand him to be referring to two truths, namely God's
riches on the one hand and God's wisdom and knowledge on the
other, and to be celebrating the depth of both (RSV, 'the depth of the

---

[1] Godet, p. 416.

riches *and* wisdom and knowledge of God'). That this second interpretation is correct (namely that God's wealth and wisdom are both being magnified) is suggested by the parallel in the next exclamation, in which Paul alludes both to God's unsearchable *judgments* (what he thinks and decides) and to his untraceable *paths* (what he does and where he goes). In fact, this distinction continues throughout the doxology – his wealth and his wisdom (33a), his judgments and his paths (33b), his revelation (34) and his gifts (35).

Paul has already written of God's wealth: 'the riches of his kindness, tolerance and patience' (2:4), 'the riches of his glory' (9:23) and the riches which the Lord Jesus bestows indiscriminately on all who call on him (10:12). Elsewhere he describes God as 'rich in mercy'[2] and refers to Christ's inexhaustible riches.[3] The dominant thought is that salvation is a gift from God's riches and that it immensely enriches those to whom it is given.

Then there is God's wisdom, which is hidden in Christ,[4] was displayed on the cross (though it appears to human beings to be folly),[5] and is unfolded in his saving purpose.[6] Thus if the wisdom of God planned salvation, the wealth of God bestows it. Moreover, God's wealth and wisdom are not only deep; they are actually unfathomable (33b). His decisions are unsearchable, and his ways inscrutable. This is the New Testament equivalent of Isaiah 55:8f. where God declares his thoughts to be higher than our thoughts, and his ways than our ways. But of course! How could finite and fallen creatures like us ever imagine that we could penetrate into the infinite mind of God? His mind (what he thinks) and his activity (what he does) are altogether beyond us.[7]

Paul continues, secondly, with *a rhetorical question*, in fact with two. The two exclamation marks of verse 33 ('Oh the depths . . . !' 'How unsearchable . . . !') are followed by the two question marks of verses 34 and 35 ('Who has known . . . ?' 'Who has ever given . . . ?'

> [34]'*Who has known the mind of the Lord?*
> *Or who has been his counsellor?*'[8]

> [35]'*Who has ever given to God,*
> *that God should repay him?*'[9]

It is frankly ludicrous, as Paul's two Old Testament quotations make clear, to imagine that we could ever teach or give God

---

[2] Eph. 2:4; *cf.* 1:7.   [3] Eph. 3:8; 3:16. *Cf.* also 2 Cor. 8:9; Phil. 4:19.
[4] Col. 2:2f.   [5] 1 Cor. 1:18ff.   [6] Eph. 1:8; 3:10.
[7] For the unfathomable nature of God's mind and mysteries see *e.g.* Jb. 5:9; 11:7; Ps. 139:6; Is. 40:28.
[8] Is. 40:13.   [9] Jb. 35:7 – 41:11.

anything. It would be absurd to claim (since his thoughts are unsearchable) that we know his mind and have offered him our advice. It would be equally absurd to claim (since his ways are inscrutable) that we have given him a gift or two and so put him in our debt. No, no. We are not God's counsellor; he is ours. We are not God's creditor; he is ours. We depend entirely on him to teach and to save us. The initiative in both revelation and redemption lies in his grace. The attempt to reverse roles would be to dethrone God and to deify ourselves. So the answer to both questions in verses 34–35 is, 'Nobody!'

Thirdly, Paul makes *a theological affirmation*: *For from him and through him and to him are all things* (36a). This is the reason for our human dependence on God. *All things* often refers to the material creation. Perhaps here, however, Paul is referring to the new creation as well, the coming into being of the new multiracial people of God. If we ask *where* all things came from in the beginning, and still come from today, the answer must be, 'From God.' If we ask *how* all things came into being and remain in being, our answer is, 'Through God.' If we ask *why* everything came into being, and where everything is going, our answer must be, 'For and to God.' These three prepositions (*ek*, 'out of' or 'from'; *dia*, 'through'; and *eis*, 'for' or 'unto') indicate that God is the creator, sustainer and heir of everything, its source, means and goal. He is the Alpha and the Omega,[10] and every letter of the alphabet in between.

Fourthly, Paul concludes with *a final ascription*: *To him be the glory for ever! Amen* (36b). It is because all things are from, through and to God that the glory must be his alone. This is why human pride is so offensive. Pride is behaving as if we were God Almighty, strutting round the earth as if we owned the place, repudiating our due dependence on God, pretending instead that all things depend on us, and thus arrogating to ourselves the glory which belongs to God alone.

It is of great importance to note from Romans 1 – 11 that theology (our belief about God) and doxology (our worship of God) should never be separated. On the one hand, there can be no doxology without theology. It is not possible to worship an unknown god. All true worship is a response to the self-revelation of God in Christ and Scripture, and arises from our reflection on who he is and what he has done. It was the tremendous truths of Romans 1 – 11 which provoked Paul's outburst of praise. The worship of God is evoked, informed and inspired by the vision of God. Worship without theology is bound to degenerate into

[10] Rev. 1:8; 21:6; 22:13.

idolatry. Hence the indispensable place of Scripture in both public worship and private devotion. It is the Word of God which calls forth the worship of God.

On the other hand, there should be no theology without doxology. There is something fundamentally flawed about a purely academic interest in God. God is not an appropriate object for cool, critical, detached, scientific observation and evaluation. No, the true knowledge of God will always lead us to worship, as it did Paul. Our place is on our faces before him in adoration.

As I believe Bishop Handley Moule said at the end of the last century, we must 'beware equally of an undevotional theology and of an untheological devotion'.

16. A manifesto of evangelism

'How beautiful are the feet of those who bring good news!' (10:15).[1]

Convinced that God has a future for both Jews and Gentiles, and that their growth into 'fulness' will be brought about by evangelism, Paul makes a forceful statement of its logic (10:14f.) and alludes in other ways to the spread of the gospel. From these chapters, therefore, it is possible to summarize Paul's teaching on evangelism to form an eight-point manifesto.

1. The need for evangelism: evangelism is necessary because until people hear and receive the gospel they are lost.
This recognition of the gravity of the human situation, which Paul argued in Romans 1 – 3, is indispensable to evangelism. All human beings in God's sight are sinful, guilty and without excuse. If they are to be saved, they must call on the name of the Lord (10:13), but in order to do this, they must be given an opportunity to hear the good news (10:14f.).

2. The scope of evangelism: the whole human race must be given the chance to hear the gospel.
Just as the heavens proclaim God's glory throughout the earth (10:18), so Christian witnesses must proclaim his grace worldwide. All nations must hear the gospel (1:5; 16:26). But so must Israel, for neither her unique privileges (9:4f.) nor her religious zeal (10:2) can be a substitute for faith in Jesus (11:23). So there is no distinction between Jews and Gentiles in respect either of their sin (3:22f.) or of the means of their salvation, for the same Lord Jesus 'richly blesses all who call on him' (10:12). There can be no question of two ways of salvation, one for Gentiles and another for Jews.

[1] Is. 52:7.

3. The incentive to evangelism: evangelism arises from the love and the longing of the heart.

Paul the patriotic Jew showed no sign of impatience, bitterness or scorn that his compatriots had rejected their Messiah. As Dr Lloyd-Jones has put it, Paul 'displays no trace of annoyance with them. There is not a suspicion of any contemptuous attitude towards them. He does not dismiss them, denounce them, attack them; he is not even irritated by them.'[2] Instead, he wrote both of his heart's anguish that they were lost (9:1f.) and of his heart's longing that they might be saved (10:1). He would be willing even to perish if thereby they might be saved. Evangelism lacks authenticity if it is not inspired by the same love.

4. The nature of evangelism: evangelism is sharing with others the good news of Christ crucified and risen.

Evangelism means spreading the evangel. Consequently, we cannot define the former without defining the latter. In 9:30 – 10:13 Paul sets over against each other the false and the true ways of salvation, and we must do the same. In particular, we need to focus on Christ and his accessibility, for he has already come, died and risen, and is readily available to simple faith (10:6ff.).

5. The logic of evangelism: evangelism demands the sending out of evangelists, so that people may call on Christ for salvation.

There can be no salvation without calling on Christ's name, no calling on his name without believing what it implies, no believing in Christ without hearing him, no hearing without the preaching of the gospel, and no preaching without preachers being sent (10:13ff.). Although all Jesus' disciples are expected to share in evangelistic outreach, he gives to some the gift and calling of an evangelist, and these the church must solemnly commission and authorize to preach.

6. The result of evangelism: evangelism brings such blessings to those who believe, that it arouses the envy of others.

Three times in these chapters Paul employs the same Greek verb *parazeloō*, to 'make envious' (10:19; 11:11, 14). Envy is the desire to have for oneself something possessed by somebody else. If that 'something' is salvation, it is understandable that people 'envy' those who have received it, that is, desire it for themselves. Many have been converted through 'envy'. One such was Robert Robinson, who later became a Baptist minister, author and hymn-writer. In 1752, at the age of seventeen, he went to hear George Whitefield

---

[2] Lloyd-Jones, vol. 9, p. 33.

preach in London, and was converted. He wrote to Whitefield: 'I went pitying the poor deluded Methodists; but came away envying their happiness'.[3]

7. *The hope for evangelism: evangelism has hope of success only if it rests on the election of God.*

Election and evangelism are not incompatible. These very chapters which contain strong teaching on election also contain clear references to the necessity both of prayer-evangelism (interceding for people to be saved, 10:1) and of preaching-evangelism (sharing the good news with others, 10:14f.). Our responsibility is to see that the gospel is preached throughout the world, so that everybody is given the opportunity to hear and to respond. For the Word of God is his appointed way of awakening faith (10:17, NEB) and so of saving those who believe.[4] Not that everybody will respond. God himself knows the painful and even humiliating trauma of patiently holding out his hands to a disobedient and obstinate people (10:21). In sum, 'so far from making evangelism pointless, the sovereignty of God in grace is the one thing that prevents evangelism from being pointless'.[5]

8. *The goal of evangelism: evangelism introduces converts into the people of God, and so brings glory to God.*

Evangelism is not an end in itself. It also unites us with the people of God. Into God's one olive tree believing Gentiles are grafted and believing Jews are grafted back, so that we all share in the same history (going back to Abraham) and the same geography (extending throughout the world). We thus rejoice in both the continuity and the solidarity of the people of God.

But the ultimate goal of evangelism is the glory of God. The gospel displays his power, proclaims his name, makes known the riches of his glory, and reveals his mercy (9:17, 22f.; 11:30ff.). There is no room for boasting; only for humble, grateful, wondering adoration. To him be the glory for ever! Amen.

---

[3] Graham W. Hughes, *With Freedom Fired* (Carey Kingsgate Press, 1955), pp. 10–12.

[4] *E.g.* 1 Cor. 1:21.

[5] J. I. Packer, *Evangelism and the Sovereignty of God* (Inter-Varsity Press, 1961), p. 106. See also R. B. Kuiper, *God-Centred Evangelism* (Banner of Truth, 1961).

D. The will of God
for changed relationships
Romans 12:1 – 15:13

One of the notable features of Paul's teaching is that he regularly combines doctrine with duty, belief with behaviour. In consequence, as in some of his other letters, he now turns in Romans 12 from exposition to exhortation, from the gospel to everyday Christian discipleship, or, as Anders Nygren put it, from the statement that 'he who through faith is righteous' to its corollary, 'he shall live'. Moreover, it is not only individual or personal ethics to which Paul now introduces his readers. He is concerned to depict the characteristics of the new community which Jesus has brought into being by his death and resurrection.

Two general aspects of Paul's instruction in Romans 12 – 15 call for comment before we consider the particulars. The first is that he integrates creed and conduct, insisting both on the practical implications of his theology and on the theological foundations of his ethic. In spite of our newness in Christ ('dead to sin but alive to God', 6:11), holiness is neither automatic nor inevitable. On the contrary, pleas for good conduct need to be issued, and reasons need to be given. Thus in chapter 12 we are told to offer our bodies to God because of his mercy (1), to serve one another because we are one body in Christ (5), and not to take revenge, because vengeance belongs to God (19). Similarly, according to chapter 13 we are to submit to the state because its officials are God's ministers wielding God's authority (1ff.), and to love our neighbour and so fulfil the law because the day of Christ's return is approaching (10f.). And in chapter 14, as we will see in detail later, we are urged not to harm our sisters and brothers in any way, because Christ died to be their saviour (15), rose to be their Lord (9f.) and is coming to be our judge (11f.). It is marvellous to see the great doctrines of the cross, the resurrection and the parousia being pressed into the service of practical, day-to-day Christian behaviour.

The second striking feature of Paul's ethical instruction in Romans 12 – 15 concerns the number of times he refers directly or indirectly to the teaching of Jesus.[1] The following table supplies the main examples.

Paul	Jesus
'Bless those who persecute you; bless and do not curse' (12:14).	'Bless those who curse you' (Luke 6:28).
'Do not repay anyone evil for evil' (12:17).	'Do not resist an evil person' (Mt. 5:39).
'Live at peace with everyone' (12:18; *cf.* 14:19).	'Blessed are the peacemakers' (Mt. 5:9). 'Be at peace with each other' (Mk. 9:50).
'If your enemy is hungry, feed him' (12:20).	'Love your enemies, do good to those who hate you' (Lk. 6:27; *cf.* verse 35 and Mt. 5:44).
'Give everyone what you owe him: if you owe taxes, pay taxes . . .' (13:7).	'Is it right to pay taxes to Caesar or not? . . . Give to Caesar what is Caesar's, and to God what is God's' (Mk. 12:14, 17).
'Love one another' (13:8).	'Love one another' (Jn. 13:34f.).
'He who loves his fellow-man has fulfilled the law' (13:8).	'Love the Lord your God . . . Love your neighbour as yourself. All the Law and the Prophets hang on these two commandments' (Mt. 22:37ff.).
'The commandments . . . are summed up in this one rule: "Love your neighbour as yourself"' (13:9).	'Do to others what you would have them do to you, for this sums up the Law and the Prophets' (Mt. 7:12).

---

[1] Dr Michael Thompson helpfully distinguishes between (a) a 'quotation', which Paul introduces by an explicit citation formula, (b) an 'allusion', which is an intentional reminder to his readers of a tradition they already know, and (c) an 'echo' or 'reminiscence', which seems to parallel Jesus' teaching but may not do so consciously in Paul's mind (Thompson, pp. 29f.). Dr Thompson concludes that in Romans 12:1 – 15:13 there are no quotations, 'only one probable allusion' (*viz.* in 12:14b), and 'three virtually certain echoes', together with several other probable ones (p. 237). Further, the effect of these echoes 'decisively favours the conclusion that dominical teachings significantly influenced Paul' (p. 238), as did Christ's example even more.

'Understanding the present time' (13:11a).	'How is it that you don't know how to interpret this present time?' (Lk. 12:56).
'Wake up from your slumber, because our salvation is nearer now . . .' (13:11b, c).	'Do not let him find you sleeping' (Mk. 13:36). 'Your redemption is drawing near' (Lk. 21:28).
'Why do you judge your brother? Let us stop passing judgment on one another' (14:10, 13).	'Do not judge, or you too will be judged' (Mt. 7:1).
'Each of us will give an account of himself to God' (14:12).	'Men will have to give an account on the day of judgment . . .' (Mt. 12:36).
'Make up your mind not to put any stumbling-block . . . in your brother's way' (14:13).	'Alas for the world that such causes of stumbling arise!' (Mt. 18:7, NEB).
'No food is unclean in itself . . . all food is clean' (14:14, 20).	'What goes into a man's mouth does not make him "unclean". (Mt. 15:10). 'In saying this, Jesus declared all foods "clean"' (Mk. 7:19).
'The kingdom of God is not . . . eating and drinking but . . . righteousness . . .' (14:17).	'Do not worry about . . . what you will eat or drink . . . But seek first God's kingdom and his righteousness' (Mt. 6:25, 33).

Turning now from these two general characteristics of Paul's teaching to its particulars, it is evident that he concentrates on our relationships, beginning with our relationship to God.

12:1–2
17.   Our relationship to God: consecrated bodies and renewed minds

Therefore, I urge you, Paul begins, probably conveying by the verb *parakaleō* a mixture of entreaty and authority. He then goes on to indicate the people to whom he is addressing his appeal, the ground on which he bases it, and what it consists of.

The people the apostle is about to exhort he calls *brothers* (1), and we can hardly doubt that his choice of this word is deliberate. Throughout the letter's earlier chapters he has been conscious of the tensions between Jews and Gentiles in the Roman church, and in chapters 9 – 11 he has been describing the roles of Israel and of the nations in the unfolding, historical plan of God. He will revert to them again for the last time in chapters 14 – 15. But now, as he develops his appeal, the distinction between the olive tree's natural and grafted branches fades into the background. Now all believers, irrespective of their ethnic origin, are brothers and sisters in the one international family of God, and so all have precisely the same vocation to be the holy, committed, humble, loving and conscientious people of God.

Secondly, the ground of Paul's appeal is indicated by his use of the conjunction *therefore* and by his reference to *God's mercy*, literally his 'mercies' in the plural (RSV), a Hebraism for the many and varied manifestations of his mercy. For eleven chapters Paul has been unfolding the mercies of God. Indeed, the gospel is precisely God's mercy to inexecusable and underserving sinners, in giving his Son to die for them, in justifying them freely by faith, in sending them his life-giving Spirit, and in making them his children. In particular, the 'key-word' of Roman 9 – 11 is 'mercy'.[1] For salvation depends 'not . . . on man's desire or effort, but on God's mercy' (9:16), and his purpose is 'to make the riches of his glory known to the objects of his mercy' (9:23). Further, as the disobedient Gentiles

---

[1] Cranfield, vol. II, p. 448. True, 'mercy' translates *oiktirmos* in 12:1 and *eleos* (or its cognate verb) in 9:16, 23 and 11:30ff. Nevertheless, although the words are different, the sense is the same.

'have now received mercy', so too disobedient Israel will 'now receive mercy' (11:30f.). 'For God has bound all men over to disobedience so that he may have mercy on them all' (11:32).

It is, then, *in view of God's mercy* (1a) that Paul issues his ethical appeal. He knows – not least from his own experience – that there is no greater incentive to holy living than a contemplation of the mercies of God. F. F. Bruce has written: 'It was well said by Thomas Erskine of Linlathen that "in the New Testament religion is grace, and ethics is gratitude". It is not by accident that in Greek one and the same noun (*charis*) does duty for both "grace" and "gratitude".'[2] God's grace, far from encouraging or condoning sin, is the spring and foundation of righteous conduct.

Thirdly, having considered the objects and the ground of Paul's appeal, we note its double nature. It concerns both our bodies and our minds, the presentation of our bodies to God and our transformation by the renewal of our minds. First, our bodies. *I urge you . . .* , he writes, *to offer your bodies as living sacrifices, holy and pleasing to God – this is your spiritual act of worship* (1b). In order to maintain the sacrificial imagery throughout the sentence, Paul uses five more and less technical terms. He represents us as a priestly people, who, in responsive gratitude for God's mercy, *offer* or present our bodies as living sacrifices. These are described as both *holy* and *pleasing to God*, which seem to be the moral equivalents to being physically unblemished or without defect, and a fragrant aroma.[3] Such an offering is our *spiritual act of worship*. 'Spiritual' translates *logikos*, which could mean either 'reasonable' (AV) or 'rational'. If the former is correct, then the offering of ourselves to God is seen as the only sensible, logical and appropriate response to him in view of his self-giving mercy. If 'rational' is correct, then it is 'the worship offered by mind and heart' (REB), spiritual as opposed to ceremonial, 'an act of intelligent worship' (JBP), in which our minds are fully engaged. Several commentators illustrate this by a delightful quotation from Epictetus, the first-century Stoic philosopher: 'If I were a nightingale, I would do what is proper to a nightingale, and if I were a swan, what is proper to a swan. In fact I am *logikos* [*sc.* a rational being], so I must praise God.'[4]

What, however, is this living sacrifice, this rational, spiritual worship? It is not to be offered in the temple courts or in the church building, but rather in home life and in the marketplace. It is the presentation of our bodies to God. This blunt reference to our bodies was calculated to shock some of Paul's Greek readers.

[2] Bruce, p. 213 footnote, quoting Thomas Erskine, *Letters* (1877), p. 16.
[3] *Cf.* Lv. 1:3, 9.
[4] Epictetus, *Discourses* I.16.20f, quoted by Cranfield, vol. 2, p. 602, and Dunn, vol. 38B, p. 711.

Brought up on Platonic thought, they will have regarded the body as an embarrassing encumbrance. Their slogan was *soma sēma estin* ('the body is a tomb'), in which the human spirit was imprisoned and from which they longed for its escape. Still today some Christians feel self-conscious about their bodies. The traditional evangelical invitation is that we give our 'hearts' to God, not our 'bodies'. Even some commentators, apparently disconcerted by Paul's earthy language, suggest as an alternative 'offer your very selves to him' (REB). But Paul is clear that the presentation of our *bodies* is our *spiritual* act of worship. It is a significant Christian paradox. No worship is pleasing to God which is purely inward, abstract and mystical; it must express itself in concrete acts of service performed by our bodies. Similarly, authentic Christian discipleship will include both the negative 'mortification' of our body's misdeeds (8:13) and the positive 'presentation' of its members to God.

Paul made it plain, in his exposure of human depravity in 3:13ff., that it reveals itself through our bodies, in tongues which practise deceit and lips which spread poison, in mouths which are full of cursing and bitterness, in feet which are swift to shed blood, and in eyes which look away from God. Conversely, Christian sanctity shows itself in the deeds of the body. So we are to offer the different parts of our bodies not to sin as 'instruments of wickedness' but to God as 'instruments of righteousness' (6:13, 16, 19). Then our feet will walk in his paths, our lips will speak the truth and spread the gospel, our tongues will bring healing, our hands will lift up those who have fallen, and perform many mundane tasks as well like cooking and cleaning, typing and mending; our arms will embrace the lonely and the unloved, our ears will listen to the cries of the distressed, and our eyes will look humbly and patiently towards God.

If the first part of Paul's appeal relates to the presentation of our bodies to God, the second relates to our transformation according to his will. *Do not conform any longer to the pattern of this world, but be transformed by the renewing of your mind. Then you will be able to test and approve what God's will is – his good, pleasing and perfect will* (2). This is Paul's version of the call to nonconformity and to holiness which is addressed to the people of God throughout Scripture. For example, God's word came to Israel through Moses: 'You must not do as they do ... in the land of Canaan where I am bringing you. Do not follow their practices. You must obey my laws ....'[5] Another example is found in the Sermon on the Mount. Surrounded by the false devotion of both Pharisees and pagans, Jesus said to his disciples: 'Do not be like them.'[6] 'We are not to be

---

[5] Lv. 18:3; *cf.* 2 Ki. 17:15; Ezk. 11:12.   [6] Mt. 6:8.

like a chameleon which takes its colour from its surroundings.'[7]
And now Paul issues the same summons to the people of God not to
be conformed to the prevailing culture, but rather to be transformed. Both verbs are present passive imperatives and denote the
continuing attitudes which we are to retain. We must go on refusing
to conform to the world's ways and go on letting ourselves be
transformed according to God's will. J. B. Phillip's paraphrase
catches the alternative: 'Don't let the world around you squeeze
you into its own mould, but let God remould your minds from
within.'

We human beings seem to be imitative by nature. We need a
model to copy, and ultimately there are only two. There is *this
world*, literally 'this age', which is passing away, and there is *God's
will*, which is *good, pleasing and perfect*. Because the two verbs
contain a different word for 'form' (*schēma* in *syschēmatizomai*,
'conform', and *morphē* in *metamorphoō*, 'transform'), earlier commentators used to argue that *schēma* meant 'outward appearance'
and *morphē* 'inward substance'. Thus Sanday and Headlam rendered Paul's appeal: 'Do not adopt the external and fleeting fashion
of this world, but be ye transformed in your inmost nature.'[8] But
because these nouns are often used interchangeably, there is now 'a
large consensus strongly of the opinion that the two verbs . . . are
more or less synonymous.'[9]

More important for our understanding of the transformation
which Paul urges is the fact that *metamorphoō* is the verb used by
Matthew and Mark of the transfiguration of Jesus. And although
the evangelists vary in saying that it was his skin, his face and his
clothing which shone, Mark is clear that he himself 'was transfigured before them'.[10] A complete change came over him. His
whole body became translucent, whose significance the disciples
would not be able to understand, Jesus implied, until after his
resurrection.[11] As for the change which takes place in the people of
God, which is envisaged in Romans 12:2 and 2 Corinthians 3:18
(the only other verses in which *metamorphoō* occurs), it is a fundamental transformation of character and conduct, away from the
standards of the world and into the image of Christ himself.

These two value systems (*this world* and *God's will*) are incompatible, even in direct collision with one another. Whether we are
thinking about the purpose of life or the meaning of life, about how
to measure greatness or how to respond to evil, about ambition, sex,
honesty, money, community, religion or anything else, the two sets
of standards diverge so completely that there is no possibility of

---

[7] Barclay, p. 157.   [8] Sanday and Headlam, p. 353.
[9] Dunn, vol. 38B, p. 712.   [10] Mk. 9:2.   [11] Mk. 9:9.

compromise. No wonder Karl Barth called Christian ethics 'the great disturbance', so violently does it challenge, interrupt and upset the tranquil *status quo*.[12]

How then does the transformation take place? *Be transformed*, Paul replies, *by the renewing of your mind*. This is because only a renewed mind can *test and approve*, that is, discern, appreciate and determine to obey, *God's will*. Although Paul does not here tell us how our mind becomes renewed, we know from his other writings that it is by a combination of the Spirit and the Word of God. Certainly regeneration by the Holy Spirit involves the renewal of every part of our humanness, which has been tainted and twisted by the fall, and this includes our mind.[13] But in addition, we need the Word of God, which is the Spirit's 'sword',[14] and which acts as an objective revelation of God's will.[15] Here then are the stages of Christian moral transformation: first our mind is renewed by the Word and Spirit of God; then we are able to discern and desire the will of God; and then we are increasingly transformed by it.

To sum up, Paul's appeal is addressed to the people of God, grounded on the mercies of God, and concerned with the will of God. Only a vision of his mercy will inspire us to present our bodies to him and allow him to transform us according to his will. In particular, his will embraces all our relationships, as Paul now goes on to show – not only to God himself (12:1–2), but also to ourselves (12:3–8), to each other (12:9–16), to evildoers and enemies (12:17–21), to the state (13:1–7), to the law (13:8–10), to the day of Christ's return (13:11–14) and to the 'weaker' members of the Christian community (14:1 – 15:13).

---

[12] Barth, pp. 424ff.

[13] *E.g.* 1 Cor. 2:14ff.; 2 Cor. 5:17; Eph. 4:20ff.; Col. 3:9f.; Tit. 3:5.

[14] Eph. 6:17.   [15] *E.g.* 1 Thes. 2:13; 4:1ff.; 2 Thes. 2:15; 3:6.

12:3-8
18. Our relationship to ourselves: thinking soberly about our gifts

The link between Paul's general appeal (1–2) and his particular instruction which now follows (3–8) seems to be the place of the mind in Christian discipleship. Our renewed mind, which is capable of discerning and approving God's will, must also be active in evaluating ourselves, our identity and our gifts. For we need to know who we are, and to have an accurate, balanced and above all sober self-image. A renewed mind is a humble mind like Christ's.[1]

The formula Paul uses to introduce his exhortation to sober Christian thinking is impressively solemn. It 'has an imperative ring'.[2] *For by the grace given me I say to every one of you . . .* (3a). 'I say to you' is reminiscent of Jesus' favourite expression, even without the 'Amen' or 'Verily' which often preceded it. Paul is addressing his Roman readers (every one of them, he claims) with the self-conscious authority of Christ's apostle. For the *grace given* him, which qualifies him to write as he does, must refer to his appointment as an apostle which he regularly attributed to God's grace (*e.g.* 1:5, 'grace and apostleship'; 15:15f.)[3]

His message to them is this: *Do not think of yourself more highly than you ought, but rather think of yourself with sober judgment* (3b). The fourfold repetition in the Greek sentence of the verb *phronein*, 'to think', makes the emphasis unmistakable. In thinking about ourselves we must avoid both too high an estimate of ourselves and (Paul might have added) too low an estimate. Instead, and positively, we are to develop a *sober judgment*. How? First by reference to our faith, and secondly by reference to our gifts.

The clause *in accordance with the measure of faith God has given you* (3c) is a well-known crux. C. E. B. Cranfield, with his customary thoroughness, says that 'measure' has seven possible meanings, 'faith' five, and 'of' two, making seventy possible combinations altogether! The main question is whether *metron*

---

[1] Phil. 2:5ff.   [2] Dunn, vol. 38B, p. 720.   [3] 1 Cor. 15:9f.; Eph. 3:7f.

('measure') means here an instrument for measuring or a measured quantity of something. If the latter is correct, as many think, the thought would be that God gives a varying amount of faith to different Christians, and, being a divine apportionment, this will keep us humble. Professor Cranfield argues, however, that *metron* here means 'a standard by which to measure ourselves'; that this for all Christians is the same, namely saving faith in Christ crucified; and that only this gospel of the cross, indeed only 'Christ himself in whom God's judgment and mercy are revealed', can enable us to measure ourselves soberly.[4]

If God's gospel is the first measure by which we should evaluate ourselves, the second is God's gifts. In order to enforce this, Paul draws an analogy between the human body and the Christian community. *Just as each of us has one body with many members, and these members do not all have the same function* (4), although (it is implied) the different functions are necessary for the health and enrichment of the whole, *so in Christ*, by our common union with him, *we who are many form one body* (5a). Although Paul stops short of saying that we 'are the body of Christ' (as he does in 1 Cor. 12:27), yet his assertion that we are 'one body in Christ' will have had enormous implications for the multi-ethnic Christian community in Rome. As one body, *each member belongs to all the others* (5b). That is, we are dependent on one another, and the one-anotherness of the Christian fellowship is enhanced by the diversity of our gifts. This metaphor of the human body, which Paul develops in different ways in different letters, enables him here to hold together the unity of the church, the plurality of the members and the variety of their gifts. The recognition that God is the giver of the gifts is indispensable if we are to 'form a sober estimate' (REB) of ourselves.

We have different gifts, Paul continues, *according to the grace given us* (6a). Just as God's grace had made Paul an apostle (3), so his grace (*charis*) bestows different gifts (*charismata*) on other members of Christ's body. Paul proceeds to give his readers a sample of seven gifts, which he urges them to exercise conscientiously for the common good. He divides them into two categories, which might be called 'speaking gifts' (prophesying, teaching and encouraging) and 'service gifts' (serving, contributing, leading and showing mercy).[5]

The first *charisma* Paul mentions here is *prophesying*, that is, speaking under divine inspiration. In Ephesians 2:20 apostles and prophets are bracketed as the foundation on which the church is

---

[4] Cranfield, vol. II, pp. 613ff.
[5] Peter makes the same distinction: 'If anyone speaks ... If anyone serves ...' (1 Pet. 4:11).

built.[6] So that reference to foundation-prophets is likely to be to the biblical prophets, including those New Testament authors who were prophets as well as apostles, such as Paul[7] and John.[8] In two lists of *charismata*, however, prophets are placed in a secondary position to the apostles,[9] suggesting that there was a lesser prophetic gift, subsidiary to that of the biblical prophets. Words spoken by such prophets were to be 'weighed' and 'tested',[10] whereas the apostles were to be believed and obeyed, and no sifting process was deemed appropriate or necessary in their case.[11] Another difference seems to have been that prophets spoke to a local situation, whereas the authority of the apostles was universal. Further, Hodge was surely right in finding 'the point of distinction' in that 'the inspiration of the apostles was abiding', whereas 'the inspiration of the prophets was occasional and transient'.[12] It is in the light of these differences that we should understand the regulation which Paul here places on the exercise of the prophetic gift: *let him use it in proportion to his faith* (6b). Some think that this is a subjective restriction, namely that the prophet should speak only so long as he is sure of his inspiration; he must not add any words of his own. But it is more likely to be an objective restriction. In this case we should note that 'faith' has the definite article, and we should translate the phrase 'in agreement with the faith'. That is, 'the prophet is to make sure that his message does not in any way contradict the Christian faith'.[13]

The remaining six gifts are more mundane. *If it (sc. a person's gift) is serving, let him serve; if it is teaching, let him teach* (7). *Serving* is *diakonia*, which is a generic word for a wide variety of ministries. For 'there are different kinds of service, but the same Lord'.[14] It is highly significant, for example, that in Jerusalem the ministry of the Word by the apostles and the ministry of tables by the seven are both called *diakonia*.[15] So whatever ministry-gift people have been given, they should concentrate on using it. Similarly, teachers should cultivate their teaching gift and develop their teaching ministry. This is arguably the most urgently needed gift in the worldwide church today, as hundreds of thousands of converts are pressing into the churches, but there are few teachers to nurture them in the faith.

Four more gifts are included in the next verse: *If it is encouraging, let him encourage* (8a). *Parakaleō* is a verb with a wide spectrum of meanings, ranging from encouraging and exhorting to comforting,

[6] *Cf.* Eph. 3:5.   [7] 1 Cor. 13:2.   [8] Rev. 1:3; 22:7, 18f.
[9] 1 Cor. 12:28; *cf.* 14:37; Eph. 4:11.
[10] 1 Cor. 14:29; 1 Thes. 5:19ff.; 1 Jn. 4:1.   [11] *E.g.* 2 Thes. 3:6ff.
[12] Hodge, p. 389.   [13] Cranfield, vol. II, p. 621.   [14] 1 Cor. 12:5.
[15] Acts 6:1ff.

conciliating or consoling. This gift may be exercised from a pulpit or platform ('the gift of stirring speech', NEB), or through writing (12:1), but more often it is used behind the scenes as 'the gift of counselling' (REB), or in offering friendship to the lonely and giving fresh courage to those who have lost heart. Barnabas, the 'son of encouragement', evidently had this gift and used it in befriending Saul of Tarsus.[16]

Next, *if it is contributing to the needs of others, let him give generously* (8b). Calvin thought this was a reference to 'the deacons who are charged with the distribution of the public property of the Church',[17] and it could certainly include these. But personal giving is involved, and this is to be done *en haplotēti*, meaning either 'with generosity', without grudging, or 'with sincerity', without ulterior motives.

If it is leadership, let him govern diligently (8c). The verb *pro-istēmi* can mean to 'care for' or 'give aid', and some commentators opt for this sense because this gift comes between 'contributing to the needs of others' and 'showing mercy'. But the more usual New Testament allusion is to leadership, whether in the home[18] or in the church.[19]

Then finally, *if it is showing mercy, let him do it cheerfully* (8d). Since our God is a merciful God (*e.g.* 12:1), his people must be merciful too. And to show mercy is to care for anybody who is in need or in distress, whether aliens, orphans and widows, who are often mentioned together in the Old Testament, or the handicapped, the sick and the dying. Moreover, mercy is not to be shown reluctantly or patronizingly, but *cheerfully*.

This list of seven spiritual gifts in Romans 12 is much less well-known than either the two overlapping lists in 1 Corinthians 12 (nine in the first list and eight in the second) or the short list of five in Ephesians 4:11. It is important to note both the similarities and the dissimilarities between them. First, all the lists agree that the *source* of the gifts is God and his grace, although in Romans it is God the Father, in Ephesians God the Son and in 1 Corinthians God the Holy Spirit. Being gifts of trinitarian grace (*charismata*), both boasting and envying are excluded. Secondly, all agree that the *purpose* of the gifts is related to the building up of the body of Christ, although Ephesians 4:12 is the most explicit, and 1 Corinthians 14:12 says that we should evaluate the gifts according to the degree to which they edify the church. Thirdly, all the lists emphasize the *variety* of the gifts, each seeming to be a random selection of them. But, whereas students of the 1 Corinthians lists tend to focus on the supernatural (tongues, prophecy, healing and

---

[16] Acts 4:36; 9:26ff.   [17] Calvin, p. 270.   [18] *E.g.* 1 Tim. 3:4f., 12.
[19] *E.g.* 1 Thes. 5:12; 1 Tim. 5:17.

miracles), in Romans 12 all the gifts apart from prophecy are either general and practical (service, teaching, encouragement and leadership) or even prosaic (giving money and doing acts of mercy). It is evident that we need to broaden our understanding of spiritual gifts.

12:9–16
19.   Our relationship to one another: love in the family of God

A number of commentators have noticed that Paul's sequence of thought in Romans 12 resembles that in 1 Corthinthians 12 – 13. 'The logic is that of 1 Corinthians 12 – 13', writes J. A. T. Robinson: 'from the fact of the body of Christ (vv. 4, 5 = 1 Cor. 12:12–27) to the diversity of ministry within it (vv. 6–8 = 1 Cor. 12:28–30) to the absolute and overriding requirement of love (vv. 9–21 = 1 Cor. 13).'[1]

Without doubt *agapē*-love now dominates the scene. So far in Romans all references to *agapē* have been to the love of God – demonstrated on the cross (5:8), poured into our hearts (5:5) and doggedly refusing to let us go (8:35, 39). But now Paul focuses on *agapē* as the essence of Christian discipleship. Romans 12 – 15 are a sustained exhortation to let love govern and shape all our relationships. Soon Paul will write about love for our enemies (12:17–21), but first he portrays it pervading the Christian community (12:9–16). This is clear from his use of the words 'one another' (three times in verses 10 and 16), 'brotherly love' (10, *philadelphia*) and 'God's people' (13). Some commentators can see in verses 9–16 only a ragbag of miscellaneous instructions, a series of epigrammatic commands with little or no connection with each other. But in fact each staccato imperative adds a fresh ingredient to the apostle's recipe for love. It seems to have twelve components.

1. *Sincerity. Love must be sincere* (9a). The word 'sincere' translates *anypokritos*, 'without hypocrisy'. The *hypokritēs* was the play-actor. But the church must not turn itself into a stage. For love is not theatre; it belongs to the real world. Indeed love and hypocrisy exclude one another. 'If love is the sum of virtue, and hypocrisy the epitome of vice,' wrote John Murray, 'what a contradiction to bring these together!'[2] Yet there is such a thing as pretence-love, which was displayed in its vilest form in the betraying kiss of Judas.[3]

[1] Robinson, p. 135.   [2] Murray, vol. II, p. 128.   [3] Lk. 22:48.

2. *Discernment. Hate what is evil; cling to what is good* (9b). It may seem strange that the exhortation to love is followed immediately by a command to hate. But we should not be surprised. For love is not the blind sentiment it is traditionally said to be. On the contrary, it is discerning. It is so passionately devoted to the beloved object that it hates every evil which is incompatible with his or her highest welfare. In fact, both verbs are strong, almost vehement. Love's 'hatred' of evil (*apostygeō*, unique here in the New Testament) expresses an aversion, an abhorrence, even a 'loathing' (REB), while love's 'clinging' to what is good (*kollaō*) expresses a sticking or bonding as if with glue.

3. *Affection. Be devoted to one another in brotherly love* (10a). Paul brings together in this verse two family words. 'Be devoted' translates the adjective *philostorgos*, which describes our natural affection for relatives, 'typically, love of parent for child'.[4] The other word is *philadelphia*, 'brotherly love', which denotes the love of brothers and sisters for each other. Both words were applied originally to blood relationships in the human family, but Paul reapplies them to the tender, warm affection which should unite the members of the family of God.

4. *Honour. Honour one another above yourselves* (10b). This is the second 'one another' exhortation in the same verse. Love in the Christian family is to express itself in mutual honour as well as in mutual affection. It is uncertain, however, whether the command is to 'esteem others more highly than yourself' (REB, as in Phil. 2:3) or whether an element of competition is implied and we should translate 'outdo one another in showing honour' (RSV). In either case we are to accord to each other the highest possible honour.

5. *Enthusiasm. Never be lacking in zeal, but keep your spiritual fervour, serving the Lord* (11). Religious 'enthusiasm' is often despised as fanatical. The word was applied in a derogatory way to the early Methodists in the eighteenth century, and R. A. Knox perpetuated the caricature in his historical study *Enthusiasm*. He portrayed 'enthusiasts' as perfectionists, given to exaggeration,[5] who will tolerate 'no weaker brethren who plod and stumble'.[6] But Paul has something different in mind when he bids the Romans not to flag (literally, 'be lazy') in zeal, for zeal is fine so long as it is according to knowledge (10:2). In telling the Romans to be 'aglow with the Spirit' (RSV, REB), he is almost certainly referring to the Holy Spirit, and the picture is not so much of a glowing lamp as of a boiling, bubbling pot. The additional clause (*serving the Lord*) may

[4] Dunn, vol. 38B, p. 740.
[5] R. A. Knox, *Enthusiasm, A Chapter in the History of Religion* (Oxford, 1950), p. 581.
[6] *Ibid.*, p. 9.

well be meant as a 'control or check in what might otherwise be interpreted as an invitation to unbridled enthusiasm'.[7] Practical commitment to the Lord Jesus, as slave to master, will keep zeal rooted in reality.

6. *Patience. Be joyful in hope, patient in affliction, faithful in prayer* (12). At the heart of this triplet is the reference to hope, namely our confident Christian expectation of the Lord's return and the glory to follow (*cf.* 5:2; 8:24f.). It is to us the source of abiding joy. But it also calls for patience, as meanwhile we endure tribulation and persevere in prayer.

7. *Generosity. Share with God's people who are in need* (13a). The verb *share* is *koinōneō*, which can mean either to share in people's needs and sufferings, or to share out our resources with them. *Koinōnokos* means generous. One is reminded of the *koinōnia* in the early Jerusalem church, whose chief expression was that its members 'had everything in common' (*koina*) in the sense that they shared their possessions with those more needy than themselves.[8]

8. *Hospitality. Practise hospitality* (13b). If generosity is shown to the needy, hospitality is shown to visitors. *Philadelphia* (love of sisters and brothers) has to be balanced by *philoxenia* (love of strangers). Both are indispensable expressions of love. Hospitality was especially important in those days, since inns were few and far between, and those that existed were often unsafe or unsavoury places. It was essential, therefore, for Christian people to open their homes to travellers, and in particular for local church leaders to do so.[9] In fact, Paul did not urge the Romans to 'practise' hospitality, but rather to 'pursue' it. Origen commented: 'We are not just to receive the stranger when he comes to us, but actually to enquire after, and look carefully for, strangers, to pursue them and search them out everywhere, lest perchance somewhere they may sit in the streets or lie without a roof over their heads.'[10]

9. *Good will. Bless those who persecute you; bless and do not curse* (14). Although our persecutors are outside the Christian community, and this verse anticipates verses 17–21, yet the call to bless them is a necessary challenge to Christian love. 'Blessing' and 'cursing' are opposites, wishing people respectively good or ill, health or harm. Paul must have known that he was echoing the teaching of Jesus, who told us not only to 'bless' those who curse us,[11] but also to 'pray' for them[12] and to 'do good' to them.[13] There is no better way to express our positive wishes for our enemies' welfare than to turn them into prayer and into action.

---

[7] Dunn, vol. 38B, p. 753. [8] Acts 2:42ff. [9] 1 Tim. 3:2; Tit. 1:8.
[10] Quoted from his commentary on Romans by Cranfield, vol. II, p. 640, footnote 1.
[11] Lk. 6:28a. [12] Lk. 6:28b; Mt. 5:44. [13] Lk. 6:27.

10. *Sympathy. Rejoice with those who rejoice; mourn with those who mourn* (15). Love never stands aloof from other people's joys or pains. Love identifies with them, sings with them and suffers with them. Love enters deeply into their experiences and their emotions, their laughter and their tears, and feels solidarity with them, whatever their mood.

11. *Harmony. Live in harmony with one another* (16a). The Greek sentence reads literally: 'Think the same thing towards one another.' That is, 'be of the same mind', and so 'live in agreement with one another' (REB). The phraseology is almost identical with Paul's appeals to the Philippians to be 'like-minded' and 'one in spirit and purpose'.[14] Once again we note the fundamental place occupied by our mind. Since Christians have a renewed mind (2), it should also be a common mind, sharing the same basic convictions and concerns. Without this common mind we cannot live or work together in harmony.

12. *Humility. Do not be proud, but be willing to associate with people of low position. Do not be conceited* (16b). Few kinds of pride are worse than snobbery. Snobs are obsessed with questions of status, with the stratification of society into 'upper' and 'lower' classes, or its division into distinctions of tribe and caste, and so with the company they keep. They forget that Jesus fraternized freely and naturally with social rejects, and calls his followers to do the same with equal freedom and naturalness. As JB puts it, 'Never be condescending, but make real friends with the poor.'

What a comprehensive picture of Christian love Paul gives us! Love is sincere, discerning, affectionate and respectful. It is both enthusiastic and patient, both generous and hospitable, both benevolent and sympathetic. It is marked by both harmony and humility. Christian churches would be happier communities if we all loved one another like that.

---

[14] Phil. 2:2.

12:17–21
20. Our relationship to our enemies: not retaliation but service

When we are moved by the mercies of God, and when our minds have been renewed to grasp his will, all our relationships become transformed. Not only do we offer our bodies to God (1–2), and develop a sober self-image (3–8), and love one another in the Christian community (9–16), but now also we serve our enemies (17–21). These have already appeared in the guise of our persecutors (14) and are about to reappear as evildoers (17). In fact, the last five verses of Romans 12 handle the question how Christians should respond to evildoers. Good and evil are contrasted throughout the whole context (*e.g.* 9, 17, 21 and 13:3–4).

The most striking feature of this final paragraph, if we add verse 14 which anticipated it, is that it contains four resounding negative imperatives:

1. 'Do not curse' (14).
2. 'Do not repay anyone evil for evil' (17).
3. 'Do not take revenge' (19).
4. 'Do not be overcome by evil' (21).

All four prohibitions say the same thing in different words. Retaliation and revenge are absolutely forbidden to the followers of Jesus. He himself never hit back in either word or deed. And in spite of our inborn retributive tendency, ranging from the child's tit for tat to the adult's more sophisticated determination to get even with an opponent, Jesus calls us instead to imitate him. To be sure, there is a place for the punishment of evildoers in the law courts, and Paul will come to this in Romans 13. But in personal conduct we are never to get our own back by injuring those who have injured us. Non-retaliation was a very early feature of the Christian ethical tradition,[1] going back to the teaching of Jesus,[2] and beyond this to the Old Testament Wisdom literature.[3]

---

[1] *Cf.* 1 Thes. 5:15; 1 Pet. 3:9. [2] *E.g.* Mt. 5:39ff.; Lk. 6:27ff.
[3] *E.g.* Pr. 20:22; 24:29.

The Christian ethic is never purely negative, however, and each of Paul's four negative imperatives is accompanied by a positive counterpart. Thus, we are not to curse but to bless (14); we are not to retaliate, but to do what is right and to live at peace (17–18); we are not to take revenge, but to leave this to God, and meanwhile to serve our enemies (19–20); and we are not to be overcome by evil, but to overcome evil with good (21).

If Paul's first antithesis between good and evil was 'bless and do not curse' (14), which we have already considered, his second begins: *Do not repay anyone evil for evil* (17a). Instead, we are to *be careful to do what is right* (*kala*, 'good things') *in the eyes of everybody* (17b), or 'see that your public behaviour is above criticism' (JBP). The reasoning seems to be that it would be anomalous to refrain from evil if at the same time we are not seen to be practising good. A further counterpart to retaliation follows, which is equally universal in its application (*everybody . . . everyone*): *If it is possible, as far as it depends on you, live at peace with everyone* (18). To refuse to repay evil is to refuse to inflame a quarrel. But this is not enough. We have also to take the initiative in positive peacemaking,[4] even if, as the two qualifications indicate ('if it is possible' and 'as far as it depends on you'), this is not always possible. For sometimes other people either are not willing to live at peace with us, or lay down a condition for reconciliation which would involve an unacceptable moral compromise.

Paul's third prohibition is: *Do not take revenge, my friends* (19a, *agapētoi*, 'beloved'; he assures them of his love because he is calling them to the way of love). To this negative Paul again opposes a positive counterpart, or actually two. The first is: *but leave room for God's wrath*. Because the Greek sentence means literally 'give place to wrath', without specifying whose wrath is in mind, some commentators have thought it was either the evildoer's ('let his anger run its course, give in to it') or the injured party's ('let your anger pass and not express itself in revenge'). But the quotation which immediately follows ('*It is mine to avenge*') shows conclusively that the reference is to God's anger, and Paul has already made us familiar with this absolute use of 'the wrath' to indicate God's wrath (*e.g.* 5:9). The RSV renders it 'leave it to the wrath of God'. Paul goes on: *for it is written: 'It is mine to avenge; I will repay,' says the Lord* (19b).[5] The word for *avenge* is *ekdikēsis*, meaning 'punishment'; it corresponds to the verb in verse 19, *do not take revenge*. Similarly, the verb *I will repay* corresponds to *do not repay* in verse 17. It is used of God's

[4] *Cf.* Mt. 5:9. [5] Dt. 32:35.

judgment, as when Jesus himself said that 'the Son of Man . . . will reward each person according to what he has done'.[6]

These verbal correspondences between what is written of God and what is forbidden to us make Paul's point plain. The very two activities which are prohibited to us (retaliation and punishment) are now said to belong to God. The reason the repayment or judging of evil is forbidden to us is not that it is wrong in itself (for evil deserves to be punished and should be), but that it is God's prerogative, not ours. We are to 'leave it to the wrath of God', which is expressed now through the state's administration of justice, since the magistrate is 'God's servant, an agent of wrath to bring punishment on the wrongdoer' (13:4), and which will be finally expressed on 'the day of God's wrath, when his righteous judgment will be revealed' (2:5).

If the first counterpart to 'do not take revenge' is 'leave it to the wrath of God', the second is the command to serve our enemy: *On the contrary, 'If your enemy is hungry, feed him; if he is thirsty, give him something to drink. In doing this, you will heap burning coals on his head'* (20).[7] Because in the Old Testament it is said that God will 'rain fiery coals' on the wicked,[8] some take the coals here as a symbol of judgment, and even argue that to serve our enemies 'will have the effect of increasing the punishment' which they will receive.[9] But the whole context cries out against this explanation, especially the very next verse and its reference to overcoming evil with good. Others suggest that the pain inflicted by the burning coals is a symbol of the shame and remorse experienced by an enemy who is rebuked by kindness. A third option is that the coals are a symbol of penitence. Recent commentators draw attention to an ancient Egyptian ritual in which a penitent would carry burning coals on his head as evidence of the reality of his repentance. In this case the coals are 'a dynamic symbol of change of mind which takes place as a result of a deed of love'.[10]

The two positive alternatives to revenge, then, are to leave any necessary punishment to God and meanwhile to get busy in serving our enemy's welfare. These are not contradictory. Moreover, both are supported by Scripture. As REB puts it, 'there is a text which reads, "Vengeance is mine, says the Lord . . . ." But there is another text: ' "If your enemy is hungry, feed him . . ." ' (19–20). Our personal responsibility is to love and serve our enemy according to his needs, and genuinely to seek his highest good. The coals of fire this

---

[6] Mt. 16:27.   [7] Pr. 25:21f.   [8] Ps. 11:6; 140:10; *cf.* 2 Esdras 16:53.
[9] Haldane, vol. 2, p. 574.
[10] This is the conclusion of William Klassen's 'Coals of Fire: Sign of Repentance or Revenge?' *New Testament Studies* 9, 1962–3, p. 349, quoted *e.g.* by Murray (vol. II, p. 143), Morris (1988, p. 455) and Dunn (vol. 38B, p. 571).

may heap on him are intended to heal, not to hurt, to win, not to alienate, in fact, to shame him into repentance. Thus Paul draws a vital distinction between the duty of private citizens to love and serve the evildoer, and the duty of public servants, as official agents of God's wrath, to bring him to trial and, if convicted, to punish him. Far from being incompatible with each other, both principles are seen operating in Jesus at the cross. On the one hand, 'when they hurled their insults at him, he did not retaliate'. On the other, 'he entrusted himself to him who judges justly', in confidence that God's justice would prevail.[11]

The fourth antithesis of good and evil, which is also a summary of Paul's argument and the climax of the chapter, is verse 21: *Do not be overcome by evil, but overcome evil with good.* A stark alternative is set before us; no neutrality, no middle way is envisaged. If we curse (14), repay evil for evil (17) or take revenge (19), then, because all these are evil responses to evil, we have given in to evil, been sucked into its sphere of influence, and been defeated, *overcome*, even 'overpowered' (JBP) by it. But if we refuse to retaliate, we can instead 'take the offensive' (JBP), and practise the positive counterparts to revenge. Then, if we bless our persecutors (14), if we ensure that we are ourselves seen to be doing good (17), if we are active in peacemaking and peacekeeping (18), if we leave all judgment to God (19), and if we love and serve our enemy, and even win him over to a better mind (20), then in these ways we have *overcome evil with good.*

In all our thinking and living it is important to keep the negative and positive counterparts together. Both are good. It is good never to retaliate, because if we repay evil for evil, we double it, adding a second evil to the first, and so increasing the tally of evil in the world. It is even better to be positive, to bless, to do good, to seek peace, and to serve and convert our enemy, because if we thus repay good for evil, we reduce the tally of evil in the world, while at the same time increasing the tally of good. To repay evil for evil is to be overcome by it; to repay good for evil is to overcome evil with good. This is the way of the cross. 'Such is the masterpiece of love.'[12]

[11] 1 Pet. 2:23; *cf.* Ps. 37:5ff.   [12] Godet, p. 439.

13:1–7
21. Our relationship to the state: conscientious citizenship

In Romans 12 Paul has developed our four basic Christian relationships, namely to God (1–2), to ourselves (3–8), to one another (9–16) and to our enemies (17–21). In Romans 13 he develops three more – to the state (conscientious citizenship, 1–7), to the law (neighbour-love as its fulfilment, 8–10), and to the day of the Lord's return (living in the 'already' and the 'not yet', 11–14).

Before we go any further, however, we need to consider a debate which has divided theologians throughout this century. It concerns the identity of the *authorities* (*exousiai*) of verse 1. It has been argued by some (beginning, it seems, with Martin Dibelius in 1909) that there is in *exousiai* a double reference, namely to the civil powers on the one hand and to cosmic forces on the other, which stand behind them and work through them. The chief protagonist of this view has been Oscar Cullmann, whose case may be summarized as follows. First, Paul undoubtedly believed in, and frequently referred to, superhuman intelligences whom he names 'principalities', 'powers', 'rulers' and 'authorities'. So these are the 'authorities' of Romans 13:1. Having been conquered and tamed by Christ, they have now 'lost their evil character', and they 'stand under and within the lordship of Christ'.[1] Secondly, it is 'certain', Cullmann writes, that in 1 Corinthians 2:8 'the rulers of this age', who if they had known God's wisdom 'would not have crucified the Lord of glory', were both 'these invisible forces and powers' and at the same time their 'effective agents, namely, the earthly rulers, the Roman administrators of Palestine'.[2] Thirdly, if we come without prejudice to Romans 13, 'it is by far the most natural thing to give to the plural *exousiai* no other sense than that which it always has for Paul, that is, the meaning of "angelic powers"', although he was also plainly writing of the state 'as the

[1] Cullmann (1962), p. 196.   [2] Cullmann (1957), p. 63.

338

executive agent of angelic powers'.[3] Indeed, these expressions ('authorities' and 'powers') were deliberately chosen, Cullmann believed, in order to make clear 'the combined meaning'.[4]

The majority of scholars have not been persuaded by these arguments, however. Three main obstacles stand in the way. First, although Paul clearly believed in cosmic principalities and powers, and although he wrote of their overthrow at the cross, he also wrote of their continuing opposition to God and his people.[5] The New Testament 'affords no evidence in support of the contention that hostile spiritual powers were re-commissioned, after being subdued, to a positive service of Christ'.[6] Secondly, 1 Corinthians 2:8 cannot bear the weight Cullmann puts on it. 'Nowhere else does the New Testament attribute the *crucifixion* to angelic beings';[7] it is always attributed to human rulers. Thirdly, the meaning of *exousiai* in Romans 13 must be determined in the end by its context, and not by its very different use elsewhere. Here we are required to submit to these 'authorities'. But nowhere else are Christian believers said to be under the principalities and powers. On the contrary, they are now under us because we are in Christ and they are under him.[8] We conclude, therefore, that the phrase 'the governing authorities' in Romans 13:1 refers to the state, together with its official representatives.

Relations between church and state have been notoriously controversial throughout the Christian centuries. To oversimplify, four main models have been tried – Erastianism (the state controls the church), theocracy (the church controls the state), Constantinianism (the compromise in which the state favours the church and the church accommodates to the state in order to retain its favour), and partnership (church and state recognize and encourage each other's distinct God-given responsibilities in a spirit of constructive collaboration). The fourth seems to accord best with Paul's teaching in Romans 13.

That church and state have different roles, and that Christians have duties to both God and the state was clearly implied in Jesus' enigmatic epigram, 'Give to Caesar what is Caesar's and to God what is God's.'[9] Now Paul enlarges on the state's God-appointed role and on the role of Christian people in relation to it, although his emphasis is on personal citizenship rather than on any particular theory of church–state relations. What he writes is specially remarkable when we recall that at that time there were no Christian authorities (global, regional or local). On the contrary, they were

---

[3] Cullmann (1962), pp. 194f.   [4] *Ibid.*, p. 196.   [5] Eph. 6:11f; *cf.* Rom. 8:37ff.
[6] Cranfield, vol. II, p. 658.   [7] Murray, vol. II, p. 254.
[8] Eph. 1:20ff.; 2:4ff.; 1 Pet. 3:22.   [9] Mk. 12:17.

Roman or Jewish, and were therefore largely unfriendly and even hostile to the church. Yet Paul regarded them as having been established by God, who required Christians to submit to them and cooperate with them. He had inherited a long-standing tradition from the Old Testament that Yahweh is sovereign over human kingdoms 'and gives them to anyone he wishes',[10] and that by his wisdom 'kings reign . . . and princes govern'.[11]

It is conceivable that Paul was responding to those 'constant disturbances', as a result of which the Emperor Claudius had 'ordered all the Jews to leave Rome',[12] and which Suetonius said in his *Life of Claudius*[13] had happened 'at the instigation of Chrestus'. We lack information about the causes of this unrest. Did some Roman Christians regard submission to Rome as incompatible with the lordship of Christ or their freedom in Christ? It seems idle to speculate.

1. The authority of the state (1–3)

Paul begins with a clear command of universal application: *Everyone must submit himself to the governing authorities* (1a). He then goes on to give the reason for this requirement. It is that the state's authority is derived from God, and this he affirms three times.

1. *There is no authority except that which God has established* (1b).

2. *The authorities that exist have been established by God* (1c).

3. *Consequently, he who rebels against the authority is rebelling against what God has instituted* (2a).

Thus the state is a divine institution with divine authority. Christians are not anarchists or subversives.

We need to be cautious, however, in our interpretation of Paul's statements. He cannot be taken to mean that all the Caligulas, Herods, Neros and Domitians of New Testament times, and all the Hitlers, Stalins, Amins and Saddams of our times, were personally appointed by God, that God is responsible for their behaviour, or that their authority is in no circumstances to be resisted. Paul means rather that all human authority is derived from God's authority, so that we can say to rulers what Jesus said to Pilate, 'You would have no power [*exousia*, authority] over me if it were not given to you from above.'[14] Pilate misused his authority to condemn Jesus; nevertheless, the authority he used to do this had been delegated to him by God.

[10] Dn. 4:17, 25, 32.   [11] Pr. 8:15f.   [12] Acts 18:2.   [13] Suetonius, 25.4.

[14] Jn. 19:11. The book of Proverbs contains several references to the existence of wicked rulers (*e.g.* 28:3, 12, 15, 16, 28), even though it affirms that it is by Wisdom that kings reign (Pr. 8:15).

Having called for submission, Paul now warns against rebellion, since rebels are not only setting themselves *against what God has instituted* (2a), but in addition *will bring judgment on themselves* (2b). In consequence, it is both right and wise to submit. Paul elaborates the wisdom of it. *For rulers hold no terror for those who do right, but for those who do wrong. Do you want to be free from fear of the one in authority? Then do what is right and he will commend you* (3). The statement that rulers commend *those who do right* and punish *those who do wrong* is not of course invariably true, as Paul knew perfectly well. Although he had himself experienced from procurators and centurions the benefits of Roman justice, he also knew about the miscarriage of justice in the condemnation of Jesus. And if all provincial courts were just, he would not have needed to appeal to Caesar.[15] So, in depicting rulers in such a good light, as commending the right and opposing the wrong, he is stating the divine ideal, not the human reality.

Yet the requirement of submission and the warning of rebellion are couched in universal terms. For this reason they have constantly been misapplied by oppressive right-wing regimes, as if Scripture gave rulers *carte blanche* to develop a tyranny and to demand unconditional obedience. Commenting on verse 2 (*he who rebels against the authority is rebelling against what God has instituted*), Oscar Cullmann has written: 'Few sayings in the New Testament have suffered as much misuse as this one. As soon as Christians, out of loyalty to the gospel of Jesus, offer resistance to a State's totalitarian claim, the representatives of that State, or their collaborationist theological advisers, are accustomed to appeal to this saying of Paul, as if Christians are here commanded to endorse and thus to abet all the crimes of a totalitarian State.'[16] But, as the context shows, 'there can be no question here of an unconditional and uncritical subjection to any and every demand of the State'.[17]

As an example of the misuse of Romans 13 I refer to an experience of Michael Cassidy, founder of African Enterprise. On 8 October 1985 he was granted an interview with President P. W. Botha in Pretoria. It was the time of the National Initiative for Reconciliation, and Michael had hoped for signs of repentance and for the assurance that apartheid would be dismantled. He was to be bitterly disappointed. This is his account of what happened: 'I was immediately aware on entry to the room that this was not to be the sort of encounter for which I had prayed. The President began by standing to read me part of Romans 13!' He evidently imagined that this passage was enough to justify unequivocal support of the

[15] Acts 25:11.   [16] Cullmann (1957), pp. 55f.   [17] *Ibid.*, p. 57.

Nationalist Government's apartheid policy.[18]

How, then, can it be shown that Paul's demand for submission is not absolute? Granted that the authority of rulers is derived from God, what happens if they abuse it, if they reverse their God-given duty, commending those who do evil and punishing those who do good? Does the requirement to submit still stand in such a morally perverse situation? No. The principle is clear. We are to submit right up to the point where obedience to the state would entail disobedience to God. But if the state commands what God forbids, or forbids what God commands, then our plain Christian duty is to resist, not to submit, to disobey the state in order to obey God. As Peter and the other apostles put it to the Sanhedrin: 'We must obey God rather than men!'[19] This is the strict meaning of civil disobedience, namely disobeying a particular human law because it is contrary to God's law. To trespass and organize a sit-in, or to obstruct the police in their duties, may also in some circumstances be justified, but it should be called 'civil protest' rather than 'civil disobedience', since in this case the laws which are being broken in order to publicize the protest are not themselves intrinsically evil.

Whenever laws are enacted which contradict God's law, civil disobedience becomes a Christian duty. There are notable examples of it in Scripture. When Pharaoh ordered the Hebrew midwives to kill the newborn boys, they refused to obey. 'The midwives ... feared God and did not do what the king of Egypt had told them to do; they let the boys live.'[20] When King Nebuchadnezzar issued an edict that all his subjects must fall down and worship his golden image, Shadrach, Meshach and Abednego refused to obey.[21] When King Darius made a decree that for thirty days nobody should pray 'to any god or man' except himself, Daniel refused to obey.[22] And when the Sanhedrin banned preaching in the name of Jesus, the apostles refused to obey.[23] All these were heroic refusals, in spite of the threats which accompanied the edicts. In each case civil disobedience involved great personal risk, including possible loss of life. In each case its purpose was 'to demonstrate their submissiveness to God, not their defiance of government'.[24]

I now cite a moving modern example. In 1957 Hendrik Verwoerd, as Minister of Native Affairs the year before he became Prime Minister of South Africa, announced the Native Laws Amendment Bill. Its 'church clause' would have prevented any racial association in 'church, school, hospital, club or any other

---

[18] Michael Cassidy, *The Passing Summer, A South African Pilgrimage in the Politics of Love* (Hodder and Stoughton, 1989), pp. 298f.
[19] Acts 5:29.　[20] Ex. 1:17.　[21] Dn. 3.　[22] Dn. 6.　[23] Acts 4:18ff.
[24] Charles W. Colson, *Kingdoms in Conflict, An Insider's Challenging View of Politics, Power and the Pulpit* (William Morrow/Zondervan, 1987), p. 251.

institution or place of entertainment'. The Anglican Archbishop of Cape Town at the time was a gentle scholar called Geoffrey Clayton. He decided with his bishops, although with reluctance and apprehension, that they must disobey. He wrote to the Prime Minister that, if the Bill were to become law, he would be 'unable to obey it or to counsel our clergy and people to do so'. The following morning he died, perhaps under the pain and strain of civil disobedience.

Further light is thrown on the ambivalent nature of the state's authority when Romans 13 is compared with Revelation 13. Some thirty years have elapsed since Romans was written, and the systematic persecution of Christians has begun under the Emperor Domitian. Now the state is no longer seen as the servant of God, wielding his authority, but as the ally of the devil (pictured as a red dragon), who has given his authority to the persecuting state (pictured as a monster emerging out of the sea). Thus Revelation 13 is a satanic parody of Romans 13. Yet both are true. 'According as the State remains within its limits or transgresses them, the Christian will describe it as the Servant of God or as the instrument of the Devil.'[25]

To sum up, we are to submit to the state's God-given authority, but it has been given for particular and not totalitarian purposes. 'The gospel is equally hostile to tyranny and anarchy.'[26]

2. The ministry of the state (4-7)

Paul makes it clear that the state's authority is with a view to its ministry. Indeed, just as he has affirmed three times that the state has authority from God, so now he affirms three times that it has a ministry from God.

1. *For he is God's servant to do you good* (4a).

2. *He is God's servant, an agent of wrath, to bring punishment* . . . (4c).

3. *The authorities are God's servants* . . . (6).

These are significant statements. If we are seeking to develop a balanced biblical understanding of the state, central to it will be the truths that the state's authority and ministry are both given to it by God. Moreover, in writing about the ministry of the state, Paul twice uses the very same word which he has used elsewhere of the ministers of the church, namely *diakonoi* (although the third time he uses *leitourgoi*, a term which usually meant 'priests' but could mean 'public servants'). We have already had occasion to note, when considering the gifts of the Spirit, that *diakonia* is a generic

[25] Cullmann (1957), p. 86.   [26] Hodge, p. 415.

343

term which can embrace a wide variety of ministries. Those who serve the state as legislators, civil servants, magistrates, police, social workers or tax-collectors are just as much 'ministers of God' as those who serve the church as pastors, teachers, evangelists or administrators.

What, then, is the ministry which God has entrusted to the state? It is concerned with good and evil, which is a recurring theme throughout Romans 12 and 13. Paul has already told us to detest what is evil and cling to what is good (12:9), to repay no-one evil for evil but rather to do public good (12:17), and not to be overcome with evil but to overcome evil with good (12:21). Now he depicts the role of the state in relation to good and evil. On the one hand, *do what is right* (*to agathon*, 'good') *and he will commend you* (3b), that is, you will have his approval. *For he is God's servant to do you good* (4a, *to agathon* again). On the other hand, *if you do wrong* (*to kakon*, 'evil'), *be afraid, for he does not bear the sword for nothing. He is God's servant, an agent of wrath to bring punishment on the wrongdoer* (the one who practises *to kakon*, 'evil', 4b).

Here, then, are the complementary ministries of the state and its accredited representatives. 'He is God's servant to do you good' (4a) and 'he is God's servant ... to bring punishment on the evildoer' (4b). The same dual role is expressed in Peter's first letter, that 'governors ... are sent by him [*sc.* the Emperor] to punish those who do wrong and to commend those who do right'.[27] Thus the state's functions are to promote and reward the good, and to restrain and punish the evil.

The restraint and punishment of evil are universally recognized as primary responsibilities of the state. Indeed (5), *it is necessary to submit to the authorities, not only because of possible punishment* (literally, 'on account of God's wrath', *i.e.* in order to avoid it) *but also because of conscience* (*i.e.* from a conscientious recognition of the state's God-given role). The apostle says nothing about what kind of sanctions and penalties the state may employ, but he would almost certainly have endorsed the principle of using 'minimum necessary force' in order to arrest criminals and bring them to justice. He also writes that the judge *does not bear the sword for nothing* (4). Since the word for 'sword' (*machaira*) has occurred earlier in the letter to indicate death (8:35), and since it was used of execution,[28] it seems clear that Paul means it here as a symbol of capital punishment. 'The sword was carried habitually, if not by, then before the higher magistrates, and symbolized the power of life and death which they had in their hands.'[29] God had justified

---

[27] 1 Pet. 2:14.   [28] *E.g.* Acts 12:2; Rev. 13:10.   [29] Denney, p. 697.

this to Noah as affirming the unique value of the life of his image-bearers.[30] The taking of human life in murder is such a heinous offence that it deserves the forfeiture of the murderer's life. Yet this does not seem to have been mandatory, since God himself protected Cain, the first murderer, from being killed.[31] Because of its finality, the risk of an innocent person being executed in error, and the termination of the opportunity to respond to the gospel, many Christians believe that, at least whenever there are mitigating circumstances or any uncertainty, the death penalty should be commuted to a life sentence. Yet I think the state should retain its right to use 'the sword', in order to bear witness both to its solemn God-given authority and to the unique sanctity of human life.

When the state punishes evildoers, it is functioning as 'the servant of God to execute his wrath' upon them (4, RSV). This expression is surely a deliberate allusion to the command in the previous chapter that we should not take revenge but 'leave room for God's wrath' (12:19), since justice belongs to him and he will punish evil. Now Paul explains one of the main ways in which he does so. God's wrath, which one day will fall on the impenitent (2:5), and is now seen in the breakdown of the social order (1:18ff.), also operates through the processes of law enforcement and the administration of justice. It is important to hold Romans 12:19 and 13:4 together. We human beings as private individuals are not authorized to take the law into our own hands and punish offenders. The punishment of evil is God's prerogative, and during the present age he exercises it through the lawcourts.

In this distinction between the role of the state and that of the individual, we may perhaps say that individuals are to live according to love rather than justice, whereas the state operates according to justice rather than love. This is by no means a wholly satisfactory formula, however, since it sets love and justice over against each other as if they are opposites and alternatives, whereas they do not exclude each other. Even in loving and serving our enemies, we should still be concerned for justice,[32] and also remember that love seeks justice for the oppressed. And even in pronouncing sentence, judges should allow justice to be tempered by love, that is, mercy. For evil is not only to be punished; it is to be overcome (12:21).

The role of the state is not only to punish evil, however; it is also to promote and reward goodness. This was certainly the case in Paul's day. Dr Bruce Winter has shown that from the fifth century BC to the second century AD there was a 'long-established tradition', well evidenced from both inscriptions and literary sources, 'which guaranteed that benefactors would be publicly praised' and

---

[30] Gn. 9:6.　　[31] Gn. 4:13ff.　　[32] 1 Pet. 2:23.

appropriately rewarded. He also shows that Paul's very words about 'doing good' in verses 3–4 occur in inscriptions relating to a public benefaction.[33]

Yet this positive function of the state is much neglected today. The state tends to be better at punishing than at rewarding, better at enforcing the law than at fostering virtue and service. At the same time, although this is a controversial area, most governments acknowledge that they have a responsibility to preserve their society's values (not least through their educational system) and to encourage citizens to share in their welfare programme by voluntary service. Most countries also have some arrangement for recognizing those of their citizens who have made a conspicuous contribution to the public good. They give them a citation or a certificate, a title, a decoration or some other token of appreciation. But they could probably improve and extend their award system, so that only outstanding merit is rewarded, and their honours become increasingly prized and coveted, like the international Nobel and Templeton awards. Perhaps citizens should be given stronger encouragement to recommend people from their community for public recognition.

Paul concludes his section on the state with a reference to the raising and paying of taxes. Taxation was widespread and varied in the ancient world, including a poll tax, land taxes, royalties on farm produce, and duty on imports and exports. Paul regarded this topic as coming under the rubric of the ministry of the state. *This is also why you pay taxes:* it is because *the authorities are God's servants, who give their full time to governing* (6), literally 'to this very thing', which in the context seems to mean not just tax-collecting but the service of God in public life. Political parties of the Right and the Left differ over the desirable size of the state's role in the nation's life, and whether it should increase or decrease taxation. All agree, however, that there are some services which the state must provide, that these have to be paid for, and that this makes taxes necessary. So Christians should accept their tax liability with good grace, paying their dues in full, both national and local, direct and indirect, and also giving proper esteem to the officials who collect and apply them. *Give everyone what you owe him: If you owe taxes, pay taxes; if revenue, then revenue; if respect, then respect; if honour, then honour* (7).

Paul gives us in these verses a very positive concept of the state. In consequence Christians, who recognize that the state's authority and ministry come from God, will do more than tolerate it as if it

---

[33] Bruce W. Winter, 'The Public Honouring of Christian Benefactors', in *Journal for the Study of the New Testament* 34 (1988), p. 93.

were a necessary evil. Conscientious Christian citizens will submit to its authority, honour its representatives, pay its taxes and pray for its welfare.[34] They will also encourage the state to fulfil its God-appointed role and, in so far as they have opportunity, actively participate in its work.

[34] See Je. 29:7; 1 Tim. 2:1ff.

22. Our relationship to the law: neighbour-love as its fulfilment

Paul turns back now from the ministry of the state (through its official representatives) to the duties of individual Christian people, particularly our responsibility to love. In fact the paragraph about the state is wedged between the two commands to love our enemy (12:20) and to love our neighbour (13:9). The fact that the state is charged with the administration of justice is in no way incompatible with our obligation to love. Three times in these three verses the apostle writes of the need to love our neighbour, and so alludes to Leviticus 19:18, 'Love your neighbour as yourself.' Indeed, he makes three affirmations about neighbour-love.

1. Love is an unpaid debt

Earlier in his letter Paul has already referred several times to the importance of paying our debts. We are in debt to the unbelieving world to share the gospel with it (1:14); we are in debt to the Holy Spirit to live a holy life (8:12f.); and we are in debt to the state to pay our taxes (13:6f.) It is in fact this reference to debt which forms the transition between verse 7 and verse 8. *Let no debt remain outstanding*, Paul writes, *except the continuing debt to love one another* (8a). That is to say, we are to be punctilious in paying our bills and meeting our tax demands. Also, before entering into a mortgage or hire-purchase arrangement, we will want to make certain that we can manage the agreed repayments punctually. But there is one debt which will always remain outstanding, because we can never pay it, and that is our duty to love. We can never stop loving somebody and say, 'I have loved enough.' Some commentators resist this interpretation on the ground that it seems to encourage us to acquiesce in our lovelessness. For we could then say: 'I accept that I must pay my debts, but Scripture says I don't have to pay my love-debt.' So, as an alternative, it is pointed out that the words *ei mē* could be translated not 'except' but 'only'. The sentence would then read literally not 'Owe nobody anything except to love one another' (the NIV's additional words 'the continuing debt' are not in the Greek text) but 'Owe nobody anything; only love one another.' The context is not favourable to such a weak anticlimax, however. It is better to understand Paul to mean that of course we must love our neighbour, as Scripture commands, even though we will always fall short of the love required of us; 'that perpetual debt of love ' (JBP) will remain.

2.   Love is the fulfilment of the law

Paul continues: *for he who loves his fellow-man* (sc. neighbour) *has fulfilled the law* (8b). The two sentences of verses 8 thus present a striking contrast. If we love our neighbour, at least in the sense of not doing him or her any harm, we may be said to have fulfilled the law even though we have not fully paid our debt.

We need to read Paul's statement about having fulfilled the law against the background of chapter 7, in which he argued that we are incapable of fulfilling it by ourselves, on account of our fallen, self-centred nature. He went on to write, however, that God has done for us what the law (weakened by our sinful nature) was unable to do. He has rescued us both from the condemnation of the law through the death of his Son, and from the bondage of the law by the power of his indwelling Spirit. For what God did was 'in order that the righteous requirements of the law might be fully met ['fulfilled' as in 13:8] in us, who do not live according to the sinful nature but according to the Spirit' (8:3f.).

Now that Paul repeats in chapter 13 his statement about our fulfilling the law, he changes his emphasis from the means of the fulfilment (the Holy Spirit) to the nature of it (love). Law and love are often thought to be incompatible. And there are significant differences between them, law being often negative ('you shall not') and love positive, law relating to particular sins and love being a comprehensive principle.

But the advocates of the 'new morality' or 'situation ethics' go considerably further than this. They insist that now 'nothing is prescribed except love'. In fact 'love is the end of law' because love is no longer needed. Love has its own 'built-in moral compass' which discerns intuitively what a true respect for persons will demand in each situation.[1] But this expresses a naïve confidence in love's infallibility. The truth is that love cannot manage on its own without an objective moral standard. That is why Paul wrote not that 'love is the end of law' but that 'love is the fulfilment of the law'. For

[1] See *e.g.* John A. T. Robinson, *Honest to God* (SCM, 1963), pp. 105ff.

love and law need each other. Love needs law for its direction, while law needs love for its inspiration.

3. Love does no harm to its neighbour

Paul now explains how it is that neighbour-love fulfils the law. He quotes the prohibitions of the second table of the law: *'Do not commit adultery,' 'Do not murder,' 'Do not steal,'* 'Do not bear false witness' (av; only a few manuscripts include this, and it is clearly a later insertion, although there seems no reason other than oversight why Paul should have left it out), and *'Do not covet'* (9a). To these he adds *and whatever other commandment there may be*, and then declares that all of them *are summed up in this one rule: 'Love your neighbour as yourself,'* as Jesus had said before him (9b).[2] Why does love sum up all the commandments? Because *love does no harm to its neighbour* (10a). Certainly the last five sins forbidden in the Ten Commandments harm people. Murder robs them of their life, adultery of their home and honour, theft of their property, and false witness of their good name, while covetousness robs society of the ideals of simplicity and contentment. All these do *harm* (*kakos*, evil) to the neighbour, whereas it is the essence of love to seek and to serve our neighbour's highest good. That is why *love is the fulfilment of the law* (10b).

It is sometimes claimed that the command to love our neighbours as ourselves is implicitly a requirement to love ourselves as well as our neighbours. But this is not so. One can say this with assurance, partly because Jesus spoke of the first and second commandment, without mentioning a third; partly because *agapē* is selfless love which cannot be turned in on the self; and partly because according to Scripture self-love is the essence of sin. Instead, we are to affirm all of ourselves which stems from the creation, while denying all of ourselves which stems from the fall. What the second commandment requires is that we love our neighbours as much as we do in fact (sinners as we are) love ourselves. This means that we will love them with a love 'as real and sincere as our sinful self-love, about the reality and sincerity of which there is no shadow of doubt'.[3] If then we truly love our neighbours, we will seek their good, not their harm, and we will thereby fulfil the law, even though we will never completely discharge our debt.

---

[2] Mt. 22:39f.; *cf.* Gal. 5:14.   [3] Cranfield, vol. II, p. 677.

13:11–14
23. Our relationship to the day: living in the 'already' and the 'not yet'

The precise point of continuity between verses 8–10 and 11–14 is not certain. *And do this*, the apostle begins, referring presumably to the commandments to love our neighbours and to refrain from harming them (8–10), and also perhaps alluding to the instructions to submit to the state and pay our taxes. But why should we *do this*? Why should we obey? Paul's purpose in this last paragraph of Romans 13 (11–14) seems to be to lay an eschatological foundation for Christian conduct. He has already told us not to 'conform any longer to the pattern of this world' (12:1). Now he urges us to remember what the time is, and then to live appropriately.

1. Understanding the time (11–12a)

One of the features of the technological society is that we are the slaves of time. We all wear watches and keep careful track of the passing time. But it is more important to know God's time, especially the *kairos*, *the present time* (11a), the existential moment of opportunity and decision. The Bible divides history into 'this age' and 'the age to come', and the New Testament authors are clear that the age to come or the kingdom of God was inaugurated by Jesus. So at present the two ages overlap. We are waiting expectantly for the parousia, when the old age will finally disappear, the period of overlap will end, and the new age of God's kingdom will be consummated. Paul makes three time references, which assume this background understanding.

First, *the hour has come* (literally, 'is already') *for you to wake up from your slumber* (11b). The time for sleep has passed. It is now time to wake up and get up.

Secondly, this is *because our salvation is nearer now than when we first believed* (11c). 'Salvation' is a comprehensive term (*e.g.* 1:16), embracing our past (justification), present (sanctification) and future (glorification). In this verse clearly our future and final salvation is in mind (8:24), what Paul has earlier depicted in terms of the freedom of glory, our final adoption as God's children, and the redemption of our bodies (8:21–23). This inheritance is nearer now than 'when we were converted' (JBP). Every day brings it closer.

Thirdly, *the night* (the old age of darkness) is well advanced (literally), so that it *is nearly over; the day* (when Christ returns) *is almost here*, on the threshold (12a). Many readers conclude that Paul was mistaken, since the night drags on, and still the day, although it dawned at Christ's coming, has not yet experienced the fulness of sunrise at his return. But this is an unnecessary judgment. First, it is antecedently unlikely that Paul pronounced the end to be imminent, because Jesus had said he did not know the time,[1] because the apostles echoed this,[2] and because they knew that worldwide evangelization,[3] the restoration of Israel (11:12ff.) and the apostasy[4] must all precede the final denouement. Secondly, what the apostles did know was that the kingdom of God came with Jesus, that the decisive salvation events which established it (his death, resurrection, exaltation and gift of the Spirit) had already taken place, and that God had nothing on his calendar before the parousia. It would be the next and the culminating event. So they were, and we are, living in 'the last days'.[5] It is in this sense that Christ is coming 'soon' (16:20).[6] We must be watchful and alert, because we do not know the time.[7]

Here, then, are the apostle's three time references. The time is already here for us to wake up (11a); now our salvation is nearer than it was (11b); and the night has nearly given place to the day (12a). It is the familiar tension between the 'now already' of Christ's first coming and the 'not yet' of his second.

2.   Understanding what is appropriate to the time (12b–14)

The *So* or 'therefore' in the middle of verse 12 marks the transition from Paul's statements about the time to his corresponding exhortations. It is not enough to understand the time; we have to behave accordingly. Paul issues three appeals. The first two are couched in the first person plural, so that he includes himself (*So let us . . . Let us . . .*), while the third changes to the second person plural and is his direct summons to his readers (*Rather, clothe yourselves . . .*). All three are double sentences, the negative and positive aspects of the appeal forming a radical antithesis.

The first continues the metaphor of night and day, darkness and light. It concerns our clothing, and what (in the light of the time) it

---

[1] Mk. 13:32.   [2] 1 Thes. 5:1f.; *cf*. Acts 1:6f.   [3] Mk. 13:10.   [4] 2 Thes. 2:1ff.
[5] *E.g.* Acts 2:17; 1 Cor. 10:11.   [6] Rev. 22:7, 12, 20.   [7] Mk. 13:35f.

is appropriate for us to wear. *So let us put aside the deeds of darkness and put on the armour of light* (12b). The picture is that, because of the hour, we must not only wake up and get up, but get dressed as well. We must take off our night clothes, *the deeds of darkness*, and put on instead, as suitable daytime equipment for the soldiers of Christ, *the armour of light*. For 'the Christian's life is not a sleep, but a battle'.[8]

From appropriate clothing Paul proceeds to appropriate behaviour. Positively, *let us behave decently* or 'becomingly' *as in the daytime*, that is, as if the day had already dawned, and turn from the kind of things people do under cover of darkness: *not in orgies and drunkenness, not in sexual immorality and debauchery, not in dissension and jealousy* (13). Opposed to decent Christian behaviour is lack of self-control in the areas of drink, sex and social relationships.

Paul's third and concluding anthithesis might be said to concern our preoccupation, what it is which engrosses our attention as Christian people. The alternative set before us is either the Lord Jesus Christ or our fallen self-centred nature: *Clothe yourselves with the Lord Jesus Christ, and do not think about how to gratify the desires of the sinful nature* (14). In Galatians Paul has written that those who are in Christ by justification and baptism 'have clothed' themselves with Christ.[9] In Romans this clothing ourselves with Christ is something we still have to do, or to keep doing. Is the clothing regarded as an adornment? If so, perhaps the thought is that we are to wear the characteristics of his teaching and example, and put on 'compassion, kindness, humility, gentleness and patience'.[10] The context, however, suggests protection rather than adornment. 'Let your armour be the Lord Jesus Christ' (JB). In any case, it is not Christlikeness only that we are to assume, but Christ himself, laying hold of him, and 'living under him as Lord'.[11]

In contrast to the beautiful and protective clothing which is Christ, Paul refers to our ugly, self-centred nature (*sarx*). It has not been eradicated; it is still there. It also still has clamant desires. Our instruction is not only not to gratify its desires, but *not to think about how to* do so, not to make any 'provision' for them (RSV), rather to be ruthless in repudiating them and putting them to death (8:13).[12]

Romans 13 began with important teaching about *how* we can be good citizens (1–7) and good neighbours (8–10); it ends with *why* we should be. There is no greater incentive to the doing of these duties than a lively expectation of the Lord's return. We will be rightly related to the state (which is God's minister) and to the law (which

---

[8] Denney, p. 699.   [9] Gal. 3:27.   [10] Col. 3:12.   [11] Ziesler (1989), p. 321.
[12] *Cf.* Gal. 5:24.

is fulfilled in loving our neighbour) only when we are rightly related to the day of Christ's coming. Although both the state and the law are divine institutions, they are provisional structures, relativized by the last day when they will cease. That day is steadily approaching. Our calling is to live in the light of it, to behave in the continuing night as if the day had dawned, to enjoy the 'now already' of the inaugurated kingdom in the certain knowledge that what is still 'not yet', namely the consummated kingdom, will soon arrive.

14:1 – 15:13
24.   Our relationship to the weak: welcoming, and not despising, judging or offending them

Both previous chapters of Romans have laid emphasis on the primacy of love, whether loving our enemies (12.9, 14, 17ff.) or loving our neighbours (13:8ff.). Now Paul supplies a lengthy example of what it means in practice to 'walk according to love' (14:15, literally). It concerns the relations between two groups in the Christian community in Rome whom he names 'the weak' and 'the strong': 'we who are strong ought to bear with the failings of the weak' (15:1).

It is important to be clear at the outset that Paul is referring to a weakness neither of will nor of character, but of 'faith' (14:1). It is a 'weakness in assurance that one's faith permits one to do certain things'.[1] So if we are trying to picture a weaker brother or sister, we must not envisage a vulnerable Christian easily overcome by temptation, but a sensitive Christian full of indecision and scruples. What the weak lack is not strength of self-control but liberty of conscience.

But who were the weak and the strong in Rome? Four main proposals have been made regarding the identity of the weak. The strong then identify themselves by contrast.

First, it is suggested that the weak were *ex-idolaters*, freshly converted from paganism, the same group in fact whom Paul had encountered in Corinth and of whom he had written in 1 Corinthians 8. Although now rescued from idolatry, their overscrupulous conscience forbade them to eat meat which, before being sold by the local butcher, had been used in sacrifice to an idol. They feared that to eat idol-meats (*eidōlothyta*) would compromise and so contaminate them.

Comparing Romans 14 with 1 Corinthians 8, there are certainly some obvious similarities. Both chapters refer to eating and abstaining, to the danger of causing the weak to stumble, to the

---

[1] Cranfield, vol. II, p. 700; *cf.* 14:2, 22f.

sanctity of the conscience, to the voluntary limitation of Christian freedom, and to 'the brother for whom Christ died'. But in Romans 14 there is no reference to idol-meats, and no hint that the question of idolatry was involved in the debate. We surely have to conclude that, although some of the same principles were involved in the two debates, the situations in Corinth and Rome were different.

The second suggestion is that the weak were *ascetics*. To be sure, 'the broad distribution of religious asceticism in antiquity is . . . well documented',[2] and ascetic ideas and practices could have infiltrated into the Roman church. Ascetic movements existed both in paganism (*e.g.* the Pythagoreans) and in Judaism (*e.g.* the Essenes). Such an asceticism might explain why the weak abstained from wine as well as meat (14:21). But beyond this the evidence is wanting.

Thirdly, C. K. Barrett has maintained that the weak were *legalists*. The phrase 'weak in faith', he proposes, 'attests a failure to grasp the fundamental principle, which page after page of this epistle emphasizes, that men are justified and reconciled to God not by vegetarianism, sabbatarianism, or teetotalism, but by faith alone'.[3] In other words, the weak (being weak in faith) regarded their observances and abstentions as good works necessary for salvation. But in Galatians Paul pronounced a solemn anathema upon anyone who in such ways distorted the gospel of grace;[4] could he have been so gentle with the weak in Rome, so lacking in indignation towards them, if the very essence of the gospel were at stake?

The fourth and most satisfactory proposal is that the weak were for the most part *Jewish Christians*, whose weakness consisted in their continuing conscientious commitment to Jewish regulations regarding diet and days. As for diet, they will have kept the Old Testament food laws, eating only clean items (14:14, 20). In addition, either they will have assured themselves that their meat was kosher (the animal having been slaughtered in the prescribed way) or, because of the difficulty of guaranteeing this, they may have abstained from meat altogether. As for special days, they will have observed both the sabbath and the Jewish festivals. All this fits a Jewish Christian context.

Paul's conciliatory attitude to the weak (not allowing the strong to despise, browbeat, condemn or damage them) is also in keeping with the Jerusalem Council's decree, which had been designed precisely to restrain the strong and safeguard the consciences of the weak. Having stated categorically that circumcision was not necessary for salvation (the central theological principle in the debate), the Council not only (tacitly) gave Jewish Christians the freedom to

[2] Käsemann, p. 365.   [3] Barrett, p. 256.   [4] Gal. 1:8f.

continue their distinctive cultural-ceremonial practices, but asked Gentile Christians in certain circumstances to abstain from practices which would offend sensitive Jewish Christian consciences (*e.g.* asking them to avoid *eidōlothyta* and non-kosher meat).[5] The apostle Paul evidently followed these guidelines in his own ministry, combining no compromise on principle with concessions on policy.[6]

Further, this understanding of the background to Romans 14:1 – 15:7, and of its purpose to enable conservative-minded Christians (mostly Jewish) and liberal-minded Christians (mostly Gentiles) to co-exist amicably in the Christian fellowship, also prepares the way for Paul's eloquent conclusion (15:5ff.). In it the weak and the strong disappear from view, Jewish and Gentile believers take their place, and this reconciled multi-ethnic community is heard 'with one heart and mouth', in glorious gospel harmony, worshipping 'the God and Father of our Lord Jesus Christ' (6ff.).

To be sure, the groups were not identical; there was some overlap. The text does not allow us to make the neat equation that 'weak = Jewish Christian' and 'strong = Gentile Christian'. For doubtless some of the weak were Gentile believers who had been 'God-fearers' on the edge of the synagogue and had grown accustomed to the traditions of Judaism, whereas some of the strong were Jewish Christians who (like Paul) had developed an educated conscience and rejoiced in their Christian freedom. Certainly this was Paul's personal position. He makes it quite clear that he believes the position of the strong to be correct (14:14, 20); he writes throughout from the perspective of the strong; and he explicitly associates himself with them when he writes, 'We who are strong . . .' (15:1).

Professor Dunn goes further. The tensions in Rome, he suggests, were 'between those who saw themselves as part of an essentially Jewish movement and therefore obligated to observe the characteristic and distinctive Jewish customs, and those who shared Paul's understanding of a gospel which transcended Jewish particularity'.[7] Although diet had always differentiated Jews from their pagan neighbours (as in the case of Daniel in Babylon),[8] 'the Maccabean crisis had made observance of these (dietary) laws a test of Jewishness, a badge of loyalty to covenant and nation'. In fact, 'dietary rules constituted one of the clearest boundary markers which distinguished Jews from Gentiles'.[9] The observance of the sabbath was another. Thus ' "eating unclean food and violating the sabbath" ranked together as the two chief hallmarks of covenant

---

[5] Acts 15:19ff., 27ff.   [6] *E.g.* Acts 16:3, 21:20ff.; Gal. 6:12ff.; 1 Cor. 9:20.
[7] Dunn, vol. 38B, p. 795.   [8] Dn. 1:3ff.   [9] Dunn, vol. 38B, p. 800.

disloyalty',[10] while strictness in both was of fundamental importance in maintaining covenant faithfulness. Therefore, James Dunn
concludes, to characterize Romans 14 – 15 as 'a discussion of
"unessentials" . . . misses the centrality and crucial nature of the
issue for earliest Christianity's self-understanding'.[11]

All this is without doubt true and well said, but only so long as
we go on immediately to clarify Paul's position in relation to it. For
vital to his strategy in these chapters is his insistence that, from a
gospel perspective, questions of diet and days are precisely *non-
essentials*. He even approaches sarcasm when he juxtaposes 'the
kingdom of God' with 'eating and drinking', as if they could be
compared (14:17), and when he pleads with the strong, 'Do not
destroy the work of God for the sake of food' (14:20).

There is a similar need for discernment today. We must not
elevate non-essentials, especially issues of custom and ceremony, to
the level of the essential and make them tests of orthodoxy and
conditions of fellowship. Nor must we marginalize fundamental
theological or moral questions as if they were only cultural and of
no great importance. Paul distinguished between these things; so
should we.

Paul does not insist that everybody else agrees with him, as he did
in the early chapters of his letter regarding the way of salvation. No,
the Roman issues were *dialogismoi* (1), 'doubtful points' (NEB) or
'disputable matters' (NIV), 'opinions' (RSV) on which it was not
necessary for all Christians to agree. The sixteenth-century Reformers called such things *adiaphora*, 'matters of indifference',
whether (as here) they were customs and ceremonies, or secondary
beliefs which are not part of the gospel or the creed. In either case
they are matters on which Scripture does not clearly pronounce. In
our day we might mention such practices as the mode of baptism
(whether by immersion or affusion), episcopal confirmation
(whether it is a legitimate part of Christian initiation), the giving and
receiving of a wedding ring (which was hotly contested by the
Puritans in the seventeenth century), and the use of cosmetics,
jewellery and alcohol, together with such beliefs as which
charismata are available and/or important, whether miraculous
'signs and wonders' are intended to be frequent or infrequent, how
Old Testament prophecy has been or will be fulfilled, when and
how the millennium will be established, the relation of history to
eschatology, and the precise nature of both heaven and hell. In these
and other issues, today as in first-century Rome, the problem is
how to handle conscientious differences in matters on which Scripture is either silent or seemingly equivocal, in such a way as to

[10] *Ibid.*, p. 805.   [11] *Ibid.*, p. 801.

prevent them from disrupting the Christian fellowship.

One further characteristic of this passage deserves our attention, namely Paul's remarkable blend of theology and ethics. He is treating some very mundane matters, yet he grounds them in the truths of the cross, the resurrection, the parousia and the judgment. Griffith Thomas appropriately entitled his exposition of Romans 14 'High Doctrines for Humble Duties'.[12]

The outline of Paul's argument in this long section (14:1 – 15:13) seems to be as follows. First, he lays down the fundamental principle of acceptance (especially the acceptance of the weak) which undergirds the whole discussion. It is positive ('Accept him'), yet qualified ('without passing judgment on disputable matters', 1). Then secondly, covering the rest of the passage, he develops three negative deductions which follow from his positive principle. He tells his readers that they must neither despise nor condemn the weak (2–13a); that they must neither offend nor destroy them (13b–23); and that they must not please themselves, but follow Christ's unselfish example (15:1–4). In conclusion he celebrates the union of Jews and Gentiles in the worship of God (15:5–13).

1.   The positive principle (1)

The positive principle is in two parts. First, *Accept him whose faith is weak* (1a). We note that there is no attempt to conceal or disguise what these brothers and sisters are. They are weak in faith (here meaning 'conviction'), immature, untaught, and (as Paul's unfolding argument makes clear) actually mistaken. Yet on that account they are to be neither ignored, nor reproached, nor (at least at this stage) corrected, but rather to be received into the fellowship. *Proslambanō* means more than to 'accept' people, in the sense of acquiescing in their existence, even in their right to belong; more even than to 'receive or accept in one's society, into one's home or circle of acquaintances' (BAGD). It means to welcome into one's fellowship and into one's heart. It implies the warmth and kindness of genuine love. Thus, it is used in the New Testament of Philemon giving to Onesimus the same welcome that he would give to the apostle,[13] of the Maltese who welcomed the bedraggled, shipwrecked company after they had swum ashore,[14] and even of Jesus who promises to welcome his people into his presence in heaven.[15]

'Acceptance' is a popular word today, and rightly so. Theologically, God's acceptance of us is quite a good contemporary term for justification. But we should be cautious about modern talk of 'unconditional acceptance', as when the concept of an 'open church'

---

[12] Griffith Thomas, p. 373.   [13] Phm. 17.   [14] Acts 28:2.   [15] Jn. 14:3.

is canvassed, in which membership is offered to everybody, with no questions asked and no conditions laid down. For though God's love is indeed unconditional, his acceptance of us is not, since it depends on our repentance and our faith in Jesus Christ. We need to bear this in mind when we consider that we are to accept the weak (14:1) since 'God has accepted him' (14:3), and to accept one another 'just as Christ accepted' us (15:7).

Secondly, having reflected on the principle of acceptance, we need to observe its qualification: *without passing judgment on disputable matters* (1b). Both Greek words have a range of meanings. *Diakriseis* (translated *passing judgment*) can mean discussions, debates, quarrels or judgments, and *dialogismoi* can mean opinions, scruples or 'the anxious internal debates of conscience'.[16] Paul is saying, then, that we must receive the weak person with a warm and genuine welcome, 'without debate over his misgivings' or scruples (REB), or 'not for the purpose of getting into quarrels about opinions' (BAGD). In other words, we are not to turn the church into a debating chamber, whose chief characteristic is argument, still less into a lawcourt in which weak persons are put in the dock, interrogated and arraigned. The welcome we give them must include respect for their opinions.

2. The negative consequences (14:2 – 15:13)

a. *Do not despise or condemn the weak person (14:2–13a)*

It may be helpful, in order that we may grasp the drift of Paul's argument, to highlight each particular theological truth on which his exhortations are based. There are four.

(i) *Welcome him because God has welcomed him (2–3)*
Paul chooses the dietary question as his first illustration of how the weak and the strong, the fearful and the free, should behave towards one another. *One man's faith allows him to eat everything*, his freedom in Christ having liberated him from unnecessary scruples about food, *but another man, whose faith is weak, eats only vegetables* (2). This is probably not because he is a vegetarian on principle or for health, but because the only foolproof way of ensuring that he never eats non-kosher meat is not to eat any meat at all. How are these Christians to regard one another? *The man who eats everything* (the strong) *must not look down on him who does not* (who is weak on account of his scruples), *and the man who does not eat everything* (the weak) *must not condemn the man*

---

[16] Moule (1894), p. 374.

who does (who is strong on account of his liberty).

It is uncertain why the strong are forbidden to 'despise' the weak, and the weak to 'condemn' the strong. Perhaps it is that, whereas the strong might be tempted to pity the weakness of the weak, the weak might regard the strong, who have abandoned Israel's time-honoured traditions, as having committed apostasy and therefore as deserving condemnation. Whether this is correct or not, the reason both the despising and the condemning of a fellow Christian are wrong is that *God has accepted him* (3). How dare we reject a person whom God has accepted? Indeed, the best way to determine what our attitude to other people should be is to determine what God's attitude to them is. This principle is better even than the golden rule. It is safe to treat others as we would like them to treat us, but it is safer still to treat them as God does. The former is a ready-made guide based on our fallen self-centredness, while the latter is a standard based on God's perfection.

(ii) Welcome him because Christ died and rose to be the Lord (4–9)
The argument moves on. If it is inappropriate to reject somebody whom God has welcomed, it is at least as inappropriate to interfere in the relationship between a master and his *oiketēs*, his household slave. *Who are you to judge someone else's servant?* (4a). In ordinary life such behaviour would be regarded as outrageous and would be deeply resented. Just so, we have no business to come between a fellow Christian and Christ, or to usurp Christ's position in his life. *To his own master he stands or falls.* For he is not responsible to us, nor are we responsible for him. *And he will stand, for the Lord is able to make him stand* (4b), giving him his approval, whether he has ours or not.

Paul now develops his second illustration of the relations between the strong and the weak. It concerns the observance or non-observance of special days, presumably Jewish festivals, whether feasts or fasts, and whether weekly, monthly or annual.[17] He begins by describing the alternatives without comment. *One man considers one day more sacred than another* (the weak); *another man considers every day alike* (the strong). The latter does not distinguish between days any more than he does between foods. To whichever group his readers might belong, Paul's first concern for them is this: *Each one should be fully convinced in his own mind* (5). Paul is not encouraging mindless behaviour. Nor is he friendly to unexamined traditions.

But assuming that each (weak and strong) has reflected on the issue and has reached a firm decision, he will then reckon his

[17] *Cf.* Gal. 4:10; Col. 2:16.

practice to be part of his Christian discipleship. *He who regards one day as special, does so to the Lord* (6a). He does it, that is, 'in honour of the Lord' (RSV, JB), with the intention of pleasing and honouring him. And the same is true of the one who regards every day alike, although Paul does not mention him in verse 6. Instead, he reverts to the question of meat and in doing so adds an important double principle, which is related to thanksgiving. *He who eats meat, eats to the Lord, for he gives thanks to God; and he who abstains, does so to the Lord and gives thanks to God* (6b). Whether one is an eater or an abstainer, the same two principles apply. If we are able to receive something from God with thanksgiving, as his gift to us, then we can offer it back, as our service to him. The two movements, from him to us and from us to him, belong together and are vital aspects of our Christian discipleship. Both are valuable and practical tests. 'Can I thank God for this? Can I do this unto the Lord?'[18]

This introduction of the Lord into our lives applies to every situation. *For none of us lives to himself alone and none of us dies to himself alone* (7). On the contrary, *If* (that is, 'while') *we live, we live to the Lord; and if* (that is, 'when') *we die, we die to the Lord. So, whether we live or die, we belong to the Lord* (8). Life and death seem to be taken as constituting together the sum total of our human being. While we continue to live on earth and when through death we begin the life of heaven, everything we have and are belongs to the Lord Jesus and must therefore be lived to his honour and glory. Why is this? Here is Paul's answer. *For this very reason, Christ died and returned to life so that he might be the Lord of both the dead and the living* (9). It is wonderful that the apostle lifts the very mundane question of our mutual relationships in the Christian community to the high theological level of the death, resurrection and consequent universal lordship of Jesus. Because he is our Lord, we must live for him. Because he is also the Lord of our fellow Christians, we must respect their relationship to him and mind our own business. For he died and rose to be Lord.

(iii)   Welcome him because he is your brother (10a)
After writing about the strong and the weak, the observers and the abstainers, the living and the dead, all in rather general and impersonal terms, Paul suddenly poses two straight questions in which he sets over against each other 'you' and 'your brother'. *You, then, why do you judge your brother? Or why do you look down on your brother?* (10a). Despising and judging fellow Christians (the same two verbs are used as in verse 3), 'the smile of disdainful contempt' and 'the frown of condemnatory judgment',[19] are both now shown

---

[18] See 1 Cor. 10:30; 1 Tim. 4:3ff.   [19] Murray, vol. II, p. 175.

up to be totally anomalous attitudes. Why? Not only because God has accepted them, because Christ has died and risen to be our common Lord, but also because they and we are related to one another in the strongest possible way, by family ties. Whether we are thinking of the weak, with all their tedious doubts and fears, or of the strong, with all their brash assurances and freedoms, they are our brothers and sisters. When we remember this, our attitude to them becomes at once less critical and impatient, more generous and tender.

(iv) Welcome him because we will all stand before God's judgment seat (10b–13a)

There is an obvious link between our not judging our brother (10a) and our having to *stand before God's judgment seat* (10b). We should not judge, because we are going to be judged. There seems to be an allusion to the word of Jesus: 'Do not judge, or you too will be judged.'[20] What kind of 'judging' was Jesus referring to, however? He was not forbidding criticism, or telling us to suspend our critical faculties. If we did that, we would not be able to obey one of his next instructions, namely to 'watch out for false prophets'.[21] No, what is prohibited to the followers of Jesus is not criticism but censoriousness, 'judging' in the sense of 'passing judgment on' or condemning. And the reason given is that we ourselves will one day appear before the Judge. In other words, we have no warrant to climb on to the bench, place our fellow human beings in the dock, and start pronouncing judgment and passing sentence, because God alone is judge and we are not, as we will be forcibly reminded when the roles are reversed.

In order to confirm this, Paul quotes from Isaiah 45:23: '*As surely as I live,*' *says the Lord* (an introductory formula which occurs before several other prophetic oracles, though not in this text), '*Every knee will bow before me; every tongue will confess to God*' (11). The emphasis is on the universality of God's jurisdiction, in that *every knee* and *every tongue* will pay homage to him. *So then,* Paul continues, in the light of this Scripture, *each of us* individually, not all of us in a mass, *will give an account of himself,* not of other people, *to God* (12). *Therefore,* because God is the Judge and we are among the judged, *let us stop passing judgment on one another* (13a), for then we shall avoid the extreme folly of trying to usurp God's prerogative and anticipate judgment day.

Four theological truths, then, undergird Paul's admonition to welcome the weak, and neither despise nor condemn them. They concern God, Christ, them and ourselves. First, God has accepted

[20] Mt. 7:1.   [21] Mt. 7:15.

them (3). Secondly, Christ died and rose to be the Lord, both theirs and ours (9). Thirdly, they are our sisters and brothers, so that we are members of the same family (10a). Fourthly, all of us will stand before God's judgment seat (10b). Any one of these truths should be enough to sanctify our relationships; the four together leave us without excuse. And there are still two to come!

b. Do not offend or destroy the weak person (14:13b–23)

In this section as in the previous one it is our relationship to the weak which is mainly in mind. In spite of three 'one another' verses (13a, 19 and 15:7), which speak of reciprocal duties between the weak and the strong, the chief emphasis throughout is on the Christian responsibility of the strong towards the weak. The argument moves on, however, from how the strong should regard the weak to how they should treat them, that is, from attitudes (not despising or condemning them) to actions (not causing them to stumble or destroying them).

Instead of passing judgment on one another, Paul writes, *make up your mind not to put any stumbling-block or obstacle in your brother's way* (13b). There is a play on words in the Greek sentence, which contains a double use of the verb *krinein*, 'to judge'. 'Let us therefore cease judging one another, but rather make this simple judgment . . .' (NEB). The judgment or decision which we are to make is to avoid putting either a hindrance (*proskomma*) or a snare (*skandalon*) in our brother's path and so causing him to trip and fall. But why? Paul goes on to lay two theological foundations for his exhortation, in addition to the four developed in verses 1–13a.

(i) Welcome him because he is your brother for whom Christ died (14–16)

Before deploying this argument for not harming the weaker brother or sister, however, Paul explains in very personal terms the dilemma which faces the strong. It is created by two truths in conflict with each other. First, *as one who is in the Lord Jesus, I am fully convinced*, as strong Christians are when they have a good doctrine of creation,[22] *that no food is unclean in itself* (14a). Paul's reference to the Lord Jesus probably does not mean that he is actually quoting him, although he is sure to have been familiar with Jesus' controversy with the Pharisees over the clean and the unclean,[23] and with the risen Lord's word to Peter not to call unclean what God has made clean.[24] The reference seems to be more general ('All that I know of the Lord Jesus convinces me that . . .', REB), and is also a

[25]1 Tim. 4:1ff.   [26]Mk. 7:14ff.   [27]Acts 10:15, 28.

claim to be in close personal union with Christ as his disciple and specially as his apostle. However he came to his conviction, it was that no food was in itself unclean. *But*, and this is the second part of the dilemma, *if anyone regards something as unclean*, because his conscience tells him it is, *then for him it is unclean* (14b), and he should not partake of it. Verse 14 refers, of course, to ceremonial or cultural (not moral) issues, for Paul is quite explicit that some of our thoughts, words and deeds are intrinsically evil.

The paradox, then, which faces the strong, is that some foods are both clean and unclean simultaneously. On the one hand, the strong are convinced that all foods are clean. On the other, the weak are convinced that they are not. How should the strong behave when two consciences are in collision? Paul's response is unambiguous. Although the strong are correct, and he shares their conviction because the Lord Jesus has endorsed it, they must not ride rough-shod over the scruples of the weak by imposing their view on them. On the contrary, they must defer to the weaker brother's conscience (even though it is mistaken) and not violate it or cause him to violate it. Here is the reason: *If your brother is distressed* (feels grief and even pain) *because of what you eat*, not only because he sees you doing something of which he disapproves, but because he is induced to follow your example against his conscience, *you are no longer acting in love* (15a), no longer walking the path of love. For love never disregards weak consciences. Love limits its own liberty out of respect for them.[5] For to wound a weaker brother's conscience is not only to distress him but to 'destroy' him, and that is totally incompatible with love. *Do not by your eating destroy your brother for whom Christ died* (15b).

Already twice Paul has referred to the weaker Christian as a 'brother' (10); now he repeats the epithet four more times (13, twice in 15, 21), and adds the poignant description *for whom Christ died*. Did Christ love him enough to die for him, and shall we not love him enough to refrain from wounding his conscience? Did Christ sacrifice himself for his well-being, and shall we assert ourselves to his harm? Did Christ die to save him, and shall we not care if we destroy him?

But what kind of 'destruction' does Paul have in mind? Professor Dunn claims that, 'as all recent commentators agree, what is in view . . . is final eschatological ruin', meaning hell.[26] I beg to disagree, for four reasons. First, are we really to believe that a Christian brother's single act against his own conscience – which in any case is not his fault but the fault of the strong who have misled him, and which is therefore an unintentional mistake, not a deliberate disobedience –

---

[25] 1 Cor. 8:9ff.   [26] Dunn, vol. 38B, p. 821.

merits eternal condemnation? No, hell is reserved only for the stubborn, the impenitent, those who wilfully persist in wrongdoing (2:5ff.). Secondly, such a view (the eternal destruction of a brother) is inconsistent with the doctrine of final perseverance, which the apostle has eloquently expressed in 8:28–39, affirming that absolutely nothing can ever separate us from God's love. The hall-mark of every authentic 'brother' or 'sister' is that he or she will, by God's steadfast love, persevere to the end. Thirdly, Paul writes in verse 15 that the strong are capable of destroying the weak; but Jesus said that God himself is the only person who can and will destroy people in hell.[27] Fourthly, the context demands a different interpretation of 'destroy'. *Apollymi* has a broad spectrum of senses which range from 'killing' to 'spoiling'. Here the opposite of to 'destroy' is to 'build up' (19f.; 15:2). Paul's warning, therefore, is that the strong who mislead the weak to go against their consciences will seriously damage their Christian discipleship. He urges the strong against causing such injury to the weak. *Do not allow what you consider good* (*i.e.* the liberty you have found in Christ) *to be spoken of as evil* (16), because you flaunt it to the detriment of the weak.

(ii) Welcome him because the kingdom of God is more important than food (17–21)

If the first theological truth which undergirds Paul's appeal to the strong for restraint is the cross of Christ, the second is the kingdom of God, that is, the gracious rule of God through Christ and by the Spirit in the lives of his people, bringing a free salvation and demanding a radical obedience. Although the kingdom of God is not as central a doctrine in the teaching of Paul as it was in the teaching of Jesus, it nevertheless occupies a prominent place.[28] The apostle's argument now is that, whenever the strong insist on using their liberty to eat whatever they like, even at the expense of the welfare of the weak, they are guilty of a grave lack of proportion. They are overestimating the importance of diet (which is trivial) and underestimating the importance of the kingdom (which is central). *For the kingdom of God is not a matter of eating and drinking, but of righteousness, peace and joy in the Holy Spirit* (17). Righteous-ness, peace and joy inspired by the Spirit are sometimes understood as the subjective conditions of being righteous, peaceful and joyful. But in the wider context of Romans it is more natural to take them as objective states, namely justification through Christ, peace with God and rejoicing in hope of God's glory (5:1f.), of which the Holy

---

[27] Mt. 10:28.
[28] *E.g.* Acts 14:22; 17:7; 19:8; 20:25; 28:23, 31; 1 Cor. 6:10; Eph. 5:5; Col. 1:13.

Spirit himself is the pledge and foretaste (8:23). And the reason for the greater significance of the kingdom is that *anyone who serves Christ in this way* (REB 'who shows himself a servant of Christ in this way'), who seeks first God's kingdom[29] and acknowledges 'that food and drink are secondary matters',[30] *is pleasing to God and approved by men* (18).

Verses 19–21 repeat, enforce and apply the same teaching about proportion or balance. They contain three exhortations. First, *let us therefore make every effort to do* (literally, 'let us then pursue') *what leads to peace and to mutual edification* (19). 'Peace' here seems to be the 'shalom' which is experienced within the Christian community, while 'edification' is building one another up in Christ. This is the positive goal which all should seek, and which the strong were neglecting in their insensitive treatment of the weak.

Secondly, *do not destroy the work of God for the sake of food* (20a). 'The work of God' could mean the individual weaker brother, but in the context it seems to refer to the Christian community. 'Destroy' translates a different verb from the one which Paul has used in verse 15. *Katalyō* means to 'tear down' or 'throw down', particularly in relation to buildings. It appears to be deliberately contrasted with the previous verse. Our responsibility is to seek to build up the fellowship (19), not to tear it down (20). And in particular we must not tear it down *for the sake of food*. In the Greek sentence this clause comes first. Surely 'for the sake of a plate of meat' (JBP) we are not going to wreck God's work! Already three times Paul has used a little irony to expose the incongruity of valuing food above peace, the health of our stomach above the health of the community; this is the fourth. Are you strong really prepared, he asks, to distress a brother *because of what you eat* (15a), to damage him spiritually *by your eating* (15b), to prize your *eating and drinking* above God's kingdom (17), and now to demolish God's work *for the sake of food* (20)?[31] There must have been some red faces among the strong as they listened to Paul's letter being read out in the assembly. His gentle sarcasm showed up their skewed perspective. They would have to re-value their values, give up insisting on their liberties at the expense of the welfare of others, and put the cross and the kingdom first.

Paul's third exhortation expresses a contrast between two kinds of behaviour, which he declares to be respectively 'wrong' and 'right', *kakos* (20b) and *kalos* (21). *All food is clean*, he affirms, a truth repeated from verse 14 except that the adjective is now *katharos* ('pure') not *koinos* ('common'), *but it is wrong (kakos) for a man to eat anything that causes someone else to stumble* (20b). This

---

[29] Mt. 6:33.   [30] Barrett, p. 265.   [31] Cf. 1 Cor. 8:8.

being so, *it is better* (*kalos*) not to eat meat or drink wine (which is here mentioned for the first time) *or to do anything else that will cause your brother to fall* (21). The statement that 'all food is clean' sounds like the slogan of the strong. And Paul agrees with it. Here is the theological truth which gave them their liberty to eat anything they liked. But there were other factors to consider, which would require them to limit the exercise of their liberty. In particular, there was the weaker brother or sister with the oversensitive, over-scrupulous conscience, who was convinced that not all food was clean. So it would be *evil* for the strong to use their liberty to harm the weak. Alternatively, it would be *good* for the strong (Paul drives the argument to its logical conclusion) to eat no meat and drink no wine, that is, to become vegetarians and total abstainers, and to go to any other extreme of renunciation, if that were necessary to serve the welfare of the weak.

Paul concludes (22–23) by drawing a distinction between belief and action, that is, between private conviction and public behaviour. *So*, he writes, as regards the private sphere, *whatever you believe about these things*, whether you are strong and believe you can eat anything, or weak and believe you cannot, *keep between yourself and God* (22a), keep it a secret. There is no need either to parade your views or to impose them on other people. As for public behaviour, there are two options, represented by two 'men' whom we quickly recognize as a strong and a weak Christian respectively. The strong Christian is blessed because his conscience approves of his eating everything, so that he can follow his conscience without any guilt feelings. *Blessed is the man who does not condemn himself by what he approves* (22b). *But the man who has doubts*, that is, the weak Christian who is plagued with misgivings because his conscience gives him vacillating signals, *is condemned if he eats* (probably by his conscience, not by God), *because his eating is not from faith; and everything that does not come from faith* (REB 'which does not arise from conviction') *is sin* (23). This final epigram exalts the significance of our conscience. Although, as we have seen, it is not infallible, it is nevertheless sacrosanct, so that to go against it (to act *not from faith*) is to sin. At the same time, alongside this explicit instruction not to violate our conscience, there is an implicit requirement to educate it.

Paul comes next to his third negative deduction from the positive principle to 'accept' the weaker brother. Having urged the strong neither to despise and judge him (14:2–13a), nor to distress and damage him (14:13b–23), he now exhorts them not to please themselves (15:1–13).

c. Do not please yourselves (15:1–13)

We who are strong, he begins. Thus for the first time he both identifies them by this name and at the same time identifies himself as one of them. What then ought the strong to do? What is their Christian responsibility towards the weak?

First, the strong *ought to bear with the failings* (literally 'weaknesses') *of the weak* (1a). Strong people are of course tempted to wield their strength to discard or crush the weak. Paul urges them instead to bear with them. The Greek verb *bastazō*, like the English verb 'bear', can mean either to 'endure' in the sense of 'tolerate', or to 'carry' and 'support'. The context suggests that the latter is correct here. One person's strength can compensate for another person's weakness.

Secondly, *we who are strong ought ... not to please ourselves* (1b). To be self-centred and self-seeking is natural to our fallen human nature. But we ought not to use our strength to serve our own advantage. As Paul has been arguing, Christians with a strong conscience must not trample on the consciences of the weak.

Thirdly, *each of us should please his neighbour for his good, to build him up* (2). Neighbour-pleasing, which Scripture commands,[32] must not be confused with 'men-pleasing', which Scripture condemns.[33] In this pejorative sense, to 'please men', usually in antithesis to pleasing God, means to flatter people in order to curry favour with them, to win their approval by some unprincipled compromise. It is always incompatible with integrity and sincerity. Perhaps it is to avoid such a possible misunderstanding that Paul qualifies his appeal to please our neighbour with the clause *for his good, to build him up* (*cf.* 14:19). Instead of causing to stumble (14:13, 20, 21), tearing down (14:20) or damaging (14:15) our neighbour, we are to build him up. Edification is a constructive alternative to demolition. And this upbuilding of the weak will doubtless include helping to educate and so strengthen their conscience.

Once again Paul adds a theological foundation to his appeal. This time it concerns Jesus Christ himself, who is now mentioned in almost every verse, and in particular his example. Why should we please our neighbour and not ourselves?

(i) Because Christ did not please himself (3–4)

This simple statement 'sums up with eloquent reticence both the meaning of the incarnation and the character of Christ's earthly life'.[34] Instead of pleasing himself, he gave himself in the service of

---

[32] Lv. 19:18; *cf.* Rom. 13:9.   [33] *E.g.* Gal. 1:10; Col. 3:22; 1 Thes. 2:4.
[34] Cranfield, vol. II, p. 732.

369

his Father and of human beings. Although he, 'being in very nature God', had the greatest right of all persons to please himself, yet 'he did not consider equality with God something to be grasped' for his own advantage, but first 'emptied himself' (rsv) of his glory and then 'humbled himself' to serve.[35]

Instead of referring specifically either to the incarnation or to some incident of his incarnate life, however, Paul quotes from Psalm 69, which vividly describes the unjust, unreasonable sufferings of a righteous man, and which is quoted of Christ four or five times in the New Testament, being regarded as a messianic prediction. Its verse 9 includes the words Paul quotes. *As it is written: 'The insults of those who insult you have fallen on me'* (3). That is to say, as an example of his refusing to please himself, Christ so completely identified himself with the name, will, cause and glory of the Father that insults intended for God fell upon him.

Christ's fulfilment of Psalm 69:9 leads Paul into a brief digression about the nature and purpose of Old Testament Scripture. *For everything that was written in the past was written to teach us, so that through endurance and the encouragement of the Scriptures we might have hope* (4). From this thoughtful statement it is legitimate to derive five truths about Scripture, which we would do well to remember.

First, its *contemporary intention*. The books of Scripture were of course primarily intended for those to and for whom they were *written in the past*. Yet the apostle is persuaded that they were also *written to teach us*.[36]

Secondly, its *inclusive value*. Having quoted only half a verse from one psalm, Paul declares that *everything* written in the past is for us, although obviously not everything is of equal value. Jesus himself spoke of 'the more important matters of the law'.[37]

Thirdly, its *Christological focus*. Paul's application of Psalm 69 to Christ is a fine example of how the risen Lord could explain to his disciples 'what was said in all the Scriptures concerning himself'.[38]

Fourthly, its *practical purpose*. Not only is it able to make us 'wise for salvation through faith in Christ Jesus',[39] but it can bring us *encouragement* with a view to *endurance*, so that *we might have hope*, looking beyond time to eternity, beyond present sufferings to future glory.

Fifthly, its *divine message*. The striking fact that 'endurance and encouragement', which in verse 4 are attributed to Scripture, in verse 5 are attributed to God, can only mean that it is God himself

---

[35] Phil. 2:6ff.   [36] *Cf.* 1 Cor. 10:11.   [37] Mt. 23:23.
[38] Lk. 24:27; *cf.* Jn. 5:39.   [39] 2 Tim. 3:15.

who encourages us through the living voice of Scripture. For God continues to speak through what he has spoken.

(ii) Because Christ is the way to united worship (5–6)

Verses 5–6 are in the form of a benediction. Paul's prayer is that *the God who gives endurance and encouragement* (through Scripture, as we have seen) may *give you a spirit of unity among yourselves*, or literally, 'may give you to think the same thing among yourselves' (5a). This can hardly be a plea that the Roman Christians may come to agree with each other about everything, since Paul has been at pains to urge the weak and the strong to accept each other in spite of their conscientious disagreement on secondary matters. It must therefore be a prayer for their unity of mind in essentials.

For Paul's petition is this: *May ... God ... give you a spirit of unity ... as you follow Christ Jesus* (5b), literally 'according to Christ Jesus'. This seems to indicate that Christian unity is unity in Christ, that the person of Jesus Christ himself is the focus of our unity, and that therefore the more we agree with him and about him, the more we will agree with one another. But what is the purpose of this unity of mind? It is in order that (*hina*) we may engage in the common worship of God: *so that with one heart and mouth you may glorify the God and Father of our Lord Jesus Christ* (6). Thus, the one mind (5) is expressed through the one heart and the one mouth (6); indeed without this unity of mind about Christ unity of heart and mouth in worship is impossible.

(iii) Because Christ accepted you (7)

With verse 7 Paul returns to the beginning, to his original and positive appeal for acceptance. Indeed, the long, closely reasoned, theological-practical argument about the strong and the weak (14:2 – 15:6) is sandwiched between the two cries, *Accept him* (14:1) and *Accept one another* (7a). Both are addressed to the whole congregation, although the first urges the church to welcome the weaker brother, while the second urges all church members to welcome each other. Both also have a theological base. The weak brother is to be accepted *for God has accepted him* (14:3), and the members are to welcome each other *just as Christ accepted you* (7a).

Moreover, Christ's acceptance of us was also *in order to bring praise to God* (7b). The entire credit for the welcome we have received goes to him who took the initiative through Christ to reconcile us to himself and to each other.

(iv) Because Chist has become a servant (8–13)

With verse 8 Paul slips almost imperceptibly from the unity of the weak and the strong through Christ to the unity of Jews and

371

Gentiles through the same Christ. Further, in both cases the unity is with a view to worship, 'so that' they 'may glorify God' together (6, 9ff.). The grammar of verses 8–9 is uncertain, however. Here is the NIV text: *For I tell you that Christ has become a servant of the Jews on behalf of God's truth, to confirm the promises made to the patriarchs* (8) *so that the Gentiles may glorify God for his mercy* (9a).

What is clear is that there are two complementary clauses, the first about *the Jews* and *God's truth* (*i.e.* truthfulness), the second about *the Gentiles* and his *mercy*. But what is the relation between them? Many commentators suspend both clauses on the solemn opening words, *I tell you*. But because the context highlights the work of Christ, it seems better to suspend them on a longer introduction, namely, *I tell you that Christ has become a servant of the Jews* . . . . Then his role as the servant of the Jews, that is, as the Jewish Messiah, is seen to have two parallel purposes, first *to confirm the promises made to the patriarchs* and secondly to incorporate the Gentiles as well. His ministry to the Jews was *on behalf of God's truth*, to demonstrate his faithfulness to his covenant promises, whereas his ministry to the Gentiles was on account of *his mercy*, his uncovenanted mercy. For, although the Old Testament contains many prophecies of the inclusion of the Gentiles, and indeed the promise to Abraham was that the nations would be blessed through his posterity, yet God had made no covenant with the Gentiles comparable to his covenant with Israel. Consequently, it was in mercy to the Gentiles, as it was in faithfulness to Israel, that Christ became a servant for the benefit of both.

This truth of the inclusion of Jews and Gentiles in the messianic community Paul now enforces with four Old Testament quotations. In each case he uses the LXX text, and he chooses one from the Law, one from the Prophets and two from the Writings, which are the three divisions of the Old Testament. All four quotations refer both to the Gentiles and to the worship of God, although each contains a slightly different emphasis. In the first, David, though king of Israel, announces his intention to praise God among the Gentiles, although it is not clear whether the nations are to be spectators only or active participants. *'Therefore I will praise you among the Gentiles; I will sing hymns to your name'* (9b = Ps. 18:49; 2 Sa. 22:50).

In the second quotation the nations are definitely participants. Moses is represented as summoning them to rejoice in company with God's people. *Again, it says, 'Rejoice, O Gentiles, with his people'* (10 = Dt. 32:43). In the third quotation the psalmist also addresses all the nations directly and bids them praise Yahweh, repeating the word 'all'. *And again, 'Praise the Lord, all you Gentiles, and sing praises to him, all you peoples'* (11 = Ps. 117:1). Then in the fourth and final verse the prophet Isaiah predicts the rise of the Messiah, descended from David, Jesse's son, who would rule the nations and win their confidence. *And again, Isaiah says, 'The Root of Jesse will spring up, one who will arise to rule over the nations; the Gentiles will hope in him'* (12 = Is. 11:10). Thus the Messiah would be simultaneously the root of Jesse and the hope of the nations.

Paul concludes the long doctrinal-ethical section of his letter with another benediction (see verse 5 for the first). *May the God of hope fill you with all joy and peace as you trust in him* (13a). The reference to joy and peace recalls the apostle's definition of the kingdom of God (14:7). Now he adds faith (*as you trust in him*) as the means by which joy and peace grow within us, and he prays that his Roman readers will be filled with both. He also anticipates that this filling will result in an overflowing: *so that you may overflow with hope by the power of the Holy Spirit* (13b). The burden of Paul's earlier benediction (5) was unity with a view to worship; the burden of this one is 'hope'. He has already expressed his assurance that the Scriptures bring us hope (4). Now he expresses his prayer-wish that *the God of hope* may cause them to *overflow with hope*. Hope of course always looks to the future. And since Paul has just quoted Isaiah's prophecy that the Messiah will be the object of the Gentiles' hope (12), we are given a clue as to what hope is in his mind. Paul is looking forward to the time the 'fulness' of both Israel and the Gentiles will have come in (11:12, 25), then to the culmination of history with the parousia, and then beyond it to the glory of the new universe which Jews and Gentiles will together inherit. Thus joy, peace, faith and hope are essential Christian qualities. If faith is the means to joy and peace, overflowing hope is their consequence, and all four are due to the power of the Holy Spirit within us.

Looking back over this whole section (14:1 – 15:13), which is largely devoted to how the strong should regard and treat the weak, it is particularly impressive to see how the apostle buttresses his ethical exhortations with solid theological arguments. Although we have noted six, three of them seem to be central. They concern the cross, the resurrection and the last judgment.

First, Christ died to be our Saviour. Since God has accepted the weaker brother (14:1, 3), and since Christ has accepted us (15:7), we must complete the triangle and accept one another. How could we possibly destroy those whom Christ died to save? The second fundamental argument is that Christ rose to be our Lord. This is explicitly stated (14:9). In consequence, all his people are his servants, and are accountable to him, the weak and the strong alike (14:6ff.). Thirdly, Christ is coming to be our judge. We will all stand before his judgment seat one day, and each of us will then give an account of himself or herself to God (14:10ff.). To presume to stand in judgment on others is to usurp the prerogative of God. These are the three acclamations which are made in many churches during the Lord's Supper: 'Christ has died! Christ is risen! Christ will come again!' They not only inform our worship; they also influence our behaviour.

As we have tried to follow the intricacies of Paul's reasoning regarding relationships between the strong and the weak, it must sometimes have seemed very remote from our own situation. Yet there are two particular principles which Paul develops, which, especially in combination, are applicable to all churches in all places at all times. The first is the principle of faith. Everything must be done 'from faith', he writes (14:23). Again, 'each one should be fully convinced in his own mind' (14:5). We need therefore to educate our consciences by the Word of God, so that we become strong in faith, growing in settled convictions and so in Christian liberty. Secondly, there is the principle of love. Everything must be done according to love (14:15). We need therefore to remember who our fellow Christians are, especially that they are our sisters and brothers for whom Christ died, so that we honour, not despise, them; serve, not harm, them; and especially respect their consciences.

One area in which this distinction between faith and love should operate is in the difference between essentials and non-essentials in Christian doctrine and practice. Although it is not always easy to distinguish between them, a safe guide is that truths on which Scripture speaks with a clear voice are essentials, whereas whenever equally biblical Christians, equally anxious to understand and obey Scripture, reach different conclusions, these must be regarded as non-essentials. Some people glory in the so-called 'comprehensiveness' of certain denominations. But there are two kinds of comprehensiveness, principled and unprincipled.

Dr Alex Vidler has described the latter as the resolve 'to hold together in juxtaposition as many varieties of Christian faith and practice as are willing to agree to differ, so that the church is regarded as a sort of league of religions [a sort of 'United Religions', he might have said today]. I have nothing to say for such an unprincipled syncretism.' The true principle of comprehension, on the other hand, he writes, 'is that a church ought to hold the fundamentals of the faith, and at the same time allow for differences of opinion and of interpretation in secondary matters, especially rites and ceremonies . . . '.[40]

[40] Alec Vidler, *Essays in Liberality* (SCM, 1957), p. 166.

In fundamentals, then, faith is primary, and we may not appeal to love as an excuse to deny essential faith. In non-fundamentals, however, love is primary, and we may not appeal to zeal for the faith as an excuse for failures in love. Faith instructs our own conscience; love respects the conscience of others. Faith gives liberty; love limits its exercise. No-one has put it better than Rupert Meldenius, a name which some believe was a *nom de plume* used by Richard Baxter:

> In essentials unity;
> In non-essentials liberty;
> In all things charity.

Conclusion: The providence of God in the ministry of Paul
Romans 15:14 – 16:27

The great exposition (chapters 1 – 11) and the great exhortation (12:1 – 15:13) are over. Paul's readers may well be thinking that his two benedictions (15:5, 13) are the conclusion of his letter. But he has not finished yet. He intends to return to the question of his relations with the Roman church, which he began to open up earlier (1:8–13). He wants to take them into his confidence about the salient characteristics of his ministry, which will throw light for them on why he has not yet visited them and on his plan to do so soon.

But first he wonders whether they may have been offended by the fact, contents or tone of his letter. Has he been presumptuous to address a church he did not found and has never visited? Has he given the impression that he regards their Christianity as defective and immature? Has he been too outspoken? The apostle seems to be experiencing a twinge of apprehension about how his letter will be received. If so, the rest of it will disarm and reassure them. He writes very personally (maintaining an 'I–you' directness throughout), affectionately ('my brothers', 15:14) and candidly. He opens his heart to them about the past, present and future of his ministry, he asks humbly for their prayers, and he sends them many greetings. In these ways he gives us insight into the outworking of God's providence in his life and work.

15:14–22
25. His apostolic service

Paul begins by expressing his confidence in his Roman readers. *I myself am convinced, my brothers*, he writes, *that you yourselves are full of goodness, complete in knowledge and competent to instruct one another* (14). He is of course engaging in a little harmless, diplomatic hyperbole. But it would be unfair to accuse him of insincerity. Nor does it seem right to describe his words as 'a courteous apology'.[1] He is simply assuring them that he knows and appreciates their qualities – their kindness (as *agathōsynē* can be rendered), their extensive Christian knowledge and their proven ability to teach and admonish one another.

If then they are such fine and gifted Christians, why has Paul thought it necessary to write to them as he has done? He supplies two reasons. First, *I have written to you quite boldly on some points, as if to remind you of them again* (15a). The apostles attached great importance to their reminding ministry. To them had been entrusted the task of formulating the gospel and thus of laying the foundations of the faith. Consequently, they kept reminding the churches of the original message and calling them back to it.[2] Paul's second reason for having written had to do with his unique ministry as the apostle to the Gentiles, to which he has already referred three times (1:5; 11:13; 12:3).[3] *I have written*, he goes on, *because of the grace God gave me* (15b) *to be a minister of Christ Jesus to the Gentiles* . . . (16a). Although he did not found the church in Rome, he nevertheless has authority to teach its members on account of his special vocation, by God's grace alone, to be the apostle to the Gentiles.

For the next seven verses Paul elaborates the nature of his ministry, drawing his readers' attention to three salient features of it.

---

[1] Sanday and Headlam, p. 403.
[2] *E.g.* Rom. 6:17; 1 Cor. 15:1ff.; Phil. 3:1; 2 Thes. 2:15; 1 Tim. 6:20; 2 Tim. 1:13f.; 3:14; Heb. 2:1; 2 Pet. 1:12ff.; 3:1; 1 Jn. 2:21ff.; Jude 3.
[3] *Cf.* Gal. 2:9; Eph. 3:2ff.

378

1. Paul's ministry was a priestly ministry (16–17)

He calls himself a *minister of Christ Jesus to the Gentiles with the priestly duty of proclaiming the gospel of God, so that the Gentiles might become an offering acceptable to God, sanctified by the Holy Spirit* (16). Many readers are taken by surprise that Paul should thus describe his service in priestly terms, but the vocabulary he uses is unambiguous. Although *leitourgos* (*minister*) usually meant a public servant, as in 13:6, yet in the biblical literature both the noun and its cognate verb *leitourgeō* are used 'exclusively of religious and ritual services' (BAGD). Thus in the New Testament they are applied both to the Jewish priesthood[4] and to Jesus our great high priest.[5] Next, the verb *hierourgeō* (*priestly duty*) means to serve as a priest (*hiereus*), especially in relation to the temple sacrifices. And Paul continues the imagery with his reference to *an offering* (*prosphora*), *acceptable to God* (*euprosdektos*, used of sacrifices)[6] and *sanctified* (used of consecrating sacrifices)[7] *by the Holy Spirit*. These five terms, directly or indirectly, all have priestly and sacrificial associations.

So what is Paul's priestly ministry, and what sacrifice does he have to offer? The answer clearly has to do with the gospel and the Gentiles. Paul regards his missionary work as a priestly ministry because he is able to offer his Gentile converts as a living sacrifice to God. It is not that he enables them to offer themselves to God (*cf.* 12:1), as some commentators suggest. For it is he himself who presents the sacrifice. Although Gentiles were rigorously excluded from the temple in Jerusalem, and were no on account permitted to share in the offering of its sacrifices, now through the gospel they themselves become a holy and acceptable offering to God. This significant development was in fulfilment of Isaiah's prophecy that diaspora Jews (of whom Paul was one) would proclaim God's glory in distant lands and bring people to Jerusalem from all the nations 'as an offering to the LORD'.[8] I wonder if Paul recalled his priestly ministry to Gentiles when less than a year later he was falsely accused of bringing one into the temple area?[9]

Although Paul's priestly ministry as apostle to the Gentiles was unique, the principle he enunciates has a vital contemporary application. All evangelists are priests, because they offer their converts to God. Indeed, it is this truth more than any other which effectively unites the church's two major roles of worship and witness. It is when we worship God, glorying in his holy name, that we are driven out to proclaim his name to the world. And when through

[4] Heb. 10:11.   [5] Heb. 8:2.   [6] *E.g.* 1 Pet. 2:5.   [7] *E.g.* Ex. 29:33ff.
[8] Is. 66:20.   [9] Acts 21:27ff.

our witness people are brought to Christ, we then offer them to God. Further, they themselves join in his worship, until they too go out to witness. Thus worship leads to witness, and witness to worship. It is a perpetual cycle. No wonder Paul is grateful for his share in this privileged ministry and breaks out: *Therefore I glory in Christ Jesus in my service to God* (17).

2. Paul's ministry was a powerful ministry (18–19a)

I will not venture to speak of anything except what Christ has accomplished through me in leading the Gentiles to obey God by what I have said and done (18) – *by the power of signs and miracles, through the power of the Spirit* (19a). This is a very valuable statement of Paul's own understanding of his ministry. The repetition of the word *dynamis* (*power*) in verse 19 justifies our calling it a 'powerful ministry'. He alludes to at least five features of it.

First, Paul describes the objective of his ministry as being to lead *the Gentiles to obey God* (*eis hypakoē*, 'with a view to obedience'). The same two Greek words occur in 1:5 and 16:26. There, however, Paul's phrase is 'unto obedience of faith among all the Gentiles'; here it is 'unto obedience of the Gentiles'. It is surprising that he now omits any reference to faith, for of course his objective is to bring people to Christ, indeed to faith in Christ (*e.g.* 1:16). Nevertheless his emphasis is on obedience, presumably because it is the indispensable consequence of saving faith, and is a vital ingredient of Christian discipleship.

Secondly, Paul refuses to recount his own exploits. All he will dare to talk about, he says, is *what Christ has accomplished through me*. To be sure, the relationship between Christ and his evangelists is variously portrayed in the New Testament, and sometimes it is seen as a collaboration (*e.g.* 'We are God's fellow-workers').[10] But Paul is not altogether comfortable to think of himself as Christ's partner; he prefers to be Christ's agent or even instrument, so that Christ works not 'with' him but 'through' him. 'We are . . . Christ's ambassadors,' he writes, 'as though God were making his appeal *through us.*'[11] It is safer to think in this way because if the work is Christ's, the glory will be Christ's as well (*cf.* 17).

Thirdly, Paul writes, what Christ has accomplished has been *by what I have said and done*, literally 'by word and deed'. This combination of words and works, the verbal and the visual, is a recognition that human beings often learn more through their eyes than through their ears. Words explain works, but works dramatize words. The public ministry of Jesus is the best example of this, and

[10] 1 Cor. 3:9; *cf.* 2 Cor. 6:1.   [11] 2 Cor. 5:20; *cf.* Acts 15:12; 21:19.

after his ascension into heaven he continued 'to do and to teach' through his apostles.[12] It would be wrong to conclude, however, that 'works' means only miracles. One of Jesus' most powerful visual aids was to take a child into his arms, and one of the early church's was their common life and care for the needy.

Fourthly, Christ's ministry through Paul was *by the power of signs and miracles*. This expression brings together the three commonest biblical terms for the supernatural. 'Signs' indicates their significance (especially in demonstrating the arrival of God's kingdom), 'powers' their character (exhibiting God's power over nature) and 'wonders' their effect (evoking people's amazement). Paul's only other use of these three words in relation to his ministry is in 2 Corinthians 12:12, where he calls them 'the things that mark an apostle' or 'the signs of a true apostle' (RSV). This is not to deny that God can perform miracles today, for it would be ludicrous to impose limitations on the creator of the universe. It is rather to acknowledge that their chief purpose was to authenticate the unique ministry of the apostles.[13] As Chrysostom put it, the signs of Paul's apostolic priesthood were 'not the long garment and the bells as they of old, nor the mitre and the turban, but signs and wonders, far more aweful than these'.[14]

Fifthly, Paul's ministry was also *through the power of the Spirit*. Since this clause is separate from the reference to the power of signs and wonders, its meaning is likely to be different too. Physical miracles are not the only way in which the power of the Holy Spirit is displayed. Indeed his usual way is through the Word of God, which is his 'sword'.[15] It is he who takes our feeble human words and confirms them with his divine power in the minds, hearts, consciences and wills of the hearers.[16] Every conversion is a power encounter, in which the Spirit through the gospel rescues and regenerates sinners.

3. Paul's ministry was a pioneer ministry (19b–22)

So, Paul continues, what Christ has accomplished through him is this: *from Jerusalem all the way around to Illyricum, I have fully proclaimed the gospel of Christ* (19b). This is Paul's succinct and modest summary of ten years of strenuous apostolic labour, including his three heroic missionary journeys. The expression *all the way around* (*kyklō*) should probably be translated 'in a circle' or 'in a circuit'. Then one can visualize, or trace on a map, the arc of Pauline evangelism encircling the Eastern Mediterranean. From Jerusalem it

---

[12] Acts 1:1.   [13] See the Acts record and *e.g.* Heb. 2:4.
[14] Chrysostom, p. 543.   [15] Eph. 6:17.   [16] *E.g.* 1 Cor. 2:4; 1 Thes. 1:5.

goes north to Syrian Antioch, then further north and west through the provinces of Asia Minor, and across the Aegean Sea to Macedonia. From there it leads south to Achaia, then east across the Aegean Sea again, and via Ephesus back to Antioch and Jerusalem.

But two questions arise. First, did no Paul begin from Antioch, rather than from Jerusalem? Yes and no. Although the first missionary journey was indeed launched from Antioch,[17] the Christian mission itself began in Jerusalem,[18] and after his conversion and commissioning Paul certainly preached in Jerusalem, albeit to Jews.[19] Secondly, did Paul ever evangelize Illyricum? It is situated on the western, Adriatic seaboard of Macedonia, and corresponds approximately to Albania and the southern part of former Yugoslavia today. Certainly Luke gives us in the Acts no account of a Pauline visit to Illyricum. But he leaves room for it, since there is a gap in his narrative of the best part of two years between his leaving Ephesus and his embarking for Jerusalem.[20] While in Macedonia at that time he may well have walked west along the Egnatian Way from Thessalonica, at least to the borders of Illyricum.

This reconstruction would justify Paul's claim to have *fully proclaimed the gospel of Christ*, or better, to have 'completed the preaching of the gospel of Christ' (REB) within this arc. This does not of course mean that Paul had 'saturated' the whole area with the gospel, as we might say today. His strategy was to evangelize the populous and influential cities, and plant churches there, and then leave to others the radiation of the gospel into the surrounding villages. So 'we understand his claim to have completed the gospel of Christ to be a claim to have completed that trail-blazing, pioneer preaching of it, which he believed it was his own special apostolic mission to accomplish'.[21]

Having plotted on the map the sweeping arc which represented his ten years of missionary outreach, Paul goes on to explain the consistent pioneer policy which lay behind it. *It has always been my ambition to preach the gospel where Christ was not known* (literally 'not named', *i.e.* 'not honoured'), *so that I would not be building on someone else's foundation* (20). Paul was quite clear, as is evident from his teaching about *charismata* (*e.g.* 12:3ff.), that Christ calls different disciples to different tasks, and endows them with different gifts to equip them. His own calling and gift as apostle to the Gentiles were to pioneer the evangelization of the Gentile world, and then leave to others, especially to local, residential presbyters, the pastoral care of the churches. He used two metaphors, agricultural and architectural, to illustrate this division of labour, especially

---

[17] Acts 13:1ff. [18] Lk. 24:47; Act 1:8; *cf.* Is. 2:13. [19] Acts 9:26ff.
[20] Acts 20:1ff. [21] Cranfield, vol. II, p. 762.

as it related to himself and Apollos in Corinth. 'I planted the seed, Apollos watered it.' Again, 'I laid a foundation as an expert builder, and someone else is building on it.'[22] It was in keeping with this policy that, positively, he would evangelize only *where Christ was not known*, and negatively, he would avoid *building on someone else's foundation*.

Rather, that is, instead of departing from his policy, he found that Scripture itself validates it, *as it is written:*

> [21]*'Those who were not told about him will see,*
> *and those who have not heard will understand.'*[23]

The prophet was writing about the mission of the Servant of the Lord to 'sprinkle many nations', so that they would see and understand what had not so far been told them. Paul sees the prophecy fulfilled in Christ, the true Servant, whom he is proclaiming to the unevangelized.

Paul concludes: *This is why I have often* ('all this time', REB) *been hindered from coming to you* (22). In the first chapter Paul wrote that he had 'many times' planned to visit them, but had so far 'been prevented' (1:13), although he did not divulge what had stopped him. Now he does. It had to do with his mission policy. On the one hand, because he was concentrating on pioneer evangelism elsewhere, he was not free to come to them. On the other hand, because the Roman church had not been founded by him, he did not feel at liberty to come and stay. Soon, however, as he is about to explain, he will visit them, since he will only be 'passing through' (24) on his way to the unevangelized field of Spain.

---

[22] 1 Cor. 3:6, 10.   [23] Isaiah 52:15.

15:23–33
26. His travel plans

Having shared with the Roman church his understanding of his special apostolic ministry, Paul now looks into the future and confides to the Romans his travel plans. He specifies three destinations. First, he is about to sail from Corinth to Jerusalem, taking with him the collection which he has long been organizing. Secondly, he is intending to go from Jerusalem to Rome, even though he will only be 'passing through' (24) rather than settling down among them for an appreciable period. Thirdly, from Rome he will travel on to Spain, determined to resume his pioneer evangelistic commitment. If he were to make all these journeys by ship, the first would be at least 800 miles, the second 1,500, and the third 700, making a minimum total of 3,000 miles, and many more if he were to travel some of the way by land rather than sea. When one reflects on the uncertainties and hazards of ancient travel, the almost nonchalant way in which Paul announces his intention to undertake these three voyages is quite extraordinary.

1. He plans to visit Rome (23–24)

Although Paul has so far been hindered from coming to Rome, now at last the time seems to be ripe for his long-awaited, long-postponed visit. A combination of three factors has facilitated it. First, his missionary service in the East Mediterranean zone is complete. *But now*, he writes, . . . *there is no more place for me to work in these regions* (23a). At first hearing this is a most surprising statement, for undoubtedly there were still many areas into which the gospel had not penetrated, and still multitudes of people who were not converted. But we must read Paul's words in verse 23 in the light of his policy explained in verse 20. He means that there is no more room in Greece and its environs for his pioneer church-planting ministry, for that initial work has been done.

Secondly, Paul writes, *I have been longing for many years to see you* (23b). He has written the same thing near the beginning of his letter: 'I long to see you' (1:11). He is not exaggerating. Nor is this a mere flash in the pan. It is a sustained, ardent desire over *many years*, which all the hindrances and frustrations have not been able to quench. It must surely come from God.

The third deciding factor in Paul's mind is that he has come to see his visit to Rome as a stepping-stone to Spain. *I plan to do so* (*sc.* visit you) *when I go to Spain* (24a). This perspective helps him to keep his resolve not to build on somebody else's foundation, for he will only be *passing through*. At the same time, he entertains a second hope: *I hope to visit you . . . and to have you assist me on my journey there* (*sc.* to Spain), *after I have enjoyed your company for a while* (24b). The verb translated *assist* (*propempō*) seems already to have become almost a technical Christian term for helping missionaries on their way. It undoubtedly meant more than good wishes and a valedictory prayer. In most cases it also involved supplying them with provisions and money,[1] and sometimes providing them as well with an escort to accompany them at least part of the way.[2] So the dictionary definition of *propempō* is to 'help on one's journey with food, money, by arranging for companions, means of travel etc.' (BAGD). Perhaps Paul hopes to establish an ongoing relationship with the Christians in Rome, so that they will continue to support him, as other churches have done previously.[3]

This conjunction of three factors must have presented itself to Paul as evidence of the providential guidance of God. It has led him to make plans to go to Rome. But first, he explains, he has another journey to make.

2. He plans to visit Jerusalem (25–27)

Now, however, I am on my way to Jerusalem in the service of the saints there (25). The expression 'I am on my way' is an attempt to catch the present tense of the verb (*poreuomai*), meaning that his departure is imminent; it has even virtually begun. His purpose in going is to 'serve the saints' there, the people of God, in this case the Jewish Christian community. To explain this to the church in Rome, he first gives the facts about the collection (26) and then draws out its significance (27).

The facts may be simply stated. *For Macedonia and Achaia* (that is, the churches of northern and southern Greece respectively) *were pleased to make a contribution for the poor among the saints in Jerusalem* (26). In order to understand this, we need to think first about the poor in Jerusalem, and then about the Christians of

---

[1] *Cf.* Tit. 3:13; 3 Jn. 6f.   [2] *E.g.* Acts 20:38; 21:5.   [3] *E.g.* Phil. 4:14ff.

Macedonia and Achaia. First, no explanation is given of the cause of poverty in Jerusalem. It may have been caused partly by the 'severe famine' which Agabus predicted.[4] But the plausible suggestion has also often been made that it was related to the economic sharing of the first church there.[5] While applauding their generosity, some have questioned their wisdom, since they sold and gave 'in the economically disastrous way of realizing capital and distributing it as income'.[6] Secondly, Paul writes that the Macedonian and Achaian Christians *were pleased to make a contribution* for the Jerusalem poor. 'Contribution' renders *koinōnia*, which means a 'common share' in anything, here in contributing to Paul's collection. His statement that the Greek Christians *were pleased* to give (an expression he repeats in verse 27) is a forgivable euphemism. They did give freely and willingly, but only because Paul had urged them to do so!

Why then did Paul conceive and initiate this freewill offering project, this *koinōnia*? Clearly he saw great significance in it, as may be seen partly from the disproportionate amount of space which he devoted to it in his letters,[7] partly from the passionate zeal with which he promoted it, and partly from his astonishing decision to add nearly 2,000 miles to his journey, in order to present the offering himself. Instead of sailing directly west from Corinth to Rome to Spain, he has made up his mind to travel first in entirely the wrong direction, that is, to go to Rome via Jerusalem!

The significance of the offering (the solidarity of God's people in Christ) was primarily neither geographical (from Greece to Judea), nor social (from the rich to the poor), nor even ethnic (from Gentiles to Jews), but both religious (from liberated radicals to traditional conservatives, that is, from the strong to the weak), and especially theological (from beneficiaries to benefactors). In other words, the so-called 'gift' was in reality a 'debt': *They were pleased to do it (sc. to make their contribution), and indeed they owe it to them. For if the Gentiles have shared in the Jews' spiritual blessings, they owe it to the Jews to share with them their material blessings* (27).

The nature of this debt Paul has already elaborated in chapter 11. Although indeed it is through Israel's transgression that 'salvation has come to the Gentiles' (11:11), he has argued, yet the Gentiles must be careful not to get boastful or arrogant (11:18–20). They must rather remember that they have inherited from the Jews enormous blessings to which they have no title. In themselves they are nothing but a wild olive shoot. But having been grafted into God's ancient olive tree, they 'now share in the nourishing sap from the olive root' (11:17). It is right therefore for Gentiles to acknowledge

---

[4] Acts 11:27ff.   [5] Acts 2:44f.; 4:32ff.   [6] Dodd, p. 230.
[7] Rom. 15:25ff.; 1 Cor. 16:1ff; and specially 2 Cor. 8 – 9.

what they owe to the Jews. When we Gentiles are thinking of the great blessings of salvation, we are hugely in debt to the Jews, and always will be. Paul sees the offering from the Gentile churches as a humble, material, symbolic demonstration of this indebtedness.

3. He plans to visit Spain (28–29)

Having explained the facts and the significance of the offering, Paul now looks beyond its presentation in Jerusalem, and hopefully its acceptance, to the long westward journey which he plans then to undertake to Spain via Rome. *So after I have completed this task and have made sure that they have received this fruit* (literally 'have sealed to them this fruit', this expression of solidarity, meaning perhaps 'have . . . officially handed over' the offering, JB), *I will go to Spain and visit you on the way* (28).

Some two years previously Paul told the Corinthians that, in keeping with his pioneer mission policy, he was hoping to 'preach the gospel in the regions beyond you'.[8] Perhaps he already had his eyes on Spain. We know from the Old Testament that for centuries before Christ the seafaring Phoenicians from Tyre and Sidon had engaged in commerce with Spain, their 'ships of Tarshish' being perhaps so called because they plied trade with Tartessus.[9] The Phoenicians also established colonies there. By the time of the Emperor Augustus 'the whole Iberian peninsula had been subjugated by the Romans and organized in . . . three provinces . . . ',[10] with many flourishing Roman colonies. Did Paul possibly look beyond Spain to the edges of the Empire, to Gaul and Germany, and even to Britain?

Whether he reached and evangelized Spain we shall probably never know. The nearest thing we have to evidence is the statement by Clement of Rome in his first letter to the Corinthians (usually dated AD 96–97) about Paul's 'noble renown' as a herald of the gospel: 'To the whole world he taught righteousness, and reaching the limits of the West he bore his witness before rulers.'[11] It may be, then, as has often been surmised, that Paul was released from his confinement in Rome, in which the Acts leaves him, and that he then resumed his missionary travels, including a visit to Spain, before being re-arrested, imprisoned and finally beheaded during the Neronian persecution.

As Paul mentally prepares for his visit to Rome, however, he is full of assurance. *I know that when I come to you, I will come in the full measure of the blessing of Christ* (29). There is no need to detect

---

[8] 2 Cor. 10:16.   [9] *Cf.* 1 Ki. 10:22.   [10] Cranfield, vol. II, p. 769.
[11] 1 Clement 5:7.

a trace of arrogance in this statement. Paul's confidence is not in himself but in Christ. That he is not trusting in himself is evident from his request for their prayers which immediately follows. He knows his weakness, his vulnerability. But he also knows the blessing of Christ.

4. He requests prayer for his visits (30–32)

I urge you, brothers, by our Lord Jesus Christ and by the love of the Spirit, to join me in my struggle by praying to God for me (30). Towards the beginning of his letter Paul assured the Roman Christians that he was constantly praying for them (1:9f.). So it is entirely appropriate that he should now ask them to pray for him. Besides, he and they are *brothers* in the family of God. He is also able to appeal to them *by our Lord Jesus Christ* (our common Lord) and *by the love of the Spirit* (our common love being the Holy Spirit's fruit).[12]

He goes on to refer to prayer as a *struggle*. It is natural that readers who are familiar with the Old Testament should recall the occasion when Jacob 'wrestled' with God.[13] But there is no suggestion here of such a struggle with God. It is more likely that Paul is thinking of our need to wrestle with the principalities and powers of darkness.[14] In point of fact, however, the apostle does not specify any adversary with whom we are to strive. It may be, therefore, that he is simply representing prayer as an activity demanding great exertion, a struggle in fact with ourselves, in which we seek to align ourselves with God's will.[15]

For what, then, does Paul ask their prayers? It concerns his visits to Jerusalem and to Rome. With regard to Jerusalem, he mentions two topics for their prayers, which relate to believers and unbelievers respectively. The first concerns the opposition of unbelievers. *Pray that I may be rescued from the unbelievers in Judea* (31a). He is aware that he has many enemies among the unbelieving Jews, who will doubtless plot and scheme for his downfall, even his death. He knows he is in danger, even for his life. He will shortly say, when *en route* for Jerusalem, 'I am ready not only to be bound, but also to die in Jerusalem for the name of the Lord Jesus.'[16] But he asks the Romans to join him in prayer for his protection and deliverance from his opponents.

Paul's second concern for his Jerusalem visit relates to the believers, the Jewish Christian community: *Pray . . . that my service in Jerusalem may be acceptable to the saints there* (31b). He realizes that it may be difficult for them to accept the offering, not in the

---

[12] Gal. 5:22.   [13] Gn. 32:24ff.   [14] Eph. 6:12.   [15] *Cf.* Col. 2:1f.; 4:12.
[16] Acts 21:13.

general sense that we all find it hard to receive gifts which place us in other people's debt, but in a much more specific sense. In accepting the gift from Paul, Jewish Christian leaders would be seen to endorse Paul's gospel and his seeming disregard of Jewish law and traditions. Yet if his offering were to be rejected, this could cause the rift between Jewish and Gentile Christians to widen irrevocably. So Paul longs that Jewish–Gentile solidarity in the body of Christ may be strengthened by the Jewish Christians' acceptance of its tangible symbol. That is why he asks the Romans to pray both that the believers will accept the gift and that unbelievers will not be able to prevent either the giving or the receiving of it.

Paul now requests prayer also for his visit to Rome. Indeed he sees the two visits to be inseparably connected. Only if his mission in Jerusalem succeeds will his voyage to Rome be possible. So he asks the Romans to pray that he may be protected and his gift accepted in Jerusalem, not only because these things are important in themselves, but also *so that by God's will I may come to you with joy and together with you be refreshed* (32). Whatever reception he is given in Jerusalem, he anticipates that afterwards he will be in need of the joy and refreshment which fellowship with the Roman Christians will bring. This time he does not mention his further plan to go on to Spain.

Paul's reference to the will of God in relation to prayer is very significant. He has prayed earlier that 'now at last by God's will the way may be opened' for him to come to Rome (1:10). Here he again prays that *by God's will* he may come to them. His use of this qualifying clause throws light on both the purpose and the character of prayer, on why and how Christians should pray.

The purpose of prayer is emphatically not to bend God's will to ours, but rather to align our will to his. The promise that our prayers will be answered is conditional on our asking 'according to his will'.[17] Consequently every prayer we pray should be a variation on the theme, 'Your will be done.'[18]

What about the character of prayer? Some people tell us, in spite of Paul's earlier statement that 'we do not know what we ought to pray for' (8:26), that we should always be precise, specific and confident in what we pray for, and that to add 'if it be your will' is a cop-out and incompatible with faith. In response, we need to distinguish between the general and the particular will of God. Since God has revealed his general will for all his people in Scripture (*e.g.* that we should control ourselves and become like Christ), we should indeed pray with definiteness and assurance about these things. But God's particular will for each of us (*e.g.* regarding a life work and a

---

[17] 1 Jn. 5:14.   [18] Mt. 6:10.

life partner) has not been revealed in Scripture, so that, in praying for guidance, it is right to add 'by God's will'. If Jesus himself did this in the garden of Gethsemane ('Not my will, but yours be done'),[19] and if Paul did it twice in his letter to the Romans, we should do it too. It is not unbelief, but a proper humility.[20]

So what happened to Paul's three prayers, in which he asked the Romans to join him, namely that he might be rescued from unbelievers in Jerusalem, that his gift might be accepted, and that he might succeed in reaching Rome? Were they answered or unanswered? Regarding the middle of the three prayers we do not know, since surprisingly Luke does not refer to the offering in his Acts narrative, although he knows about it, because he accompanied Paul to Jerusalem and records Paul's statement (when on trial before Felix) that he had come to Jerusalem 'to bring my people gifts for the poor'.[21] The probability is that the gifts were accepted.

What, then, about the other two petitions? Both received a qualified 'Yes': the first 'Yes and no', the second 'Yes but'. Was Paul delivered from unbelievers in Jerusalem? 'No', in the sense that he was arrested, tried and imprisoned, but also 'yes' because he was three times rescued from lynching,[22] once from flogging[23] and once from a plot to kill him.[24] Then did he reach Rome? Yes indeed, as Jesus had promised him he would,[25] but neither when nor how he had expected, for he arrived about three years later, as a prisoner, and after an almost fatal shipwreck.

So prayer is an essential Christian activity, and it is good to ask people to pray for us and with us, as Paul did. But there is nothing automatic about prayer. Praying is not like using a coin-operated machine or a cash dispenser. The struggle involved in prayer lies in the process of coming to discern God's will and to desire it above everything else. Then God will work things out providentially according to his will, for which we have prayed. That is why I have called this concluding section 'The Providence of God in the Ministry of Paul'.

Paul ends this part of his letter with a third benediction, in which, having asked for their prayers, he prays for them again. *The God of peace be with you all. Amen* (33). That he chooses this time to call God *the God of peace* or reconciliation, that peace (shalom) is a central Jewish concern, and that he deliberately writes not 'with you' but *with you all* are three suggestive pointers. They seem to indicate that Paul's mind is preoccupied to

---

[19] Lk. 22:42.   [20] *Cf.* Jas. 4:15.   [21] Acts 24:17.
[22] Acts 21:30ff.; 22:22ff.; 23:10.   [23] Acts 22:25ff.   [24] Acts 23:12ff.
[25] Acts 23:11.

the end with Jewish–Gentile unity. As Professor Dunn has aptly put it, 'Paul the Jew, who is also apostle to the Gentiles, says the Jewish benediction over his Gentile readers.'[26]

---

[26] Dunn, vol. 38B, p. 884.

16:1–16
27.   His commendation and greetings

'I think', wrote Chrysostom, 'that many even of those who have the appearance of being extremely good men, hasten over this part of the epistle as superfluous ... Yet', he went on, 'the gold founders' people are careful even about the little fragments ... it is possible even from bare names to find a great treasure.' Brunner went further and called Romans 16 'one of the most instructive chapters of the New Testament', because it encourages personal relationships of love in the church. Chrysostom and Brunner are right.[1] Even in the genealogies of both the Old and the New Testaments, and in Paul's list of those who send or receive greetings, there are truths to ponder and lessons to learn.

1.   A commendation (1–2)

¹I commend to you our sister Phoebe, a servant of the church in Cenchrea. ²I ask you to receive her in the Lord in a way worthy of the saints and to give her any help she may need from you, for she has been a great help to many people, including me.

It seems very likely that Phoebe was entrusted with the responsible task of carrying Paul's letter to its destination in Rome, although other business was apparently taking her to the city as well, perhaps commerce or 'quite probably a law suit'.[2] So she needed a 'letter of commendation' to take with her, which would introduce her to the Christians in Rome. Such letters were common in the ancient world, and necessary to protect people from charlatans. They are several times mentioned in the New Testament.[3] In

---

[1] Chrysostom, p. 553; Brunner, p. 126. See 'The Roman Christians of Romans 16' by Peter Lampe, in Donfried, pp. 216ff.

[2] Dunn, vol. 38B, pp. 888f. This opinion is based on the fact that *pragma* (2) is used of a lawsuit in 1 Cor. 6:1.

[3] *E.g.* Acts 18:27; 2 Cor. 3:1.

his testimonial for Phoebe Paul asks the Roman church both *to receive her*, giving her a worthy Christian welcome and hospitality, and *to give her any help she may need*, as a stranger in the capital city, presumably in connection with her other business.

Before and after these requests Paul supplies some information about Phoebe, 'so placing on each side of the needs of this blessed woman', writes Chrysostom, 'her praises'.[4] Indeed, he goes on, 'see how many ways he takes to give her dignity'. First, he calls her *our sister*, 'and it is no slight thing to be called the sister of Paul'.[5] Secondly, he acknowledges her as *a servant* ('minister', REB) *of the church in Cenchrea* (1), which was Corinth's eastern port at the head of the Saronic Gulf. This general meaning of *diakonos* may be correct here. On the other hand, we know that the office of 'deacon' already existed, in however undeveloped a form.[6] So RSV and NIV margin call Phoebe a 'deaconess', and Professor Cranfield regards this not only as 'very much more natural' but as 'virtually certain'.[7] Thirdly, *she has been a great help to many people*, including Paul (2). This phrase renders *prostatis*, which can mean 'patroness' or 'benefactress'. Phoebe was evidently a woman of means, who had used her wealth to support the church and the apostle.

2. Many greetings (3–16)

³*Greet Priscilla and Aquila, my fellow-workers in Christ Jesus.*
    ⁴*They risked their lives for me. Not only I but all the churches of the Gentiles are grateful to them.*
⁵*Greet also the church that meets at their house.*
 Greet my dear friend Epenetus, who was the first convert to Christ in the province of Asia.
⁶*Greet Mary, who worked very hard for you.*
⁷*Greet Andronicus and Junias, my relatives who have been in prison with me. They are outstanding among the apostles, and they were in Christ before I was.*
⁸*Greet Ampliatus, whom I love in the Lord.*
⁹*Greet Urbanus, our fellow-worker in Christ, and my dear friend Stachys.*
¹⁰*Greet Apelles, tested and approved in Christ.*
 Greet those who belong to the household of Aristobulus.
¹¹*Greet Herodion, my relative.*
 Greet those in the household of Narcissus who are in the Lord.
¹²*Greet Tryphena and Tryphosa, those women who work hard in the Lord.*

---

[4] Chrysostom, p. 550.   [5] *Ibid.*, p. 549.   [6] *E.g.* Phil. 1:1; 1 Tim. 3:8, 11.
[7] Cranfield, vol. II, p. 781.

> *Greet my dear friend Persis, another woman who has worked very hard in the Lord.*
> [13]*Greet Rufus, chosen in the Lord, and his mother, who has been a mother to me, too.*
> [14]*Greet Asyncritus, Phlegon, Hermes, Patrobas, Hermas and the brothers with them.*
> [15]*Greet Philologus, Julia, Nereus and his sister, and Olympas and all the saints with them.*
> [16]*Greet one another with a holy kiss.*
> *All the churches of Christ send greetings.*

Thus Paul sends greetings to twenty-six individuals, twenty-four of whom he names, adding in most cases an appreciative personal reference. Scholars have naturally wondered how the apostle could know so many people so well in a church he had never visited. Some have therefore developed the theory that these greetings were in reality sent to Ephesus, not Rome. For Paul had stayed three years in Ephesus and knew it well. Further, his first greeting was sent to Priscilla and Aquila (3), who had accompanied him to Ephesus, and his second to Epenetus, whom he describes as *the first convert to Christ in the province of Asia* (5), Ephesus being the provincial capital. On the other hand, there is no manuscript evidence that these greetings were ever detached from their place in Romans; the names fit Rome better than Ephesus; and if Paul had sent this list of greetings to Ephesus, it would have been too short rather than too long.

As for the question how Paul could have known so many Roman Christians, travel was more frequent in those days than many realize. Aquila and Priscilla are a case in point. New Testament references to them tell us that Aquila came from Pontus on the southern shore of the Black Sea, that he and Priscilla lived in Italy until the Emperor Claudius expelled the Jews from Rome in AD 49, that they then moved to Corinth where Paul met them and stayed with them, and that they travelled with him to Ephesus, which is perhaps where *they risked their lives* for him (4). It is not in the least unlikely that after Claudius' death in AD 54 they returned to Rome, which is where they received Paul's greeting.[8] Perhaps a number of other Jewish and Jewish-Christian refugees from Rome met Paul during their exile and returned to Rome after Claudius' edict had been rescinded.

Reflecting on the names and circumstances of the people Paul greets, one is particularly impressed by the unity and diversity of the church to which they belonged.

---

[8] Acts 18:1ff., 18, 26; 1 Cor. 16:19.

a.   The diversity of the church

The Roman Christians were diverse in race, rank and gender. As for race, we know already that the church in Rome had both Jewish and Gentile members, and this is confirmed by the list. Certainly Aquila and Priscilla were Jewish Christians, and so were Paul's *syngeneis* (7 and 11), which is less likely to mean his *relatives* than his 'kinsfolk' or 'those of his own race' (as in 9:3). But it is equally clear that others on his list were Gentiles.

The social status of his Roman friends is uncertain. On the one hand, inscriptions indicate that Ampliatus (8), Urbanus (9), Hermes (14), Philologus and Julia (15) were common names for slaves. On the other, some at least were freed people, and others had links with persons of distinction. For example, commentators consider it quite likely that the Aristobulus mentioned (10) was the grandson of Herod the Great and friend of the Emperor Claudius, and that Narcissus (11) was none other than the well-known, rich and powerful freedman who exercised great influence on Claudius. It is not of course that these celebrities had themselves become Christians, and in any case they were probably dead by now, but their households had clearly remained in being, and there were Christians in them. J. B. Lightfoot concludes his interesting note on 'Caesar's Household'[9] with these words: 'We seem to have established a fair presumption that among the salutations in the Epistle to the Romans some members at least of the imperial household are included.'[10]

More distinguished, though in a different and nobler way, was Rufus (13), for he may well have been the son of Simon of Cyrene, who carried Jesus' cross to Golgotha. At least Mark, whose gospel was written in or for Rome, is the only evangelist who mentions that Simon's sons were Alexander and Rufus, and he does it in such a way as to imply that they were already well known to his readers in Rome.[11]

But the most interesting and instructive aspect of church diversity in Rome is that of gender. Nine out of the twenty-six persons greeted are women: Priscilla (3), Mary (6), probably Junia (7), Tryphena and Tryphosa, who may have been twin sisters, and Persis (12), Rufus' mother (13), Julia and Nereus' sister (15). Paul evidently thinks highly of them all. He singles out four (Mary, Tryphena, Tryphosa and Persis) as having 'worked hard'. The verb *kopiaō* implies strong exertion, is used of all four of them, and is not

[9] Phil. 4:22.
[10] J. B. Lightfoot, *St Paul's Epistle to the Philippians* (Macmillan, 1868; 8th edn., 1885), p. 177.
[11] Mk. 15:21.

applied to anybody else on the list. Paul does not specify what kind of hard work they did.

Two names call for special attention. The first is Priscilla, who in verse 3 and in three other New Testament verses is named in front of her husband.[12] Whether the reason was spiritual (that she was converted before him or was more active in Christian service than he) or social (that she was a woman of standing in the community) or temperamental (that she was the dominant personality), Paul appears to recognize and not to criticize her leadership.

The other woman to be considered is mentioned in verse 7: *Greet Andronicus and Junias*. In the Greek sentence the second name is *Iounian*, which could be the accusative of either Junias (masculine) or Junia (feminine). Commentators are agreed that the latter is much more likely to be correct, since the former name is unknown elsewhere. Perhaps then Andronicus and Junia were a married couple, about whom Paul tells us four things: they are his kinsfolk, that is, Jewish people; they have at some point been his fellow prisoners; they were converted before he was; and they *are outstanding among the apostles*. In which of its two senses is Paul using the word 'apostles'? The commonest New Testament application of the word is to 'the apostles of Christ', meaning the Twelve (Matthias having replaced Judas), together with Paul and James, a very small group whom Christ had personally appointed and equipped to be the teachers of the church.

The much less frequent use of the term designates 'the apostles of the churches'.[13] This must have been a considerably larger group, who were sent out by churches as what we would call 'missionaries', like Epaphroditus who was an 'apostle' of the Philippian church,[14] or like Barnabas and Saul who had been sent out by the church of Antioch.[15] If then by 'apostles' in Romans 16:7 Paul is referring to the apostles of Christ, we must translate that they were 'outstanding in the eyes of the apostles' or 'highly esteemed by the apostles', for it is impossible to suppose that an otherwise unknown couple have taken their place alongside the apostles Peter, Paul, John and James. Since this translation slightly strains the Greek, however, it is probably better to understand 'apostles' as meaning 'apostles of the churches', and to conclude that Andronicus and Junia were indeed outstanding missionaries.

The prominent place occupied by women in Paul's entourage shows that he was not at all the male chauvinist of popular fantasy. Does it also throw light on the vexed question of the ministry of women? As we have seen, among the women Paul greets four were

---

[12] Acts 18:18, 26; 2 Tim. 4:19.   [13] 2 Cor. 8:23.
[14] Phil. 2:25, literally 'your apostle'.   [15] Acts 13:1ff.; 14:4, 14; *cf*. 1 Thes. 2:6.

hard workers in the Lord's service. Priscilla was one of Paul's 'fellow-workers', Junia was a well-known missionary, and Phoebe may have been a deaconess. On the other hand, it has to be said that none of them is called a presbyter in the church, even though an argument from silence can never be decisive.

b. The unity of the church

Alongside the Roman church's diversity in race, rank and sex, it experienced a profound unity which transcended its differences. For 'there is neither Jew nor Greek, slave nor free, male nor female, for you are all one in Christ Jesus'.[16] Moreover, the list of greetings contains several indications of this fundamental unity of the people of God. Four times Paul describes his friends as being *in Christ* (3, 7, 9, 10) and five times as *in the Lord* (8, 11, twice in 12, 13). Twice he uses the family language of 'sister' and 'brother' (1, 14). In addition, he is not inhibited from calling people 'beloved' or 'my beloved' (5, 8, 9, 2). He also mentions two experiences which strengthen Christian unity, namely being fellow workers (3, 9) and fellow sufferers (4, 7).

How then in practice was the Roman church's unity in diversity displayed? We know that they met in houses or household churches, for Paul probably refers to such six times (5, 10, 11, 14, 15; cf. 23).[17] How was membership of these determined? We cannot suppose that they met according to sex or rank, so that there were different house churches for men and women, for slaves and free. What about race, however? It would be understandable if Jewish Christians and Gentile Christians, and specially the weak and the strong, wanted to meet with their own people, because culture and customs are a strong cement to fellowship. But did they? I think not. The toleration of ethnic division in the Roman house churches would be entirely incompatible with Paul's sustained argument in chapters 14 – 15, and with its climax. How could the church members 'accept one another', and how 'with one heart and mouth . . . glorify the God and Father of our Lord Jesus Christ' (15:6f.) if they worshipped in different, ethnically segregated house churches? Such an arrangement would contradict the church's unity in diversity.

The same is true today. It is of course a fact that people like to worship with their own kith and kin, and with their own kind, as experts in church growth remind us; and it may be necessary to acquiesce in different congregations according to language, which is the most formidable barrier of all. But heterogeneity is of the essence of the church, since it is the one and only community in the

---

[16] Gal. 3:28.   [17] *Cf.* Acts 12:12; 1 Cor. 16:19; Col. 4:15; Phm. 2.

world in which Christ has broken down all dividing walls. The vision we have been given of the church triumphant is of a company drawn from 'every nation, tribe, people and language', who are all singing God's praises in unison.[18] So we must declare that a homogeneous church is a defective church, which must work penitently and perseveringly towards heterogeneity.[19]

Paul concludes his list of individual greetings with two universals. The first is that, although only a few of them have been greeted by name, they must all *greet one another with a holy kiss* (16a). The apostles Paul and Peter both insisted on this,[20] and the Church Fathers took it up. Justin Martyr wrote that 'on finishing the prayers we greet each other with a kiss',[21] and Tertullian seems to have been the first to call it a 'kiss of peace'.[22] The logic is that our verbal greeting needs to be confirmed by a visible and tangible gesture, although what form the 'kiss' should take will vary according to culture. For those of us who live in the West, J. B. Phillips paraphrases: 'Give one another a hearty handshake all round for my sake.'

Paul's second universal follows: *all the churches of Christ send greetings* (16b). But how can he speak for all the churches? Is this mere rhetoric? No, he is probably writing representatively. Since he is about to set sail for Jerusalem, we know that those appointed by the churches to carry and deliver the offering have just assembled in Corinth. Luke tells us that they included delegates from Berea, Thessalonica, Derbe, Lystra and Ephesus.[23] Perhaps he has asked them if he may send their churches' greetings to Rome.

---

[18] Rev. 7:9ff.
[19] See *The Pasadena Consultation on the Homogeneous Unit Principle* (Lausanne Occasional Paper no. 1, 1978).
[20] 1 Cor. 16:20; 2 Cor. 13:12; 1 Thes. 5:26; 1 Pet. 5:14.
[21] Justin Martyr, *Apology* I.65.   [22] Tertullian, *On Prayer*, 14.   [23] Acts 20:4.

16:17–27
28. His warnings, messages and doxology

Some find Paul's transition from greeting to warnings very abrupt, and the tone of his admonition so harsh as to be inconsistent with the rest of his letter, and especially with his gentle handling of the weak. They therefore wonder if verses 17–20 were written by another hand than Paul's. But it is readily understandable that his mind should move from the Roman church's unity in diversity (to be expressed in the kiss of peace) to the menace of those who were threatening divisions. Moreover, Paul's conciliatory attitude to the weak reflected his respect for sensitive consciences; his severity to the false teachers was aroused by their deliberate mischief in disrupting the fellowship and contradicting apostolic teaching. Having said this, we still do not know who they were. Paul's language is too indefinite to permit certainty. All we can say is that, since they served themselves instead of Christ (18), they had antinomian tendencies.

1. Paul's warnings (17–20)

Paul begins his exhortation with the same words which he has used to introduce an earlier one: *I urge you, brothers* (17, *cf.* 12:1). He issues a threefold appeal – to vigilance, to separation and to discernment.

First, Paul pleads for vigilance: *watch out for* (JB 'be on your guard against') *those who cause divisions and put obstacles in your way*, hindering your progress, *that are* (both of them) *contrary to the teaching you have learned* (17). Of course some *divisions* are inevitable, like those caused by loyalty to Christ,[1] and so are some *obstacles* (*skandala*), especially the stumbling-block of the cross (9:32f.).[2] Paul urges the Romans to look out for those who cause them because they contradict the teaching of the apostles. He takes

[1] See Mt. 10:34ff.   [2] 1 Cor. 1:23.

it for granted, even thus early in the church's history, that there is a doctrinal and ethical norm which the Romans must follow, not contradict; it is preserved for us in the New Testament.

Secondly, Paul calls for separation from those who deliberately depart from the apostolic faith. *Keep away from them*, he writes. There is no question of approaching them with a holy kiss, but rather of standing aloof, and even turning away.[3] Why is this? What is the essence of their deviation? Paul tells us. *For such people are not serving our Lord Christ, but their own appetites* (18a), literally 'their own belly' (av). This is very unlikely to be an allusion to the controversy over the Jewish food laws. It is rather a graphic metaphor of self-indulgence (as in Phil. 3:19, 'their god is their stomach'). The expression is used 'in the sense of serving oneself, of being the willing slave of one's egotism'.[4] These false teachers have no love for Christ, and no wish to be his willing slaves. Instead, they are 'utterly self-centred' (jbp), and also have a baneful effect on the gullible. *By smooth talk and flattery they deceive the minds of naïve people* (18b). Better, 'they seduce the minds of simple people with smooth and specious words' (reb).

Thirdly, Paul urges the Romans to grow in discernment. On the whole he is very pleased with them. *Everyone has heard about your obedience*, he says, *so I am full of joy over you* (19a). Nevertheless, there are two kinds of obedience, blind and discerning, and he longs for them to develop the latter: *but I want you to be wise about what is good, and innocent about what is evil* (19b). To be wise in regard to good is to recognize it, love it and follow it. With regard to evil, however, he wants them to be unsophisticated, even guileless, so completely should they shy away from any experience of it. J. B. Phillips captures the contrast well: 'I want to see you experts in good, and not even beginners in evil.'

Here then are three valuable tests to apply to different systems of doctrine and ethics – biblical, Christological and moral tests. We could put them in the form of questions about any kind of teaching we come across. Does it agree with Scripture? Does it glorify the Lord Christ? Does it promote goodness?

In verse 20 Paul adds an assurance to his warning. He has written about good and evil; he wants the Roman Christians to know that there is no doubt about the ultimate outcome, the triumph of good over evil. He detects the strategy of Satan behind the activity of the false teachers, and he is confident that the devil is going to be overthrown. *The God of peace will soon crush Satan under your feet*

---

[3] For similar commands see 1 Cor. 5:11; 2 Thes. 3:6, 14; 2 Tim. 3:5; Tit. 3:10. They relate not to trivial matters, but to inveterate and impenitent offenders, who deliberately turn away from plain apostolic truth, and who ignore repeated warnings.

[4] Cranfield, vol. II, p. 800.

(20a). That is, God 'will throw him under your feet, that you may trample upon him'.[5] He has already been decisively defeated; but he has not yet conceded his defeat.

It may seem strange that in the context Paul refers to 'the God of peace' (as in 15:33), since enjoying peace and crushing Satan do not sound altogether compatible with each other. But God's peace allows no appeasement of the devil. It is only through the destruction of evil that true peace can be attained.

Probably there is an allusion to Genesis 3:15, where God promised that the seed of the woman (namely the Christ) would crush the serpent's head. But there is surely a further reference to man, male and female, whom God created and to whom he gave dominion. As the psalmist put it, God has 'put everything under his feet'.[6] So far this has been fulfilled only in Christ, since God has put 'all things under his feet'.[7] Yet still his exaltation is incomplete, for, while he reigns, he also waits for his enemies to be made his footstool.[8] That this will happen 'soon' is not necessarily a time reference, but rather a statement that God has planned nothing to occupy the space between the ascension and the parousia. The parousia is the very next event on his calendar. Meanwhile, the Romans should expect regular interim victories over Satan, partial crushings of him under their feet.

Such victories would be impossible, however, apart from grace. So Paul adds: *The grace of our Lord Jesus be with you* (20b).

2. Paul's messages (21–24)

Having sent his own personal greetings to twenty-six individuals in Rome (3–16), Paul now passes on messages from eight named people, who are with him in Corinth. He begins with one extremely well-known name, followed by three apparently unknown ones. *Timothy, my fellow-worker, sends his greetings to you, as do Lucius, Jason and Sosipater, my relatives* (21). If anybody deserved to be called Paul's 'fellow-worker', that person was Timothy. For the last eight years Timothy had been Paul's constant travelling companion and had undertaken several special missions at Paul's request. The apostle evidently had a warm affection for his young assistant. Having led him to Christ, he regarded him as his son in the faith.[9] He was now in Corinth, about to set sail for Jerusalem with the offering from the Greek churches.[10]

From his fellow worker Paul turns to three of his fellow countrymen, as his 'relatives' should probably be understood. We

[5] Sanday and Headlam, p. 431.   [6] Ps. 8:6.   [7] Eph. 1:22; cf. Heb. 2:8f.
[8] Ps. 110:1, and its many New Testament applications to Christ.
[9] *E.g.* 1 Cor. 4:17.   [10] Acts 20:4.

cannot for certain identify any of them, although many guesses have been made, some more plausible than others. For example, although there is nothing to link *Lucius* with the 'Lucius of Cyrene' who was in Antioch with Paul ten years previously,[11] it is tempting to identify him as Luke the evangelist, since we know from one of his tell-tale 'we' passages that he was in Corinth at the time.[12] The only difficulty is that Luke was a Gentile. But then 'my fellow-countrymen' could refer only to Jason and Sosipater. This Jason could quite easily be the Jason who had been Paul's landlord in Thessalonica,[13] and Sosipater could be the Berean church's delegate to Jerusalem, whose name was abbreviated to Sopater,[14] for he too was in Corinth at the time.

At this point Paul allows his scribe, to whom he has been dictating this letter, to write his own greeting. *I, Tertius, who wrote down this letter, greet you in the Lord* (22).

Next comes a message from Paul's host in Corinth. *Gaius, whose hospitality I and the whole church here enjoy, sends you his greetings* (23a). Several men called Gaius appear in the New Testament, for it was a common name. It would be natural, however, to identify this one with the Corinthian whom Paul had baptized.[15] Some scholars have further suggested that his full Roman name was Gaius Titius Justus, in which case he had a large house next to the synagogue, into which he had welcomed Paul after the Jews had rejected his gospel.[16] It is then understandable that Paul would again be his house guest, and that the church would also meet in his home.

Two further people complete the series of messages from Corinth. *Erastus, who is the city's director of public works* (RSV 'the city treasurer'), *and our brother Quartus send you their greetings* (23b). Of Quartus nothing is known, although F. F. Bruce asks if it would be 'excessively far-fetched' to think of him as Tertius' younger brother, since *tertius* means 'third' and *quartus* 'fourth'.[17] In response, C. E. B. Cranfield dubs Bruce's guess 'an exercise of free fancy'. Erastus, on the other hand, however we should translate 'the *oikonomos* of the city', seems to have been a responsible local government official. Perhaps he was the *aedile*, the magistrate in charge of public works, whose name is still clearly legible in a first-century Latin inscription on a marble pavement close to the ruins of old Corinth. It is difficult to see, however, how he could at the same time have been one of Paul's itinerant helpers who on one occasion was sent 'to Macedonia',[18] although on another he 'stayed in Corinth'.[19]

---

[11] Acts 13:1. [12] Acts 20:5f. [13] Acts 17:5ff. [14] Acts 20:4.
[15] 1 Cor. 1:14. [16] Acts 18:7. [17] Bruce, p. 266. [18] Acts 19:22.
[19] 2 Tim. 4:20.

3. Paul's doxology (25–27)

Paul's doxology is an eloquent and appropriate conclusion to his letter, for he takes up its central themes, summarizes them and relates them to one another.[20] Although the grammar of the doxology is not easy to unravel, it contains profound truths about God and the gospel. It consists of four parts which focus respectively on the power of God, the gospel of Christ, the evangelization of the nations and the praise of God's wisdom.

First, Paul writes of *the power of God*. *Now to him who is able* (*dynamenō*, has the *dynamis*) *to establish you* . . . . Although this accurately translates the Greek, it is an awkward introduction, and JB does better to begin with a noun: 'Glory be to him who is able . . .!' It can hardly be an accident that Romans begins and ends with a reference to the power of God through the gospel. If the gospel is God's power to save (1:16), it is also God's power to establish. *Stērizō* (to establish) is almost a technical term for nurturing new converts and strengthening young churches. Luke uses it in the Acts (or rather the cognate verb *epistērizō*) of Paul and his fellow missionaries, who deliberately revisited the churches they had planted, in order to 'establish' them.[21] And Paul himself uses the verb in his letters in relation to making Christians firm, strong and stable, whether in their faith (against error), in their holiness (against temptation) or in their courage (against persecution).[22] So the vision conjured up by the doxology's opening words is of God's ability to establish the multi-ethnic church in Rome, of which Paul has been dreaming, and to strengthen its members in truth, holiness and unity.

Secondly, Paul writes of *the gospel of Christ*. For God is able to establish you, he says, *by* (literally 'according to') *my gospel and the proclamation of Jesus Christ, according to the revelation of the*

[20] Complex textual questions surround the end of Romans in general and the doxology in particular. The manuscript evidence suggests that two editions of Romans were in circulation, a longer and a shorter. Origen wrote that Marcion, the second-century heretic, on account of his hostility to the Old Testament and Judaism, was responsible for the shorter edition which omitted the last two chapters. Other scholars suggest that Paul himself authorized the publication of two editions, one with and one without the long list of greetings. The doxology (verses 25–27) and the grace (verses 20 and 27) also occur in different places. The standard commentaries provide the details. So does Dr Bruce Metzger in his *Textual Commentary* (pp. 533ff., 540). Despite the textual uncertainties, the authenticity of Romans 16 is not in doubt, and the themes of the doxology at the end of the letter dovetail beautifully with those of its introduction. For a stout defence of the integrity of Rom. 16 see Donfried, 'A Short Note on Romans 16', pp. 44ff., 119f.

[21] *E.g.* Acts 14:21f.; 15:41; 18:23.

[22] *E.g.* Rom. 1:11; 1 Cor. 1:8; 2 Cor. 1:21; Col. 2:7; 1 Thes. 3:2, 13; 2 Thes. 2:17; 3:7.

mystery hidden for long ages past (25), *but now revealed . . .* (26a). The Greek sentence has three coordinate clauses, namely 'according to my gospel', 'and [according to] the proclamation of Jesus Christ', and 'according to the revelation of the mystery'. But the first two are almost identical, since Paul's gospel was essentially a proclamation (*kērygma*) of Christ. What Paul is affirming is that God's power to establish the church is part of his gospel, of his proclamation. This reminds us of the first three verses of his letter, in which he described himself as 'set apart for the gospel of God . . . regarding his Son'. Now he refers to 'the gospel of God' as 'my gospel' (*cf.* 2:16), because it had been revealed and entrusted to him by God, and the gospel 'regarding his Son' he calls 'the proclamation of Jesus Christ'.

The third coordinate clause ('according to the revelation of the mystery') emphasizes the fact that his gospel is revealed truth. It is a 'mystery', that is to say, a truth or cluster of truths *hidden for long ages past, but now revealed.* What is included in the 'mystery' Paul does not here explain. But he does elsewhere. God's secret, hitherto concealed but now revealed, is essentially Jesus Christ himself in his fulness,[23] and in particular Christ for and in the Gentiles,[24] so that Gentiles now have an equal share with Israel in God's promise.[25] The mystery also includes good news for Jews as well as Gentiles, namely that one day 'all Israel will be saved' (11:25f.). And it looks forward to the future glory,[26] when God will bring all things together under one head, Christ.[27] Thus the mystery begins, continues and ends with Christ.

Thirdly, Paul writes of *the evangelization of the nations.* It is important to grasp that Paul is stating three truths about the mystery, which are summed up by the verbs *hidden, revealed* and *made known.* It is not just that the mystery was long concealed, but has now been revealed, namely through the life, death, resurrection and exaltation of Jesus. The third fact is that this good news must be, and is already being, made known throughout the world: *made known through the prophetic writings by the command of the eternal God, so that all nations might believe and obey him* (26b).

Consider now four significant features of the universal 'making known' of the gospel mystery, which are strongly reminiscent of the letter's opening paragraph (1:1–5). Both passages (the introduction and the doxology) refer to the Scriptures, the commission of God to evangelize, the obedience of faith, and all the nations.

First, the mystery is being made known *through the prophetic writings*, which must mean Old Testament Scripture. But how can

---

[23] Col. 2:2.   [24] Col. 1:27.   [25] Eph. 3:6ff.; 6:19f.   [26] 1 Cor. 2:7ff.
[27] Eph. 1:9f.

God be making known his mystery through the Old Testament now, when it has been in existence for centuries? The answer seems to be that, following the saving events of Christ, God has given his people a new Christological understanding of the Old Testament as bearing witness to Christ (*cf.* 1:2; 3:21). In consequence, it is through the apostolic declaration that 'the Christ is Jesus'[28] that the gospel is spreading.

Second, the clause *by the command of the eternal God* must refer to the universal commission to preach the gospel, for behind the risen Christ who gave it there stood the eternal God, whose everlasting purpose it is to save and unite Jews and Gentiles in Christ.

Third, the clause 'unto obedience of faith' (translated *might believe and obey him*) comes next in the Greek text. It is identical with 1:5. The proper response to the gospel is faith, as Paul has stressed throughout his letter, but it is a faith which itself is obedient and which issues in a life of obedience.

Fourth, the contemporary 'making known' of God's mystery is for *all nations*, so that they will believe and obey. No limit is placed on the beneficiaries of the gospel; it is intended for everybody.

So this fourfold scheme of the making known of the gospel through Scripture, by God's command, unto obedience of faith, for all the nations, exactly corresponds to the letter's opening, which refers to the gospel as being, among other things, according to the Scriptures, through the grace and apostleship given to Paul and others, unto obedience of faith, and for all the nations.

Finally, Paul concludes *in praise of God's wisdom: to the only wise God be glory for ever through Jesus Christ! Amen* (27). God's wisdom is seen in Christ himself, 'in whom are hidden all the treasures of wisdom and knowledge',[29] above all in his cross which, though foolish to human beings, is the wisdom of God,[30] in God's decision to save the world not through its own wisdom but through the folly of the gospel,[31] in the extraordinary phenomenon of the emerging multiracial, multicultural church;[32] and in his purpose ultimately to unite everything under Christ.[33] No wonder Paul has already broken out in praise of God's wisdom: 'Oh, the depth of the riches of the wisdom and knowledge of God!' (11:33). No wonder he does it again at the end of his letter. Indeed, God's redeemed people will spend eternity ascribing to him 'praise and glory and wisdom and thanks and honour and power and strength'.[34] That is, they will worship him for his power and wisdom displayed in salvation.

It is fair then to say that the major themes of Paul's letter are

---

[28] *Cf.* Acts 17:1ff.   [29] Col. 2:3; *cf.* 1 Cor. 1:30.   [30] 1 Cor. 1:24.
[31] 1 Cor. 1:21.   [32] Eph. 3:10.   [33] Eph. 1:8ff.   [34] Rev. 7:12.

encapsulated in the doxology: the power of God to save and to establish; the gospel and the mystery, once hidden and now revealed, which are Christ crucified and risen; the Christ-centred witness of Old Testament Scripture; the commission of God to make the good news universally known; the summons to all the nations to respond with the obedience of faith and the saving wisdom of God, to whom all glory is due for ever.

Study guide to *The Message of Romans*

David Stone

The aim of this study guide is to help you get to the heart of what the author has written and to challenge you to apply what you learn to your own life. The questions have been designed for use by individuals or by small groups of Christians meeting, perhaps for an hour or two each week, to study, discuss and pray together.

The guide provides material for each of the sections in the book. When used by a group with limited time, the leader should decide beforehand which questions are most appropriate for the group to discuss during the meeting and which should perhaps be left for group members to work through by themselves or in smaller groups during the week.

In order to be able to contribute fully and learn from the group meetings, each member of the group needs to read through the section or sections under discussion, together with the passages in the letter to which they refer.

It is important not to let these studies become merely academic exercises. Guard against this by making time to think through and discuss how what you discover *works out in practice* for you. Make sure you begin and end each study by focusing on God in praise and prayer. Ask the Holy Spirit to speak to you through your discussion together.

Preliminary essay (pp. 19–43)

1. The influence of the letter

1 John Stott quotes the impact of Romans on five church leaders. To what extent can you identify with the questions they faced? How did the letter help them? How might it help you? Spend some time praying that this will happen as you study.

'There is no saying what may happen when people begin to study the letter to the Romans . . . !' (p. 23, quoting F. F. Bruce).

---

2. New perspectives on old traditions

2 What has 'long been taken for granted' as the 'apostle's chief emphasis in Romans' (p. 24)?

3 John Stott draws our attention to the views of several scholars (pp. 24ff.). Can you try to sum up their assessments of what

Romans is really all about? What do you think of their arguments?

4   What can we be 'profoundly thankful for' (p. 31) in these modern views of Romans? Why?

3. Paul's purposes in writing

5   How do the three places which Paul intends to visit help us to assess why he writes as he does (pp. 32ff.)?

6   What is the controversy whose 'echoes . . . may be heard rumbling throughout Romans' (p. 35)? Are you aware of a similar tension in your own church? How does Paul answer it?

4. A brief overview of Romans

7   We shall come in more detail to the different points John Stott makes later on. For now, trace through his summary of this letter (pp. 36ff.). In what ways does this relate (a) to your past experience and (b) to your present questions?

Introduction: The gospel of God and Paul's eagerness to share it
Romans 1:1–17

1:1–6
1. Paul and the gospel (pp. 46–54)

1   What is 'particularly striking' (p. 47) about Paul's description of himself as 'slave' and 'apostle'? What do the two terms tell us about Paul's view of his calling (pp. 47f.)?

1. The origin of the gospel is God

2   What is 'the first and most basic conviction which underlies all authentic evangelism' (p. 48)? Why is this?

2. The attestation of the gospel is Scripture

3   According to what Paul says here, why is the Old Testament so important (p. 48f.)? Does it have this significance for you?

3. The substance of the gospel is Jesus Christ

4   What do verses 3–4 say about the double identity of Jesus (pp.

49ff.)? How does what Paul says shed light on these two aspects? Why are they both so important?

4. The scope of the gospel is all the nations

5   As he states the purposes of his apostleship, what 'further aspects of the gospel' does Paul disclose here (pp. 51f.)? What implications does this have for you?

5. The purpose of the gospel is the obedience of faith

6   Paul's gospel demands, literally, 'the obedience of faith' (verse 5). How would you answer the suggestion that this contradicts his emphasis elsewhere that justification is through faith alone (p. 52f.)?

6. The goal of the gospel is the honour of Christ's name

7   What is 'the highest of all missionary motives' (p. 53)? How does your experience of evangelism match up to this?

1:7–13
2. Paul and the Romans (pp. 55–57)

1   In what way does this passage underline Paul's conviction that 'all believers in Christ, Gentiles as well as Jews, now belong to the covenant people of God' (p. 56)?
2   What can we learn from the way he describes his feelings for his Roman readers (pp. 56f.)?

1:14–17
3. Paul and evangelism (pp. 58–65)

1. The gospel is a debt to the world (14–15)

1   Why might we expect Paul to have been reluctant to preach the gospel in Rome (p. 59)? What was it that overcame these factors? How can this help us?

'People nowadays tend to regard evangelism as an optional extra and consider (if they engage in it) that they are conferring a favour on God; Paul spoke of it as an obligation' (p. 58).

---

2. *The gospel is God's power for salvation (16)*

2   Are you at all 'ashamed of the gospel' (p. 60)? Why? What is the antidote to this?

3. *The gospel reveals God's righteousness (17)*

3   What different answers have been given to the question what Paul means by (a) *the righteousness of God* and (b) *from faith to faith* in verse 17 (pp. 61ff.)? Which are more likely to be correct? Why?
4   How should we translate Paul's quotation from Habbakuk (pp. 64f.)? Why?

A.   The wrath of God against all humankind
Romans 1:18 – 3:20

1   'Nothing keeps people away from Christ more than . . .' what (p. 67)? Can you give examples of this from your own experience? What is the answer?

1:18–32
4. Depraved Gentile society (pp. 69–79)

1   To what extent does talk of the wrath of God cause you 'embarrassment and even incredulity' (p. 71)? Why is this? How may such reactions be avoided?

1. *What is the wrath of God?*

2   How did C. H. Dodd and A. T. Hanson seek to overcome the 'problem' of God's wrath (pp. 71f.)? Does their solution work?

2. *Against what is God's wrath revealed?*

3   What is the connection between revelation and God's wrath (pp. 72ff.)?

3. *How is God's wrath revealed?*

4   Can you identify the three ways in which God's wrath is revealed (pp. 74f.)? In what ways have you experienced those that are active now?
5   For which 'modern obsession' (p. 76) are you most tempted to *exchange the glory of the living God*? How can this be avoided?

6 Do verses 26–27 'describe and condemn all homosexual behaviour' (pp. 77f.)? How has this view been challenged? What do you think?

> The 'essence [of Paul's portrayal of depraved Gentile society] lies in the antithesis between what people know and what they do' (p. 79).

2:1–16
5. Critical moralizers (pp. 80–89)

1 The common assumption is that Paul is addressing a Jew in these verses. Why might this not be the case (pp. 80f.)? How might we more accurately define his target?

1. God's judgment is inescapable (1–4)

2 What 'strange human foible' does Paul uncover in these verses (p. 82)? Is it one you share?

2. God's judgment is righteous (5–11)

3 If salvation is by faith alone, why is judgment according to works (pp. 83f.)?

> 'The presence or absence of saving faith in our hearts will be disclosed by the presence or absence of good works of love in our lives' (p. 84).

4 Which two paths does Paul contrast in verses 7–10 (p. 84)? Which are you on? How do you know?

3. God's judgment is impartial (12–16)

5 By what criteria does God judge (a) Jews and (b) Gentiles (pp. 85ff.)?

6 In talking about Gentiles, what does Paul mean by saying that *the requirements of the law are written on their hearts* (verse 15; pp. 86f.)?

7 What 'three further truths about judgment day' (pp. 87f.) does Paul add in verse 16? How do you respond to these?

'We cheapen the gospel if we represent it as a deliverance only from unhappiness, fear, guilt and other felt needs, instead of as a rescue from the coming wrath' (p. 88).

---

4. Conclusion: God's judgment and God's law

8 How would you answer the suggestion that verses 12–16 hold out the hope that some people might gain salvation by living good lives (p. 88)?
9 Do you ever feel that Christian involvement in society is a case of 'Christians trying to force their standards on an unwilling public' (p. 89)? How does what Paul says here help?

2:17 – 3:8
6. Self-confident Jews (pp. 90–98)

1. The law (17–24)

1 What 'double relation' (p. 91) do Jewish people have to the law? How does Paul 'turn the tables on them'?

'If we set ourselves up as either teachers or judges of others, we can have no excuse if we do not teach or judge ourselves' (p. 92).

---

2. Circumcision (25–29)

2 Can you think of any 'magical ceremony or . . . charm' (p. 92) that people rely on today in order to exempt them from God's judgment, as some Jews in Paul's day relied on their circumcision?
3 What 'fourfold contrast' does Paul draw as he redefines what it means to be a Jew (p. 94)?

3. Some Jewish objections (3:1–8)

4   If 'being an ethnic Jew has no value in protecting from God's judgment' (p. 96), what value does it have?
5   What are the other three objections to what he has been saying that Paul deals with here (pp. 96ff.)?
6   What does 'apologetics' mean? How does what Paul writes here emphasize the importance of this aspect of evangelism (p. 98)?

3:9–10
7. The whole human race (pp. 99–105)

1   What is the possible contradiction between verses 1 and 9 (p. 99)? How may it be resolved?
2   What are the 'three features of this grim biblical picture' which stand out in verses 10–18 (pp. 100f.)?
3   Which expression has, according to James Dunn, 'frequently been misunderstood' (p. 102)? What is the difference between the traditional and modern interpretations of this phrase? Which do you think is right? Why does it matter?
4   How does John Stott suggest we should respond to Paul's indictment of universal sin and guilt (pp. 104f)?

B. The grace of God in the gospel
Romans 3:21 – 8:39

3:21 – 4:25
8. God's righteousness revealed and illustrated (pp. 108–137)

1. God's righteousness revealed in Christ (3:21–26)

1   What do these verses teach about *righteousness from God* (pp. 108f.)?
2   Can you define (a) justification and (b) sanctification? Why is the distinction between them important (pp. 110ff.)?

'No formulation of the gospel is biblical which removes the initiative from God and attributes it either to us or even to Christ' (pp. 111f.).

---

3 Why is the statement that *God . . . justifies the wicked* (4:5; p. 112) so 'startling'? How then can God do it?
4 What parallels can you identify between the picture of 'redemption' and our situation as sinners (p. 113)?
5 What does 'propitiation' mean (pp. 113ff.)? Why do some people react against this as a translation of the Greek word *hilastērion*? What alternatives are suggested? Why are these unsatisfactory?

'God himself gave himself to save us from himself'
(p. 115).

---

6 Apart from redeeming sinners and propitiating God, what else does Paul identify here as achieved by the cross (pp. 116f.)?
7 Why is it 'vital to affirm that there is nothing meritorious about faith' (p. 117)?
8 How does John Stott defend his statement that 'Justification . . . is the heart of the gospel and unique to Christianity' (p. 118)? Where does this leave other religions?

2. God's righteousness defended against criticism (3:27–31)

9 What effect does justification by faith have on boasting (pp. 119f.)? Why? What do you take pride in?
10 In what ways does the doctrine of justification by faith *uphold the law* (verse 31, p. 121)?

3. God's righteousness illustrated in Abraham (4:1–25)

11 'Paul wants Jewish Christians to grasp that his gospel of justification is no novelty . . . and he wants Gentile Christians to appreciate the rich spiritual heritage they have entered by faith in Jesus' (p. 122). Why does Paul choose Abraham as his main example of justification (pp. 122f.)?
12 How does Paul show that Abraham was justified by faith rather than works (pp. 124ff.)?
13 'Justification involves a double counting, crediting, or reckoning'. To what is John Stott referring? How is this relevant to you?
14 What does Paul draw from the fact that Abraham was justified long before he was circumcised (pp. 124f.)? Why would this have embarrassed his Jewish opponents?
15 On what three points does Paul base his assertion that God's promise to Abraham was 'received and inherited by faith, not law' (pp. 131f.)?

'The law ... divides. Only the gospel of grace and faith can unite, by ... levelling everybody at the foot of Christ's cross' (p. 132).

16 What then was it that enabled Abraham to believe God (pp. 132ff.)? What enables *you* to believe in God? How does faith grow?
17 In what ways is verse 25 'a comprehensive statement of the gospel' (Hodge, quoted on p. 135)?

'Faith is not burying our heads in the sand, or screwing ourselves up to believe what we know is not true, or even whistling in the dark to keep our spirits up. On the contrary, faith is a reasoning trust. There can be no believing without thinking' (p. 136).

5:1 – 6:23
9. God's people united in Christ (pp. 138–188)

1. *The results of justification (5:1–11)*

1 What 'six bold assertions' are true of all whom God has justified (pp. 139ff.)? What does each one of them mean for you?
2 'Justified believers enjoy a blessing far greater than ... an occasional audience with the king' (p. 140). In what way?
3 What do you hope for in the future? Does it include what Paul has in mind here (pp. 140f.)?
4 What is your attitude to suffering? According to Paul, what should it be? Why (pp. 141f.)?
5 What 'important lessons' (p. 142) does verse 5 teach us about the work of the Holy Spirit in the life of the Christian? Does this refer to 'unusual and overpowering experiences which are given only to some' (p. 143) or is it more general? Why?
6 What are the 'two major means by which we come to be sure that God loves us' (p. 142) which Paul mentions here? How important is each of them to you?
7 How does Paul portray those for whom Christ died (pp. 144f.)? In what ways do you qualify?

'The integration of the historical ministry of God's Son (on the cross) with the contemporary ministry of his Spirit (in our hearts) is one of the most wholesome and satisfying features of the gospel' (p. 146).

---

8 Why is the 'correct answer' (p. 146) to the question 'Have you been saved?' both 'Yes' and 'No'? What does this mean?

9 What is the difference between Jewish boasting in God which Paul mentions in 2:17 and the Christian boasting in God he writes about in 5:11 (pp. 147f.) Which more characterizes you?

10 What is 'the major mark of justified believers' (p. 148)? Is it in your case? Why?

2. The two humanities, in Adam and in Christ (5:12–21)

11 What 'two particular links' (p. 148) are there between verses 1–11 and verses 12–21?

12 What are the two possible answers (pp. 148f.) to the question arising from verse 12: 'In what sense have all sinned so that all die?' Which is more likely to be correct? Why? Why is this important?

13 'The concept of our having sinned in Adam is certainly foreign to the mindset of western individualism' (p. 153). How does it strike you? What problems does it solve? And how do you answer those it creates?

14 What differences does Paul draw out between Adam and Christ (pp. 154ff.)?

15 What parallels does Paul draw out between the effects of Adam and Christ (pp. 156ff.)?

16 What is meant by 'universalism'? Why might it be thought that Paul is teaching it here? How do we know that this is not the case (pp. 158ff.)?

'Christ will raise to life many more than Adam will drag to death' (p. 161).

---

17 What is it about Paul's teaching here that 'should be a great spur to world evangelization' (p. 162)? Does it have this effect on you?

18 Given the probability that there are 'symbolical elements in the Bible's first three chapters' (p. 163), why does John Stott believe we should regard Adam and Eve as historical characters? To what problems does this give rise? How might they be solved?

19 Paul says in verse 12 that death entered the world through sin. How can the difficulties this statement raises be dealt with?

3. United to Christ and enslaved to God (6:1–23)

20 How might Paul's gospel seem 'to stimulate people to sin more than ever' (p. 167)? What is Paul's answer to this objection?

'Have we never caught ourselves making light of our failures on the ground that God will excuse and forgive them?' (p. 167).

---

21 What popular view does John Stott set out of what it means to 'die to sin' (pp. 169ff.)? Why should this view be rejected? What *does* it mean, then?

'It is not the literal impossibility of sin in believers which Paul is declaring, but the moral incongruity of it' (p. 169).

---

22 'The death and resurrection of Jesus Christ are not only historical facts and significant doctrines, but also personal experiences' (p. 174). In what ways is this true for you?

23 What is the relationship between our freedom from the tyranny of sin on the one hand and the crucifixion of Jesus on the other (pp. 175ff.)?

24 What are the 'two quite distinct ways in which the New Testament speaks of crucifixion in relation to holiness' (p. 176)? Why is this distinction important?

25 What does it mean for you to 'live with' Christ (verse 8, p. 178)?

26 What differences does John Stott draw out between the death and resurrection of Jesus (pp. 178f.)? How do these differences relate to our understanding of what it means to live as a Christian?

27 What is 'the major secret of holy living' (p. 180)? Have you discovered it?

28 What does John Stott describe as 'the ultimate secret of freedom from sin' (p. 181)? How does it work out in practice?

29 In verses 15–23 Paul deals again with the question whether grace encourages sin. What 'two significant shifts of emphasis' (p. 182) are there compared with his answer in verses 1–14?

30 How does the picture of slavery help us to understand life before and after someone becomes a Christian (pp. 182ff.)? In what ways is it unhelpful? Why then does Paul use it (p. 185)?

31 In what four stages does Paul sum up his readers' experience (p. 184)? How have these been true of you?

32 What contrasts does Paul draw out between slavery to sin and slavery to righteousness (p. 186)?

'Our heavenly Father says ... to us every day: "My dear child, you must always remember who you are"' (p. 188).

7:1–25
10. God's law in Christian discipleship (pp. 189–215)

1 For what reason is Romans 7 'well known to most Christian people' (p. 189)? Why is this potentially misleading? What is Paul's real focus in this chapter?

2 In what sense are Christians 'not under law' (pp. 191f.)? And in what sense do we still have obligations to it?

3 What are the 'three possible attitudes to the law' (pp. 191f.) outlined by John Stott? What are the strengths and weaknesses of each?

1. Release from the law: a marriage metaphor (1–6)

4 What truths about a Christian's relationship to God's law are illuminated by Paul's discussion of marriage here (p. 193)?

5 Some commentators suggest that Paul's mention of *fruit* in verse 4 continues the marriage metaphor and refers to the birth of children. Is this 'unmistakably' so or is the idea 'grotesque' (pp. 195f.)? Why?

2. A defence of the law: a past experience (7–13)

6 Why would what Paul has just said about the law 'have sounded to some like full-blown antinomianism' (p. 198)? How does Paul defend himself?

7   What suggestions have been made about the identity of the 'I' in verses 7–13 (pp. 198ff.)? Which do you think is correct? Why?
8   Paul denies that the law is sin (verse 7). What then is the relationship between the two (pp. 201ff.)? What experience have you had of the different aspects John Stott draws out?
9   How does this passage reveal 'the extreme sinfulness of sin' (p. 204)?

3. The weakness of the law: a continuing conflict (14–25)

10 What 'important truth lies behind the whole final section of Romans 7' (p. 205)?
11 What suggestions have been made about the identity of the *wretched man* Paul writes about? What are their strengths and weaknesses (pp. 206ff.)?
12 What is John Stott's solution (pp. 208ff.)? What evidence does he give to support it? If he is right, how is what Paul says relevant for us today?
13 What lies behind the conflict Paul describes here (pp. 211ff.)?
14 Can you trace out the 'double reality' which Paul depicts 'four times in four different ways' (pp. 213f.)?
15 'When we are seeking a legitimate application of Romans 7 to ourselves today, we are likely to find verses 4–6 to be crucial' (p. 214). Why? How do these verses help?

8:1–39
11. God's Spirit in God's children (pp. 216–260)

1. The ministry of God's Spirit (1–17)

1   What are the two privileges of salvation that Paul sets out here (pp. 217f.)? How do these apply to you?
2   Can you list the five expressions Paul uses to describe what God did to bring us salvation (pp. 219f.)? What else does the way he puts this tell us?
3   What is 'the ultimate purpose of God's action through Christ' (p. 221)? Need this contradict what Paul has already said? Why?

Our obedience to the law ' . . . is so important to God that he sent his Son to die for us and his Spirit to live in us, in order to secure it' (p. 222).

---

4 What differences are there between those whose mindset is characterized by the flesh and those whose mindset is characterized by the Spirit (pp. 223ff.)?

5 Why is verse 9 'of great importance in relation to our doctrine of the Holy Spirit' (p. 224)?

6 What 'two major consequences' of the Holy Spirit's indwelling does Paul focus on here (pp. 224ff.)?

7 How does verse 13 clarify the meaning, means and motive 'mortification' (pp. 228ff.)? In what ways do you need to *put to death the misdeeds of the body*?

8 What 'four pieces of evidence' does Paul assemble to demonstrate that we are God's children (pp. 230ff.)?

9 How does the Holy Spirit 'lead us to holiness' (pp. 230f.)? In particular, is he violent or gentle? How does this fit in with your experience?

10 What does the cry '*Abba*, Father' tell us about the nature of our relationship to God (pp. 233f.)? How deeply do you experience this?

2. The glory of God's children (18–27)

11 What contrasts does Paul draw out between the sufferings and glory of God's children (pp. 237f.)?

12 What does Paul mean by *the creation* and its destiny (p. 238)?

13 What five 'aspects of our half-saved condition' does Paul go on to highlight (pp. 242f.)?

'*We are to wait neither so eagerly that we lose our patience, nor so patiently that we lose our expectation, but eagerly and patiently together*' (p. 243).

---

14 How does the Holy Spirit help us in our weakness (pp. 244f.)? How can we help him to help us more effectively?

3. The steadfastness of God's love (28–39)

15 What are the 'five truths about God's providence' (pp. 247f.) which Paul lists in verse 28? How do we know them to be true?

16 What does it mean to suggest that God's 'foreknowledge is the basis of his predestination' (p. 248)? Why can't this be right? What could foreknowledge mean, then?

> *'Clearly ... a decision is involved in the process of becoming a Christian, but it is God's decision before it can be ours'* (p. 249).

---

17 What might 'predestination' mean? What are some of the objections to this doctrine (pp. 249f.)? How may they be answered?

18 'Evangelism (the preaching of the gospel), far from being rendered superfluous by God's predestination, is indispensable ...' (p. 252). Why? Is this how you see it?

19 List some of the things you would set out in response to the question 'Who is against you?' How does the way Paul asks the question render it unanswerable (pp. 254f.)?

20 What needs do you have? How can you be sure that God will meet them (p. 255)?

21 Why does every accusation and condemnation aimed at the Christian ultimately fail (pp. 255ff.)?

22 What experience do you have of the things Paul sets out as candidates for separating us from Christ's love (pp. 257ff.)? Why can't they do so?

> *'Christian people are not guaranteed immunity to temptation, tribulation or tragedy, but we are promised victory over them. God's pledge is not that suffering will never afflict us, but that it will never separate us from his love'* (p. 259).

C. The plan of God for Jews and Gentiles
Romans 9 – 11

9:1–33
12. Israel's fall: God's purpose of election (pp. 263–278)

1 What is it that Paul affirms so strongly at the beginning of this chapter (pp. 264f.)? Why?

STUDY GUIDE

2   Can you identify the eight unique privileges enjoyed by Israel (pp. 264f.)? What privileges have you had which would make your rejection of God all 'the more poignant'?

3   One explanation of widespread Jewish rejection of Christ is that God's promises have failed. How does Paul rebut this (pp. 266ff.)? What evidence does he give?

4   Concerning election, 'we need to remember two truths' (p. 268). What does John Stott have in mind? How do they help?

5   How does Paul refute the charge that for God to choose some and not others is unjust (pp. 268f.)?

'The wonder is not that some are saved and others not, but that anybody is saved at all' (p. 269).

---

6   What further question concerning election does Paul go on to deal with in verses 19–29 (pp. 27ff.)? What are his three responses?

7   Paul goes on to quote from Hosea and Isaiah. Why? What do we need to remember 'in order to understand Paul's handling of these texts' (pp. 273ff.)?

8   What is 'completely topsy-turvy' about the situation Paul has been describing (pp. 276f.)? How has this come about? How does Paul provide biblical support for what he has written?

9   'This chapter about Israel's unbelief begins with God's purpose of election (6–29) and concludes by attributing Israel's fall to her own pride (30–33)' (p. 277). How would you answer someone who suggested that Paul is contradicting himself?

10:1–21
13. Israel's fault: God's dismay over her disobedience (pp. 279–290)

1. Israel's ignorance of the righteousness of God (1–4)

1   What can all too easily be wrong with religious sincerity (pp. 279f.)? What examples of this can you think of?

2   What do you think Paul means in verse 3 when he writes about Israel's ignorance of *the righteousness that comes from God* and her search to *establish* her *own righteousness* (pp. 280ff.)?

2. Alternative ways of righteousness (5–13)

3　What is the problem with trying to achieve *the righteousness that is by the law* (verse 5; p. 282)? What is the alternative?

4　How do verses 6–8 fit in to Paul's argument (pp. 282ff.)? Is Paul's use of this text legitimate? Why?

5　How do verses 11–13 'build on this' (pp. 284f.)?

3. The necessity of evangelism (14–15)

6　How does Paul 'demonstrate the indispensable necessity of evangelism' (p. 285)?

4. The reason for Israel's unbelief (16–21)

7　In spite of evangelism, many of Paul's fellow Israelites do not believe. What reasons does Paul suggest and then reject (pp. 287ff.)? Why?

8　What then *is* the reason for Israel's unbelief (pp. 288ff.)? How does Paul back up his conclusion?

11:1–32
14. Israel's future: God's long-term design (pp. 291–315)

1　What basic theme of this chapter is revealed by Paul's questions in verses 1 and 11 (p. 291?)?

1. The present situation (1–10)

2　Can you identify the four strands of evidence which Paul gives in order to show that God has not turned his back on his people Israel (pp. 292f.)?

3　What do you understand by *The others were hardened* in verse 7 (pp. 293f.)? How would you answer the suggestion that it is unreasonable of God to harden people's hearts?

2. The future prospect (11–32)

4　What is 'Paul's sequence of thought in this paragraph' (p. 295)? How is this evident from his own ministry?

5　Why is Paul's statement in verse 14 'remarkable' and 'surprising' (p. 297)? How can it be explained?

6　What might Paul's reference to 'life from the dead' in verse 15 mean (pp. 298f.)? Which do you think is more likely? Why?

7 What 'two complementary lessons' (p. 300) does Paul draw from the allegory of the olive tree? How is what he says relevant for you?

'It is when we have false or fantasy images of ourselves that we grow proud. Conversely, knowledge is conducive to humility, for humility is honesty, not hypocrisy. The complete antidote to pride is truth' (p. 302).

---

8 What does Paul mean by *this mystery* in verse 25 (p. 302)? Can you trace out the three truths he mentions?
9 What does the statement *all Israel will be saved* (verse 26) mean (pp. 303f.)? How does what follows help our understanding?
10 Why are some Christians reluctant to engage in missionary activity among Jews (pp. 300f.)? What theological basis does such a stance have? How do you think Paul would respond?
11 How do verses 28–32 give us 'confidence that God has neither rejected his people (1–2) nor allowed them to fall beyond recovery (11)' (p. 305)?
12 Some suggest that verse 32 supports universalism, the idea that, in the end, everyone will be saved. Do you think this is right (pp. 307f.)? Why?

11:33–36
15. Doxology (pp. 309–312)

1 What do you notice about Paul's worship here (pp. 309ff.)? Does it differ from yours? In what ways? Why?
2 How can we ensure that our belief about God and our worship of God are never separated (pp. 311f.)? Why is this so important? Which do you tend to focus on more? Why?

'Beware equally of an undevotional theology and of an untheological devotion' (p. 312, quoting Bishop Handley Moule).

---

16. A manifesto of evangelism (pp. 313–315)

1 How do your own beliefs about evangelism, and your practice of it, measure up to the seven points set out here?

D. The will of God for changed relationships
Romans 12:1 – 15:13

12:1–2
17. Our relationship to God: consecrated bodies and renewed minds (pp. 320–324)

1 Paul makes his appeal on the grounds of *God's mercy* (verse 1). How would you define and describe God's mercy to you (pp. 321f.)?

'There is no greater incentive to holy living than a contemplation of the mercies of God' (p. 321).

---

2 Why would the idea of worship as 'the presentation of our bodies' to God (p. 322) have come as a shock to Paul's Greek readers? What does it mean in practice for you?
3 In what ways do you tend to 'be conformed to the prevailing culture' (p. 323)? How in practice can you overcome this tendency?

12:3–8
18. Our relationship to ourselves: thinking soberly about our gifts (pp. 325–329)

1 Why is it so important for us to have a sober judgment of ourselves (pp. 325ff.)? What two criteria are we to use? What do you conclude about yourself in the light of these?
2 What does Paul mean by requiring someone with a prophetic gift to *use it in proportion to his faith* (verse 6; p. 327)?
3 What is 'arguably the most urgently needed gift in the worldwide church today' (p. 327)? Why?

4   In the light of these verses, in what ways do you 'need to broaden [your] understanding of spiritual gifts' (p. 329)?

12:9–16
19. Our relationship to one another: love in the family of God (pp. 330–333)

1   What are the ingredients in Paul's 'recipe for love' (pp. 330ff.)? Which are especially relevant for you?

12:17–21
20. Our relationship to our enemies: not retaliation but service (pp. 334–337)

1   'Retaliation and revenge are absolutely forbidden to the followers of Jesus' (p. 334). Why? Do you find this easy to accept?
2   What can we learn from the four positive counterparts that accompany Paul's four negative imperatives (pp. 336f.)?
3   In the light of what Paul has said about revenge, what does the reference to *burning coals* in verse 20 mean (p. 336)?

12:1–7
21. Our relationship to the state: conscientious citizenship (pp. 338–347)

1   What do scholars like Oscar Cullman suggest Paul means by *authorities* in verse 1 (pp. 338f.)? Are they correct? Why?
2   Why is what Paul writes here 'particularly remarkable' (pp. 339f.)? How is this observation relevant to us?

1. The authority of the state (1–3)

3   In what way do we 'need to be cautious' (p. 340) in the way we interpret what Paul says about the state as a divine institution with divine authority? What are the limits of the state's authority?
4   'Whenever laws are enacted which contradict God's law, civil disobedience becomes a Christian duty' (p. 342). What examples of this, ancient and modern, can you think of?

2. The ministry of the state (4–7)

5   What jobs has God entrusted to the state (pp. 343f.)?

'Those who serve the state as legislators, civil servants, magistrates, police, social workers or tax-collectors are just as much "ministers of God" as those who serve the church as pastors, teachers, evangelists or administrators' (p. 344).

---

6   What does Paul say which has a bearing on the issue of capital punishment (pp. 344f.)? What do you think? Why?
7   What 'positive function of the state is much neglected today' (p. 346)? Why is this? How can it be encouraged?

13:8–10
22. Our relationship to the law: neighbour-love as its fulfilment (pp. 348–350)

1. Love is an unpaid debt

1   Why can we 'never stop loving somebody and say, "I have loved enough"' (p. 348)?

2. Love is the fulfilment of the law

2   Why are law and love 'often thought to be incompatible' (p. 349)? Why is it, on the contrary, that each needs the other?

3. Love does no harm to its neighbour

3   Why is love 'the fulfilment of the law' (verse 10; p. 350)?
4   In order to love my neighbour, do I need to love myself (p. 350)? In what sense?

13:11–14
23. Our relationship to the day: living in the 'already' and the 'not yet' (pp. 351–354)

1. Understanding the time (11–12a)

1 How would you answer someone who claimed that subsequent history shows Paul to have been mistaken in stating that *the night is nearly over* (verse 11; p. 352)?

2. Understanding what is appropriate to the time (12b–14)

2 What are we to *put on* or *clothe* ourselves with, and what are we to avoid (verses 12b–13; pp. 352f.)? Why?

3 How is it possible to avoid gratifying *the desires of the sinful nature* (verse 14; p. 353)?

14:1 – 15:13
24. Our relationship to the weak: welcoming, and not despising, judging or offending them (pp. 355–375)

1 What sort of weak people is Paul referring to here (pp. 355ff.)? What different suggestions have been made as to their identity? Which is most likely?

2 How do we distinguish essentials and non-essentials (p. 358)? What non-essentials are you aware of which threaten to disrupt Christian unity in your circle?

1. The positive principle (1)

3 Does accepting 'the weak' mean accepting everyone without question (pp. 359f.)? Why not?

4 Does your church tend to be 'a debating chamber' (p. 360)? How can this be overcome?

2. The negative consequences (14:2 – 15:13)

5 What is 'the best way to determine what our attitude to other people should be' (p. 361)? As you reflect on some of the people with whom you differ, how does this change your way of thinking?

6 What principles does Paul advise us to use in determining whether or not a particular course of action is right (p. 362)?

7 What other reasons does Paul give for welcoming the weaker

brother (pp. 362ff.)?

8 As the argument moves from the attitudes of the strong to their actions, what further reasons does Paul set out for welcoming the weak (pp. 364f.)?

9 What is 'the dilemma which faces the strong' (p. 364)? Can you think of any circumstances in which a similar dilemma faces you? How is it to be resolved?

10 What does Paul mean by his warning that the strong might *destroy* the weak if they exercise their freedom insensitively (pp. 365f.)?

11 What is the Christian responsibility of the strong to the weak (pp. 369ff.)? How does Paul back up his instructions on this point?

12 What five important truths emerge from Paul's 'brief digression about the nature and purpose of Old Testament Scripture' (p. 370)?

13 How does Paul support the rightness of including the Gentiles together with the Jews as God's people (pp. 372f.)?

14 What specific *hope* does Paul seem to have in mind as he concludes this section (p. 373)? Is it one you share?

15 What 'two particular principles' set out by Paul in chapters 14 – 15 'are applicable to all churches in all places at all times' (p. 374)?

Conclusion: The providence of God in the ministry of Paul
Romans 15:14 – 16:27

15:14–22
25. His apostolic service (pp. 377–383)

1 What gives Paul the right to write as he does (p. 378)? To what extent do Christian leaders today have the same responsibility?

1. Paul's ministry was a priestly ministry (16–17)

2 What truth is it that 'more than any other . . . effectively unites the church's two major roles of worship and witness' (p. 379)? How does this happen?

2. Paul's ministry was a powerful ministry (18–19a)

3 In what ways are these verses 'a very valuable statement of Paul's own understanding of his ministry' (p. 380)? What do they have to teach us today?

3. Paul's ministry was a pioneer ministry (19b–22)

4   What was the 'consistent pioneer policy' (p. 382) behind Paul's ministry?

15:23–33
26. His travel plans (pp. 384–391)

1. He plans to visit Rome (23–24)

1   How is it that Paul is now able to visit Rome (pp. 384f.)?

2. He plans to visit Jerusalem (25–27)

2   Why is Paul so keen to go out of his way to Jerusalem (pp. 385f.)? What does this tell us about his major concerns?

3. He plans to visit Spain (28–29)

3   What do we know about Paul's intended destination, and the fulfilment of his plans (pp. 387f.)?

4. He requests prayer for his visits (30–32)

4   What does Paul specifically request prayer for (pp. 388f.)? What does this tell us about his priorities? How do yours compare?
5   What does his addition of the qualifying clause *by God's will* (verse 32) tell us about the purpose and character of prayer (pp. 389f.)?

'The struggle involved in prayer lies in the process of coming to discern God's will and to desire it above everything else' (p. 390).

16:1–16
27. His commendation and greetings (pp. 392–398)

1. A commendation (1–2)

1   What made Phoebe worthy of commendation by Paul (pp. 392f.)?

2. Many greetings (3–16)

2 How have scholars sought to explain how Paul knew 'so many people so well in a church he had never visited' (p. 394)? What do you think?

3 What is 'the most interesting and instructive aspect of church diversity in Rome' (p. 395)? What does this have to teach us today?

16:17–27
28. His warnings, messages and doxology (pp. 399–406)

1. Paul's warnings (17–20)

1 Do you think Paul would issue the same warnings today? Why (pp. 399f.)?

2 What are the 'three valuable tests' which we are urged to apply to teaching we come across (p. 400)? How do they derive from what Paul has said?

3 'Enjoying peace and crushing Satan do not sound altogether compatible with each other' (p. 401). Why, though, is it important to hold them together?

2. Paul's messages (21–24)

4 What do we know about the quality of some of the relationships that underline these greetings (pp. 401f.)?

3. Paul's doxology (25–27)

5 What is the 'fourfold scheme of the making known of the gospel' (p. 405) that this doxology contains? How does it tie in with the opening of the letter?